D0400271

TERRORISM

TERRORISM

A HISTORY

Randall D. Law

polity

Copyright © Randall D. Law 2009

The right of Randall D. Law to be identified as Author of this Work has been asserted in accordance with the UK Copyright, Designs and Patents Act 1988.

First published in 2009 by Polity Press, Reprinted in 2010 (twice), 2011 (three times), 2013 (twice), 2014

Polity Press
65 Bridge Street
Cambridge CB2 1UR, UK.

Polity Press
350 Main Street
Malden, MA 02148, USA

All rights reserved. Except for the quotation of short passages for the purpose of criticism and review, no part of this publication may be reproduced, stored in a retrieval system, or transmitted, in any form or by any means, electronic, mechanical, photocopying, recording or otherwise, without the prior permission of the publisher.

ISBN-13: 978-0-7456-4037-2
ISBN-13: 978-0-7456-4038-9(pb)

A catalogue record for this book is available from the British Library.

Typeset in 10 on 12 pt Sabon
by Servis Filmsetting Ltd, Stockport, Cheshire.
Printed and bound in the USA by Edwards Brothers, Inc.

The publisher has used its best endeavours to ensure that the URLs for external websites referred to in this book are correct and active at the time of going to press. However, the publisher has no responsibility for the websites and can make no guarantee that a site will remain live or that the content is or will remain appropriate.

Every effort has been made to trace all copyright holders, but if any have been inadvertently overlooked the publishers will be pleased to include any necessary credits in any subsequent reprint or edition.

For further information on Polity, visit our website: www.politybooks.com

Contents

Acknowledgments	vii
List of Abbreviations	ix
Chronology	xi
Introduction	1
1 Terror and Tyrannicide in the Ancient World	11
2 Terror and Tyrannicide in the Middle Ages	32
3 Terror and Tyrannicide in the Early Modern Era in Europe	47
4 The Dawn of Revolutionary Terrorism	57
5 Russian Revolutionary Terrorism	74
6 The Era of the European *Attentat*	98
7 Labor, Anarchy, and Terror in America	114
8 White Supremacy and American Racial Terrorism	126
9 The Dawn of Ethno-Nationalist Terrorism	142
10 The Era of State Terror	160

11 Decolonization and Ethno-Nationalist Terrorism from the   178
   1930s to the Early 1960s

12 Decolonization and Ethno-Nationalist Terrorism from the   217
   Late 1960s to the Present

13 The Era of Leftist and International Terrorism   254

14 The Rise of Jihadist Terrorism   281

15 Alternative Terrorisms   316

16 9/11, the War on Terror, and Recent Trends in Terrorism   330

Index   343

Acknowledgments

It is with great pleasure that I recount the extensive support I have received over the course of this project. My approach to teaching and scholarship reflects my abiding faith in the power of a liberal arts education. Thus it should not be a surprise that this book grew out of a course I began teaching in 2002; in fact, the course and the book's growth have been closely intertwined. I thank my students at Northwestern College of Iowa and Birmingham-Southern College, in Birmingham, Alabama, where I have taught since 2003. They have asked the questions that have in large part provoked the writing of this book.

I wish to thank the faculty, staff, librarians, and administrators of Birmingham-Southern for their extraordinary support. In particular, I want to thank my fellow historians at BSC: Guy Hubbs, Mark Lester, Matt Levey, Bill Nicholas, and Victoria Ott. I cannot imagine a more stimulating, friendly, and supportive group; every one of them read the manuscript in whole or in part and provided extensive critique and commentary. The book is much better for their input, but, of course, any errors of fact or interpretation are mine alone. Other colleagues at Birmingham-Southern read and commented on chapters or sparked my imagination with their ideas. They include Amy Cottrill, Vince Gawronski, Michael McInturff, Sam Pezzillo, Gail Smith, and David Ullrich. While studying at BSC, Daniel Mauldin worked as my research assistant and developed ideas that I incorporated into my coverage of Ireland's Troubles.

Those beyond my campus who have provided valuable information, advice, and/or support include Colonel Tony Abati (USMC), Laura Anderson, Mark Brighton, Stuart Finkel, Steven Isaac, Lynn Patyk, Colonel Ed Rowe (US Army, ret.), and Thomas Sharp. I would particularly like to thank Gregory Miller and Stephen Shellman for twice inviting me to teach at the annual Summer Workshop on Teaching about Terrorism. I am convinced that I learned as much as I taught during those encounters with presenters and participants. While in graduate school at Georgetown University I worked with three outstanding teacher-scholars who continue to influence me a decade later: Catherine Evtuhov, in whose course I first began to explore Russian and European terrorism in comparative perspective; David Goldfrank, who always helped me to see above, around, and behind every issue I sought to tackle; and Richard Stites, who filled me with a passion for scholarship and effective historical writing.

The good folks at Polity, especially Andrea Drugan and Jonathan Skerrett, have provided indispensable advice, generous support, and not a little bit of patience in working with me on this book.

Every member of my family has graced me not only with their considerably learned advice, but also their unflagging emotional and logistical support. To my parents, Elmo and Patricia Law, and my in-laws, Barbara Delman Wolfson and Lewis Wolfson – thank you. My greatest thanks – and debt – are due to my wife, Hannah Wolfson, without whom this project would not have been conceived, sustained, and completed. This book is dedicated to my son, Alexander Ward Law, who is my source of so much happiness in the present and so much hope for the future.

Abbreviations

ALF	Animal Liberation Front (US)
ANFO	Ammonium nitrate and fuel oil bomb
ATF	Bureau of Alcohol, Tobacco, and Firearms (US)
BMG	Baader-Meinhof Gang (West Germany)
CIA	Central Intelligence Agency (US)
COINTELPRO	Counterintelligence program of FBI (US)
ELF	Earth Liberation Front (US)
EOKA	National Organization of Cypriot Fighters
ETA	Basque Nation and Liberty (Spain)
FARC	Revolutionary Armed Forces of Colombia
FBI	Federal Bureau of Investigation (US)
FLN	National Liberation Front (Algeria)
GAL	Anti-Terrorist Liberation Groups (Spain)
GIA	Armed Islamic Group (Algeria)
GSG 9	Border Guard Group 9, West German counter-terrorism unit
HSRA	Hindustan Socialist Republican Association (India)
IMRO	Internal Macedonian Revolutionary Organization (Balkans)
IDF	Israel Defense Forces
IRA	Irish Republican Army
KKK	Ku Klux Klan (US)
KPD	Communist Party of Germany
LEHI	Fighters for the Freedom of Israel
LTTE	Liberation Tigers of Tamil Eelam (Sri Lanka)
MCP	Malayan Communist Party
NATO	North Atlantic Treaty Organization

NRBC	Nuclear, radiological, biological, or chemical weapons
NSA	National Security Agency (US)
OAS	Secret Army Organization (Algeria)
PFLP	Popular Front for the Liberation of Palestine
PIRA	Provisional Irish Republican Army
PLO	Palestine Liberation Organization
RAF	Red Army Faction (West Germany)
RIC	Royal Irish Constabulary
RUC	Royal Ulster Constabulary (Northern Ireland)
SA	Storm Division of Nazi Party (Germany)
SDLP	Social Democratic and Labour Party (Northern Ireland)
SDS	Students for a Democratic Society (US)
SLA	Symbionese Liberation Army (US)
SPD	Social Democratic Party of Germany
SRs	Party of Socialists–Revolutionaries (Russia)
UN	United Nations
Unabomber	University Airline Bomber (US)
UUP	Ulster Unionist Party (Northern Ireland)
UVF	Ulster Volunteer Force (Northern Ireland)

Chronology

647 BCE	Assyrian Emperor Assurnasirpal II terrorizes the city of Susa
514 BCE	Assassination of Athenian tyrant Hippias by Harmodius and Aristogeiton
63 BCE	Catiline Conspiracy
58 BCE	Tribuneship of Clodius Pulcher
44 BCE	Assassination of Julius Caesar by Roman senators
66–70	Jewish-Roman War
73	Fall of Masada
1090s	First Assassin leader, Hassan-i Sabbah, seizes the castle of Alamut
1159	Publication of *Policraticus* (*The Statesman's Book*) by John of Salisbury
1256	Destruction of Alamut and Assassins by Mongols
1407	Assassination of Louis, the French Duke of Orléans
1532	Publication of *The Prince* by Niccolò Machiavelli
1534–5	Anabaptist reign of terror in Münster, Germany
1605	Gunpowder Plot of Guy Fawkes
1649	Execution of England's King Charles I
1793–4	Jacobins' Reign of Terror during the French Revolution
1795	First documented use of the word "terrorist," by Edmund Burke
1811–16	Luddite violence in England
1820s	Carbonari uprisings in Italy, France, and Spain
1828	Publication of *The Conspiracy of Equals* by Filippo Buonarroti
1849	Publication of "Murder" by Karl Heinzen

1850   Publication of *History of Secret Societies in France*
            by Lucien de la Hodde
1857   Carlo Pisacane introduces the term "propaganda of
            the deed"
1858   Assassination attempt on Napoleon III by Felice
            Orsini
1860s   Development of nitroglycerin by Alfred Nobel
1867   National organizational meeting of Ku Klux Klan
1869   Sergei Nechaev Affair and publication of *The
            Catechism of the Revolutionist* by Nechaev
1876–9   Execution of Molly Maguires
1877   End of US Reconstruction
1878   Assassination attempt on Teodor Trepov by Vera
            Zasulich
1879   Johann Most begins publishing *Die Freiheit*
            (*Freedom*)
1881   Assassination of Alexander II by the People's Will
1882   Phoenix Park murders committed by Irish National
            Invincibles
1886   Haymarket Riot
1892–4   Bombings by François-Claudins Ravachol, Emile
            Henry, and Auguste Vaillant
1893   Bombing of Barcelona's opera house by Santiago
            Salvador French
1901   Assassination of US President William McKinley by
            Leon Czolgosz
1902–5   High-profile assassinations by Combat Organization
            of the Socialists-Revolutionaries
1905–7   Russian Revolution of 1905
1907   Publication of *The Secret Agent* by Joseph Conrad
            and *The Man Who Was Thursday* by G.K.
            Chesterton
1908   Alipore Bomb Conspiracy in India
1914   Assassination of Archduke Franz Ferdinand by
            Gavrilo Princip
1915   Formation of second Ku Klux Klan
1916   Easter Uprising in Dublin, Ireland
1918–20   Russian Civil War and Red Terror
1919   Galleanists' bombing campaign
1920   Wall Street bombing
1920   IRA attacks on British during Black and Tan
            War
1928   Formation of Muslim Brotherhood in Egypt

1929	Attack on Indian Legislative Assembly by the Hindustan Socialist Republican Association
1933	Reichstag Fire
1934	Assassination of Yugoslavian King Alexander I by Ustaše and Internal Macedonian Revolutionary Organization
1934	Assassination of Sergei Kirov by Leonid Nikolaev
1936–8	Great Terror and Stalinist Show Trials
1937	League of Nations issues Convention on the Prevention and Punishment of Terrorism
1938	Irgun market bombings in Palestine
1938	Night of Broken Glass (*Kristallnacht*)
1944	Assassination of Lord Moyne by LEHI agents
1946	Bombing of Jerusalem's King David Hotel by Irgun
1948	Formation of Israel, First Arab–Israeli War, and Arab *Nakba*
1948–60	Malayan Emergency
1953–9	Mau Mau Insurrection
1954–62	Algerian War of Independence
1955–9	Terrorist campaign of National Organization of Cypriot Fighters
1956–7	Battle of Algiers
1960–2	Terror campaign of Secret Army Organization in Algeria and France
1961	Publication of *The Wretched of the Earth* by Frantz Fanon
1963	Bombing of Sixteenth Street Baptist Church in Birmingham, Alabama
1966	Execution of Sayyid Qutb in Egypt
1967	Six Day War in Middle East
1968	First hijacking by Popular Front for the Liberation of Palestine
1968–72	Urban guerrilla campaign of Tupamaros of Uruguay
1969	British troops return to Northern Ireland
1969	Publication of *Mini-Manual of the Urban Guerrilla* by Carlos Marighella
1969	Bombing of Milan's Piazza Fontana by Italian neo-fascists
1970	Bombings by the Weather Underground
1972	Provisional Irish Republican Army detonates twenty-two bombs in Belfast
1972	Munich Olympics Massacre by Black September

1973	Assassination of Luis Carrero Blanco, Prime Minister of Spain, by ETA
1974	Robbery of Hibernia Bank by Symbionese Liberation Army and Patty Hearst
1975	Publication of *The Monkey Wrench Gang* by Edward Abbey
1977	German Autumn of Red Army Faction trial and terrorism
1978	Kidnapping and murder of Aldo Moro by Red Brigades of Italy
1978	Publication of *The Turner Diaries* by William Pierce
1979	Iranian Revolution and start of Tehran hostage crisis
1979	Seizure of Grand Mosque of Mecca by Juhayman al-Utaybi and followers
1979	Soviet invasion of Afghanistan and beginning of mujahideen campaign
1980	Bombing of Bologna train station, Italy, by Armed Revolutionary Nuclei
1980–81	Hunger strike by Provisional Irish Republican Army inmates
1980s	Spain's "Dirty War" against ETA
1981	Publication of *The Terror Network* by Claire Sterling
1981	Assassination of Egypt's President Anwar Sadat by al-Jihad
1983	Bombing of US Marine and French paratrooper barracks in Beirut by Hezbollah/Islamic Jihad
1984	Salmonella attack in Dalles, Oregon, by followers of Bhagwan Shree Rajneesh
1985	Seajacking of *Achille Lauro* by PLO
1987	Remembrance Day bombing in Enniskillen, Northern Ireland, by PIRA
1987	Hamas formed during first Palestinian Intifada
1988	Bombing of Pan Am flight over Lockerbie, Scotland, by Libyan agents
1988	Yasser Arafat renounces terrorism
1988	Creation of al-Qaeda by Osama bin Laden
1991	Assassination of Rajiv Gandhi, the Prime Minister of India, by Tamil Tigers
1992	Baltic Exchange bombing in London by Provisional Irish Republican Army
1992	Capture of Abimael Gúzman, leader of the Shining Path, by Peruvian police

1992	Ruby Ridge, Idaho, shootout between survivalists and US marshals
1992–2000	Terrorist campaign of Armed Islamic Group during Algerian Civil War
1993	FBI siege of Branch Davidian compound near Waco, Texas
1993	Bombing of World Trade Center by Ramzi Yousef
1993	Hamas carries out first suicide bombing against Israel
1995	Sarin gas attack on Tokyo subway by Aum Shinrikyo cult
1995	Bombing of Murrah Federal Building in Oklahoma City by Timothy McVeigh
1995	Arrest of Theodore Kaczynski, the Unabomber
1996	Osama bin Laden "declares war" against United States
1996–8	Bombings of Atlanta Summer Olympics and abortion clinics by Eric Rudolph
1997	Luxor Temple massacre in Egypt
1998	Good Friday accords in Northern Ireland
1998	Fires set at Vail Ski Resort by Earth Liberation Front cell
1998	Bombings of US embassies in Nairobi, Kenya, and Dar es Salaam, Tanzania, by al-Qaeda
2001	9/11 attacks on World Trade Center and Pentagon by al-Qaeda
2001	Anthrax attacks in US
2002	Chechen terrorists seize Dubrovka Theatre in Moscow
2002	Bombings at resorts in Bali, Indonesia, by the Islamic Group
2004	Bombings of commuter trains in Madrid, Spain, by al-Qaeda-inspired jihadists
2005	Bombings of public transportation in London by al-Qaeda-inspired jihadists
2006	Bombing of al-Askari Mosque in Samarra, Iraq, by al-Qaeda in Iraq

Introduction

Terrorism is as old as human civilization . . . and as new as this morning's headlines. For some, it seems obvious that individuals and organizations have used terrorism for millennia, while others insist real terrorism has only been around for decades. Both camps are right – up to a point. The weapons, methods, and goals of terrorists constantly change, but core features have remained since the earliest times.

Clodius Pulcher, the Roman patrician who used murderous gangs to intimidate his opponents; the dagger-wielding Sicarii of Judea who hoped to provoke a war with the Romans; twelfth-century assassins who killed and terrorized their Muslim rivals; medieval scholars who quoted scripture to justify killing rulers – all these are examples of terrorism, and all predate the advent of the word "terrorism" in revolutionary France. Since the 1790s, terrorism has been used by Italian secret societies hoping to establish a liberal democratic state, Russian revolutionaries eager to introduce socialism, and European anarchists keen to abolish all governments. American workers intimidated industrialists with terrorism, while German fascists used it to open the way to a semi-legal seizure of power. Zionists and Arabs alike have employed it in attempts to win themselves states in Palestine. Cults have hoped to trigger the apocalypse, and environmental extremists have sought to save wilderness. More recently, an American hated the government so much that he blew up a federal building in Oklahoma City. And nineteen Arabs loved death so much that they piloted planes into American landmarks, killing three thousand people. All of these actors and events are unique, but every single one belongs to the history of terrorism.

When I started teaching a course on the subject soon after September 11, 2001, I could not find a book for my students that told this story in a clear chronological fashion, that provided a sufficient analytical framework, that made use of the most recent scholarly work, and that was comprehensive but succinct. My goal has been to provide students and readers with that book, a true history of terrorism.

But what is terrorism? Any discussion of the subject must start with a definition, which means we immediately venture into a minefield. Scores of definitions have been proposed, and the chaos extends beyond academia. For example, although terrorism is defined in the US legal code, every significant American governmental entity – the State, Defense, and Treasury Departments, the Federal Bureau of Investigation, the Central Intelligence Agency, the National Security Agency, and the Drug Enforcement Administration – has its own unique definition. Under these circumstances, most people are likely to react along the lines of Justice Potter Stewart, who tried to define pornography by claiming "I know it when I see it."

The problem is that scholars, policy analysts, and laypeople alike tend to use the word "terrorism" in mutually exclusive ways. On the one hand, we use it normatively, as a moral judgment against violence that is inherently wrong. On the other hand, we imagine we are using it analytically, as an objective descriptor. Our understanding of terrorism is rooted in an emotional reaction and moral revulsion. But this understanding undermines our efforts to define and analyze what we also try to pretend is a neutral phenomenon. We thus end up with a definition that may satisfy our rational search for clarity but fails to match how the term is used in practice. For instance, what does it do to our definitional clarity when we note that the Israelis and Palestinians call each other terrorists, as do Osama bin Laden and George Bush? The term packs more wallop as an epithet than it does as an analytical term. What to do, short of descending into the cheeky relativism of that well-worn cliché that one person's terrorist is another's freedom fighter?

Perhaps we should begin with a definition consisting of just one criterion. For example, suppose we define the term as violence against civilians. For nearly all such deceptively simple definitions, at least two examples exist that make its application problematic: one that excludes something we want to call terrorism (in our example, for instance, Hezbollah's 1983 attack on the Marine barracks in Beirut) and one that demands we label something terrorism that we do not want to (the Allied bombing of German cities in the Second World War). If we string together enough criteria to produce a compound definition, it robs the word of many of the ways we actually use it. Such jury-rigged definitions also tend to be narrowly applicable to certain times, places, and circumstances, restricting us, for example, to imagining terrorism as a sub-state force, even though nation-states have often employed terrorist methods.

Another complicating factor is that people, misled by the word's suffix, tend to mistake the core nature of terrorism. Terrorism is not an ideology and does not exist as a specific worldview, a system of thought, or a political program. In this regard, it is not comparable to liberalism, conservatism, capitalism, socialism, or any of the other myriad "isms" that populate our history books, despite terrorism's existence as one of the defining phenomena of the modern era. Looked at another way, terrorists are always something else, be they communists, nationalists, or fascists (among many possibilities). Terrorism is a *tactic*, a means to an end – although often one that eventually overshadows the putative goals toward which its users ostensibly strive.

I begin with two core assertions well founded in the broad literature on the topic. The first is that individuals or groups choose to commit terrorist acts as part of a process of rational and conscious decision-making within particular political and cultural contexts. Thus, terrorism is not, as it is often colloquially described, a kind of madness – although individual terrorists have certainly been known to exhibit the signs of various forms of mental illness. My second basic assertion is that terrorism is a communicative act intended to influence the behavior of one or more audiences. I address this point in more detail below.

Rather than trying to pigeonhole this elusive phenomenon with an artificially precise definition, I will explore terrorism in three different ways, illuminating it from three different angles: as a set of tactics; as an act of symbolic and provocative violence; and as cultural construct.

The first approach to terrorism over the course of the book describes the emergence and development of what we could call the terrorist toolbox: a list of behaviors, tactics, and methods typically associated with terrorism. I will also explore elements of common definitions, such as violence against civilians, various methods of organization, the dependence on conspiratorial existence, the use of fear, interaction with the media, and so on. Such an approach is helpful in identifying tactics and the influence of technological change, though it may fail to distinguish terrorism from other forms of violence, such as crime, war, or guerrilla activity.

The second approach I take is to explore terrorism as violent theatre that fundamentally relies on symbolism and provocation. Terrorists choose targets not for their military value, but for their ability to create an extreme reaction – often fear – and their utility in prodding others to act. Many terrorists have hoped their feats would lure their enemy into self-destructive behavior. For instance, the Marxist Tupamaros of Uruguay tried to use terrorism to provoke the state into revealing itself as the fascist entity they believed it was. Other groups use terrorism to inspire the masses to rise up in revolution, such as European and Russian anarchists and populists did in the late nineteenth century. Others have hoped to attract international attention through spectacular acts of violence – the Palestine Liberation Organization's strategy in the late 1960s and much of the 1970s. A more limited goal has often been to keep the spirit of opposition alive and convince the enemy it is not worth the lives, the resources, or the time to stay engaged. This was the plan behind Irgun's terrorism in British Palestine in the 1940s.

This approach highlights the role of ideology and motive and distinguishes terrorism from other forms of violence. And since it has essentially just one criterion – the presence of symbolic, provocative violence – it is flexible and can be applied over decades and even centuries, revealing continuities in the practice. This approach does rely on the assumption that terrorism is a rational, consciously chosen strategy with, broadly speaking, political aims. Organizations whose members have regarded violence as a sacramental act, such as the organization responsible for the Tokyo subway gas attack in 1995, often appear to act out of wholly religious aims, but these are always articulated within a particular historical and cultural context, however bizarre it might appear to outsiders. Moreover, this approach can reveal the different roles of leaders and followers in terrorist groups. For instance, al-Qaeda's foot soldiers see their acts as sacramental but their leaders are far more calculating.

The third approach is the most abstract, exploring how the term "terrorism" itself has evolved over the centuries. In this sense, the word has no meaning except that which has been invested into it. Such an approach acknowledges that terrorism is a word used to deem another's goals or methods illegitimate within a particular matrix of culture, history, or perception. One political scientist used such an approach to observe, "An action of violence is labeled 'terrorist' when its psychological effects are out of proportion to its purely physical result" (Raymond Aron, *Peace and War: A Theory of International Relations* (Doubleday, 1966), 170). Sometimes the process is unconscious and merely the result of changing norms about legitimate violence. More often, the terrorist label is a conscious effort by governments, dominant populations, or influential organizations to frame debates, find scapegoats, and vilify enemies. Only when we take these dimensions into account can we understand the strained distinctions sometimes drawn between terrorism and wartime collateral damage or "legitimate" guerrilla movements. Such contexts also help explain the ways in which "terrorism" and various forms of political violence find themselves at the center of broader contests of legitimacy between governments or rival organizations.

All three of these approaches yield results only when an instance of terrorism – whatever its guise – is presented in context. Therefore, the fundamental goal of this book is to provide the reader with a comprehensive history of terrorism in which the major actors and organizations are presented alongside the salient details of the political, social, cultural, religious, and economic environments that gave their acts meaning. In other words, this book interweaves the history of terrorism and the history of the societies that spawned it.

Terrorism as I have described it above naturally hinges on the ability of violent actors to ensure that news of their acts and intentions reach their target audiences, sometimes through direct impact, but most probably and more effectively through rumors, government responses, newspapers, television, entertainment sources, and countless other forms of information dissemination. In this sense, the media, broadly imagined, provides the oxygen without which terrorists cannot survive. The noted television journalist Ted Koppel famously remarked that "without television, terrorism becomes rather like the philosopher's hypothetical tree falling in the forest: no one hears it fall and therefore it has no reason for being" (quoted in Zulaika and Douglass, 7). Thus, woven into my book's narrative is the critically important story of the relationship between terrorism and the media.

I accept without proof or caveat the assertion that no scholarly discipline has a monopoly on the truth or ultimately provides more valuable insights into the workings of the world. Yet different disciplines have different strengths and weaknesses; and the domination of any field of interest by any one discipline produces certain distorting effects. The study of terrorism is an excellent case in point. "Terrorism studies" within academia and the broader debates about terrorism and counterterrorism raging in our society today have been dominated by social scientists, journalists, policy experts, and political pundits. First, the end of the Cold War and the events of 9/11 created the impression that terrorism was the contemporary world's most pressing challenge (a fact that clouded the historical origins of terrorism); and issues that demand complicated, resource-intensive government responses tend to invite more attention from social scientists. Secondly, historians' natural predisposition against generalizing and theorizing has limited their ability or desire to tackle the broad sweep of the history of terrorism. Furthermore, the sheer scale and breadth of the history of terrorism – from ancient Judea to medieval Europe to modern Latin America – leads most historians to focus on a particular time and place rather than tackling a global, epoch-spanning theme like terrorism. In turn, the limited forays by historians into the subject reinforce the general belief that terrorism can be narrowly construed as a contemporary problem requiring only practical solutions. Historians have tended to concede the point, even though terrorism is as old as humanity itself.

The constant push for governmental plans that will "solve" terrorism has exacerbated the turn to social science because policy initiatives and the social sciences share a common starting point: clear definitions that enable the collection of quantifiable data sets. Criteria-driven definitions of terrorism have produced extraordinary insights into the nature of the phenomenon. Examples of this can be found in every issue of the journal *Studies in Conflict and Terrorism*, as well as more general publications such as the *American Political Science Review*. Perhaps the best book in this vein is Walter Enders and Todd Sandler, *The Political Economy of Terrorism*. Unfortunately, the definitions that suit today's political purposes also shape the long-term debates, unintentionally marginalizing the contributions of those in history and the humanities who may ask philosophical questions about the very construction of our perception of terrorism. I reiterate: neither approach is right or wrong. But problems arise when the field is dominated by one outlook, and the search for workable definitions of terrorism has taken on an outsized importance. I do not criticize that effort; I merely seek to help provide some balance to it. Rather than starting with definitions of terrorism designed to produce quantifiable data, I trace the emergence, evolution, and manipulation of the definitions of terrorism.

Of course, it is impossible to write an all-inclusive history of terrorism that addresses every group, movement, and event relevant to the subject. So what guided my selection of material to include in this text? Why is *this* terrorist group worthy of inclusion, but not *that* one? The most important point to recognize is that my understanding of terrorism, as described above, does not revolve around traditional definitions or clearly demarcated criteria. I have not let a checklist of definitional elements build my pool of actors and events and thus my narrative. Rather – and remember the three approaches I described earlier – I have included individuals and groups that have contributed in particularly important ways to the forms of conspiratorial organization, the specific justifications, the innovative uses of technology, or the pioneering of new tactics in the history of terrorism. For instance, although the People's Will of Russia killed only a few people in the 1870s and 1880s, the group warrants inclusion for its pioneering use of underground cells, its deliberate attempt to use terror to cultivate a heroic public persona, and its influence on subsequent generations of Russian terrorists.

I have also included the most illustrative historical examples of terrorism as a specific form of provocative and symbolic violence, as well as examples that demonstrate how terrorism frequently overlaps with other types of violence, such as war, guerrilla activity, crime, and psychopathic behavior. For example, long before the invention of the word terrorism, the Sicarii of ancient Judea used violence for its impact on distant audiences, not its military utility against its targets. And although the 1960s Brazilian revolutionary Carlos Marighella never carried out a significant terrorist attack himself, he devised a widely emulated strategy of using provocative violence to build a revolutionary movement.

In addition, since terrorism has long been used as an epithet to delegitimize groups, ideologies, motives, and forms of violence deemed deviant or dangerous by the dominant powers, I have included a generous selection of actors denounced as terrorists who would not otherwise meet such definitional a criterion. Most historians, for instance, dismiss the notion that a formal organization plotted the violence that erupted at the Haymarket in Chicago in 1886; nonetheless, the authorities' allegations about shadowy conspiracies inaugurated an obsession with leftist terrorism in the United States that lasted for two generations.

Because I am not wedded to definitions of terrorism that hinge on a particular terrorist profile, I am free to investigate the use of so-called state terror where it has influenced the history of terrorism. The French Jacobins of the 1790s, for example, used terror against civilians only *after* they seized state power – but in so doing laid the foundation for revolutionary terrorism and inspired the first use of the word "terrorist." Furthermore, Soviet and Nazi violence appears in this context to be a near mirror image except in scale of the sort of sub-state terrorism that had stalked Europe for decades: revolutionaries and state actors alike killed to achieve aims beyond just destroying their enemies. I have chosen not to provide lengthy accounts of later purveyors of state terror, such as the far right regimes of Argentina, Spain, and South Africa because those governments typically mimicked earlier patterns.

This understanding of terrorism as, variously, a set of tools, a commitment to symbolic violence, and a contest for legitimacy also demands that counter-terrorism be treated as a critical component of its history. First, counter-terror has a dual meaning, since states engaging in it not only try to destroy terrorists, but also often terrorize the populations that harbor terrorists. Second, poorly executed counter-terrorism enables terrorism, since terrorists can often capitalize on a population's anger, fear, or humiliation; at the same time, successful counter-terrorism demands a clear understanding of the factors that make terrorism possible. Thus, the two phenomena are always intertwined. This book does not purport to be a comprehensive history of counter-terrorism. Yet in several instances I have included descriptions and analyses of counter-terror efforts where the links between terrorism and counter-terrorism are very clear and where the consequences of poorly executed counter-terror are especially negative. The example of the French in Algeria in the 1950s and 1960s is particularly illuminating on both counts.

My intent has been to produce a highly readable and useful narrative history of terrorism that is sensitive to the twin concerns of historians: the march of time and differences of place. The temporal and geographic sweep of this subject, however, demands that the historian find a way to address simultaneous narrative threads. My solution has been to stick generally to a chronological treatment of terrorism, deviating from that when necessary to trace consecutively simultaneous developments in multiple places. I frequently juggle two or more storylines within a chapter, such as in Chapter 2, which addresses developments in Europe and the Islamic world during the Middle Ages. I have resorted twice to a more drastic solution when simultaneous developments were particularly detail-rich and distinct. From the 1860s to the 1910s, for instance, terrorism was used by Russian revolutionaries, European anarchists, American racists, and Irish ethno-nationalist separatists. Likewise, during the second half of the twentieth century, terrorism was a byproduct of decolonization and ethno-nationalist struggles, leftist millenarianism, the rise of Islamism/jihadism, radical environmentalism, and the American Patriot movement. For each of these two time periods I pursue individual narrative threads one at a time. I encourage the reader to turn to the chronology of important dates for these chapters in particular.

Because I have chosen to prioritize the overall chronology of the history of terrorism, the history of several groups, movements, and regions is separated across two or more chapters. I have adopted this method of organization in the case of the IRA because nearly fifty years separated the activity of the IRA of Michael Collins and the Black and Tan War from that of the Provisional IRA of the 1970s and beyond. In the case of the Middle East, the story of Irgun and LEHI is presented alongside other mid-century opponents of the British Empire, while the PLO is laid out as a separate but intertwined struggle that touches the present. The story of jihadism is presented in yet another chapter because its proponents provide such a stark alternative to the PLO's secular ethno-nationalism. The white supremacist beliefs of the Reconstruction-era Ku Klux Klan obviously have much in common with recent American militia activity, but they are discussed in separate chapters because they are divided by a century of history that includes the end of the Cold War and the emergence of the urban guerrilla movement – two historical developments that have as much to do with the last two decades of militia violence as does earlier American racism.

On a final organizational note, some recent terrorist groups (ALF/ELF, militias, etc.) get relatively short shrift if judged solely in terms of their current importance. Some readers might ask why Russian revolutionaries of the 1870s and Algerian ethno-nationalist separatists of the 1950s are accorded more space than terrorists active today. The reasons are many: these groups were the pioneers that developed the tactics and made terrorism the tool it is today; they are rarely covered in sufficient detail in texts on modern terrorism; and many complementary works are available on contemporary terrorism. In short, I have allocated space and attention to individuals, groups, and movements based on their overall historical significance rather than body counts or their current scale of activity.

The perceptive reader will note that I abstain throughout the text from presenting this work as a set of "historical lessons" about terrorism. The past teaches us nothing on its own; rather, it is our interpretations of history that are significant and guide us in our future action. But we extract blueprints for action at our peril, for the same circumstances never occur twice. The human record – both at the national and personal levels – is strewn with the wreckage of "lessons" and their blueprints misapplied. Indeed, one of the major storylines of this book is the repeated effort by various authorities to apply blueprints in the effort to combat and curtail terrorism. The results are often disastrous. As an historian, what motivates me is the search for richer, more incisive questions – questions that can illuminate the present through an informed exploration of the past. My hope is that the pages that follow will prompt readers to ask those questions.

Bibliography

The best single-volume introductions to contemporary terrorism are Jonathan R. White, *Terrorism: An Introduction*, 4th edn. (Thomson Wadsworth, 2002); and Bruce Hoffman, *Inside Terrorism* (Columbia University Press, 1998). As mentioned above, the best survey of terrorism from the social science perspective is Walter Enders and Todd Sandler, *The Political Economy of Terrorism* (Cambridge University Press, 2006). Another valuable work in this vein is Neil J. Smelser, *The Faces of Terrorism: Social and Psychological Dimensions* (Princeton University Press, 2007).

A trailblazing article on terrorism that has influenced my work significantly is David Fromkin, "The Strategy of Terrorism," *Foreign Affairs* 53:4 (July 1975), 683–98. The first true attempt to present a history of terrorism is Walter Laqueur, *A History of Terrorism* (Transaction, 2001 [1977]). It remains highly valuable, but some of its material is out of date, and it is not organized chronologically. An excellent work, both for the editor's methodological introduction and its authors' various chapters, is Martha Crenshaw [Henderson], ed., *Terrorism in Context* (Pennsylvania State University Press, 2001 [1995]). More recent surveys are Gérard Chaliand and Arnaud Blin, eds., *The History of Terrorism* (University of California Press, 2007); and Michael Burleigh, *Blood and Rage: A Cultural History of Terrorism* (Harper Press, 2008). A useful edited work that draws on a number of disciplines is Walter Reich, ed., *Origins of Terrorism: Psychologies, Ideologies, Theologies, States of Mind* (Woodrow Wilson Center Press, 1998 [1990]).

The best anthology of primary sources is Walter Laqueur, ed., *Voices of Terror: Manifestos, Writings and Manuals of al Qaeda, Hamas, and Other Terrorists from around the World and throughout the Ages* (Reed Press, 2004). Another useful collection is Isaac Cronin, ed., *Confronting Fear: A History of Terrorism* (Thunder's Mouth Press, 2002).

The best study of terrorism as a social and cultural construct is Joseba Zulaika and William A. Douglass, *Terror and Taboo: The Follies, Fables, and Faces of Terrorism* (Routledge, 1996). Another valuable work is Philip Jenkins, *Images of Terror* (Aldine de Gruyter, 2003).

I
Terror and Tyrannicide in the Ancient World

There are few examples of terrorism in the ancient world that would warrant inclusion in a history of the subject if we were limited by most of the modern definitions of the phenomenon. As soon as we begin to speak of terrorism as symbolic violence intended to achieve its users' aims indirectly through fear or intimidation, then we can begin to see many pre-modern antecedents to what otherwise seems to be a purely modern phenomenon. And if we acknowledge that the term "terrorism" is often used by a society's dominant political and cultural authorities to condemn forms of violence regarded as fundamentally illegitimate, then we can discern even more proto-terrorism in the pre-modern world. Finally, if one is keen to trace the emergence of many common traits associated with terrorism, then one might well be surprised at how much continuity exists between the ancient and modern worlds. In other words, if "terrorism" as we know it did not exist for the ancients, surely many of its characteristics would have seemed awfully familiar.

The Assyrians

The Assyrians were perhaps the ancient world's fiercest and most violent people. Their empire in the ninth to the seventh centuries BCE was the largest of its day and the most highly militarized society yet seen in the world. Faced with a dearth of resources, the Assyrians conquered those with material assets and large populations and then ruled their far-flung and diverse empire through systematic terror. The military was organized to terrify its enemies, using large formations of chariots and cavalry designed to awe as much as to destroy. The king employed his personal bodyguard to police the bureaucracy; disloyal government agents were recalled and executed; and when the Assyrians' enemies and their leaders resisted or revolted, they were cruelly tortured and killed.

For the first time in recorded history, these acts were publicized in order to warn potential enemies; in fact, the Assyrians are often cited as the earliest practitioners of psychological warfare. The Emperor Assurnasirpal II bragged of how he skinned alive, impaled, burned, mutilated, blinded, and decapitated the leaders and many of the citizens of the rebellious city of Susa. "All the other survivors I left to die of thirst in the desert," he wrote (quoted in Bradford, *With Arrow, Sword, and Spear*, 42). This brutal treatment was meted out with such regularity that the word "Assyrian" became synonymous with cruelty to one's neighbors. The Assyrians were eventually undone by their own methods in the seventh century BCE, when the burden of living under the Assyrians became so great that their native auxiliary troops revolted. Assyria's neighbors seized the opportunity and toppled the empire.

Warfare in Ancient Greece

Elsewhere, cultures differentiated between acceptable and unacceptable forms of violence, a precursor to later societies' efforts to differentiate between terror, a normal weapon of war, and terrorism, an illegitimate weapon used by immoral agents. In Greece, war was fought according to commonly accepted rules and then celebrated in myth, literature, and history. The Greeks recognized a code of conduct marked by an emphasis on arête (manliness, bravery, and skill) and heroic hand-to-hand combat. This usually meant that city-states sent phalanxes of heavy infantry to grind it out against each other until one broke and fled the field. Wars were decided by short, vicious, and decisive battles in which both sides committed all their troops. They were to be fought during the summer on wide open plains, and certain times and targets – such as the Olympics and civilians, priests, heralds, and holy sites – were off-limits. Unorthodox tactics that we might today call guerrilla warfare or even terrorism were frowned upon and worse, punished by history and the gods. In Homer's *Odyssey*, for example, Achilles' desecration of the body of the vanquished Hector tarnishes his reputation and leads to his downfall. After all, a Greek warrior was to fight honorably with every drop of energy, skill, and resolve, but recognize defeat and submit to the benevolent victor.

Yet the Greeks violated their own norms when it served their political and military purposes, so that, despite cultural taboos, terror like the Assyrians' was not alien to the Greeks. One of the most disturbing examples is Alexander the Great's response to the Theban revolt of 335 BCE: he sold nearly all the citizens into slavery and razed the city to the ground, sparing only the priests, their temples, and the descendants of the ancient poet Pindar. The lesson was not lost on the city of Athens, which was also in revolt. It immediately sent a delegation to Alexander begging for peace. Practicality thus trumped morality when it came to warfare and violence.

Warfare in Ancient India

Only in the case of ancient India, however, were tactics such as assassination openly accepted as legitimate forms of warfare. This is but one of the many startling suggestions presented in the *Arthashastra* (best translated as *The Science of Wealth*). Its author was Kautilya (aka Chanakya), kingmaker and counselor to Chandragupta, who ruled late in the fourth century BCE and rid India of the Greeks in the years after the death of Alexander the Great. Unlike other ancient Indian texts, which are primarily religious and ethical in orientation, the *Arthashastra* is largely secular and practical. In its emphasis on the "natural" needs of the state and on ends rather than means, some have noted a strong similarity to Machiavelli's *The Prince*. Kautilya described four categories of conflict resolution, the first three of which are diplomacy; "open war," or conventional combat similar to that of the Greek phalanxes; and "concealed war," which is dependent on maneuver, surprise, and deception and resembles modern guerrilla war.

Kautilya's fourth category is "silent" or "clandestine war," that is, covert operations and assassination. Although he regarded open battle as more "righteous," Kautilya favored clandestine war, for it allowed for larger victories at smaller costs. "A single assassin can achieve, with weapons, fire or poison, more than a fully mobilized army," he noted (*Arthashastra*, 507). Kautilya wrote at length about the assassination of rulers and high officials but also sketched a few scenarios involving terror against the broader population. One script instructed secret agents to assassinate community leaders and rob wealthy citizens while spreading rumors that these were punishments exacted by a regent or an ambitious viceroy. Another called for agents to set fire to palaces, city gates and granaries and kill guards while planting rumors of courtly intrigue, thus "rousing the people" against the ruler's underlings (*Arthashastra*, 527). In the most extraordinary scenario, Kautilya spins out a remarkable plan for defeating a besieged city. Agents costumed as demon-serpents and flesh-eating were-tigers should terrorize civilians to lure the enemy king outside the city walls to perform rites of appeasement, whereupon he could be ambushed and killed (*Arthashastra*, 535–6).

The meaning of Kautilya's text was not lost on his benefactor, the Emperor Chandragupta, who used guerrilla warfare in the early stages of forging his empire. In his war against Alexander the Great's successors, Chandragupta reputedly had Greek officials assassinated (Boesche, *The First Great Political Realist*, 9) and, fearing he was also the target of such attempts, is said never to have slept in the same bed on consecutive nights.

Tyrannicide

The emperor's dilemma – a ruler cannot assassinate his enemies without expecting to become a target himself – was recognized by contemporary authors in many civilizations. Ancient civilized societies were strongly hierarchical in organization, with nobles, priests, and warriors superior to commoners and slaves in quantifiable ways. King Hammurabi of Babylon, for instance, made this a cornerstone of his famous code, which only levied a fine if a person killed someone of a lower rank. An intact hierarchy was the glue that held ancient societies together, guaranteeing prosperity and social stability. Killing a ruler was therefore the most serious of crimes, because it set a dangerous precedent by reminding everyone that rulers were mortal and – even worse – vulnerable. The rate of political assassination that defied hierarchy could thus serve as a barometer of the health of a body politic. Rome, for example, witnessed few political murders until the assassination of the Gracchus brothers in the late second century BCE, killings that serve as a convenient marker for the beginning of the Republic's descent into blood-soaked political in-fighting.

Ancient history nonetheless abounds with examples of regicide, real and mythical. Sometimes killing a ruler was regarded as necessary, even good because some were meant to die. Ancient apologists for the murder of an illegitimate ruler would deem it a "tyrannicide" – that is, the murder of a tyrant. Though the introduction of the word "terrorism" was still centuries away, we can see the modern rhetorical dynamic at work, at least in regard to the phenomenon of assassination. The two terms approach the same issue from opposite sides. In the last century, the word "terrorism" has become a slur, damning certain sorts of unconventional political violence deemed illegitimate; while in the ancient world, the word "tyrannicide" was praise, blessing those acts of unconventional political violence designated as legitimate. Over the last two centuries, these terms have formed two sides of the same coin: proponents of what society deems terrorism justify their acts with the rhetoric and ethical arguments of tyrannicide.

The Ancient Hebrews

Kautilya did not define the moral circumstances that permitted regicide and other assassinations – utility was his main yardstick. Others were keen to contextualize political murder, whether through suggestion or strict guidelines. Some of the oldest descriptions of justifiable assassination come to us through Hebraic scripture. In fact, one can find few stretches of literature with more blood-stained pages.

The most famous stories come from the time when the Hebrews were ruled not by kings who drew their legitimacy from genealogy, but by men known as judges who received their mandate from Yahweh, as God was known to the Hebrews. Though celebrated as the people responsible for the concept of monotheism, the Hebrews frequently ran afoul of their Lord by engaging in idolatry, worshiping rival gods, or lapsing into other unseemly behavior. Yahweh's punishment, as recorded in scripture, was often to send a foreign tyrant to conquer and enslave the Hebrews, who – after the sufficient return of piety, obedience, and humility – would eventually be rewarded with a hero to deliver them from the tyrant. As the medieval scholar John of Salisbury wrote, "penitence annihilates, drives out and kills those tyrants whom sins obtain, introduce and encourage" (Salisbury, *Policraticus*, 207). The "deliverer" Ehud committed the first Hebraic tyrannicide against Eglon, king of Moab, initiating his act with the startling words, "I have a message from God for you" (Judges 3:20).

The most extraordinary tale of assassination comes from the Book of Judith. It recounts the invasion of Judah by Holofernes, the Assyrian king Nebuchadnezzar's most trusted general. With the Assyrians on the brink of victory, salvation for the Hebrews comes from an unlikely source, the widow Judith. She prays to the Lord for the strength to save her people and her land, and he grants her beauty "to entice the eyes of all men who might see her." This beauty helps her gain entry into the Assyrian camp and the tent of Holofernes himself. While trying to seduce her, he falls asleep, drunk on wine, whereupon Judith beheads him with his own sword. Both Jews and Protestants have assigned the Book of Judith deuterocanonical or apocryphal status, in part because of its unclear authorship and many historical anachronisms. The apocryphal nature of Judith's heroism, however, has not deterred apologists for tyrannicide through the ages from exploiting her story. Medieval

Figure 1.1: Caravaggio, *Judith Beheading Holofernes* (1598)
(ibilio.org)

authors, for example, turned to it to argue that deception, treachery, and even the appeal to lustful prurience were acceptable when used to do God's work.

Historians are on more stable ground when it comes to using scripture to tell the bloody story of the Hebrew kingdoms of Israel (in the North) and Judah (in the South) from the death of Solomon in 922 BCE to the beginning of the Babylonian Captivity in the sixth century BCE. The record reveals a catalog of assassinations and intrigues nearly unrivaled in human history. Of the forty kings who ruled during these three and a half centuries, twelve were victims of regicide (many more died in battle, from suicide, or by other violent means). In most instances, scripture notes that the ruler had warranted death for doing "evil in the eyes of the Lord" (see, for example, 1 Kings 15:26). Sometimes the details are nearly too gruesome to bear, as with Jehu's assassination of Jezebel: "some of her blood spattered the wall and the horses as they trampled her underfoot . . . But when they went out to bury her, they found nothing except her skull, her feet and her hands . . ." Jehu's response: "This is the word of the Lord . . . On the plot of ground at Jezreel dogs will devour Jezebel's flesh" (2 Kings 9:33–7).

These tales of blood and assassination from Judges and Kings served to clarify the Hebrews' history to themselves. Religious scholars generally believe that these books achieved their final form during the Babylonian Captivity in the sixth century BCE. The author or authors of these books set out to answer a simple question: how could Yahweh allow his chosen people to be led away into brutal and humiliating captivity? The author(s) of the histories answered clearly: the Hebrews repeatedly defied their God and received the punishment they deserved, for which the earlier tales of tyranny and tyrannicide were merely table-setters. Thus, the violence of these scriptural histories was metaphorical, even educational. Just as tyrants were meant to punish the Hebrews and their rulers for idolatry, polytheism, and other sins, the violence meted out in the act of tyrannicide reminded all of the cost of sin (particularly polytheism and idolatry) and the possibility of redemption. Clearly, great evil was sometimes done in the name of establishing a future good. Ultimately, however, stories of regicide and rebellion were more successful at reinforcing Hebraic monotheism than creating universal norms for the ethical behavior of rulers and subjects. An indication of this can be seen in the fact that by the time of the Hebrews' last prophets, reverence for the Lord was more clearly attained – and even valued – than was political stability.

Tyrannicide in Ancient Greece

The Greeks also grappled with the idea of justifiable assassination and left behind colorful tales of tyrannicide. There is the murder of the tyrant Phalaris of Acragas (in Sicily) by Telemachos in 554 BCE; the assassination of Polycrates of Samos by Cambyses in 515 BCE; the murder of Jason of Pherae in 370 BCE; the poisoning of Dionysius I of Syracuse by his son, Dionysius II, in 367 BCE; the killing of Dion of Syracuse, who overthrew Dionysius II, by Callippus in 354 BCE; the murder of Clearchus of Heraclea by Chion and Leonidas in 353 BCE; and the death of Oxyathres of Heraclea at the hands of Lysimachus in 284 BCE.

To the earliest Greeks, the word tyrant was morally neutral. It simply referred to a leader who came to power by force, typically by overthrowing a polis' traditional form of government, which in the eighth to sixth centuries BCE was monarchy or oligarchy. The typical Greek tyrant courted popular favor by persecuting aristocrats, canceling the debts of the poor, and putting commoners to work on public works projects. They were often regarded by contemporaries as just and kind rulers.

In time, the term tyrant began to acquire nasty connotations, a development marked by the emergence of a rich literature justifying tyrannicide. The growth of Athenian democracy led citizens to view tyrants as usurpers, not just of the people's political power, but also of their property and honor. Eventually, the growth of new legal institutions and norms led more Greeks to condemn tyranny as a violation of the natural order and illegitimate by definition.

The evolving Greek attitude toward tyrannicide can be traced in reference to the most famous instance of it, the murder of Hipparchus, a younger brother of the Athenian tyrant Hippias, in 514 BCE by the lovers Harmodius and Aristogeiton. After the eventual overthrow of Hippias himself, the assassins of Hipparchus were celebrated as "the Liberators" and "the Tyrannicides" (tyrannophonoi). The sculptor Antenor fashioned a monument to the two that stood in the Agora of Athens; it was Athens' first political monument and is often described as the first statue to honor humans. The feat was also the subject of a poem by Callistratus that in turn became a popular Athenian drinking song. "They killed a tyrant," it declared, "and made Athens a place of equality under the law" (quoted in Taylor, The Tyrant Slayers, xiii).

The great Greek historians Herodotus and Thucydides took some of the luster off the reputations of the heroic lovers by noting some of the historical inconsistencies in the story. In any case, there is considerable evidence that Athenians of the fifth century BCE knew the facts, yet persisted in their hero worship (Monoson, Plato's Democratic Entanglements, 27–8). Aristotle ventured a reassessment of this famous killing as well, claiming that Hippias and Hipparchus were actually quite "temperate" in their rule. This was not merely an act of righting the historical record for Aristotle; rather, it was a striking illustration of what made his dissection of the phenomenon of tyrannicide the most influential in the ancient and medieval world. The danger was that criminal murder could easily be pitched as tyrannicide. Such, essentially, had been the case with the two lovers, according to Aristotle, who protested that the pair were nothing but demagogues. For Aristotle, the key was to construct a rationale that praised tyrannicide but only in the most egregious cases of tyrannical abuse.

This he did in Book V of Politics. There, Aristotle made clear that a tyrant was such because of the manner of his rule, not the mere circumstances of how he came to power. To illustrate his point he drew from dozens of real-life examples. The common elements were the morally debauched and mentally disordered character of the tyrant (a key feature of Plato's earlier description of tyranny), his perversion of the traditional political practices of the polis, and his assault on the honor, wealth, and rights of the citizens. As Oszkár Jászi and John D. Lewis note, "the test was ethical rather than legal." Quite tellingly, Aristotle – just as Plato before him – dwelt little on making an explicit case for tyrannicide. As far as both were concerned, the killing of a tyrant was the natural response to the tyrant's transgressions. "Hatred of tyrants," Aristotle wrote, "is inevitable," as was, presumably, the effort by some to be rid of them. He described the motives of historical tyrant-slayers and remarked off-handedly that "high honors are awarded to one who kills a tyrant" (Jászi and Lewis, *Against the Tyrant*, 7).

Tyrannicide, Terror, and Political Violence in Ancient Rome

Across the Ionian Sea, the Romans began their ascent to greatness awash in political murder, or so their later historians claimed in a process that they indirectly acknowledged was conscious myth-making. The purpose of this mythology-as-history was, in part, to establish beyond doubt in the eyes of the Republic the liabilities of Rome's early monarchy and, by extension, monarchy as a whole. According to this "history," Rome's eighth-century founders, the twins Romulus and Remus, had a falling out that ended in the latter's murder and the former's emergence as the first of the so-called "seven kings of Rome." The biographer Plutarch specu-lated that Romulus became a tyrant and was murdered by the Senate, the advisory council of patricians he created. The sixth Roman king, Servius Tullius, was also murdered, in this case by his daughter and her husband, who ran him down in a chariot on an avenue that came to be known as Wicked Lane (*Vicus Sceleratus*). Whereas the Athenians held up Harmodius and Aristogeiton as models of citizenly duty, the Romans downplayed the feats of patriotic assassins. A partial explanation can be found in Roman reverence for authority, the law, and custom. Romans were aware of the fragile balance struck in the Republic between elite and mass, between oligarchy and democracy. To them, the cure for tyranny could easily be worse than the disease.

At the end of the sixth century BCE, the Senate expelled the last Roman king and established the Republic, at which time the duties of the monarch were divided between two consuls who served year-long terms. One of the first two consuls was Lucius Junius Brutus, whose first act, according to the Roman historian Livy, was to require Romans "to swear a solemn oath never to allow any man to be king in Rome" (*From the Founding of the City*, Book 2, Chapter 1). Brutus' second consular colleague was Valerius Publicola, who introduced a law stating that the public was enti-tled to kill any man who declared himself a king of Rome.

Perhaps such declarations were enough, for Roman politicians and theoreticians rarely engaged in discussions of tyranny and tyrannicide for the next five centuries. And, whereas the Greeks frequently killed tyrants – particularly in the century before and after the age of Pericles – Rome was nearly free of the phenomenon of political murder or assassination from the time of its emergence from the founding of the Republic until the second century BCE.

There are only three known cases of tyrannicide in this time period – the patricians Cassius and Manlius and the wealthy plebeian Maelius – and all are poorly documented. In each instance, a wealthy politician allegedly sought monarchical power by using his riches to court favor with plebeians. Grasping after kingship – the greatest offense against justice in the Roman Republic – was a violation of tradition, not law. As such, these killings were reputedly carried out by citizens, not the state. Today we might call this vigilante justice.

In war and international diplomacy, the Romans developed a strong animus against the targeted killing of foreign dignitaries. The reason for this stigma is hard to pinpoint. Some have noted that the Roman personal code of conduct so valued personal bravery and skill in group arms that assassination was seen as unmanly. The Romans also developed a taste for the sort of total victory that only came from crushing one's enemy on the battlefield.

Ironically, the conquest of a Mediterranean empire through military prowess signaled the beginning of the end of the fine balances that limited the domestic use of political violence and made the Republic viable. The influx of slaves undermined the security and value of the plebeian Roman soldier-farmer-citizen, and the introduction of generals made powerful by the loyalty of their legions destroyed the traditional political process. The dramatic proliferation of political murders in the second and first centuries BCE was both cause and consequence of further political decline. The first two victims were the brothers Tiberius and Gaius Gracchus, the most prominent of the so-called *populares* who championed the causes of the poor but were denounced as demagogues by Rome's elite. Angry senators beat Tiberius to death, along with up to three hundred of his supporters, in 133 BCE. Twelve years later, the Senate granted one of their own emergency powers that were used to besiege Gaius, who committed suicide rather than submit, and his followers on the Aventine Hill in Rome.

This sequence of plebeian challenge and reactionary patrician violence – sometimes sanctioned, often extra-legal – became a common feature of Roman politics, with each bloody cycle further degrading the traditional restraints and checks and balances that had been hallmarks of Rome's success (Boatwright *et al.*, *The Romans*, 165). Lintott claims that in the years after the death of Tiberius Gracchus, the stories of the patriotic murders of Cassius, Maelius, and Manlius were re-circulated, but in altered forms suggesting that patrician magistrates were responsible for meting out the tyrants' punishments. The goal was narrowly to circum-scribe tyrannicide as a patrician prerogative. Still, with the emergence of more and more *populares* in the Senate eager to court the masses to gain power, the specter of internecine violence, terror, and civil war grew.

The consulships of the patrician general Sulla and his chief rivals, Marius, Cinna, and Marius the Younger, were a watershed in the decline of the Republic and the introduction of wide-scale political violence. Twice (in 87 and 82 BCE) Sulla waged civil wars against his enemies. In the wake of the first, Sulla prevailed upon the Senate to declare Marius and eleven others "enemies of the people of Rome" (*hostes populi Romani*) without benefit of a trial. Most of the condemned escaped, including Marius, but Sulla had set in motion the use of extra-judicial decrees to destroy oppo-nents and terrorize their supporters. Between the two civil wars and in Sulla's absence, Marius and Cinna engineered their elections as consuls, after which they immediately rounded up and executed over one hundred noble supporters of Sulla and then displayed their heads in the Forum as a lesson to all. Sulla's return from exile at the head of a new army triggered the second civil war that ended with his victory. Horrified by the violence and desperate for stability, the Senate conferred on Sulla the title of dicta-tor and granted him sweeping authority to rule by decree. The Senate had done this in previous emergencies, but never for longer than six months at a time. This time there was no term limit attached. The newly chris-tened dictator quickly put his powers to use against his enemies, primarily through "proscription." Such a declaration stripped the victim of citizen-ship and condemned him to death without a trial. Rewards were given to informers and those who killed the proscribed, while those who sheltered them were punished. During Sulla's reign of violence – the ancient world's most infamous precursor to modern day state terror – an estimated 500 to 1,500 senators and equestrians who had opposed him died. So great was the violence that one of his associates, Senator Lutatius Catulus, asked Sulla whether he planned to kill everyone.

Cicero and the Last Decades of the Roman Republic

Over the next two decades, outbreaks of violence and rumors of civil war and conspiracy were common. In 63 BCE, the disgruntled patrician Catiline planned a campaign of terror consisting of arson, hostage-taking, and assassination that was to culminate in an armed coup in Rome. As he secretly massed the army that would cap his revolution, Catiline's con-spiracy was unmasked by the consul and famed orator Marcus Tullius Cicero. The Senate, at Cicero's urging, executed Catiline's associates who could be found in the city. Within a few months, armies sent by the Senate destroyed the rebel's army. Catiline himself was killed and his head displayed in Rome.

Our knowledge of the history of the Catiline conspiracy is unfortunately based almost entirely on the works of Sallust, an historian with his own axe to grind against the rebel, and Cicero himself. Sallust attributed to Catiline an inflammatory speech in which he roused his supporters to imagine themselves not as the "mere mob" described by the Senate, but as the opponents of "those, to whom, if the state were in a sound condition, we should be a terror" (Sallust, *The Catilinarian Conspiracy*, Chapters 20 and 22).

One of the principal words with which Cicero denounced Catiline and his fellow conspirators was *latro*. In earlier centuries, it had meant simply "pirate" or "robber" but by Cicero's time had come to mean something more than "bandit" and less than "rebel" – in other words, someone whose engagement in criminal acts rose above simple thievery and posed a threat to the state, but whose motive remained personal and financial, not political or ideological. The status of a *latro* was murky: no longer was he protected by the rights of citizenship, whether by choice or act of state, nor was he dignified with recognition as an enemy combatant. Cicero and others, including the later historian Livy, notably contrasted *latrocinia* (a *latro*'s activity, often translated as "brigandage") to *bellum iustum*, a "just war" that was fought by legitimate means and for legitimate purposes. While *latro* had a technical meaning, it was just as useful to Romans as a metaphor. As Brent Shaw has noted, the term was "used deliberately to cast doubt on hostile persons, principally political enemies" (23). For the Romans, *latro* most likely conjured up the same feelings of fear, disgust, and anger that are today triggered by the word "terrorist." In fact, Cicero and Sallust's accounts of the Catiline conspiracy are best understood not as descriptions of the real Catiline and his plot, but rather as the ancient world's most successful example of the public vilification of what today would commonly be called a terrorist.

The last decades of the Republic also witnessed a new kind of violence in Rome, the virtually unchecked activity of gangs of thugs whose mayhem was part political, part criminal. The closest modern day parallel is Hitler's SA, members of which were known as Brownshirts. The Roman practice of clientage meant that patricians always had a pool of eager partisans willing to agitate on their behalf. This sort of impromptu violent behavior was part and parcel of Rome's political life – particularly bloody examples were the disturbances associated with the Gracchi in 133 and 122. By the 60s BCE, the swelling ranks of disaffected soldiers and unassociated plebeians became a tempting target for those of means who were able to hire them.

The man most responsible for organized gang terror was Clodius Pulcher, a patrician of the famed Claudius family, who renounced his rank and adopted the plebeian spelling of the name so that he could be elected tribune of the people. Before that, he was most known for being caught in drag while attending a religious service to which no men were admitted. As tribune in 58 BCE, Clodius actively recruited urban toughs, freedmen (immigrants who were not citizens), slaves, soldiers, and even gladiators into semi-official gangs and used them to terrorize his opponents in both the Senate and the Tribal Assembly. Even after the end of his one-year tribunate, Clodius remained the master of Rome's streets and a critical figure in Roman politics. His enemies, most notably the conservative Tribune Annius Milo, pursued the only path available to them: the recruitment of their own rival gangs. Running battles raged in Rome's narrow and winding streets. After one particularly violent battle, Cicero recorded that "the Tiber was full of citizens' corpses. The public sewers were choked with them and the blood that streamed from the Forum had to be mopped up with sponges" (quoted in Everitt, *Cicero*, 149).

The Republic's descent into bloody civil strife horrified Cicero. His reaction, however, was not to decry all such violence, but to justify certain manifestations of it – really for the first time in Roman history – with an eye toward limiting its application. Injustice demands remedy, he stated, and it is good and necessary when a tyrant is overthrown by the populace, "as long as it has sense and wisdom . . . and applies itself to maintaining the constitution which it has established. But" – and here is Cicero's critical caveat – "if ever the people has raised its forces against a just king and robbed him of his throne, or, as has frequently happened, has tasted the blood of its legitimate nobles, and subjected the whole Commonwealth to its own license, you can imagine no flood or conflagration so terrible, or any whose violence is harder to appease than this unbridled insolence of the populace" (Cicero, *On the Commonwealth*, I, 42). Not surprisingly, Cicero's warning did little to lessen the bloodshed.

Julius Caesar and the End of the Roman Republic

In fact, Rome's drama of terror and tyrannicide was moving toward its climax: the assassination of Julius Caesar remains history's most celebrated act of tyrannicide, and the defense mounted by Cicero of the murder remains one of its most influential.

Long-simmering tensions between the joint rulers Julius Caesar and Pompey Magnus erupted into civil war in 50 BCE. After nearly three years of fighting across the length of the Republic, Pompey was killed and his forces defeated. Caesar returned to Rome and embarked on an ambitious program of debt cancellation and public building designed, like the Gracchi's eighty years before, to win popular support and aid the urban poor. He was appointed dictator for life in February 44 BCE, in part because he packed the Senate with supporters. But patrician hatred of him increased. Many feared and hated him as a populist and demagogue: some for personal slights, others for his open contempt for the Republic's obsolete rituals and institutions, some for his attacks on or simple avoidance of traditional senatorial privileges, still others for the idea that he aspired to be king.

For some senators, the new title was the last straw. Marcus Junius Brutus – one of Caesar's closest friends and the descendant of Lucius Junius Brutus, the author of the oath against tyranny – hatched a plot along with his brother-in-law Cassius Longinus. Details of the conspiracy and the eventual assassination are confused, in part because of the existence of so many accounts and later retellings, most famously Plutarch's and Shakespeare's. What is known, though, is that the group of conspirators – who tellingly dubbed themselves "the Liberators" (*Liberatores*) – included about sixty men, all drawn from the Senate. Their plot was inspired by a mixture of patriotism and self-interest, but the goal was universal: to restore the power of the *optimates*, the conservative senatorial "constitutionalists." Meanwhile, Caesar apparently became so fatalistic he dismissed his bodyguards and mingled freely with the public. In the days preceding the planned attack, the conspiracy became Rome's worst-kept secret, and several people tried to warn Caesar, to no avail. On March 15 – the Ides of March – Caesar was lured to the Senate and attacked. By prior arrangement, all of the conspirators tried to land a blow, and in the maelstrom several senators wounded each other. Caesar may have only received one fatal blow, but the cumulative effect was enough. Much has been made of his apparent death wish, but more should be made of the simplicity, even amateurishness, of the plot. The assassination was hardly inevitable; in fact, its success was a comedy of errors.

The plotters' hopes for the return of senatorial privilege and Republican stability were swiftly dashed. A triumvirate of strong men formed – consisting of Caesar's grand-nephew and heir, Octavian; Caesar's most trusted lieutenant, Mark Antony; and the general Lepidus – and a new round of civil war quickly followed. Rome became calm only with the final destruction of the Republic and transformation into the Empire under Octavian, who became known as Augustus Caesar.

The reality of the murder's aftermath, like its planning, is hard to separate from later embellishments and outright fictions. It can be argued, in fact, that the true significance of the assassination lies not in its immediate results – many have argued that a new bout of patrician in-fighting was likely whatever Caesar's fate – but rather in the amount of interpretation and conscious myth-making that it provoked. In time, Caesar became more important as a symbol than as a man.

The most influential description of the assassination was composed decades after the fact by Plutarch (46–127 CE), who wrote biographies that are more accurately described as morality tales than histories. In his "Life of Brutus," Plutarch praised the conspirators against Caesar as men driven by their unstinting love of the Republic and singled out Brutus for exceptional glory as "an heroic soul and a truly intrepid and unquailing spirit" who "had no private quarrel with Caesar, but went into the risk singly for the liberty of his country" (*Lives*, "Comparison of Brutus and Dion"). Plutarch's narration of the assassination itself laid out the blueprint for a properly conceived and executed tyrannicide, especially since Brutus insisted the violence be limited to Caesar's killing, although many conspirators wanted to kill Antony as well.

The theoretical justification for Caesar's murder was enshrined much more quickly, courtesy of Cicero, and displays the same essential features. Cicero had publicly held his tongue about Caesar during his lifetime and even offered some mild praise because of the dictator's efforts to rebuild Rome and care for the poor. In the end, however, Cicero became convinced that Caesar aspired to kingship or, at the least, complete emasculation of the Senate. The orator and statesman was not part of the conspiracy, but he came to support the assassination after the fact, claiming that Caesar had sought to become king. In *De Officiis* (*On Duties*), Cicero claimed that natural laws govern human morality and demand certain actions, even when they might appear to violate the state's laws. To illustrate, he drew upon the recent assassination of Caesar:

> What more atrocious crime can there be than to kill a fellow-man, and especially an intimate friend? But if anyone kills a tyrant — be he never so intimate a friend — he has not laden his soul with guilt, has he? The Roman People, at all events, are not of that opinion; for of all glorious deeds they hold such a one to be the most noble. (*De Officiis*, Book III, 19–20)

Cicero's argument perfectly encapsulated the ancient world's attitude toward tyrannicide: tyranny is a perversion of nature, and tyrannicide is the moral and expedient corrective. The removal of the tyrant and the tyrant alone – violence beyond his person would be immoral – allows the body politic to return to its natural state, just as a surgeon, according to Cicero, might amputate a diseased limb. That the ancients went to such great lengths to justify tyrannicide and lionize its best exemplars demonstrates their fear that the practice would be indiscriminately applied.

Yet the killing of tyrants – like most forms of violence – was rarely as neat and tidy as Cicero and other ancients wished. In fact, it tended to open Pandora's box and loosen existing restraints on violence. If he could speak from beyond the grave, Cicero himself might well attest to that. During the chaos that followed Caesar's death, he once again emerged as a popular leader of the Senate. When Octavian and Antony swiftly moved to destroy the assassins of Caesar and supporters of the conspiracy, Cicero fled Rome, but was caught and executed in 43 BCE. His head and hands were cut off, returned to Rome, and displayed in the Forum – the same punishment given Catiline twenty years earlier.

The birth of the Empire under Augustus (Octavian) Caesar brought stability to Rome, but the concentration of power in the Emperor's court also created new opportunities for murder and mayhem among the elite. Although the volume of such political violence during the Empire dwarfed that of the Republic, most of it can be categorized as palace intrigue, revenge killings, or imperial sadism. A few of the murders, such as the assassination of the notorious Caligula in 41 CE and of the only marginally less cruel Domitian in 96 CE, had some of the trappings of tyrannicide, but might just as easily have been the products of personal animosities; to be sure, neither of them re-established senatorial rule or appreciably changed Roman political culture. Noteworthy, however, is the effort of commentators to portray these murders as something more elevated. The historian Suetonius, for example, wrote that Caligula's assassination was foretold by a bolt of lightning that hit the Capitol in Capua on the Ides of March. This portent was likely included to draw a link between this justifiable tyrannicide and that of Julius Caesar. In any case, the Empire survived, but emperors frequently found themselves the victims of their own bodyguards. From 192 to 244 CE, half of the emperors who served (seven of fourteen) were murdered by the Praetorian Guard or its prefect. These were hardly tyrannicides, however, for the responsible parties rarely made the barest pretense of killing for any reason other than personal advancement; nor did historians, chroniclers, or theoreticians of tyrannicide make any attempt to justify any of these murders as the defense of liberty.

Terrorism in Judea: The Case of the Sicarii

A very different brand of violence – one that we would readily recognize as terrorism – emerged in the area known variously as Israel, Judea, and Palestine. But first, some background. The Jews of the Eastern Mediterranean had already been living under a string of foreign rulers for centuries when the Syrians seized Israel from the Ptolemy dynasty in 168 BCE and quickly instituted the worship of Greek and other pagan gods. The following year, the Jewish priest Mattathias and his sons, including

Judah the Maccabee, "gave vent to righteous anger" and struck down both the Syrian officer who would force them to worship an idol and a fellow Jew who stepped forward to answer the Syrian's call (1 Maccabees 2:24). This was perhaps the first documented instance of revolutionary terrorism, that is, an act of violence not intended to destroy an enemy, but rather to inspire others to rise up. "Let everyone who is zealous for the law and supports the covenant come out with me!" cried Mattathias, thus beginning what came to be known as the Maccabee revolt, a popular uprising that culminated several years later in the establishment of the Jewish Hasmonean dynasty.

The Hasmoneans found it easier to live up to Mattathias' violent precedent than his reputed religious purity. After several bouts of familial civil war, one monarch appealed to Rome for help in 64 BCE, an act which turned Israel into a client state and the Hasmoneans into puppets. In order to maintain their privileged position, the priests of the Jerusalem Temple and their supporters, known as Sadducees, collaborated with the Romans. In the first decade of the Common Era, a small movement began to proclaim "no masters above God" and violently agitated against both Romans and Sadducees. Another symptom of discontent was the prevalence of banditry, some of it carried out by Jewish "Robin Hoods" angered by the region's painful social and economic inequalities. Increasing tensions and violence culminated in the outbreak of open and ill-fated revolt in 66 CE. The so-called Jewish War ended four years later with the Roman conquest of Jerusalem and the destruction of the Second Temple. The dramatic epilogue came in the siege and suicide of nearly one thousand holdouts at the mountain fortress of Masada in 73 CE.

These events provided the stage for the ancient world's most notorious and controversial terrorist group, the Sicarii. Acrimonious debate surrounds them even today, largely because virtually all knowledge of the Sicarii comes from a single source laden with biases. That man is Josephus, a Jewish general who defected to the Roman side, acquired Roman citizenship, and eventually wrote a history of the revolt, *The Jewish War*. According to Josephus, the Sicarii began operating in the 50s CE. As the newest adherents to the doctrine of "no masters above God," their goal was the liberation of Judea and its people from Rome. They were sure that God was on their side, a conviction nearly apocalyptic in its intensity. Their use of distinctive daggers similar to the Roman *sicae* gave the Sicarii their name, and their use of these weapons distinguished them from run-of-the-mill bandits or even traditional revolutionaries. The Sicarii assassinated prominent Jews who collaborated with the Romans, often in daylight and in the midst of large crowds. According to Josephus, "The first to have his throat cut by them was Jonathan the high priest, and after him many were murdered every day. More terrible than the crimes themselves was the fear they aroused, every man hourly expecting death, as in war" (Josephus, *The Jewish War*, 147). The Sicarii also kidnapped and ransomed prominent Sadducees in order to raise money, gain the release of captured compatriots, and further spread a sense of chaos and instability. In the countryside, the Sicarii attacked pro-Roman Jewish gentry and looted their property. The Sicarii understood that they were few in number and apparently hoped to foment an uprising against the Romans by demonstrating the authorities' vulnerability. Some historians have also surmised that the Sicarii hoped to provoke a harsh crackdown by the Sadducees, which would in turn push the Jewish population into rebellion. That the Sicarii targeted only fellow Jews can be explained by the fact that few Roman officials lived in Judea at the time. Some have conjectured that this strategy is proof that the Sicarii were motivated by social and economic concerns as well, since it was the Sadducees and rural Jewish gentry, after all, who most benefited from Roman rule.

In any case, Sicarii terrorism contributed significantly to the outbreak of a revolt in Jerusalem against the Romans and their Temple allies in 66 CE. The Sicarii leader Menachem briefly led the insurgency but was assassinated by rivals when, in the words of Josephus, he "turned to savagery and . . . became unbearably tyrannical" (Josephus, *The Jewish War*, 167). As with many modern terrorists, Menachem's fanaticism and violence made him a poor candidate to lead a broader movement. His death also spelled the end of the Sicarii's brief involvement in the Jewish revolt in Jerusalem. Before the Romans even arrived in large numbers, the Sicarii fled the city, a persecuted minority within the rebellion. At this point, leadership of the revolt was seized by the so-called Zealots, a Jewish faction often confused with the Sicarii.

The Sicarii sat out the war in the mountaintop fortress of Masada, which they captured shortly after their flight from Jerusalem. At Masada, the Sicarii were driven to criminal acts to survive their desert exile. Josephus describes one raid on the village of Engedi in which the Sicarii "butchered" 700 women and children, "stripped the houses bare, seized the ripest of the crops, and brought the loot to Masada" (Josephus, *The Jewish War*, 266). This episode, like the entire Roman–Jewish War that the Sicarii helped to foment, demonstrates well a timeless trait of terrorists: their willingness to see the civilians they claim to represent as ultimately expendable, necessary sacrifices to the greater cause.

Stocked with fresh supplies, the Sicarii, "who left no word unspoken, no deed untried, to insult and destroy the objects of their foul plots," continued to carry out terrorist attacks "against those prepared to submit to Rome, [but] in reality this was a mere excuse, intended to cloak their barbarity and avarice" (Josephus, *The Jewish War*, 393–4). Only after the Romans captured Jerusalem, destroyed the Second Temple, and crushed the rebellion – killing as many as 1.3 million in the process – did they turn their attention to the Sicarii at Masada. There, the Romans erected a wall around the fortress and began a siege. Though the defenders had enough food and water to last for some time, it quickly became clear that the end was preordained. In a long speech preserved by a survivor, the Sicarii leader Eleazar ben Yair convinced his followers to die by their own hands rather than become Roman slaves. The ensuing mass suicide of nearly one thousand is further testament to the Sicarii's fanaticism, perhaps even their conviction that the apocalypse was at hand.

There are two curious epilogues to the Sicarii's putative "last stand" at Masada. Some Sicarii made their way to Alexandria, Egypt, where they tried to create a second uprising against the Romans, again using assassination and terror. Alexandria's Jews, knowing what happened to Jerusalem and its Jewish community when the Romans were finally provoked into a full-scale invasion, ferreted out the Sicarii on their own initiative and turned them over to the Romans. Meanwhile, in Cyrene (eastern Libya), a rabble rouser named Jonathan whipped up discontent among the poor. Fearing the start of a new wave of Sicarii-inspired terrorism, the local Jews reported his existence to the Roman governor, Catullus, who promptly rounded up Jonathan and his rag-tag band. At some point, Jonathan and Catullus entered into a plot – the former to save his life, the latter to gain fame and fortune – that involved Jonathan's denunciation of Cyrene's wealthiest and most powerful Jews as his terrorist backers. Catullus used the unmasking of this contrived conspiracy to murder three thousand local notables and confiscate their possessions, likely the first time in history that a very public fear of terrorism was used for a ruthless politician's personal ends (Josephus, *The Jewish War*, 405–8).

Within the history of terrorism, the Sicarii are also significant as subjects of what we might call "terrorism discourse." For example, we have no evidence that the Sicarii called themselves by that name. Most likely, the term is of Josephus' invention since the word Sicarii was Latin, not Greek or Hebrew – that is, from the language of the victors, not the terrorists or rebels. More than a century before Josephus and the Jewish–Roman war, the word *sicarius* had come to mean "assassin," appearing as such in the name of a Roman law from the days of Sulla intended to punish murderers-for-hire and those that supplied them with equipment. Cicero also used it to refer to a member of an armed gang that killed for financial gain (Brighton, "The Sicarii in Josephus' Judean War," 84). We can gain even more insight into Josephus' use of the term by noting the other words that he frequently used to describe the Sicarii. Both the Greek *lestai* and the Latin *latro* can mean bandit; but during the late Republic and early Empire, as described above, the term *latro* was applied to enemies that were more than a criminal but less than a state.

In other words, if the word "terrorist" had been available to Josephus, we can be sure he would have applied it to the Sicarii, a classic case of the victors using the epithet to frame a narrative in a way that strikes at the heart of a cause's legitimacy. For we must remember that despite his defection to the Romans, Josephus remained a Jewish patriot. In his twenty-one-volume history of the Jews, *The Antiquities*, he presented his coreligionists as the noble, just, and intelligent followers of a tradition of world-wide significance. *The Jewish War* was thus his effort to rescue that tradition from the thugs he believed had hijacked it.

And yet, for decades the modern state of Israel lionized the Sicarii as the heroic defenders of Masada and Jewish independence. Until recently, in fact, recruits were solemnly sworn into Israeli armored units atop the mountain. The historical and rhetorical treatment given the Sicarii, therefore, provides one of the first and best examples of the semantic relativism summarized in the cliché that one person's terrorist is another's freedom fighter.

Bibliography

Good works on early warfare include Richard Gabriel, *The Culture of War: Invention and Early Development* (Greenwood, 1990); Victor Davis Hanson, *Carnage and Culture: Landmark Battles in the Rise of Western Power* (Anchor Books, 2002 [2001]); Alfred S. Bradford, *With Arrow, Sword, and Spear: A History of Warfare in the Ancient World* (Praeger, 2001); and John Lynn, *Battle: A History of Combat and Culture*, rev. updated edn. (Basic Books, 2004), which contains a short but excellent treatment of Kautilya, the Indian Machiavelli. Kautilya's work, *The Arthashastra*, ed., trans., and introduced by L. N. Rangarajan (Penguin, 1992) is available in English. The best study of Kautilya is Roger Boesche, *The First Great Political Realist: Kautilya and His "Arthashastra"* (Lexington Books, 2002).

Two excellent and wide-ranging dissections of the theory and history of tyranny and tyrannicide are Roger Boesche, *Theories of Tyranny from Plato to Arendt* (Pennsylvania State University Press, 1996); and Oszkár Jászi and John D. Lewis, *Against the Tyrant: The Tradition and Theory of Tyrannicide* (The Free Press, 1957). Another very useful survey covering the history of assassination and, by extension, tyranny and tyrannicide, is Franklin L. Ford, *Political Murder: From Tyrannicide to Terrorism* (Harvard University Press, 1985).

Boesche and Jászi/Lewis are excellent on the Greeks. Two useful monographs, particularly on the Greek tyrannicides Harmodius and

Aristogeiton, are S. Sara Monoson, *Plato's Democratic Entanglements: Athenian Politics and the Practice of Philosophy* (Princeton, 2000); and Michael W. Taylor, *The Tyrant Slayers: The Heroic Image in Fifth Century B.C. Athenian Art and Politics*, 2nd edn. (Ayer, 1991).

A solid and stimulating survey of Roman history is Mary T. Boatwright *et al.*, *The Romans: From Village to Empire* (Oxford, 2004). Anthony Everitt, *Cicero: The Life and Times of Rome's Greatest Politician* (Random House, 2001), provides a good introduction to Cicero. Two works that illuminate the role of the mob and political violence in the waning days of the Roman Republic are A. W. Lintott, *Violence in Republican Rome* (Oxford, 1968); and Fergus Millar, *The Crowd in Rome in the Late Republic* (University of Michigan Press, 1998). Brent Shaw, "Bandits in the Roman Empire," *Past and Present*, no. 105 (Nov. 1984), 3–52, provides a helpful analysis of the Latin term *latrocinia* and its uses as a political weapon.

The Sicarii and the Jewish War have generated a large amount of scholarship – not all of it helpful. Excellent introductions to the Sicarii are Richard A. Horsley, "The Sicarii: Ancient Jewish 'Terrorists'," *Journal of Religion*, vol. 59, no. 4 (Oct. 1979), 435–58; and David C. Rapoport, "Fear and Trembling: Terrorism in Three Religious Traditions," *American Political Science Review*, vol. 78, no. 3 (Sept. 1984), 658–77. The latter is a path-breaking article on terrorism that explores the history of religiously inspired terrorism by examining the Sicarii, the Assassins, and the Thugs (of early modern India). A first-rate analysis of Josephus' treatment of the Sicarii is Mark Brighton's unpublished dissertation, "The Sicarii in Josephus' Judean War" (University of California, Irvine, 2005). As for Josephus' work itself, it is available in many editions; I used *The Jewish War*, trans. G. A. Williamson, rev. edn. (Penguin, 1981). An outstanding study of the modern creation and political uses of the myth of heroic resistance at Masada is Nachman Ben-Yehuda, *The Masada Myth* (University of Wisconsin Press, 1995).

2

Terror and Tyrannicide in the Middle Ages

Political terror and the theory and practice of righteous killing figured prominently in both the Islamic world and Christian Europe in the centuries between the collapse of Roman rule in the West and the dawning of the modern era. Beneath that broad statement, however, lurk important differences.

During the High Middle Ages in Europe, conflicts between Church and state led to new justifications of tyrannicide – that is, apologies for violence otherwise rejected as unacceptable. During the late Middle Ages and the early modern era – from the fourteenth to the eighteenth centuries – several major developments transformed Europe and intensified interest in both the theory and practice of tyrannicide. The splitting of the Western Church and emerging ideas about popular sovereignty empowered individuals to protest their subservience to traditional authorities deemed illegitimate. Both changes provided additional justifications for tyrannicide and contributed to the modern understanding of terrorism.

Church, State, and Violence in Medieval Europe

With the decline and collapse of the Western Roman Empire in the fifth century, a new set of realities dominated Europe. Infrastructure decayed, central authority disintegrated, and literacy and education nearly vanished. State power and the rule of law disappeared. In their absence arose rule by a patchwork of Germanic tribes nominally ruled by monarchs, but political power in feudal Europe was really exercised effectively only at the local level. Given this state of affairs, it is often difficult to differentiate between private murder and political assassination. Most killings were the result of personal feuds or disagreements over inheritance and property; matters of precedent or abstract principle rarely figured.

In this political and legal vacuum, the Church – the only possible universal authority – tried to impose some stability and a moral compass. The Church regarded itself as the sole interpreter of scripture and had representatives throughout Europe, from village priests to bishops and archbishops in major cities to the Pope in Rome. The Church operated hundreds of monasteries and was one of the largest landowners in Europe, untaxed and not subject to local laws.

In theory, the Church's ideas about violence, authority, and tyranny were of supreme importance. Christ's teachings on these subjects were unambiguous: suffer all violence passively and submit to temporal authority meekly. The Apostle Paul stated the proposition even more forcefully when he wrote to the Christians in Rome that "everyone must submit himself to the governing authorities . . . [for they] have been established by God. Consequently, he who rebels against the authority is rebelling against what God has instituted" (Romans 13:1–2). The early Church Fathers expanded on these statements. Augustine of Hippo, for example, stated that Roman citizens should obey their rulers since the good ones ruled in God's name and evil ones delivered humanity's well-earned punishment.

Although a full-blown Christian doctrine of tyrannicide was long in coming, theologians did believe one could not be compelled to follow a tyrant who violated divine laws. The fourth-century Bishop of Constantinople, John Chrysostom, said Christ ordained the office, not the ruler who inhabited it. Even more influential was Augustine's verdict that the doings of the city of Rome were by definition criminal, at best irrelevant, and certainly consigned to the way of all flesh. Toward this end, he praised the brave words – preserved by Cicero – of a pirate to Alexander the Great: "Because I [seize property] with a petty ship, I am called a robber [latro], while you who do it with a great fleet are proclaimed emperor" (City of God, Book IV, Chapter 4). How could it be wrong, Augustine's reader might have asked, to oppose such injustice and criminality?

In addition, popes and other Church leaders found it necessary to remind monarchs that their endorsement of temporal rule was not absolute. When the Roman Emperor Theodosius I massacred thousands of Greek civilians in 390, the Bishop of Milan successfully threatened him with excommunication if he did not repent. "Notice whether [monarchs] rule lawfully," said the ninth-century Pope Nicholas I. "Otherwise they are rather to be considered tyrants than kings: tyrants whom we ought rather to resist and assail than to obey" (quoted in Jászi and Lewis, Against the Tyrant, 15).

John of Salisbury and Tyrannicide in the High Middle Ages

Such pronouncements took on new weight in the High Middle Ages, when dynastic rulers began to gather up lands, develop bureaucracies and royal courts, and find new ways to raise revenue. While powerful national monarchs could provide greater stability in their realms, they also threatened the traditional rights of aristocrats and the Church. In particular, Church lands and wealth were tempting targets to money-hungry kings, who also wanted to subject the clergy to royal laws. Popes fought back; Gregory VII, for instance, declared in the eleventh century that, as God's representative on Earth, he had the power to depose kings through excommunication. In England, the conflict between Church and State turned violent in 1170, when Henry II's knights murdered the country's highest religious official, Thomas Becket, who had steadfastly defended the Church's authority.

John of Salisbury – Becket's secretary, an English diplomat, church official, and one of the greatest scholars of his day – witnessed the murder. A decade earlier, he had written *Policraticus* ("The Statesman's Book"), in which he sought to clarify the sources of political legitimacy in an age of heightened monarchical authority. His nightmare scenario was an incompetent or unrighteous king atop a powerful throne.

Like most other great intellectuals of his time, John of Salisbury practiced scholasticism, the dominant school of Church teaching in the eleventh to thirteenth centuries. Influenced by the Greek and Roman Stoics, Scholastics sought to reconcile divine and natural law and saw faith and reason as twin paths to the same ultimate truth. They dwelt on the notion that a just ruler was obliged to secure the "common good," although most failed to define it. That had serious implications for those trying to determine a Christian's obligations to monarchical authority. If, as written in Romans 2:15, every man should exercise moral responsibility in accordance with "the requirements of the law . . . written on their hearts" (Romans 2:15), was there not room to criticize tyrannical authority – or perhaps even a duty to act? If so, anti-authoritarian acts almost had to be couched in religious terms to provide the requisite justification. The victim had to "deserve" to die in God's eyes, thus alleviating the killer of all culpability.

"Between a tyrant and a prince," John of Salisbury wrote, "there is this single difference . . . The prince fights for the laws and the liberty of his people; the tyrant thinks nothing done unless he brings the laws to nought and reduces the people to slavery." The result? A proper king was "a kind of likeness of divinity," while a tyrant has "the likeness of the devil" (quoted in Jászi and Lewis, *Against the Tyrant*, 20). He added that the best remedy for the oppressed is to pray humbly, and God will remove "the scourge with which they are afflicted" (John of Salisbury, *Policraticus*, 209). But he also strikingly endorsed a violent solution, declaring that "it has been honorable to kill [tyrants] if they could not be otherwise restrained" (John of Salisbury, *Policraticus*, 205). His evidence came mostly from the Bible, from which he quoted at length the stories of the tyrant Eglon and his assassin, Ehud; the general Sisera and the Israelite deliverer Jael; and the Assyrian Holofernes and his killer, Judith, whose story he translated in a way to suggest the beauty that tempted her victim was the result of divine intervention. At the same time, he warned against the use of poison, for it was used by "infidels," or killing those to whom participants had sworn oaths of fealty.

John of Salisbury's influence can be seen in medieval England's most important political document, the Magna Carta of 1215. Although the Magna Carta is often considered a democratic manifesto, it is more properly understood as a contract between the English monarch and his nobles. In the agreement, the nobles ceded to the king general authority over the state in exchange for privileged status within it. The terms masked the aristocracy's defeat while crystallizing high and late medieval political thought, and the document solidified medieval Europe's definition of tyrant as a king who violated his subjects' traditional rights and privileges.

The Theory of Tyrannicide in the Late Middle Ages

When Europeans conquered Muslim lands in Spain and the Eastern Mediterranean during the Crusades, they rediscovered Aristotle, whose works had mostly been lost to the West since the fifth century collapse of Rome. New translations of the ancient world's greatest authority on tyranny were commissioned and welcomed by medieval intellectuals who recast his descriptions of tyrants in scholastic terms, cementing the belief that tyranny was a deviation from both divine and natural law. Examples may be found in the works of the philosopher Aegidius Romanus (d. 1316) and the jurists Bartolo da Sassoferrato (d. 1357) and Luca da Penna (d. 1390).

If tyranny was so roundly condemned, why was tyrannicide not more common? In fact, why was it so rarely practiced at all? Although it was a violent age, strong biases existed against the use of planned violence against monarchs. Most Europeans, commoners and nobles alike, were constrained by the widespread fear that political violence might unleash social unrest. "The vices of the powerful are to be tolerated, because with them rests the prospect of public safety," wrote John of Salisbury

(*Policraticus*, 131). Pre-Reformation scholars usually explored the question of tyrannicide not in response to a spate of such murders, but rather as a byproduct of debates over political legitimacy.

A new appreciation for tyrannicide's appeal – and thus danger – emerged in the thirteenth century. Thomas Aquinas, Medieval Europe's greatest scholar, condemned tyranny in ringing terms but was ambivalent about tyrannicide. On one occasion he approvingly cited Cicero's endorsement of Caesar's murder and stated that when there is no other recourse, "he who kills the tyrant for the liberation of his country is praised and receives a reward" (quoted in Jászi and Lewis, *Against the Tyrant*, 26). But he later drew a distinction that took on great significance for medieval audiences. He allowed for the killing of tyrants who ruled without legitimate title and authority (*ex defectu tituli*), but condemned the murder of those with the proper title, even if they ruled cruelly (*ex parte exercitii*). Ambiguity eventually disappeared altogether when he proposed that prayer and patience were better responses, since the cure for tyranny was likely to be worse than the disease. A failed tyrannicide might push a tyrant to greater cruelty; a successful one might precipitate civil war. Thomas warned that the precedent was more likely to lead evil men to commit poorly justified tyrannicide than good men to carry out appropriate ones. He concluded that it was safer to demand that tyrannicide only be exercised by the country's "public authorities" instead of private individuals. Given the paucity of authorities besides the king who were prepared to speak or act on behalf of the kingdom, such a mechanism could really only be of use to a later age.

Tyrannicide vs. Murder

In fifteenth-century France we come upon one of the few tests of tyrannicide theory in medieval Europe. The reign of King Charles VI was at low tide during the Hundred Years War with England. Weak in mind and body, he was reduced to the status of mere observer as the rival ducal houses of Orléans and Burgundy fought for supremacy. In 1407, assassins sent by Jean the Fearless, the duke of Burgundy and cousin of the king, murdered Louis, the duke of Orléans and the king's brother. This was the first murder within the ruling family of France in hundreds of years, and it prompted a royal inquest. Jean's advocate, the Sorbonne professor Jean Petit, admitted that his patron was responsible for Louis' murder, but quoted nearly every ancient and medieval authority on tyrannicide, producing the Procrustean claim that "it is lawful for any subject, without any order or command, according to moral, divine, and natural law, to kill or cause to be killed a traitor and disloyal tyrant. It is not only lawful, but honorable and meritorious" (quoted in Jászi and Lewis, *Against the Tyrant*, 29). Despite the fact that the particulars of the case were specious – Petit said that Louis would surely *have become* a tyrant if not prevented by Jean – a stacked audience secured Burgundy's vindication.

The Chancellor of the Sorbonne, Jean Gerson, was horrified by Petit's excuse of tyrannicide in the service of base political murder. Several years later, during a lull in Burgundian influence, the Chancellor denounced Petit's claim and offered in its place an exceedingly qualified view of tyrannicide, capped off with the plea that even when the tyrant deserved death, he "ought rather to be left to the judgment of God than killed by private authority or by sedition" (quoted in Jászi and Lewis, *Against the Tyrant*, 30). The Council of Constance, convened by the Church in 1415, vaguely condemned tyrannicide without naming Petit. A brutal response to Jean's deed and Petit's justification came in 1419 when the Duke of Burgundy was himself assassinated by soldiers of the Dauphin, a validation of Aquinas' fears that tyrannicide might unleash the floodgates of political violence. This episode also foreshadowed the much greater tension between tyrannicide theory and murderous practice that would emerge over the next few centuries in Europe.

State Terror in Medieval Europe

At the same time, another variety of medieval violence also anticipated violence in the modern age: state terror. Extaordinarily brutal acts were designed and carried out, then as now, as public spectacles meant to teach unmistakable lessons. One of the first examples grew out of a decades-long conflict between rival Frankish kingdoms in the sixth and early seventh centuries. In 613, Queen Brunhilda of Austrasia – who repeatedly had opponents assassinated and who was accused of incest and other sordid crimes – was killed by her enemies, but only after she was tied to wild horses who dragged her through the streets for three days.

The Norman kings of England were particularly adept at the use of state terror. During the winter of 1069–70, William the Conqueror engineered a famine in Northern England that put an end to that region's resistance to its new Norman lord. Half a century later, William's son, Henry I, invited to London scores of officials responsible for minting coins, then ordered the public castration of those he determined had cheapened his money by using too little silver. Henry's nephew, Stephen, hanged the entire garrisons of rebellious forts and cities during the lengthy civil war that dominated his reign. King John of England added a new twist to the use of state-sponsored terror: he cleverly orchestrated the disappearance of enemies so gruesome that rumors of what happened to them were even more effective deterrents than public mutilations or executions. His use of this tactic against nobles helped spur the revolt that led to his defeat and the signing of the Magna Carta.

Terror, Terrorism, and Tyrannicide in the Medieval Islamic World

Within the Islamic world, the source of violence lay within Islam's defining principle: *tawhid*, meaning unity or oneness. The term primarily refers to Islamic monotheism, but *tawhid* also means there are no clear distinctions between secular and religious authority. Although Westerners typically translate the term *sharia* as "Islamic law," a more accurate definition is God's will for humanity – immutable, eternal, and binding. As such, *tawhid* leaves no room for "politics" as we know them. Another factor is Islam's fundamental and age-old orientation toward social justice, violations of which are naturally translated into religious terms.

Another critical source of violence is that Muhammad and the leaders that followed him for several generations set an example of territorial conquest and theocratic rule. Since the death of the Prophet, sectarian rivalries have been the greatest source of Islamic "political" violence, tyrannicide, and terrorism. The Qur'an demands obedience to Islamic rulers, but at least two *hadith* (sayings and actions attributed to Muhammad) obligate Muslims to disobey heretical leaders. Tyrannicide thus has deep roots in Islamic tradition.

Schisms in Islam

The empire and religious community that Muhammad forged in the seventh century CE was led after his death by a series of caliphs ("successors" in Arabic), and the enormous medieval Islamic empires they ruled were called caliphates. The first four caliphs were chosen by consensus among Muhammad's companions, but thereafter the position became hereditary. Three of the first four caliphs were assassinated, and the death of the third, Uthman, was a clear case of tyrannicide. Many accused him of ruling as a king because he abandoned Arab traditions of leadership, favored kin over the community of believers, and violated religious duties and norms. Uthman's successor was Ali, Muhammad's cousin and son-in-law.

Religious violence appeared in many guises in Islam's early years. The Kharijites ("seceders" in Arabic) branded as apostates all Muslims who committed a serious sin. The result of this excommunication (*takfir* in Arabic – the word is once again in circulation today) was not unlike Roman proscription, for the Kharijites believed that killing such an individual was allowed or even required by believers. Ali was assassinated at the hands of a Kharijite who thus "punished" him for accepting arbitration in a dispute with a rival when he should have asserted his claim as Muhammad's rightful heir. Today's Kharijites have rejected violent behavior and their ancient name, but the practice of proscription is alive and well today in the hands of other Muslims. The most notorious example has been the fatwa issued in 1989 by the Iranian leader Ayatollah Khomeini calling for the death of the author Salman Rushdie and his publisher.

From the death of Muhammad in 632 CE, Islam has been divided against itself over claims about leadership of the community of believers (known as the *umma* in Arabic) and the source of religious authority. Most Muslims followed the medieval caliphs and regarded them as regular mortals who drew their authority from their ability to uphold *sharia*. They came to call themselves Sunnis, after the Arabic word meaning tradition. In Sunni societies, theological doctrine has been left to the *ulama*, the community of elected religious scholars. Today, most Muslims – perhaps 85–90 percent – are Sunni.

A smaller number of Muslims, both then and now, rejected the Sunni attitude toward religious leadership. When Muhammad died, they regarded Ali as the Prophet's natural successor. Thus they came to be known as Shia, a shortening of the Arabic phrase meaning the Party of Ali. In each generation, Shiites followed an Imam ("leader" in Arabic) descended from the Prophet and regarded as the infallible source of religious and political guidance. From the beginning, Shiites pressed their claim that they were truer Muslims since they followed their Imam and relied on only the Quran and *hadith* for direction. In the centuries after the death of Muhammad, Sunnis and Shiites openly battled each other. The conflict, though, was one-sided. Sunnis – always the majority – persecuted Shiites as extremists who practiced mysticism, idolatrously worshipped their Imams, and, much worse, would never accept the rule of the caliphs. Sunnis also killed many of the first Imams, heightening the antagonism.

The Assassins

Islam's many schisms gave rise to the Assassins, the most notorious of medieval Islamic factions and one of the most illuminating pre-modern examples of terrorism. Although all evidence indicates that the Assassins only targeted rival military, political, and religious leaders, they practiced something much broader than tyrannicide. In fact, they appear in many ways to be forerunners of today's jihadists.

With the decline of the Shiite-dominated Fatimid dynasty in Egypt, the great Sunni empire of the Abbasid caliphate and its eventual overlords, the Seljuk Turks, stepped up their persecution of scattered Shia communities. Meanwhile, a new group led by Hassan-i Sabbah emerged in distant Persia in the 1090s to carry the Shiite banner. Sabbah's group was itself an offshoot of the eighth-century Ismaili sect of Shia Islam. The so-called "new teaching" of Sabbah was notable for its uncompromising attitude, and his Ismaili followers displayed unquestioning obedience, fervent proselytizing, and a willingness to embrace martyrdom at the hands of Sunnis. With his sect on the verge of extinction, Sabbah retreated to the mountains of Persia just south of the Caspian Sea, seized the castle of Alamut, and carved out his own mini-state. Sabbah's Ismailis found a cause and a name when they backed Nizar, a candidate for the Imamate and the Fatimid throne. The Nizaris grew in number, seized more territory, and sent missionaries to modern day Syria. They raised armies and sent diplomats, behaving in all outward ways as a Muslim principality. In territory ruled by the Sunni Abbasids or Seljuks, Nizaris formed a significant minority but their fanaticism invited even greater persecution, which further radicalized the sect. After Nizar's death, Sabbah claimed to know the hidden location of the living Imam and spoke on his behalf. In his hands, the hidden Imam became the sole source of legitimacy, truth, and revelation. Sabbah's group became convinced that their mission was to purify Islam, and they retreated further and further into mysticism and secret rituals.

Most importantly, Sabbah committed the Assassins – as Europeans came to call them for their chosen method – to a campaign of terror and violence. The Nizaris didn't hope to eliminate all of their opponents, but they used murder to destroy those who threatened their missionary zeal, to remind themselves of their uncompromising revolutionary drive, and to radicalize the broader Muslim world. The Nizaris regarded assassinations as a tool of public influence, and usually carried them out in full view in courts, city squares, or mosques. Their first victim was Nizam al-Mulk, a Seljuk Turk minister who persecuted the sect for its "vice, mischief, murder and heresy" (Nizam, *The Book of Government*, 188). Upon receiving the news that Nizam was dead, Sabbah reputedly announced, "The killing of this devil is the beginning of bliss" (quoted in Lewis, *The Assassins*, 47). The fact that Sabbah's assassins often killed after insinuating themselves into their victims' retinues heightened their fearsome reputation and further spread terror; Sabbah seems never to have lacked for volunteers. At Alamut, the Nizaris kept a list of victims and showered honor on the names of each one's killer. Like today's jihadism, Nizari fanaticism attracted recruits even as it alienated the broader population. In the Persian city of Isfahan, for example, Nizaris seized power and carried out a brief reign of terror that ended only when they were overthrown and killed by crowds. Within fifty years of the sect's creation, few adherents could be found in most urban areas.

Many scholars have speculated on why the Nizaris leaned so heavily on assassination. Some have pointed out that justification for such a technique could be found in the life of the Prophet himself, who had once urged followers to murder a particularly sharp-tongued Jewish poet who had written some nasty verses about Muhammad and the Muslims (Rapoport, "Fear and Trembling," 667–8). Assassination also made strategic sense in the Muslim world, where power was always personal and the death of a Sultan could throw his lands into chaos, providing significant opportunities to an organization of limited military means.

Whatever the reason for their dedication to the tactic, there is evidence of fifty assassinations carried out by the Nizaris before Sabbah's death in 1124 (Lewis, *The Assassins*, 51). Victims included Sunni religious figures, as well as Abbasid and Seljuk princes, governors, judges, diplomats, and nobles. The fear the Nizaris generated was pervasive. According to a Muslim chronicler, "No commander or officer [at the court of the Seljuk Sultan] dared to leave his house unprotected; they wore armor under clothes, and even the vizier Abu'l-Hasan wore a mail shirt under his clothes" (quoted in Lewis, *The Assassins*, 50). The Nizaris cultivated an extensive network of agents among their enemies in a manner analogous to today's terrorist cells. The Assassins also benefited from widely circulated tales of Sabbah's monk-like asceticism and a fanaticism so intense that he had both of his sons executed. Sunni and Shiite alike came to understand that such devotion brooked no compromise.

The Nizaris were so feared, they didn't necessarily have to kill. For example, the Seljuk Sultan supposedly awoke one morning from a drunken stupor to find a dagger stuck in the ground beside him. Sabbah soon sent him a message claiming that had he wished it, the dagger would have been left in the Sultan's chest. Fearing for his life, the Sultan granted the Nizaris the right to tax the residents around Alamut and to assess tolls on local travelers.

Fear of the Nizaris also drove their enemies to use excessively violent, even counter-productive strategies. Seljuk campaigns against Nizari strongholds often led to the unintentional destruction of surrounding Sunni communities, and little encouragement from Sultans and other anti-Ismaili leaders was necessary to touch off public lynchings of suspected Nizaris by civilians and soldiers alike. When Sunnis managed to re-capture Nizari castles, the Assassin commanders were often subjected to the most gruesome torture. The head of the fortress near Isfahan, for example, was flayed alive and his head was sent to Baghdad, the capital.

The animosity between the Nizaris of Alamut and the Fatimids of Egypt – another group with Ismaili roots – was, if anything, even more ferocious than that between the Nizaris and Sunnis. It is another example, in Bernard Lewis' words, of "that special, intimate hatred that exists between rival branches of the same religion" (*The Assassins*, 59). In 1122 the Egyptians, having gotten wind of a Nizari plot to assassinate the Fatimid caliph and his vizier, al-Ma'mun, responded with a counter-terrorism scheme of extraordinary reach. At Asqalan, on the frontier of the caliphate, al-Ma'mun instructed the local governor to dismiss all officials not known in the community and to investigate all travelers entering the city. Every caravan traveling to Cairo became the subject of a detailed dossier; al-Ma'mun also ordered a complete census of Cairo and forbade the population to change residences without his approval. As a result, "there was nothing concerning the affairs of anyone in old or new Cairo that was hidden from him" (quoted in Lewis, *The Assassins*, 59–61). The Fatimids seized Nizari agents, including the tutor of the caliph's children. But the vizier's strategy failed in the long term: the Assassins killed Caliph al-Amir, regarded by the Nizaris as an apostate of the first order, in 1130.

Muslim and Western Perceptions of the Assassins

We have evidence of the cultural resonance of the Nizaris' terrorist campaign, particularly in the language used to describe the group. Sabbah's followers called themselves *fedayeen* – fighters willing to sacrifice themselves for a cause – but were given a host of other names by the Sunni Muslim opponents who sought to undermine them in the court of public opinion. In fact, Sunni Arab writers typically only mentioned the violent acts of the *fedayeen*, rarely discussing their religious beliefs or motives. A twelfth-century historian described them as having "no brains in their skulls and no conviction in their hearts" or criminals trying to acquire religious cover for their violent acts (quoted in Saleh, "The Use of Bāṭinī, Fidā'ī and Hashīshī," 38). Other contemporaries claimed they killed for profit, slandered them as "gnostics" and branded Sabbah a demagogue. The Nizaris' millenarian appeal to the poor and discontented challenged the traditional social and economic hierarchy. And invented tales of Nizari licentiousness and communal possession of women and wealth alienated both Sunnis and the more moderate Twelver Shiites – so called for their recognition of a total of twelve Imams descended from Muhammad.

The most famous and lasting name for the *fedayeen*, Assassins, has been difficult to decipher. Some contemporary stories describe the *fedayeen* as hashish addicts who used the drug to steel themselves for attacks. In his travels through the Middle East in the thirteenth century, Marco Polo encountered the more fanciful tale that Sabbah, whom Polo referred to as the Old Man of the Mountain, drugged his followers and ushered them into a lush secret garden filled with beautiful women, a taste of the Paradise to come if they followed his instructions to kill for Allah. Polo rendered a local Syrian word for a hashish user, *hashishiyyin*, as "ashishin," which entered English and other European languages as "assassin." In all likelihood, local Muslims probably called the Nizaris *hashishiyyin* not to describe drug use, but what they regarded as utterly irrational behavior. Given the paucity of hard facts about the secretive sect, Polo's memoir helped create an image and a name for the Assassins in the West. The earliest use of the word "assassin" for a paid murderer also dates from around this time.

Marco Polo's account of the Assassins was so influential, in part, because it corroborated stories already circulated by the Crusaders. When the warriors of the First Crusade conquered Jerusalem in 1099 – less than a decade after the capture of Alamut – Europeans became

Figure 2.1: *The Old Man of the Mountain Giving Instructions to his Followers*, from a fifteenth century edition of Marco Polo's *Travels* (Project Gutenberg)

neighbors of the Syrian Nizaris. The Assassins killed several Christian leaders, most notably Count Raymond II of Tripoli (in Syria, not Libya) and Marquis Conrad of Montferrat, one of the contenders for rule of the Crusader Kingdom of Jerusalem. Fear that the Nizaris were focused on killing Christians compelled the Crusaders to pay tribute to the Assassins of Syria, and wild stories circulated about Assassin plots reaching all the way to Europe itself. The most notorious was the fabricated story of a Nizari conspiracy to murder French King Louis IX in Paris. It would not be the last time that narcissism and ignorance clouded the West's ability to appreciate the extent and ferocity of intra-Muslim discord.

Sabbah personally anointed his successor, on whose watch the Nizaris assassinated an Abbasid caliph and several of his prefects. At this point, leadership of the Nizaris became hereditary. Followers of the third Assassin ruler engaged in fewer assassinations, but managed to fell a caliph, a sultan, and several other prominent officials. The fourth Assassin leader dispensed with earlier theological niceties and claimed that he himself was the Imam. His heirs continued these claims into the thirteenth century.

It is worth reminding ourselves that with but a few exceptions, the Nizaris eschewed arson, kidnapping, massacres, or the targeting of civilians during their two centuries of activity. Assassination, for all intents and purposes, was their sole unorthodox means of promoting their agenda. Nonetheless, the Assassins' ability to inspire fear was so great that they reputedly convinced the great Sunni general Saladin, better known in the West for his rivalry with Christian Crusaders, to leave them alone even as he destroyed other Shia sects. One source alleges that the Nizaris even infiltrated his personal bodyguard.

In 1256, the Assassins at last met their match in the Mongols. Like the Assyrians and Alexander the Great before them, terror was a critical element in the Mongols' extraordinary expansion of empire. As they relentlessly spread from their homeland north of China across Central Asia, Russia, and Persia, they destroyed cities and slaughtered citizens, allowing a few survivors to escape so they could dissuade their neighbors from resisting.

This strategy elicited the surrender of the last Assassin Imam, Rukn al-Din, and the commanders of most Nizari castles. To prevent a revival of the sect, the Mongols dismantled the fortress of Alamut and killed up to 100,000 Nizaris. The few that remained went into hiding and were eventually absorbed back into the larger Ismaili sect, which exists to this day. The Persian Sunni historian Juvayni witnessed the fall of one of the Assassins' castles and gleefully described the death of their last Imam: "Of him and his stock no trace was left, and he and his kindred became but a tale on men's lips and a tradition in the world" (quoted in Lewis, *Assassins*, 95).

The rise of jihadist terrorism in recent decades has led modern Western writers to spill much ink comparing today's Islamists to the Nizaris. In fact, the same analytical minefields await those analyzing either group, most significantly when it comes to questions of motives. To a Western audience, the Nizaris can appear as either starry-eyed religious fanatics or cynical political opportunists. But neither response suffices, because, as noted above, the question is specious in light of the Muslim principle of *tawhid*. The Nizaris had heaven on their minds, but they certainly recognized pragmatic considerations. Thus every assassination bore the three-fold meaning of a sacramental act, publicity-seeking propaganda, and the practical removal of an enemy. The Nizaris could speak the language of territory, trade, and taxation, to be sure – even to the point of forming a mini-state – because *sharia* addresses all those subjects regarded by Westerners as "secular." The Nizaris simply parted ways with their fellow Muslims in their degree of commitment to Islam as an on-going revolution. In the context of Islam, this meant millenarianism, monasticism, and martyrdom.

Like many later terrorist organizations, the most remarkable thing about the Assassins is the stark contrast between the fear they gener-ated in their opponents and their ultimate failure to achieve their goals. Although they managed to strike terror into the hearts of Sunni leaders for two centuries, they never captured populated areas nor did much to slow the expansion of Sunni influence. And although the Assassins were established to defend Nizari Shiism, their final defeat nearly proved fatal for their sect.

Bibliography

Three studies on the history of tyranny, tyrannicide, and political murder mentioned in the last chapter are equally indispensable for this one: Boesche, *Theories of Tyranny*; Jászi and Lewis, *Against the Tyrant*; and Ford, *Political Murder*. John of Salisbury's magnum opus is readily available in English: *Policraticus*, ed. and trans. Cary J. Nederman (Cambridge, 1990).

There is a wealth of fine studies available on Islam and the Middle East. I leaned heavily on John L. Esposito, ed., *The Oxford Dictionary of Islam* (Oxford, 2003); Arthur Goldschmidt, Jr., *A Concise History of the Middle East*, 7th edn. (Westview Press, 2002); Bernard Lewis, *The Political Language of Islam* (University of Chicago Press, 1988); and Maxine Rodinson, *Muhammad* (Pantheon Books, 1980 [1961]). The standard work on the Assassins is Bernard Lewis, *The Assassins: A*

Radical Sect in Islam, reprint edn. (Oxford, 1987 [1967]). Other helpful works on the subject are Farhad Daftary, *The Assassin Legends: Myths of the Isma'ilis* (I. B. Taurus, 1994); Marshall G. S. Hodgson, *The Secret Order of Assassins* (University of Pennsylvania Press, 2005 [1955]); David C. Rapoport, "Fear and Trembling: Terrorism in Three Religious Traditions" (cited in Chapter 1); and Shakib Saleh, "The Use of Bātīnī, Fidā'ī and Hashīshī," *Studia Islamica*, no. 82 (October 1995), 35–43. The work of Nizam al-Mulk, a persecutor and victim of the Assassins, is available in English: *The Book of Government or Rules for Kings*, trans. Hubert Darke (Routledge, 1978 [1960]).

3

Terror and Tyrannicide in the Early Modern Era in Europe

Historians have applied the designation "early modern" to the period in Europe between the Middle Ages and the French and Industrial Revolutions, roughly the fifteenth to eighteenth centuries. In general, this was a time of transition during which many of the modern world's most distinctive elements began to emerge. This can also be said of terrorism, for during these years we can discern the origins of the empowerment of the individual – as opposed to medieval Europe's emphasis on communal interests – as well as, paradoxically, increasing belief in national identity rather than royal sovereignty. During the early modern era there was still no bright line demarcating secular from religious tyrannicide. Men of religious conviction came to see God's hand and God's purpose at work in transforming *this* world; while moved by religion, they were increasingly fixated on justice in the here-and-now. Tyrannicide melded religious and secular concerns; fanatical, other-worldly millenarianism mingled easily with anger at human injustice. The secure truths of the black-and-white world of violent apocalyptic thought could serve secular ends without compromise.

The Renaissance and Tyrannicide

During the Italian Renaissance, the political, economic, and cultural leaders of Northern Italy's great cities were motivated by a new range of interests. Whereas the pillars of medieval life were community, inheritance, and land, the Renaissance world valued the individual, education, and commerce. The Renaissance elite were especially inspired by the ancient Greeks and Romans. Although Christianity remained influential during the Renaissance, it faced competition from a new pragmatism and a revived humanism.

It is no accident that during the Renaissance tyranny increased dramatically in Italy. Papal and foreign intervention stymied national unity, while commercial interests often backed local despots in a desperate bid for stability, and mercenary warlords called *condottieri* assembled states by conquest. Milan, for instance, was ruled by two despotic dynasties in the fourteenth and fifteenth centuries, the Visconti and the Sforza, each of which produced a number of individuals renowned for their cruelty and ambition. The most notorious of Renaissance despots was Cesare Borgia, who briefly fashioned a duchy in central Italy but died at the age of thirty-one.

That the era spawned a number of famous tyrannicides should not be surprising. Because rulers of the Italian city-states owed their positions to guile more often than heredity, the natural medieval deference toward titles was less present. Just as importantly, infatuation with all things Greco-Roman revived the classical era's republican sentiments and its endorsement of tyrannicide. Renaissance episodes of tyrannicide include the assassinations of Giovanni Maria Visconti in 1412 and Alessandro de Medici in 1537. Equally notable despite its failure was the anti-Medici conspiracy of 1513, which ended with the capture of both would-be assassins. While awaiting execution, one of the conspirators, Pietro Paolo Boscoli, begged his friend, "pray get Brutus out of my head, so that I may make this step entirely as beseems a good Christian" (quoted in Ford, *Political Murder*, 138).

Greeks and Romans were not the only touchstones invoked. Cosimo de Medici commissioned Donatello to sculpt a statue depicting Judith's murder of the tyrant Holofernes. The fact that he imagined Judith's heroic act as a symbol of the Medicis' defense of Florentine liberty made for delicious irony when the statue was moved to a more prominent position upon the expulsion of the Medici in 1494. The sculpture's new caption read: "The citizens have erected this example of the salvation of the republic" (quoted in Jászi and Lewis, *Against the Tyrant*, 39). Across Italy, a popular saying maintained that "he who gives his own life can take a tyrant's" (quoted in Padover, "Patterns of Assassination," 684).

State-Sponsored Assassination in the Renaissance

Targeted assassination was also a tool of those already in power. Venice's secretive ruling body, the Council of Ten, reportedly relied so heavily on assassination that it created a bureaucratic apparatus devoted to the task. This body's work is shrouded in myth, and the list of Venice's rumored targets reads as a veritable who's who of Renaissance Europe. What we do know is that the Council's rumored commitment to assassination as state policy led scores of potential assassins to apply for work, including one Brother John of Ragusa who stated that he would kill the King of Spain for 150 ducats (not including travel expenses!). The humanist scholar Thomas More explicitly endorsed assassination as a moral and effective alternative to war since it led to far fewer deaths and held leaders responsible for their state's policies (Ward Thomas, "Norms and Security," 110). During the mid sixteenth century, an anonymous Italian authored an extraordinary text on assassination cumbersomely entitled *Of the Right that Princes Have to Compass the Lives of Their Enemies' Allies*. "In every State," the author wrote, "political expediency rules absolutely in its own right . . . Hence for great princes that is lawful and customary which is absolutely forbidden and impossible for others . . . " (quoted in Padover, "Patterns of Assassination," 688–9).

Machiavelli

When it comes to Renaissance political writers and their evaluations of assassination and tyrannicide, the contrast with the Middle Ages is stark and illuminating. In the earlier period, tyrannicide was often invoked as a sidebar to abstract considerations of princely authority, but was rarely practiced. Conversely, as the frequency of real tyrannicide grew during the Renaissance, fewer writers explicitly endorsed it. In fact, Dante symbolically condemned tyrannicide in *The Divine Comedy* by placing Brutus and Cassius along with Judas in the jaws of Lucifer himself at the center of the ninth circle of hell.

The political theorist Niccolò Machiavelli (d. 1527) was likewise ill at ease about tyrannicide. Although most people use the epithet derived from his name to indicate a love of treachery and power, he was, in fact, a realist motivated by a desire for effective Italian governance. While allowing that some tyrannicides genuinely seek their country's liberty, he noted that most are motivated by greed or revenge and usually lead to chaos or more repression because mobs rarely back tyrant slayers. Although only vaguely possessed of an interest in "the common good," Machiavelli was something of a pre-modern utilitarian, rejecting tyrannicide as counter-productive. If anything, he was more likely to defend the tyrants' practices as more conducive to good governance and social cohesion.

This is where Machiavelli introduced something quite new: the science of terror. He picked through history and contemporary Italian politics for episodes that he could use to illustrate how an effective ruler might carefully calibrate public acts of violence for maximum effect. The best example involved Machiavelli's hero, Cesare Borgia, who installed a "cruel, efficient" Spaniard, Remirro de Orco, to pacify and stabilize Borgia's newly won territory of Romagna. After this was accomplished, Borgia had Remirro killed, knowing that his lieutenant's cruelty would soon cause resentment. "One morning," Machiavelli relates, "Remirro's body was found cut in two pieces on the piazza at Cesena, with a block of wood and a bloody knife beside it. The brutality of this spectacle kept the people of the Romagna for a time appeased and stupefied" (*The Prince*, 57–8). In the long sweep of history, Borgia's use of a blood-soaked spectacle to influence his people is not remarkable; neither, particularly, is Machiavelli's enthusiastic endorsement of it as effective governance. What is noteworthy is that he primarily appreciated it *as a piece of theatre*.

The Reformation and Tyrannicide

Over the next several centuries, the rise of royal absolutism and its justification, the divine right of kings, bolstered the case for total subservience to authority. Yet the situation was volatile because of frequent dynastic turmoil, continuing royal encroachment on aristocratic privilege, new economic disparities, and heightened awareness of national identities. Starting in 1517, a new element introduced a level of passion that plunged Europe into nearly unprecedented violence. This was Martin Luther's challenge to Church dogma and Papal authority, which led to the emergence of "monarchomachs" – literally "fighters against monarchs." Within a few years, he broke with the Church, which soon found itself divided at first between Catholics and Lutherans, then also Calvinists, then a bewildering variety of sects, each claiming it had a monopoly on the truth. For a century and a half, Europe was wracked by war. While there were many reasons for the conflicts, sectarian dissension lent many an almost genocidal tone. Not surprisingly, tyrannicide took on new meanings and importance during these years. In particular, a new question was added to those proposed earlier by John of Salisbury: What if the ruler is a heretic in the eyes of his people?

Luther and John Calvin, the most important theologians of Protestantism, bluntly reiterated the early apostolic doctrine that resistance to authority was always forbidden. In his response to the Peasants' Revolt of 1525, Luther described tyrannicide as the gateway to mob rule.

Luther and Calvin's followers, however, were not nearly so tolerant. John Knox, the clergyman who introduced Calvinism to Scotland, led the way in articulating an early modern religious duty to resist despotism. Thrown in prison for his praise of several Calvinists' murder of an English cardinal, Knox became convinced that the acceptance of rule by heretics was spiritual treason. In *The First Blast of the Trumpet against the Monstrous Regiment of Women* (1558), he proclaimed it a Christian duty to remove "Bloody" Mary Tudor from the throne of England for her persecution of Protestants. In a later work extolling the virtues of resistance to tyranny, he boldly stated, "It is not only lawful to punish to the death . . . labor to subvert the true Religion, but the Magistrates and People are bound so to do, unless they will provoke the wrath of God against themselves" (quoted in Jászi and Lewis, *Against the Tyrant*, 49). In an era of spiritual pluralism, the call to preserve the "true religion" through violence was a recipe for political murder on a scale previously unseen in Europe.

The French Wars of Religion

The historian Franklin Ford has produced a three and a half page list of assassinations and political murders from 1535 to 1649. His list reflects the fact that although the bloodiest conflict of the era, the Thirty Years War, was fought in Germany and central Europe, the states that produced the most assassinations and theoretical justifications thereof were France and England. In France in the sixteenth century, Huguenots – French Calvinists – formed a sizeable minority, up to ten percent of the population in overwhelmingly Catholic France. Mutual fear and suspicion led to much violence and even bouts of open civil war between Catholics and Huguenots. The low point of the French wars of religion came on St. Bartholomew's Day in 1572, when King Charles IX and his mother orchestrated the assassination of nearly all the prominent Huguenots in Paris. These murders unleashed the anti-Protestant fury of the Parisian populace, which then proceeded to slaughter thousands more Huguenots. The killing spread to other French cities and lasted for months, not ending the Huguenot threat but convincing them all the more how intolerable Catholic rule was.

Two years later, in his book *Franco-Gallia*, the Huguenot François Hotman creatively asserted the king's right to rule came from the people, who could rescind it if he became a tyrant. A blunter argument along these lines appeared in 1577 under the pseudonym Junius Brutus, a name that still packed an enormous symbolic punch. The most likely author was Philippe de Mornay, scholar and advisor to Henry of Navarre, who was a Huguenot aristocrat, a miraculous survivor of the St. Bartholomew's

Day Massacre in Paris, and, amazingly, heir to the French throne. Mornay's book, *A Defense of Liberty against Tyrants*, was written in the shadow of the massacre and cast Catholic crimes in the most dastardly light. "It is then lawful for Israel to resist the king, who would overthrow the law of God and abolish His church," wrote Mornay. "And not only so, but also the people ought to know that in neglecting to perform this duty, they make themselves culpable of the same crime, and shall bear the like punishment with their king" (quoted in Laqueur, *Voices*, 30). Mornay's call for tyrannicide and civil war was qualified by the notion that the right to resist did not belong to private individuals, but rather to nobles and clerics acting on their behalf.

In this era of great religious hatred, most of the assassinations ostensibly inspired by sectarian strife turn out on closer examination to be the result of political disputes, such as aristocratic competition for influence at the king's court. Such was the case in 1584 with the murder of William of Orange, the principal leader of the successful Dutch revolt against Spain. The Spanish king, Philip II, had openly proclaimed a bounty for William's murder and found a taker in Balthasar Gérard (who used a pistol; perhaps the first assassination by such means in history). Gérard claimed that he had committed "an act acceptable to God," but the murder is more properly called state-sponsored assassination. His four-day punishment at the hands of the Dutch was as brutal as any on record: his arms were ripped from the sockets; his body was cut all over and covered in salt; both hands were cut off; chunks of flesh were torn from his body with hot pincers; and his bowels were ripped from his body and burned before his eyes. Finally, Gérard was quartered alive.

English Tyrannicide in Theory and Practice

Across the Channel, "Bloody" Mary's persecution of Protestant dissenters produced many apologists for tyrannicide, including the Calvinists Christopher Goodman and John Knox, the Anglican John Ponet, and the early constitutionalist George Buchanan, all of whom appealed to both English tradition and divine law. At the same time, the reign of Elizabeth I (1558–1603) is noteworthy for the number of Catholic plots hatched against her. Philip II of Spain – the author of the assassination of William of Orange in 1584 – was behind most of them, but these were not merely the product of economic and political rivalries. In 1570, Pope Pius V issued an edict that excommunicated Elizabeth and called on the faithful to remove her from power by any means necessary. Ten years later, Pope Sixtus V renewed the call, declaring that "there is no doubt that

Figure 3.1: Contemporary drawing of the Gunpowder Plot conspirators
(© Bettmann/CORBIS)

whosoever sends her out of the world with pious intention of doing God service, not only does not sin but gains merit" (quoted in Jászi and Lewis, *Against the Tyrant*, 76). The parallel with Roman proscription and the Kharijite practice of *takfir* is unmistakable.

Elizabeth's death in 1603 without heir brought her cousin James VI of Scotland to the throne. James – who ruled England as James I – was the target of one of the most spectacular assassination attempts in European history, the Gunpowder Plot. A band of Catholic conspirators smuggled 1800 pounds of gunpowder into a cellar below the House of Lords in the Westminster Palace complex. The munitions expert Guy Fawkes planned to detonate the explosives on the opening day of Parliament, November 5, 1605; conspirators in the English Midlands planned then to stage a revolt that they hoped would spawn a popular rebellion and the elevation of a Catholic monarch. Twentieth-century forensics tests and re-enactments have concluded that the force of the explosion would likely have killed James and all members of Lords and Commons and devastated an area perhaps a mile in diameter. Authorities were tipped off to the plan on the night of November 4 and discovered Fawkes beneath Westminster, matches and fuses in hand. Under torture, he revealed the details of the plot and the names of his co-conspirators. After a perfunctory trial, the would-be regicides were hanged until nearly dead and then drawn and quartered in the yard of the palace they had hoped to destroy.

In the 1980s, the graphic novel *V for Vendetta* (and a movie based on it in 2005) projected a Fawkes-like plot into the twenty-first century, imagining the Gunpowder Plot as a stunning pre-modern example of terrorism. Some have derided the comparison as misplaced and the use of the term terrorism as anachronistic, but we could at least apply the modern term "asymmetric warfare." Fawkes and his small number of conspirators relied on surprise and technology to facilitate a massive attack that they hoped would produce an extraordinary number of casualties, including many innocent "collateral" deaths. The use of the attack to signal a revolt and the hope that it would precipitate a popular rebellion bring us even closer to the modern meaning of terrorism.

The English Civil War

There is no doubt about the importance to the history of terrorism of the English Civil War, which broke out in 1642 after decades of increasing tension over religion and royal authority. The war was fought between Parliament – dominated by Puritans (English radical Protestants) who sought religious reformation and the restoration of traditional English liberties – and the English King Charles I, a barely closeted Catholic who believed that it was his right to rule as he saw fit. Parliament's army, led by Oliver Cromwell, defeated Charles and his supporters in 1645, promptly abolished the monarchy, and then put Charles on trial "as a tyrant, a traitor, and murderer, and a public enemy of the Commonwealth of England" (quoted in Ford, *Political Murder*, 178). Charles' execution in 1649 was the culmination of centuries of tyrannicide theory and an event without precedent. While plenty of kings and emperors had been assassinated, none were killed after being tried by former subjects who styled themselves as the ruler's peers.

This staggering assertion of traditional liberties and popular sovereignty set in motion a tumultuous period in English history. Cromwell emerged as a military dictator who disbanded Parliament and imposed a harsh theocratic regime. Some, such as Edward Saxby, a colonel in Cromwell's New Model Army, turned against the man they had once supported. Saxby backed a number of plots to dispose of the newest tyrant, including a failed plan to detonate a bomb under Whitehall Palace, the home of Cromwell and his retinue. Saxby himself was captured and died in prison before he could be executed by his rival. His fame primarily rests on his authorship in 1657 of a short pamphlet, "Killing No Murder," which he hoped would rouse a rebellion against Cromwell. In it, Saxby painfully acknowledged that the tyrannicide of 1649 made Cromwell possible, but he argued that Charles' execution also increased English intolerance for tyranny. To those who feared that tyrannicide in the hands of the people was a recipe for even greater disasters, Saxby sarcastically answered,

"One would think the world bewitched. I am fallen into a ditch, where I shall certainly perish if I lie, but I refuse to be helped out for fear of falling into another; I . . . let the disease kill me, because there is hazard in the cure" (quoted in Jászi and Lewis, *Against the Tyrant*, 85). Saxby draped his secular justification for rebellion and tyrannicide with religious, even apocalyptic language (Laqueur, *Voices*, 42).

Such recourse to traditional law and divine rhetoric alike had been the norm for centuries, but by the end of the century, a new emphasis was placed on humanistic reason. In 1689 the Englishman John Locke penned his classic statement of liberal political philosophy. Governments exist through the consent of the governed, he argued, and the people maintain the right to rebel if their governments fail to protect their natural rights of life, liberty, and property. Locke's argument was entirely naturalistic and remains a cornerstone of modern republicanism, but the path had been cleared by the earlier theorists of tyrannicide who had long assailed the absolute rights of monarchs.

Review of Tyrannicide in Medieval and Early Modern Europe

With but a few exceptions, both the theoretical and practical target of tyrannicide in the medieval and early modern world was a single person deemed personally responsible for the grave state of national affairs. His or her death was presented as an act that would restore affairs to their proper and previous state of health. The goal was the return to the *status quo ante*, and the death of the offending tyrant was most surely not intended as a purely symbolic act. Likewise, tyrannicide was not revolutionary, since its purpose was not the creation of new political, social, and cultural norms. In all these particulars, there is much continuity in the history of tyrannicide from the ancient to the early modern world, and it is not surprising that biblical tyrannicides and Caesar's assassination continued to exert a strong hold on the medieval and early modern imagination.

Assassination – as practiced by both individuals and states – remains an important tactic of the modern terrorist. There is also much continuity from the Middle Ages to the modern period in the explanations proffered by tyrant-slayers and their apologists. The justifications range, then as now, from sectarian to democratic, but the real similarity lies in the rhetoric, which was and is uncompromising, fanatical, and often apocalyptic. But just as importantly, the discourse of medieval and early modern tyrannicide employed the same mechanism as the social construction of terrorism in the modern era. In both cases, the goal is the delineation of legitimate political violence. Most pre-modern political and intellectual authorities condemned popular violence against the elite, but then went to great lengths – often engaging in the most torturous of mental gymnastics – to rescue certain acts of violence they deemed legitimate, even praiseworthy, namely tyrannicides. In the modern era, the story has more frequently been the opposite: certain forms of violence are condemned as terrorism when the goals of the group using them are deemed illegitimate.

Historical eras are not divided one from the other by bright red lines, and during the medieval and early modern periods we can discern two elements that foreshadow later developments: the existence of brutal but brief reigns of terror and the organization of secret societies. Both will be discussed in the next chapter because they are so clearly linked to the emergence of revolutionary terror and terrorism.

Bibliography

Two works on the history of tyranny, tyrannicide, and political murder mentioned in earlier chapters are once again highly valuable for this period: Jászi and Lewis, *Against the Tyrant*; and Ford, *Political Murder*.

The classic by Jacob Burckhardt, *The Civilization of the Renaissance in Italy* (New American Library, 1960), provides many good descriptions of Renaissance-era tyranny and tyrannicide. Two articles that provide interesting details about assassination during the period are Ward Thomas, "Norms and Security: The Case of International Assassination," *International Security*, vol. 25, no. 1 (summer 2000), 105–33; and Saul K. Padover, "Patterns of Assassination in Occupied Territory," *Public Opinion Quarterly*, vol. 7, no. 4 (winter 1943), 680–93.

A popular, but well done, work on a prominent sixteenth-century assassination is Lisa Jardine, *The Awful End of Prince William the Silent* (HarperCollins, 2005). Excerpts from Junius Brutus and Edward Saxby can be found in the extremely valuable collection of primary sources assembled by one of the pioneering figures of terrorism studies, Walter Laqueur, ed., *Voices of Terror* (Reed Press, 2004). A helpful article on French tyrannicide is Orest Ranum, "The French Ritual of Tyrannicide in the Late Sixteenth Century," *Sixteenth Century Journal*, vol. 11, no. 1 (spring, 1980), 63–82.

4

The Dawn of Revolutionary Terrorism

The critical differences between pre-modern tyrannicide and modern terrorism have been, first, the nature and scope of targets, and second, the purpose of the violence. The subjects of tyrannicide were kings and high magistrates; when they fell, they did so alone. The goal was the elimination of specific obstacles to stability, the natural order, and traditional justice. The fitting image remained, after Cicero, the amputation of a gangrenous limb. On the other hand, terrorists have typically targeted broader populations – not merely tyrants, but those who enable or benefit from entire political or economic systems, and all with the goal of fashioning a new world. Such a transformation was fitting given that the very basis of political legitimacy was recast in the seventeenth, eighteenth, and nineteenth centuries, particularly in the cauldron of the French Revolution. Under the influence of the Enlightenment and dramatic political events, significant numbers of Europeans came to believe that sovereignty naturally resided in nations, not monarchs. Moreover, they came to accept that revolutions could remake the world on a more rational basis. If this involved the extermination of entire populations tied to the Old Order, so be it. This was the birth of revolutionary terrorism.

The Anabaptists of Münster and Secret Societies

Two important elements of what became revolutionary terrorism surfaced before the Estates-General met in Versailles in 1789. The first was the appearance of the revolutionary "reign of terror." Massacres of civilians are as old as humanity itself, of course. Those already mentioned in these pages were typically the product of vengeful armies (such as the case of the Assyrians) or the political machinations of tyrants (such as Clodius Pulcher). Altogether different was the violence visited upon the German city of Münster in 1534–5 by radical Protestants known as Anabaptists. As part of their effort to establish a shining city on the hill, the Anabaptists practiced polygamy, abolished money, and regulated all sexual relations. To enforce the new order, city leaders organized book burnings and executed dissenters in elaborate ceremonies. In the weeks before the city fell to the Lutherans and Catholics who had suspended their own feud out of horror at the Anabaptist experiment, public executions were an almost daily occurrence. When the city was taken in June 1535, the conquerors tortured and killed every surviving Anabaptist leader. All too easily dismissed as simply cultish delusion, Münster under the Anabaptists was a foreshadowing of the secularist nightmare that engulfed Paris two and a half centuries later.

Another foreshadowing of modern terrorism was the appearance of secret societies in Ireland in the eighteenth century that used real and symbolic violence to protect landowners' efforts to kick poor tenant farmers off the land they worked. The Whiteboys – so-called because of the clothing they wore so they could recognize one another in the dark – leveled stone walls built to enclose common land, destroyed orchards, and extorted money and arms. Occasionally they roughed up or even killed tax collectors and landlords. The authorities passed laws and mounted punitive raids, but the Whiteboys could usually depend on locals to hide them. The Whiteboys' demands were hardly revolutionary: they wanted the return of traditional rights and practices, not the creation of new utopian communities. The Anglican authorities, however, tended to impute sectarian motives to the Whiteboys and characterized their violence as the leading edge of much larger Catholic plots. Much of the significance of these Irish secret societies lies in the influence they exercised on the formation of later explicitly sectarian and political groups such as the Orange Order and the Fenians. The Molly Maguires who supposedly terrorized the coal mine operators of Pennsylvania in the 1860s and 1870s can also be understood as the descendants of the Whiteboys.

Tyranny as a System

What would make these and other elements add up to something revolutionary was the addition of a new understanding of the nature of tyranny, one that imagined it as the product of a system and outlook and not just the actions of a single individual. Locke had done away with medieval distinctions when he proposed that tyranny was the suppression of the will of the governed, whether or not the tyrant became ruler legitimately. The Enlightenment writer Montesquieu expanded on this when he introduced the political concept of the separation of powers, asserting that it is the unchecked growth of power, regardless of who wields it, that enables despotism. American revolutionaries made the idea a cornerstone of the US Constitution and opposition to tyranny the watchword of their new republic. Benjamin Franklin lobbied unsuccessfully for the seal of the United States to bear the motto "Resistance to Tyrants is Obedience to God," a phrase made famous by John Bradshaw, the Englishman who oversaw the trial of Charles I. Thomas Jefferson took it as his own personal seal, only substituting "Rebellion" for "Resistance." Commenting on Shays' Rebellion of 1786–7, Jefferson famously asked, "What country can preserve its liberties, if their rulers are not warned from time to time that this people preserve the spirit of resistance? . . . The tree of liberty must be refreshed from time to time with the blood of patriots and tyrants. It is its natural manure" (letter to William Smith, November 13, 1787).

L'Ancien Régime and the French Revolution

The decisive break away from mere tyrannicide and toward terrorism in its modern guise came during the French Revolution. Under the Old Order," France had no representative legislative assemblies, no political parties, and no formal constitution, and its people enjoyed few civil liberties. Instead, the French king – Louis XVI in 1789 – was the source of all sovereignty, his power resting on and guaranteeing the continuance of a socio-political system that assigned tremendous privileges to nobles and representatives of the Catholic Church. The other 98 percent of the population paid taxes to the state, tithes to the Church, and feudal dues to landowners, and were conscripted into the army. Peasants hoped for affordable food and a reduced tax burden, while educated professionals known as the bourgeoisie wanted civil liberties, secure property rights, and a role in governing the country. Many of the bourgeoisie were motivated by Enlightenment principles, the cornerstone of which was the belief that the application of human reason and experience was the way to human progress.

The start of the Revolution is usually dated to June 1789, when representatives of the commoners walked out of the king's advisory body and declared themselves the National Assembly. Claiming they spoke for the entire nation, they bluntly stated that they would not disband until France had a constitution that curtailed the power of the king. What stayed the hand of the king and his army was the emergence of a new kind of popular violence directed against the very symbols of royal power, not just against the king's agents. The best example of this was a Parisian mob's seizure of the fortress of the Bastille on July 14, 1789. In the countryside, peasants burned down aristocrats' mansions, destroyed government offices that held records of their debts, and triggered a mass exodus of the nobility in what came to be known as the "Great Fear."

From the summer of 1789 to 1792, the National Assembly dismantled the Old Order. They abolished the class system; declared that sovereignty resided in the nation, not the king; limited the power and influence of the Catholic Church; and eventually created a constitutional monarchy. The kings, nobles, and churchmen of France's neighbors soon grew fearful that their own subjects would demand such reforms. Thus, by 1792, France was at war with its neighbors who were eager to snuff out the Revolution.

The Revolution Turns Radical

Cooperation – alleged and real – between foreign states and France's dispossessed elite stoked the belief that the Revolution was threatened by a vast conspiracy of internal and external counter-revolutionaries. As news reached Paris of French defeats, panic and anger propelled a new generation of radicals into France's new legislature, the Convention. In September 1792, the monarchy was abolished and France became a republic. Within months, Louis XVI was put on trial by the state, found guilty, and executed, like Charles I a century and a half earlier. There was clearly no going back for revolutionary France.

Meanwhile, the Convention had come to be dominated by the Jacobins, a group of representatives known for their allegiance to the Enlightenment writer Jean-Jacques Rousseau, who believed that humans could only be made truly free through the imposition of strict social and economic equality. The Jacobins curried favor with the most vocal Parisian poor, known as the *sans-culottes*, by adopting the latter's demands for public works programs, price controls on basic necessities funded by seizures and forced loans, and the death penalty for hoarders and speculators – in other words, a brand of justice that went far beyond the political and legal gains made in the early years of the revolution.

An important step in the creation of a dictatorship more bloody and domineering than the monarchy it replaced was an assassination destined to take its place among the most famous in history. In July 1793, Charlotte Corday, a moderate republican, stabbed to death Jean-Paul Marat, a radical journalist and close associate of the Jacobins. When questioned, Corday proudly declared that she had acted alone. "I knew

Figure 4.1: Jacques-Louis David, *The Death of Marat* (1793)
(Wikimedia Commons)

that [Marat] was perverting France," she said to her interrogators. "I have killed one man to save a hundred thousand." Some compared Corday to Brutus, but many more turned Marat into a martyr, pointing to his death as proof that the Revolution was under attack. Many in the streets and the Convention believed them. Thus the murder stands at the very boundary of the eras of tyrannicide and terrorism: although it was conceived as a single murder to restore health to the body politic, it was understood by revolutionaries as an assault on society.

The Reign of Terror

In short order, the Jacobins constructed a centralized revolutionary dictatorship whose key public figure was Maximilien Robespierre. Known for his ascetic lifestyle and ruthless commitment to the Revolution, he was the most prominent of the figures that came to be associated with the Reign of Terror (*la Grande Terreur* in French), instituted ostensibly to protect the Revolution. On September 5, the Convention issued a decree that proclaimed "terror is the order of the day." Twelve days later, the Convention passed the Law on Suspects which targeted for arrest those who "either by their conduct, their contacts, their words or their writings, showed themselves to be supporters of tyranny . . . or to be enemies of liberty" (quoted in Doyle, *The Oxford History of the French Revolution*, 251). The law was deliberately phrased in a vague manner to give maximum flexibility to the authorities as they sought out counter-revolutionaries.

Official rolls list 16,000 victims killed in the pursuit of revolutionary justice for the ten months beginning September 1793, but the real toll could easily be double that. The guillotine was the favored means of execution, but when it could not kill quickly enough, the hastily convicted were shot by firing squad or blown apart by grape shot from cannons. Outside Paris, so-called "Revolutionary Armies" – really glorified mobs – were formed to crack down on hoarders, round up suspects, and terrorize potential counter-revolutionaries. Those arrested were turned over to local watch committees that pronounced verdicts, often based on little more than appearance and hearsay. The number of those imprisoned but not executed is even harder to identify concretely; some estimates reach 500,000.

Revolutionary violence and the Terror itself was not monolithic. In fact, we can discern three strains of violence during the Reign of Terror. The first was a campaign of intimidation against those accused of speculation and hoarding; this was the economic program of the *sans-culottes* and reflected the anger unleashed in the summer of 1789. These demands were inflamed by fear and war and manipulated by the Jacobins to justify a second, broader political terror against those accused of conspiring with France's foreign enemies. In practice, this meant anyone who stood against the Jacobins on both the left and right.

"Virtue and Terror"

In the Terror's last stage, Robespierre increasingly used violence in a
third manner as an instrument of social and cultural transformation. Its
target was anyone broadly associated with the Old Order, people whose
mere presence represented an obstacle to the creation of a nation of
free and equal patriots. This occurred in the first half of 1794, after the
tide had turned in France's war against its neighbors and after most of
the Revolution's open political enemies were already dead. Robespierre
laid out the principles guiding the Terror in an infamous speech to the
Convention in February. Its most quoted passage can still raise the hairs
on one's neck today:

> If the mainspring of popular government in peacetime is virtue, the main-
> spring of popular government in revolution is virtue and terror both:
> virtue, without which terror is disastrous; terror, without which virtue
> is powerless. Terror is nothing but prompt, severe, inflexible justice; it is
> therefore an emanation of virtue; it is not so much a specific principle as
> a consequence of the general principle of democracy applied to the home-
> land's most pressing needs. (Robespierre, *Virtue and Terror*, 115)

Such a justification meant that in the mouths of the Jacobins, the
"system of terror" (*le régime de terreur*) had a thoroughly positive
meaning, as did the word that they occasionally used to describe themselves: *les terroristes*.

What Robespierre described was a dictatorship of the majority, with
the minority left naked and unprotected. Since the goal was an undi-
vided nation, dissent became indistinguishable from treason. Virtue was
defined as self-abnegation, a devotion to civic duty, and a boundless
love of the fatherland. And although virtue sprang from the people, it
transcended them, rendering individuals expendable in furtherance of
a vision of mythic, perfect unity. The destruction of entire categories of
individuals could be ordained by the will of the collective, which in a time
of revolution, Robespierre proclaimed, could only be exercised by the
centralized revolutionary government. Such is always the language of the
terrorist propelled by absolute obedience to a cause.

In June and July 1794, the killing reached a fever pitch in Paris
as dozens were killed every day on the guillotine in the Place de la
Révolution. Every member of the Convention came to feel threatened
by the Terror, an atmosphere which Robespierre did nothing to dispel.
On July 27 (9 Thermidor, according to the Revolutionary calendar),
Robespierre's terror turned full circle when his numerous opponents in
the Convention orchestrated his sudden arrest, trial, and execution.

Jean Lambert Tallien, one of the organizers of Robespierre's fall, spoke to the essence of the Jacobins' regime: "if the government of terror pursues a few citizens for their presumed intentions, it will frighten all citizens" (Mason and Rizzo, *The French Revoluition*, 264, 266). Tallien understood that the Terror was an exercise in highly symbolic violence. Robespierre and his partisans could not physically destroy all their enemies; therefore, they had to cow the population, especially those whose secret hatred of republicanism and the Revolution might turn into open revolt in the future. This is at the heart of Robespierre's obsession with what we would today call "thought crime." Thus, we could say that the Terror was perversely educational since a primary goal was to shape the mind and behavior of the populace. This was the advent of modern terrorism, if not in form, then in function.

Another lesson of the French Revolution is that terror often tends to lead to more terror, because it coarsens political dialogue and destroys traditional barriers against the use of large-scale violence to solve major political and ideological questions. The use of terror sets precedents that are hard to undo, particularly when they are as visceral as the public execution of thousands.

The End of the Revolution

The specter of *terroristes* waiting in the wings, eager to return, was enough to impel most former victims of the Terror to dispatch their victimizers quickly after they were swept from power. A baser motive, of course, was revenge. Within twenty-four hours of Robespierre's execution, more than eighty of his closest collaborators went to the guillotine. One man who watched the proceedings commented that although he was standing more than "a hundred paces from the place of execution, the blood of the victims streamed beneath [his] feet" (quoted in Doyle, *The Oxford History of the French Revolution*, 281). Several weeks later, Paris found itself in the grip of counter-revolutionary "white" terror carried out by gangs of the so-called Gilded Youth, freshly released upper-class prisoners who terrorized the former terrorists, all while flaunting the clothes and manners that had been the object of so much derision in recent years.

The government that succeeded the Convention was quite unstable, eventually giving way in 1799 to a coup by the military hero Napoleon Bonaparte. Napoleon ruled as a dictator, but one who enjoyed great popularity because of his militant appeals to nationalism and his support of progressive ideas. Under Napoleon, France was frequently at war with its neighbors; wherever the French armies were victorious, the moderate ideals of the Revolution took root. The most important of these was nationalism, which appeared in two equally important guises. The first was the belief in popular sovereignty, a development that began to put dynastic rulers on the defensive everywhere. The second manifestation of nationalism was the increasing tendency of people to understand themselves primarily as members of ethnic groups defined by language, territory, history, and culture. As Napoleon's conquests chipped away at legally defined class structures and other traditional sources of authority, national identities tended to fill the void, particularly when French armies stayed around long after the battles were over. In 1815, Napoleon was defeated by his European rivals and exiled to the small island of St. Helena.

The Restoration and Conservatism

The leaders of Europe who met at the Congress of Vienna to plot a post-Napoleonic course restored a king to France, returned land to French nobles, and swore to act in unison to defend the traditional pillars of power against the ideas that had been unleashed by the French Revolution. It seemed that the dream of national states governed by free and sovereign peoples was dead. But the genie could not be returned to the bottle so easily, and new challenges to the status quo emerged everywhere.

The rulers of Restoration Europe repeatedly used force to repress these challenges. The newly emerging ideology of the traditional elite was conservatism, and it was principally defined by a fear of insurrection, social upheaval, and political terror. The father of the movement was Edmund Burke, a political philosopher and member of the English House of Commons. Burke rejected the notion that rights were unalienable (and thus perceptible to all through rational inquiry), proclaiming instead that they were historical creations. Thus he defended "English liberty" as an organic development, but condemned the French Revolution as a radical egalitarian revolt against the traditional social and political order of France. In 1790 he presciently predicted that it would end in a blood-drenched and demagogic democracy more despotic than the monarchy it unseated. It is, in fact, Burke who seems to have translated the term *terroriste* into English when in 1795 he denounced French revolutionaries as "thousands of those hell hounds called terrorists . . . let loose on the people" (Letter IV to Earl Fitzwilliam). In the hands of many leaders of Restoration Europe, conservatism became reactionary dogma, a kneejerk rejection of anything that smacked of political or social progress.

Revolutionary Secret Societies

For a brief period in the 1810s and 1820s, secret groups devoted to the ideals of the French Revolution sprouted across Europe. Most of these societies – whose exotic names included the Delphic Society, the Friends of Virtue, the Republican Brother Protectors, and the Society of the Black Pin – were in Germany and Italy, where demands for popular sovereignty expressed the desire for national unification as much as for political liberty, legal equality, and economic opportunity. Although these groups met with almost no success, the specter of shadowy left-wing conspiracies stalked Europe and set off an obsessive hunt for subversive elements.

Many revolutionary groups grew out of others that had existed for decades, particularly the Freemasons. The group allegedly has ancient origins, but its modern version was founded in London in 1717. Members – perhaps 100,000 of them in France alone by 1789 – were organized into lodges that became shelters for frank debates about the political and intellectual issues of the day, particularly those associated with the Enlightenment. Most governments in Europe tolerated the Freemasons since they largely avoided political activism.

The purpose and function of modern secret societies changed in 1776 when Adam Weishaupt, a shadowy Bavarian law professor about whom much more is speculated than known, founded the Illuminati. He and his organization were dedicated to the destruction of all religions and monarchies in favor of a radical egalitarian social order. If reports concerning the Illuminati are to be believed – a big "if" – the group's few members, perhaps four thousand at its peak, were organized into cells throughout Europe. Weishaupt's strategy was to expand through Freemason lodges – a secret society harboring a secret society! He hoped for a peaceful transition rather than bloody revolution, but his obsession with secrecy, deception, and ritual encouraged the growth of outlandish suspicions and outright myths about violent Illuminati intentions.

Weishaupt and the Illuminati's contribution to the history of terrorism rests not in a violent plot or extraordinary act, but rather in the reaction they engendered. In fact, Weishaupt's organization would probably have slipped into oblivion were it not for the French Revolution, which fueled a fear of Enlightenment ideas and raised the specter of rapid, comprehensive, and violent political and social change. In the 1790s, conservative authorities searched far and wide across Europe for traces of a vast conspiracy organized by secret societies that threatened to destroy traditional ways. Little evidence was to be found, and, in most instances, the secret societies that were unearthed were comically small and/or inept. And yet the fear of conspiracies lived on.

Babeuf and Buonarroti

Not only did the French Revolution produce the revolutionary agenda, it produced professional revolutionaries who devoted themselves full-time to the agenda's realization. Such revolutionaries became fixtures of the European imagination.

The prototype was François-Noel Babeuf, a hot-tempered radical whose proto-communist egalitarian sentiments put him far to the left of the Jacobins during the Reign of Terror. The fall of Robespierre seems to have pushed Babeuf to the conclusion that revolutionary terror remained the only way to usher in true democracy. Babeuf set about organizing a coup. His vehicle was to be a "secret directory" of committed revolutionaries concealed within a broader organization responsible for propaganda and recruitment. Babeuf's strategy was to stage a coup d'état that would in turn trigger an uprising of the poor and disenfranchised. Violence and terror were to be the real midwives, however: "Let everything return to chaos," Babeuf demanded, "that out of chaos may arise a new and regenerated world" (quoted in Jászi and Lewis, *Against the Tyrant*, 129). A well-placed informer tipped off the authorities, however, and Babeuf was arrested in May 1796 and executed the following year.

One of his co-conspirators, Filippo Buonarroti, turned Babeuf's life into a legend when he published a romanticized history of the abortive coup, *The Conspiracy of Equals*, in 1828. Two types of reader eagerly drank up the book's contents: the police and revolutionary conspirators. Although Europe's secret societies were actually lapsing into inactivity, the book established in the minds of the authorities the belief that a single, unbroken chain of conspiracies stretched from the 1780s down to the living present. And for revolutionaries throughout the nineteenth century, Buonarroti's description of Babeuf re-invented the Jacobins as a conspiratorial organization and sanctified the great leader (now, more than ever, necessary in the years after 1815, when the conservative authorities knew full well the dangers that threatened their grip on power) who could lead the people against the repressive regime. It also encouraged conspirators to believe that the sowing of chaos might be enough to prompt a true revolution.

The Carbonari

The greatest proponents of such a doctrine in this era inhabited the radical fringe of the Carbonari, itself a widespread, loosely bound secret society. The first of its chapters appeared in Italy around 1806 and from there spread into France, Spain, and Greece. The Carbonari program was liberal and nationalist; by 1814, hundreds of chapters had sprung up across the continent. Although they were founded on a vaguely anti-Napoleonic platform, they quickly moved into opposition to the restored monarchies of 1815. Their practices and ornate rites, which borrowed heavily from Masonic lore, included oaths of secrecy, large doses of Christian symbolism, and multiple grades through which initiates climbed. Estimates of Carbonari membership in 1820 range from a rather conservative 24,000 to a hard-to-believe 642,000.

In the most radical lodges and at the uppermost grades, there is evidence that the Italian Carbonari were devoted to the destruction of tyrannical governments and the establishment of a united, democratic, egalitarian Italian republic. In some of these lodges, initiation ceremonies made use of imaginative and symbolic props, such as a cross "to crucify the tyrant," a hatchet to "cut his head from his body," and a shovel to "scatter his ashes to the wind" (Rath, "The Carbonari," 362).

Most of what little we know about the inner workings of the Carbonari comes from *Memoirs of the Secret Societies of the South of Italy*, published in 1821 by Jakob Bartholdy, a Prussian diplomat in Italy. Bartholdy wisely called for avoiding the use of "the prison and the scaffold" to combat the Carbonari, since persecution only lent revolutionaries an air of mystery and taboo which brought in new recruits. He instead advocated lifting "the veil of secrecy" (quoted in Roberts, *The Mythology of the Secret Societies*, 336). His book was filled with so many horrifying details, however, it could not help but increase the authorities' paranoia. Bartholdy, for instance, attributed several fires, prison breaks, and knife attacks (but only one murder) to the Carbonari and described one lodge's plan for a revolt that involved more prison breaks, assaults on "public treasuries . . . [and] the habitations of rich private individuals," and the murder of the Carbonari's known enemies (Laqueur, *Voices*, 51–2).

In the early 1820s, the Carbonari were involved in uprisings in Italy, France, and Spain. In some cases they were briefly successful because they had recruited young officers who persuaded their soldiers to follow them in revolt. The sort of proto-terrorism described by Bartholdy did not figure in any of these uprisings, however; these were classic putsches carried out by elites with few connections to the peasantry or urban laborers. In any event, the successful uprisings were quickly overturned by Great Power interventions. Within several years, most Carbonari lodges were destroyed by police infiltration or disenchantment.

The Authorities and Revolutionary Terrorism

Europe's rulers had nary a moment to rest, however, for new challenges were emerging against the status quo. Mounting social and economic tension and the spread of nationalism were making possible truly popular rebellions far more dangerous than the putschism of the 1820s. In that sense, the revolutions of 1830 in France, Belgium, and Poland and those of 1848–9 across much of Europe heralded a return to the revolutionary spirit of 1789.

The rise of revolutionary fervor convinced the conservative authorities that radical conspiracies still lurked behind every corner. Such fears were fueled by the revelations of Lucien de la Hodde, a journalist, spy, and police provocateur who infiltrated several French secret societies in the 1830s and 1840s. His *History of Secret Societies in France* (1856) was one of the first serious attempts to analyze terrorism and propose strategies to counter it. Hodde, himself a Burkean conservative, claimed that secret societies were mostly composed of radical demagogues who hoped to take advantage of the erosion of the masses' traditional obedience to authority. He believed that students, immigrants, and criminals were particularly susceptible to the siren song of revolution. Despite his concerns, he ultimately concluded that "secret societies may raise a mob, but can never accomplish a revolution." The greatest danger to public order arises "when the strength of the revolutionary monster is exhausted," for that is when "his instincts drive him to willful murder and assassination" (Hodde, *History of Secret Societies*, 33, 196). Hodde recognized that terrorism is typically a weapon of last resort, a tactic used by groups that have largely been defeated. Therefore, he claimed, the police should act – to forestall not the overthrow of government but casualties among the general population. Toward this end, police agents should infiltrate secret societies and be willing to participate in violent activity in order to snag conspirators.

The Luddites

Secret societies in the wake of the French Revolution and the Restoration were not just interested in nationalist insurrections. Anger at economic dislocation prompted a very different sort of early terrorism: assaults on machinery. During the Industrial Revolution, the spread of textile machines operated by minimally trained workers threatened the livelihood of skilled knitters and other workers. From 1811 to 1816, bands of English artisans sabotaged thousands of mechanized looms and destroyed several wool and cotton mills in emulation of their almost certainly mythical leader, Ned Ludd, who supposedly destroyed two knitting machines in the 1770s. The so-called "Luddites" issued manifestos demanding the protection of traditional labor and boasting of the creation of armed detachments to be used in the event of an insurrection. They also issued threats against mill owners themselves, but there were few such attacks.

Such was the fear, however, that the industrialist John Heathcote built an early "panic room" under his house in the event of a Luddite attack. And when Prime Minister Spencer Perceval was assassinated in May 1812 by what later turned out to be an insane merchant, initial speculation connected the murder to Luddism. In the press and among local magistrates, the movement provoked many charges of Jacobinism, a term that packed the rhetorical punch of "terrorism" today. Among the middle and upper classes, Luddism became synonymous with senseless mob violence and became an epithet to be hurled against all opponents of modernization. The English government took the threat seriously because of the economic damage and the threat to public order. Legislators designated industrial sabotage and membership in secret societies as capital crimes, and local authorities followed up on the threat by executing seventeen Luddites in York in 1813.

Heinzen and Conspiratorial Terrorism

In the case of the Luddites, the Carbonari, and other secret societies, their tactics were the result of the great odds they faced. The symbolic violence that all these groups used and threatened was largely an answer to their enemies' near monopoly on the use of force. But violence could also be a response to what was perceived as an assault on moral law itself. The eighteenth-century Whiteboys and Robespierre had made such claims indirectly, but more than fifty years later, no one had provided a very satisfying theoretical framework for conspiratorial terrorism.

The first modern revolutionary to attempt that was Karl Heinzen, a Prussian radical democrat and writer who fled his homeland after his participation in the upheavals of 1848–9 left him a wanted man. While exiled in Switzerland, he published a series of articles entitled "Murder," in which he outlined his extraordinary doctrine. Killing, Heinzen wrote, is always immoral, but in practice it is frequently depicted otherwise. In terms that echoed Augustine's famous confrontation between Alexander and the pirate, Heinzen noted that the state's soldiers are praised for killing in battle, its patriots lionized for acts of tyrannicide, and its hangmen excused for executing criminals, while revolutionaries who fight for democracy are denounced and hunted down. Because states, themselves simply the expression of the interests of the wealthy, had thus shown the concepts of morality and justice to be relative, governments could not legitimately reference those standards when violently oppressing their opponents.

And why, therefore, should violence be denied to freedom-fighters, the true moral forces of their age? Heinzen asked. "Let us, then, be practical," he wrote, "let us call ourselves murderers as our enemies do, let us take the moral horror out of this great historical tool." Revolutionaries and democrats should wage war against rich, well-armed states by using terror, conspiratorial organization, and destructive new technologies to level the playing field. In this vein, Heinzen celebrated the invention of fulminating silver, a highly unstable explosive compound that could "blow whole towns into the air." Revolutionaries should not hesitate, he continued, "to blow up half a continent or spill a sea of blood in order to finish off the barbarian party." In such a way, he concluded, "the path to Humanity" could pass successfully "through the zenith of Barbarity" (Laqueur, *Voices*, 58, 62, 67).

Heinzen's ideas were put into action – if only on a limited scale – by a multinational conspiracy orchestrated by the Italian nationalist Felice Orsini. His target was Napoleon III, the French emperor who had intervened in Italy in 1849 to restore the pope's temporal authority. The story of the unsuccessful attempt is particularly interesting because, like Charlotte Corday's murder of Jean-Paul Marat, it lies at the border of two brands of political violence. Although Orsini imagined the assassination as a classic tyrannicide – during his trial, he declared "I acted as Brutus did" – the killing was intended to further a revolutionary cause, the unification of Italy (quoted in Ford, *Political Murder*, 223). We can only guess at the reason why the plotters chose to use bombs constructed from fulminate of mercury, a recent invention. Perhaps they believed it would prove to be more effective at destroying a well-guarded target; or maybe because they understood the impact such a dramatic attack would have on the public and other revolutionaries. What their decision undoubtedly reveals was the conspirators' willingness to shed the blood of many to make a point, a stance claimed by Heinzen but disturbingly realized by the anarchist assassins of Russia and Western Europe around the turn of the century. And blood there was aplenty on January 14, 1858. As the imperial carriage of Napoleon III and the Empress Eugénie rolled to a stop outside the Paris Opera, assassins threw three bombs, killing eight and wounding 148, over two-thirds of whom were civilian bystanders. Amazingly, the imperial couple suffered only a few cuts. The Empress was even heard, allegedly, to mutter about "the risks of our trade" as she descended from the wrecked carriage (quoted in Packe, *The Bombs of Orsini*, 259). Many others in the decades to follow – civilian and ruler alike – would not be so lucky. The age of terror had dawned in Europe.

One factor that was to make it effective – even possible – in ways that had never before been contemplated was dramatic growth in the field of mass communications in the second half of the nineteenth century. Several inventors patented telegraph machines and codes for communicating messages in the 1830s, but it took several decades for such systems to make possible rapid communication across continents. An astounding advance was made in 1866 when the first transatlantic cable entered commercial use. Meanwhile, newspapers were beginning to reach mass audiences, a product of increased literacy, the rise of civic engagement, and technological advances. Alongside the relatively independent and objective journalism of such papers as *The Times* of London, *The New York Times*, *Le Figaro* in France, and the *Frankfurter Zeitung* of Germany, there existed scores of tabloid-style "penny press" papers which often enjoyed larger circulations and provided even more lurid descriptions of terrorist violence.

Bibliography

The classic study of religious apocalypticism, with an excellent chapter on the Anabaptists of Münster, is Norman Cohn, *The Pursuit of the Millennium* (Secker & Warburg, 1957).

For a theoretical understanding of the early modern understanding of "tyranny as a system," see Jászi and Lewis, *Against the Tyrant*.

Perhaps no subject in Western history has been covered as thoroughly as the French Revolution. An excellent place to start is William Doyle, *The Oxford History of the French Revolution*, 2nd edn. (Oxford, 2002). Somewhat more polemical, but highly illuminating is Simon Schama, *Citizens: A Chronicle of the French Revolution* (Knopf, 1989). The classic study of the Reign of Terror is R. R. Palmer, *Twelve Who Ruled: The Year of the Terror in the French Revolution* (Atheneum, 1965 [1941]). Two recent, stimulating additions to the literature are David Andress, *The Terror: The Merciless War for Freedom in Revolutionary France* (Farrar, Straus & Giroux, 2005); and Eli Sagan, *Citizens and Cannibals: The French Revolution, the Struggle for Modernity, and the Origins of Ideological Terror* (Rowman & Littlefield, 2001). A helpful collection of primary sources is Laura Mason and Tracey Rizzo, eds., *The French Revolution: A Document Collection* (Houghton Mifflin,

1999). Robespierre's famous speech on revolutionary terror, along with a valuable analysis, can be found in Maximilien Robespierre, *Virtue and Terror*, Introduction by Slavoj Žižek (Verso, 2007).

Studies of secret societies usually tend toward the fantastical and conspiratorial, rather than the historical. Two important exceptions are J. M. Roberts, *The Mythology of the Secret Societies* (Charles Scribner's Sons, 1972); and R. John Rath, "The Carbonari: Their Origins, Initiation Rites, and Aims," *American Historical Review*, vol. 69, no. 2 (Jan., 1964), 353–70. Lucien de la Hodde's work on secret societies is extremely valuable and available in English: *History of Secret Societies and of the Republican Party of France from 1830 to 1848* (J. B. Lippincott & Co., 1856).

An excellent study of the Luddites is Malcolm I. Thomis, *The Luddites: Machine-breaking in Regency England* (David & Charles Archon Books, 1970).

The standard biographies of two critical nineteenth-century figures are old, but solid: Carl Wittke, *Against the Current: The Life of Karl Heinzen (1809–80)* (University of Chicago Press, 1945); and Michael St. John Packe, *The Bombs of Orsini* (Secker & Warburg, 1957).

5

Russian Revolutionary Terrorism

French Revolutionaries introduced the language and purpose of modern terrorism in the late eighteenth century, but only after seizing power. During the next several decades, radical visionaries developed elaborate justifications for using terrorism as a tool to gain power, while secret societies tentatively explored the means of doing so. During the second half of the nineteenth century and the first few decades of the twentieth, the number of groups devoted to the use of terrorism grew rapidly, as did the number of guises in which terrorism appeared. In the next five chapters we will examine the nearly simultaneous development of five aspects of modern terrorism: revolutionary terrorism in Russia, anarchist terrorism in Europe, labor-related terrorism in the United States, reactionary white supremacist terrorism in the United States, and ethno-nationalist terrorism around the world.

If any country can claim to be the birthplace of modern terrorism, it is Russia. There, beginning in the 1860s, three generations of radicals introduced the language, justifications, means, and strategies that shaped the use of modern political violence.

The Russian Empire

During the nineteenth century, Russia was surely the most backward of the great states of Europe. The Russian tsar ruled absolutely over a country in which hereditary nobles possessed great wealth and privilege and 85 percent of the population was made up of poor, illiterate peasant farmers shackled to the land through private serfdom or state servitude. There were no elections, no representative assemblies, no legal political parties or trade unions, and virtually no recognized civil rights. The government relied on nobles, the army, the police, and censorship to preserve the status quo. The reform-minded intelligentsia, drawn from the middle classes, was marginalized. The only possible source of reform short of complete revolution came from the top. Thus it was Tsar Alexander II who emancipated privately held serfs in 1861, the first of a series of administrative and judicial changes that the tsar hoped would modernize his country without diminishing his authority. The so-called Great Reforms transformed Russia, but in ways that alienated much of the public. Serfs were liberated from their masters, but were forced to take on enormous payments to the state, which had compensated landowners for the loss of free labor. Reforms whetted the appetite of peasants and intelligentsia alike for more far-reaching reforms, the sort that typically could only be gained through revolution. This fresh resentment helped nourish the roots of terrorism in Russia.

Alexander II enabled the growth of terrorism in another way by easing restrictions on censorship as part of the Great Reforms. While academic journals had been published for decades, these publications had to address political and social issues in roundabout ways. New journals that appeared in the 1860s, such as the *Russian Messenger*, had more latitude to report and comment on contemporary events, including terrorism. Of even greater significance is the fact that Russian daily newspapers began to attract more readers than did academic journals in the 1870s and 1880s. The issues addressed were not necessarily different, but the tone was. The daily press required large circulations, which were built, in part, on lurid descriptions of assassinations and other violent acts. Terrorists now had the megaphones they needed to reach their audiences.

The educated public was the source of the organized opposition to the tsarist state, and it fell, broadly speaking, into four categories: liberalism, populism, Marxism, and anarchism. Liberals made up a large segment of the intelligentsia and middle classes and believed that the way forward for Russia lay along the European path of constitutions, representative institutions, and industrialization. Russian liberals generally hoped for peaceful, evolutionary change; thus their ambivalence toward terrorism in the 1900s and 1910s – during the third generation of Russian terrorism – is a significant story, one to which we will return later.

Populism and Nihilism

One set of opponents saw in the communal traditions of Russia's enormous peasantry the possibility of agrarian socialism. They opposed both the exploitation of the people by the reactionary monarchy and the liberal bourgeoisie. Because they were focused on "the people" (*narod*), they became known as "Populists" (*narodniki*). Populists were typically young, often students, well educated, and from the middle classes. Although they were far from uniform in their beliefs, they tended to believe that all arable land should be reapportioned among the peasantry and managed by local communes. Populists had faith in the idea of a massive transformation of Russia by the peasants themselves from the ground up – a proposition that made sense on the surface, given that Russia in the third quarter of the nineteenth century was still overwhelmingly rural and agrarian. Most Populists also understood that this would somehow be linked to a political revolution, most likely a violent one.

In the 1860s, a fashionable brand of quasi-populism dubbed nihilism took hold of the Empire's youth. Nihilists were radicals more interested in individual revolt and the rejection of tradition than with overtly political or social solutions; today we would call them the counterculture. Nihilism was centered in radical student groups that thrived on the cultish world of literary heroes, martyrdom, and the mystique of conspiratorial activity. Very quickly, nihilism became the *scourge de jour* of polite society, a development reinforced by the publication in 1863 of Nikolai Chernyshevsky's novel *What Is to Be Done?* The novel – deemed so important by Lenin that he reused the title for one of his most significant polemical tracts – is essentially the story of a love triangle, complete with descriptions of communal living, cooperative economic ventures, and radical politics. While the novel's proto-feminist heroine garnered the most attention from progressives, a minor character captivated student radicals. Rakhmetov is an extreme nihilist who renounces love and trains himself for revolutionary feats by sleeping on a bed of nails. Although he does not use violence, Rakhmetov inspired two generations of Russian revolutionaries who found in him a blueprint for selfless and fanatical devotion to radical social transformation.

Russian Marxism and Anarchism

Frustrated by the conservatism of Russian peasants and impressed by the emergence of a new urban working class, some Populists turned to Karl Marx's doctrines (typically known to its practitioners as social democracy) in the 1870s and 1880s. Out of the Russian Marxists, of course, came Lenin and the Bolsheviks. They embraced terrorism in a circumscribed fashion while in the underground, but became terrorists "from above" after seizing the Russian state in 1917.

But it is with another ideological movement – anarchism – that the story of Russian terrorism properly begins. Anarchism had very few adherents mid-century but grew in such importance that early in the twentieth century it inspired thousands of terrorist acts. Mikhail Bakunin (d. 1876) is regarded as one of the fathers of the anarchist movement. Although born into an aristocratic Russian family, Bakunin accepted Marx's contention that governments, religions, and the various manifestations of culture are products of the class struggle. And they agreed that the oppressors in the centuries-old drama of haves vs. have-nots were fated to be overthrown in a cataclysmic revolution that would usher in a new era of peace, prosperity, justice, and equality. They differed, however, in that Marx envisioned at that point a brief period of rule by a "dictatorship of the proletariat," during which accounts would be settled and the way would be paved for the new society, while Bakunin insisted that government itself was and always had been the problem. He opposed all forms of authority, believing that in the proper environment, every human could live in accordance with the natural laws of social organization.

Bakunin presented two faces to his followers. On the one hand, he was decidedly romantic in his adoration of peasants and the lumpen proletariat as a "powder keg" of "noble savages" who need only be nudged in order to bring down the state. In particular, he praised the bandit as the most perfect revolutionary: "[he] is the people's hero, defender, and savior. He is the implacable enemy of the state and the whole social and civil order set up by the state" (quoted in Laqueur, *Voices*, 68). Any assault against the state was desirable, any blow that could inspire more blows was a step forward, even if it was carried out by a criminal. After all, such designations came from the state, whose sole concern was the protection of property. "Everything in this fight is equally sanctified by the revolution. [Never mind that those destined to perish] will call it terrorism!" (quoted in Laqueur, *Voices*, 70). Like Heinzen, Bakunin turned society's condemnation of terrorists as criminals on its head, openly embracing criminals as the perfect revolutionary terrorists. Bakunin's promotion of individual terror gained him the most followers among those committed to political violence.

Sergei Nechaev and the Professional Revolutionary

On the other hand, Bakunin sometimes longed for the post-revolutionary emergence of an organically whole community devoted to absolute equality. À la Rousseau, individuals would be free from the effluvia of the modern world that destroy spiritual wholeness and sow dissension. When he indulged this fantasy, he imagined that his new world would come about not through spontaneous rebellion but through a carefully executed revolution, whose path would be opened and eased by the chaos created by bandits/terrorists/revolutionaries. This side of Bakunin is best illustrated by his cooperation with the shadowy Russian revolutionary Sergei Nechaev.

Nechaev was born a commoner near Moscow in 1847. Bitterness, alienation, and a thirst for revenge dominated his outlook, but he was also energetic and charismatic. Above all, he reveled in the chic terrorist mystique that was all the rage in nihilistic student circles in the 1860s. He first became involved with radical groups while studying at Moscow State University, where he was strongly influenced by the example of Dmitrii Karakazov, a mentally ill nihilist who was executed for a comically inept assassination attempt against the tsar in 1866. Circumstances drove Nechaev briefly into Swiss exile, where he met Bakunin. Both were egoists and avid self-promoters, and both claimed to be heads of nonexistent revolutionary movements of international proportions. This was clearly a match made in anarchist heaven.

During their brief time together in 1869, Nechaev wrote a pamphlet entitled *The Catechism of the Revolutionist*. In it, he spelled out how to construct a secret organization dedicated to revolution and "pitiless destruction" using self-contained and insulated cells – a strategy light years beyond the theatrical oath-making and Masonic ritual of the Carbonari. Although there is no evidence that he had read Heinzen's manifesto, Nechaev's pamphlet seems to pick up where "Murder" left off. Since the state has perverted the very concepts of morality and legality in its oppression of the "people," the revolutionary should be bound by no ethical precept, except to act in such a way as to further the revolution, he explained. Nechaev proposed that the perfect revolutionary should cut himself off utterly from family, friends, and conventional society; abandon the possibility of love or emotional attachment; and dedicate himself entirely to the acquisition of the skills necessary for conspiratorial activity and the success of the revolution. Nechaev maintained that the revolution would be made on behalf of the people, but he regarded the poor and downtrodden as the expendable pawns of a repressive system. Unable to understand their own true interests or the sacrifices of the revolutionary martyrs, the masses were more likely to turn opponents of the state over to the police than to aid them in their work.

Nechaev's pamphlet wasted no ink on ideology or speculation about the shape of post-revolutionary society, merely assuming that the revolution would solve all. In prototypical terrorist fashion, *The Catechism* denies the possibility of compromise: the revolution will be total or it will be nothing. This is also the logic behind the pamphlet's infamous line: "The revolutionary is a doomed man" (Laqueur, *Voices*, 71). Either he will die making the revolution or he will be rendered irrelevant by its success, since there would be no more need of someone skilled only in the science of destruction and death.

Nechaev was not merely a theorist. After bouncing around from one to another radical but non-violent group, he formed his own revolutionary cell, the People's Vengeance, dedicated to overthrowing tsarism and liberating the people. The group was small – perhaps a few hundred – and soon every member's name was replaced by a number, as per instructions in *The Catechism*. In 1869, Nechaev denounced an increasingly recalcitrant colleague to the other members of the cell, who then murdered him to preserve their secrecy. Nechaev fled Russia shortly after the crime was discovered, but was caught in Switzerland in 1873 and extradited back to Russia, where he was found guilty of the murder and died in prison in 1882.

The Nechaev affair, as it came to be called, was a humiliating blow to a revolutionary movement that for all its conspiratorial activity still thought largely in conventional moral terms. Furthermore, it was painfully clear that revolutionary terrorism had produced few accomplishments. The result was a widespread abandonment of violence in favor of more peaceful propagandizing and agitational work. The Russian novelist Fyodor Dostoevsky heard of the Nechaev affair and used it as inspiration for his novel *The Devils* (published in 1872 and frequently translated as *The Possessed*). The novel's central character is Pyotr Verkhovensky, a manic, power-hungry revolutionary devoted to conspiratorial activity. The radical cell he leads plots the death of one of its members and sows destruction in a small provincial town. Another peripheral revolutionary, the nihilist Nikolai Stavrogin, rapes a ten-year-old girl and pushes her into suicide. Dostoevsky was one of many contemporary novelists who condemned the nihilism and revolutionary violence of the 1860s and early 1870s through fiction, but he was unique in both his background and talent. He was a radical in his youth, but after arrest, exile, and an intense spiritual awakening became quite conservative, denouncing atheism and political radicalism as morally corrupt European imports. In his hands, the Nechaev affair became the point of departure for a metaphysical rumination on the descent of the modern world into an orgy of self-destruction. To Dostoevsky, revolutionary terrorism was the outgrowth of secularism, and ideologies that justified conspiratorial violence were mere cover for self-aggrandizement and chaos-loving criminality.

Populism into Terrorism

Dostoevsky believed that terrorism was more a result than a cause of the troubled times, a deeply cynical and idiosyncratic stance that put him at odds with the generally idealistic tenor of the era. The agitprop movement spawned by the embarrassment of the Nechaev affair and the failure of revolutionary terrorism culminated in 1874's summer of "going to the people," when thousands of university students and young folk traveled to the countryside to live and work among the peasantry. Russian peasants were mostly illiterate, suspicious, and tightly knit, however; they beat up many students as dangerous outsiders and turned some in to the local police. The ringleaders of the summer of 1874 were convicted of various revolutionary activities and given harsh sentences. In the cities, where beefed-up police work took a heavy toll on the ranks of the agitators, Populists began to conceive of terrorism as an extension of self-defense, and thus a weapon against the police. These radicals knifed, shot, and bombed their way up the hierarchy of police spies, gendarmes, administrators, and governors-general. Rural propagandists were much slower to embrace political violence since they believed that violence simply invited more police attention to their agitational work.

Nonetheless, proponents of rural propaganda and urban violence agreed on the creation of an umbrella organization, which was given the Populist name Land and Liberty. Despite the fact that the two wings of the group increasingly competed for funds, recruits, and attention, the terrorist faction of Land and Liberty did not reject the grand strategy of preparing for a social revolution through the slow cultivation of the peasantry's insurrectionary potential. What the terrorists came to believe was that tsarism's machinery of repression made productive propaganda work impossible at the moment. In time, they embraced the notion that the political revolution would have to precede the social one. The terrorists of Land and Liberty and its successor, the People's Will, essentially practiced political assassination – as opposed to indiscriminate mass terror – but in their hands it was not mere tyrannicide. This was revolutionary terror meant to pave the way for the creation of a new world of peasant communalism, not a return to a *status quo ante*. According to pamphlets and articles published by Land and Liberty terrorists such as Nikolai Morozov, the goal of the organization was to demonstrate the weakness of the government, inspire the peasants to revolution, and keep alive the spirit of insurrection.

Police documents and the memoirs of other terrorists, however, paint a rather different portrait: of individuals motivated by revenge, seduced by the lure of adrenaline and heroic action, and validated by the close-knit bonds of conspiratorial comradeship. As Lev Tikhomirov, a member of Land and Liberty, later noted, the dedication to violence preceded the effort to justify it. To some radicals, the willingness to carry out violent acts became the sole mark of revolutionary legitimacy. For instance, in the arguments that tore Land and Liberty apart in 1879, Tikhomirov suggested that the rural propagandists were not real revolutionaries, a slur that he recognized was useful at recruiting terrorists from the ranks of peaceful activists.

Revolutionary Heroes: Zasulich and Kravchinsky

The story of Vera Zasulich, author of the era's most celebrated attack, illustrates the role that violence played at the nexus of social discontent, personal politics, and revolutionary mystique. Zasulich's commitment to the Populist program was minimal; what motivated her was the search for purpose and belonging, left cold, as she was, by the limited roles available to young women from the lower gentry. Revolutionary activism brought her membership in a community that provided meaning, identity, and opportunity for action. Even then, what roused her to violence was the notorious beating of an imprisoned fellow revolutionary by General Teodor Trepov, the governor of St. Petersburg. In January 1878, Zasulich shot Trepov as an act of revenge and revolutionary self-defense, but she only managed to wound him and was arrested in the process.

Zasulich and her defense counsel used her public trial to denounce the regime and publicize its brutishness. So great was the skill of her lawyers and so deep the public sympathy for anti-government activists, that she was acquitted by the jury. Terrorists – no longer tainted by the Nechaev affair – had been transformed into heroic freedom fighters. The public's change of mood was reflected in a contemporary poem, "The Threshold," by the well-known novelist Ivan Turgenev (author of *Fathers and Sons*). In it, he describes a young woman who readies herself to take the plunge into revolutionary activity. In a page right out of Nechaev's *Catechism*, a disembodied voice asks whether she is prepared to accept "total alienation [and] loneliness" and "to commit crimes." When she crosses the threshold, onlookers shout "fool!" and "saint!" (quoted in Pomper, "Russian Revolutionary Terrorism," 78–9). Notably, no one attacks her underlying motive. Turgenev's suggestion was that Russian public opinion differed not in its general disapproval of the tsar's government, but only in the effective means of opposition.

This line was echoed by that year's other most celebrated political assassin, Sergei Kravchinsky, who operated under the revolutionary nom-de-guerre Stepniak. He, like Zasulich, was another Populist who turned to violence in the late 1870s. In 1878, he stabbed to death General Nikolai Mezentsev, the head of the tsar's political police, on a St. Petersburg street. Kravchinsky eventually fled abroad and spent most of the rest of his life in London, where he became the chief source of information in the West about the Russian revolutionary movement. Kravchinsky admitted that the terrorists' goal was not to overthrow the government but rather to "render its position untenable." And although the terrorists were few in number, "the universal discontent will provide them with pecuniary means," while the widely circulated tales of the terrorists' heroism and bravery would furnish "an immense and inexhaustible source of new recruits" (Stepniak-Kravchinsky, 256–7).

The first reaction to Mezentsev's assassination was an announcement that all terrorists would be tried in military courts and, second, a series of appeals to the Russian population to turn against the "criminals in its midst" (quoted in Ulam, 295). The response was, at best, lukewarm. Two provincial assemblies went so far as to announce that they were powerless to thwart terrorism if the government refused to establish representative institutions or to grant basic civil liberties. A cartoon from 1880 expressed the popular bemusement over the panic spreading through elite circles: over the caption "Next season's fashions," three well-to-do Russians promenade in suits of armor, walking sticks, and parasols. The government's discombobulation and society's response proved to many the utility of terrorism, for these were results far beyond what the propagandists of 1874 had ever achieved.

The People's Will and the Assassination of Alexander II

Land and Liberty, always an uneasy alliance of urban terrorists and rural agitators, split in 1879, largely over the use of terrorism, particularly the decision during the summer to focus all efforts on the goal of assassinating Alexander II. Out of this rupture was born the revolutionary group Narodnaia Volia (translated variously as the People's Will or the People's Liberty). The group had perhaps five hundred members in about fifty cities across the Russian Empire. Beyond this, it had several thousand supporters who supplied safe houses and financial and moral support. The program of the People's Will was targeted assassination, but there was much disagreement about the specific purpose that violence was to serve. A few members, principally Nikolai Morozov, argued for a wide open campaign of terrorism that would unleash chaos and provoke a peasant rebellion, while others argued that the People's Will should use terrorism to seize power and rule from above, given the passivity of the Russian masses. Most of the People's Will, such as its nominal leader Lev Tikhomirov, steered the group along a middle course. He refused to endorse a specific political endgame, arguing that the purpose of terrorism was symbolic. Since revolution was impossible until the peasants gave up their belief in the tsar as a distant but benevolent father figure, terrorism, he proposed, could undermine the legitimacy of the tsar and lead the people to see the terrorists as their benefactors.

What all could agree on was the romance of political violence. Although Morozov left the People's Will in frustration when his political views were rejected by his colleagues, his description of the purposes of terror summarized the group's mood: "the terroristic movement . . . should make the struggle popular, historical, and grandiose." Terrorist strikes provide justice against despots, he opined, but more importantly, such attacks tell the people "about the powerful love of freedom which is capable of making a hero out of a man, which can give people gigantic strength to accomplish almost superhuman deeds" (Laqueur, *Voices*, 78–9).

The People's Will killed two provincial governors, but gave up such attempts on lesser officials in favor of an all-out effort to assassinate the tsar. This goal increasingly consumed all the time, effort, and resources of the People's Will, rendering almost quaint the group's debates about the nature of the revolution that would follow an assassination. The demands of plotting the tsar's death while avoiding discovery forced the People's Will to become the modern era's first professional conspiratorial terrorist organization. As such, its influence was pronounced even on those subversive organizations that disavowed terrorism. The group's division of labor was impressive: there were specialists in target surveillance, forging documents, smuggling equipment, and counter-espionage against the police. Furthermore, the group divided itself into cells, about whose existence the rank-and-file members were, in theory, mutually ignorant.

The decision to use high explosives was just as important as the organization of the conspiracy and likewise full of historical significance. Assassins had previously used bombs made out of gunpowder or fulminate of mercury, but with only limited success (Orsini's attack in 1858 had killed many, but not its target). Enter the Swedish inventor, Alfred Nobel, who developed an efficient process for manufacturing a much more powerful and concentrated explosive, nitroglycerin, in the 1860s and two devastatingly effective means of conveyance, dynamite (patented in 1867) and gelignite (1876). Originally developed for mining, these explosives were quickly appropriated for military and terrorist use. There were many disadvantages, however. Explosives were expensive, hard to obtain, and difficult to transport and handle. The resultant bombs – themselves tricky to fashion – were quite heavy, thus requiring the terrorist to get close to his target, which nearly ensured that the assassin would be wounded, killed, or captured in the attack. Nonetheless, when the People's Will considered using revolvers to kill the tsar, they decided against it, since, according to one member, "it would have been interpreted as an ordinary murder, and would not have expressed a new stage in the revolutionary movement" (quoted in Iviansky, "Individual Terror," 6).

On March 1, 1881, Alexander II was killed when his royal sleigh was attacked in the streets of St. Petersburg. After an earlier attempt killed eleven bystanders, the leaders of the People's Will decided to use small, hand-held explosives designed to injure as few people besides the target as possible. One assassin died in the attack. Five more were arrested and quickly hanged. Wholesale arrests swept up almost all members of the People's Will. Needless to say, no popular revolution erupted. The new tsar, Alexander III, began to roll back his father's reforms, which he blamed for the growth of the revolutionary movement. He also erected a cathedral – popularly known as Christ the Savior on the Spilled Blood – on the exact spot where his father was murdered. The cathedral, replete with onion domes and colorful mosaics, was constructed in the pre-modern Muscovite style and thus presented a direct challenge to both liberals and radicals who hoped for a turn away from authoritarian rule.

Figure 5.1: The Church of the Savior on the Spilled Blood, St. Petersburg (© Richard Klune/Corbis)

The period between the assassination of Alexander II in 1881 and the start of the new century is usually characterized as merely the downtime between the revolutionary terrorism of the People's Will and its most notable successor, the Party of Socialist–Revolutionaries. The ground was being prepared for more violence, however. In particular, the Russian state was losing the allegiance of much of society. A devastating famine in 1891–2 revealed the vast indifference and incompetence of the government, while curtailment of Alexander II's reforms alienated the liberal intelligentsia. Pogroms – anti-Semitic violence carried out by right-wing nationalist groups often linked to the government – drove more people into the arms of terrorists. Meanwhile, rapid industrialization was creating a sizable and deeply embittered working class that was vulnerable to the radical propaganda of Russian Marxists. The cycle that played out in the 1860s and 1870s repeated itself in the 1880s and 1890s: educational and agitational work meant to prepare peasants and workers for a broad social revolution produced little progress, eventually yielding to the urge to use conspiratorial violence in pursuit of a political revolution. Another factor that contributed to the slide toward violence was the survival of the mystique of revolutionary terrorism.

Propaganda of the Deed

An additional element that contributed to the persistence of such mystique was the development of a doctrine widely known as "propaganda of the deed." The phrase was first used by the Italian anarcho-socialist Carlo Pisacane who, like Bakunin, believed insurrection was instinctual among the poor and needed only an inspirational shove by a group of professional, elite revolutionaries. His own experience did not bear this out: his effort in 1857 to rouse the peasants of Southern Italy failed when they killed his small band of invaders. He committed suicide out of disillusionment, but his 1857 testament provided fodder for countless others. "Propaganda of the idea is a chimera," he wrote. "The education of the people is an absurdity. Ideas result from deeds, not the latter from the former . . . . The only work a citizen can do for the good of the country is that of cooperating with the material revolution: therefore, conspiracies, plots, attempts, etc., are that series of deeds through which Italy proceeds toward her goal" (quoted in Nunzio Pernicone, *Italian Anarchism*, 13).

Such ideas underpinned much of Bakunin's work, and he began to use the phrase propaganda of the deed in the last years of his life. The doctrine achieved wide circulation in the 1870s and 1880s when it was endorsed and articulated by Peter Kropotkin (d. 1921), who, alongside

Bakunin, stands as the most important theorist of anarchism. Kropotkin, like Heinzen before him, accepted the premise that governments used legal and moral precepts as justifications for violence that benefited the privileged. He also believed that the bourgeois capitalist state used its cultural and social domination to erect psychological barriers against revolution in the minds of workers and peasants. Only propaganda of the deed, claimed Kropotkin, could destroy those barriers and radicalize the masses. Although he was likely thinking of demonstrations and other subversive acts, he did not shy away from endorsing violence: "permanent revolt by word of mouth, in writing, by the dagger, the rifle, dynamite . . . Everything is good for us which falls outside legality" (quoted in Joll, *The Anarchists*, 109). Even when individual propagandists are silenced for their deeds, the act of government repression could further the cause by, in turn, provoking new acts of revolt. Kropotkin thus understood well the cornerstone of the modern terrorist's strategy that the properly chosen terrorist act is, above all else, symbolic and provocative. For this reason, Kropotkin praised the terrorists of the People's Will from his European exile, but not without chiding them for having too narrowly focused on assassination at the expense of agitation among the people.

The Socialist–Revolutionaries and the Combat Organization

Propaganda of the deed certainly figured prominently in the thinking of leaders of the Party of Socialist–Revolutionaries, the organization most responsible for the re-emergence of systematic terror in Russia. The group (frequently referred to as the SRs) formed in 1901 and was dedicated to the establishment of a socialist state based on the communal traditions of rural Russia. The SRs were the direct heirs of Land and Liberty with one important difference: whereas the debate over the use of terrorism led to the earlier group's split, the SRs' leaders emphasized the compatibility of terror and peaceful agitation, stating that the role of terrorism and political assassination would be to revolutionize the masses and "awaken even the sleepiest philistines . . . and force them, even against their will, to think politically." The SRs also stated that, as with earlier Russian conspiratorial groups, terrorism would be used to defend the movement against the authorities while sowing "disorganization" in the ranks of the government, perhaps even to the point of forcing it to make concessions (quoted in Geifman, *Thou Shalt Kill*, 46–7).

The Party of Socialist–Revolutionaries was a national, albeit illegal, party with local chapters and a large, open membership. Because SR leaders understood that such a structure would make conspiratorial work impossible, they created a separate organization devoted to terrorism, the Combat Organization. Its members were officially under the control of the SRs' Central Committee, but had their own treasury, chose their own targets, and carried out their operations with the barest of input from the Central Committee, which glorified the Combat Organization's acts while maintaining a discreet distance. In time, the members of the Combat Organization, like Land and Liberty's terrorists, came to see themselves as the party's only true revolutionaries, the only ones willing to take action and put their lives on the line. As they grew ever more disdainful of the soft-handed folk who filled the ranks of the mass party, the Combat Organization's terrorists developed a separate identity and a loyalty to their own far above any to the parent party. Just as significantly, the distorting effect of their cloistered, conspiratorial lifestyle drove members of the Combat Organization to become more loyal to the primacy of violence than to any specific ideological stance.

The Combat Organization pulled off a range of spectacular assassinations from 1902 to 1905, including two ministers of internal affairs; the governor of Ufa province; several other police and government officials; and even the tsar's own uncle, the Grand Duke Sergei Aleksandrovich, who was Moscow's governor general. The targets were well chosen, for their deaths were not mourned, even by those from the political center and right. An English newspaper correspondent reported that one minister's demise "was received with semi-public rejoicings. I met nobody who regretted his assassination or condemned the authors" (quoted in Asprey, *War in the Shadows*, I:292). These killings made the Combat Organization the darlings of the revolutionary movement and helped produce a steady stream of money and recruits. Many, it seems, agreed with the courtroom speech made by Ivan Kaliaev, the murderer of the Grand Duke:

> We are two warring camps. You – the representatives of the imperial government, the hired servants of capital and oppression. I – one of the avengers of the people, a socialist and revolutionary . . . You have declared war upon the people. We have accepted your challenge (quoted in Asprey, *War in the Shadows*, I:292).

Kaliaev's combination of eloquence, bravado, and self-abnegation – not to mention his obligatory death sentence – made him a revolutionary martyr of the first order.

The Combat Organization's most effective organizer was Boris Savinkov, who, as the group's deputy leader, planned the assassination of Internal Affairs Minister von Plehve and the Grand Duke Sergei. Immediately after he ceased his violent activities, Savinkov embarked on a career as an author, publishing a memoir and two semi-autobiographical novels under the pen name of "V. Ropshin." The memoir is a fairly straight forward affair, but the novels are distinguished by their astonishing cynicism. Savinkov's semi-fictional assassins are motivated by almost everything but devotion to socialism or the liberation of Russia's peasants. Some characters thirst for revenge, others flirt with existentialism and spirituality. The "hero" of the second novel, *What Never Happened: A Novel of the Revolution* (1912), is driven by, at first, his own self-importance and then later, his need to prove himself. Whether the novels were intended by Savinkov as admissions of guilt or error is unclear. The bottom line is that Savinkov brutally demystified Russia's tradition of romantic revolutionaries stretching back to Zasulich and Rakhmetov and left behind portraits of ideologically barren terrorists who worshiped violence.

The Revolution of 1905

The Combat Organization has received the lion's share of attention concerning terrorism during the waning days of the Russian Empire. In fact, the group was responsible for only a handful of victims during this violent era. What had been a carefully orchestrated campaign of targeted assassination waged by the Combat Organization turned into a terrorist free-for-all of staggering and historical proportions. The turning point came on January 9, 1905, when Cossacks and police massacred hundreds of peaceful demonstrators in St. Petersburg. As news of "Bloody Sunday" spread, workers went on strike, liberal intellectuals organized public protests, peasants staged uprisings, and soldiers and sailors occasionally mutinied – a collective upheaval that has come to be known as the Revolution of 1905. With Russia teetering on the brink of total collapse in the fall, the tsar relented and issued the October Manifesto, which promised a parliament, a constitution, and guaranteed civil liberties. This action largely appeased the intelligentsia and middle-class professionals who had gotten what they wanted. Even the SRs briefly suspended all terrorist activities. The radicals and the lower classes continued to seethe, however, because the Manifesto failed to address economic grievances. Strikes and peasant disturbances continued apace, and order was not restored throughout the Empire until 1907.

The government arrested enough members of the Combat Organization in March 1905 to effectively shut down the group. But the chaos that rapidly engulfed the Empire swamped the government's ability to maintain order. Emboldened by both the evaporation of civil authority and the sense that liberation was near at hand, terrorists began an unprecedented wave of political violence. In fact, violence dramatically increased after the October Manifesto. Smelling blood, extremists thought the time had come to launch a final assault upon the citadel of oppression. The result was a vicious cycle from fall 1905 to spring 1907: terrorist violence begat more chaos, which inspired more violence.

The extent of terrorism beggars the imagination. One contemporary source calculated that seventeen thousand people were killed or wounded from 1901 to 1916, a figure which includes at least thirty-three governors and seven generals or admirals. The majority of the victims – more than nine thousand, over one-third of whom were government officials – came in the period 1905–7. Police estimated that terrorists killed or wounded an average of eighteen victims per day in 1907. These statistics do not include politically motivated robberies – dubbed "expropriations" or "exes." During just the year beginning October 1905, there were nearly two thousand robberies which netted a total of seven million rubles (Geifman, *Thou Shalt Kill*, 21–2).

Most of this violence was perpetrated by members of local groups. This began with the SRs themselves. Unlike the People's Will, the Party of Socialist–Revolutionaries did not demand that all of its terror operations be centrally directed. Although the Combat Organization was responsible for the SR's highest profile assassinations, local cells, dubbed "flying detachments," were allowed and even encouraged to carry out their own attacks. That 80 percent of the members of these groups were not even official members of the Party highlights the fact that terrorism during this period became less and less linked to ideological stance. The SR flying detachments were responsible for some high-profile killings, sometimes on the orders of the Central Committee. From October 1905 to July 1906, while the SRs declared a truce against the government in order to evaluate the results of the October Manifesto, the flying detachments killed local officials, notables, and police spies on its own initiative, against the express wishes of the Central Committee.

"A New Type of Revolutionary"

The SRs' flying detachments were but one segment of a larger campaign against state and society in Russia characterized by a new coarseness and brutality. The liberal writer Peter Struve understood this when he remarked that "a new type of revolutionary" had come to dominate the movement. The typical Russian terrorist of the 1870s and 1880s was educated, middle class, and interested in ideological and theoretical rationales for terrorism. In particular, they tended to discriminate between their targets, whose deaths they considered morally justified, and innocent bystanders, whose deaths they hoped to avoid. Terrorists of this earlier generation also generally sought to limit "collateral" damage because they hoped to cultivate public sympathy and build support for the revolutionary movement. Not so with Struve's "new type" of terrorist who, he noted, was a blend of "revolutionary and bandit [marked by] the liberation of revolutionary psychology from all moral restraints" (quoted in Geifman, *Thou Shalt Kill*, 6).

Such violence was the particular hallmark of the anarchists. Although there were very few of them in Russia before the 1905 Revolution, anarchist groups "sprang up like mushrooms after a rain" in 1905–7, in the words of one anarchist (quoted in Avrich, *The Russian Anarchists*, 42). While many Russian anarchists heeded Kropotkin's warning against random violence unconnected to the liberation of the masses, others gravitated toward Bakunin and his endorsement of all violence as essentially revolutionary. Many of these anarchists could be found in the Black Banner, a very loose federation of independent local chapters. Black Banner anarchists embraced terrorism as a means of promoting more chaos, a force they believed would directly precipitate a free, new world. This strategy even acquired a name: "motiveless terror." Tellingly, the one nineteenth-century Russian terrorist whose stock rose was Sergei Nechaev. Gone was the effort to justify individual acts of violence or even to discriminate between degrees of authoritarian guilt. Black Bannerists believed conscripted soldiers and government clerks deserved death just as much as did the tsar. Likewise, in their promotion of economic terror they equally condemned factory owners, middle managers, and minor owners of property. A typical anarchist manifesto from 1909 screeched out the Black Banner creed succinctly: "Take the picks and hammers! Undermine the foundations of venerable towns! Everything is ours, outside us is only death . . . All to the street! Forward! Destroy! Kill!" Not surprisingly, the Black Banner attracted many people with a limited understanding of anarchist theory. No matter: the awareness of intellectual justifications of violence was unnecessary. All that was required to make a good revolutionary was to have "combat in his blood," as one anarchist put it (quoted in Geifman, *Thou Shalt Kill*, 125, 134).

Even more troubling was the presence in the movement of many who used anarchism and revolution as covers for blatantly criminal behavior. Anarchist leaders, in fact, went to great lengths to recruit thieves, arsonists, and murderers into their ranks. Some of the more principled anarchists understood that the purveyors of indiscriminate killing and robbing discredited the broader movement, but they had little power to rein in what one moderate anarchist called the "bombthrower-expropriators" (quoted in Avrich, *Russian Anarchists*, 60).

Although there were far more SRs and Marxists in the years 1905–7, anarcho-terrorists produced far more mayhem and death (there were probably never more than five thousand active anarchists in the Russian Empire, including those of the peaceful variety). The result was a bacchanal of violence that broke down the distinctions among crime, terrorism, guerrilla fighting, revolution, and civil war. Anarchists and members of other ideologically vague groups attacked everything that smacked of the old order. They fired shots and threw bombs at police, soldiers, and patrolling Cossacks. They freed prisoners and killed their guards. They invaded churches and attacked priests. They robbed banks and armored cars. They held hostages and ransomed their captives. They launched bombs into restaurants, cafes, theatres, and shops. They attacked bureaucrats in their offices, in their homes, and on the streets. No endorsement was necessary from a group; personal initiative was frequently the cause of action. When threatened with capture, many committed suicide, some quite dramatically through self-immolation. The southwestern industrial city of Odessa (in modern-day Ukraine) was particularly wracked by anarcho-terrorist violence. One of the era's most infamous attacks occurred in December 1905, when several dozen people were wounded by anarchists throwing bombs into the city's Café Libman. Terrorists had chosen the target because they believed the bourgeoisie congregated there. In reality, it was a hangout for artisans and intellectuals. Anarchists in Odessa also stalked policemen, randomly shot into crowds, and threw bombs in streetcars and trains that defied calls for general strikes. In the city's port, terrorists blew up merchant steamers and killed unpopular captains.

Marxism and Terrorism

Russian Marxists condemned assassinations, bombings, and revenge-killings, but their concern was not morality. History was made through the class struggle, they maintained, not the actions of isolated cells of terrorists. In 1911, Lev Trotsky got to the heart of the matter: "if we rise against terrorist acts, it is only because individual revenge does not satisfy us" (Trotsky, "Why Marxists Oppose Individual Terrorism"). The chilling implication was that state terror as practiced by the Jacobins could be effective and wholly satisfying.

In fact, Marxists retreated from even this denunciation of individual terror when circumstances warranted. In the wake of the 1905 Revolution, Lenin recognized that terrorism was appropriate in two circumstances: as a means of generating popular support among workers and peasants for the Bolshevik cause, and as a means of raising money necessary for the party's operations. The result was that local

Bolsheviks carried out assassinations of police, police spies, and petty officials throughout the Empire, but never on the scale of the SRs or anarchists. Where the Bolsheviks emerged as second to none was in the field of "revolutionary expropriations." Bolshevik cells carried out dozens of robberies to fund the party's conspiratorial activities, particularly in the South. The most notorious theft took place in 1907 when the robbery of a state bank stagecoach in Tiflis, Georgia, netted 250,000 rubles, money that was immediately sent to the Bolshevik Party in exile. A behind-the-scenes coordinator of these Bolshevik "exes" in the Caucasus was none other than Joseph Stalin. The future dictator, in fact, used the nickname Koba, a Robin Hood figure from a mid nineteenth-century Georgian novel.

Responses to Terrorism

Terrorist groups thrived during this time, in part because of the benevolent neutrality of liberal politicians and the middle classes they represented. The largest liberal organization, the Constitutional Democrats (known as the Kadets), refused time and time again to denounce terrorism. Like the onlookers in Turgenev's 1878 poem, "The Threshold," the Kadets sympathized with Russia's anti-tsarist terrorists in the belief that they faced a common enemy. Unwilling to throw bombs themselves, the Kadets tolerated and encouraged it in others. That a "liberal" movement sympathized with terrorism says much for the political environment in Russia at the time. In 1906, Russia's new parliament, not just its Kadet faction, decided against issuing a statement officially condemning terrorism and "political murders."

Meanwhile, the educated public was exposed to terrorism through the press on a scale never before experienced in Russia. Many daily newspapers routinely ran summaries of terrorist attacks throughout the Empire. Readers were able, at a glance, to note the variety, lethality, and scale of terrorism in Russia. And given that anarchists and others were no longer targeting just government officials and police – as Russian terrorists had typically done before 1905 – news of attacks served the double function of terrorizing the state and much of society.

The educated public responded to the prevalence of terrorism with a large dose of gallows humor. A frequently heard joke posed the question, "What is the difference between European ministers and ours?" The answer: "European ministers get thrown out of office, and ours get blown out." Like today, the fear of terrorism was such that it was perceived as a genuine threat to all, not just politicians or the wealthy. "Luck is like a bomb," went another joke. "It can strike one man today, another tomorrow" (quoted in Geifman, *Thou Shalt Kill*, 57, 16).

While many Russian intellectuals supported or at least sympathized with revolutionary terrorism, some sought to explore the moral consequences of terrorism for society. In reviewing Savinkov's first novel, the contemporary literary critic S. Andrianov described the corrosive effect of terrorism. For the individual who uses it, "there occurs the same horror that takes place in a society morally crushed by tyranny: both oppressor and oppressed are isolated and corrupted" (quoted in Kelly, "Self-Censorship," 204).

Other authors, particularly those of the avant-garde, used terrorism as a metaphor, holding it up as a mirror of society. The most famous example is Andrei Bely's disturbing comic masterpiece *Petersburg*, published in 1913. The plot concerns a hapless revolutionary charged with assassinating a high-level bureaucrat, who happens to be his father. In fact, the story is secondary to the absurdist descriptions of St. Petersburg as a city perched on the edge of destruction. In this regard, Bely borrows from nineteenth-century Russian literature's abundant treatments of floods, a stock metaphor used to describe Petersburg (a city vulnerable to floods because of its location on a swamp) as a metropolis threatened by its own progress and undone by hubris. Bely updates the metaphor by substituting terrorism, a more topical phenomenon that would convey horror and dread.

The chaos led some Russians to take matters into their own hands. Amid the growing violence of 1905 and 1906, hundreds of independent, locally organized right-wing cells, known as Black Hundreds, carried out pogroms against Jews and liberal groups. Sometimes the behavior of these groups became indistinguishable from that of the revolutionary terrorists – except that the reactionaries were almost never punished by the government, a move that most Russians interpreted as tacit approval of right-wing violence.

Russian Counter-Terrorism

The scale and ferocity of left-wing violence overwhelmed the tsarist government, but the necessity of dealing with much larger – and more prosaic – revolutionary threats, such as demonstrations, general strikes, peasant uprisings, and military mutinies, hampered the state's ability to address the terrorist threat. Another factor was that the notoriously underpaid police often found themselves outgunned and outhustled by better armed and better motivated terrorists. Even when the police could get their hands on terrorists, the tsarist state continued to treat terrorism as a political crime, a designation that brought with it relatively lenient sentences.

The government began to use field courts-martial to combat terrorism in 1906. These bodies carried out sentences within hours of convening, often mere hours after the crime was committed; defendants were denied counsel, public hearings, and appeals. By April 1907, when the courts were done away with, roughly eleven hundred field trials had been held, and more than one thousand people had been shot by military firing squads or hanged. The use of such tribunals reflected the state's increasing inclination to view counter-terrorism in military terms, as simply part of the larger effort to suppress internal enemies during and after the 1905 Revolution. Throughout the Empire, soldiers replaced or augmented police, whether on patrol, protecting likely targets, or guarding prisons. During the winter of 1906/7, however, the government reorganized the Empire's counter-terrorism apparatus with an emphasis on inter-agency cooperation and intelligence gathering, reforms that made the police more capable of distinguishing between terrorists and the merely discontented.

That might have been the case, but the brutality and pseudo-legality of the field courts-martial attracted the attention of moderates and leftists, and provided vivid proof of how little interest the tsar had in a true constitutional system. No less a public figure than Leo Tolstoy condemned the military tribunals in an essay entitled "I Cannot Keep Silent!" The execution of women and juveniles brought forth particularly strong reactions from the public, including its moderate and even conservative elements. There is also evidence of declining military morale as soldiers were called upon to carry out police duties against civilians, tasks for which the troops had never been trained. Historians continue to debate whether constitutionalism could have succeeded in Russia. What seems clear is that the state's counter-terrorism tactics undermined its efforts to win support from the public. A police report from 1901, in fact, had recognized that the goal of some revolutionary terrorists was to provoke the authorities into brutal repression that would radicalize the population. Awareness of this strategy did not in and of itself provide the antidote.

Troops and military courts were undoubtedly effective in helping to curtail terrorist activity, as was the use of double agents, the most famous of whom, Evno Azev, was for a time actually head of the SRs' Combat Organization. Azev's work meant that the government was able to thwart every assassination plot of the Combat Organization from 1906 to 1908. The public revelation of the Azev Affair seriously damaged the reputation of the entire terrorist movement but also horrified the public, which wondered just how far the government would apparently go in combating terrorism.

The largest factor contributing to the eventual decline of terrorist activity in 1908 and beyond was the steep fall in revolutionary activity by 1907. As the number of major demonstrations, strikes, and spontaneous revolts waned and then ceased and the prospects of a revolutionary victory became more remote, the cycle of violence and chaos was finally broken. Violence still continued at a lesser rate, however; by 1912, the police registered "only" eighty-two terrorist acts for the entire year.

Russian revolutionary terrorists never succeeded in inspiring a popular revolution. When the end came for the tsarist state during the First World War, it was, in fact, the result of a popular uprising, but one brought on largely by governmental incompetence and a disastrous and unpopular war. Nonetheless, revolutionary terrorism in Russia contributed significantly to what came to pass in 1917. Assassination robbed the country of thousands of civil servants and paralyzed tens of thousands more with fear, a state of affairs that presumably decreased the government's effectiveness. Counter-terrorism measures diverted extensive resources and gobbled up the state's meager supply of moral capital and political legitimacy with the educated public. The intelligentsia contributed their fair share to the Russian tragedy as well: alienated from the government to the point that they were seduced by the terrorists' promise of tough action and quick results, the moderate and leftist intelligentsia virtually gave up on helping to build the sort of state that could have withstood the challenges of the war years. Last but not least, terrorism during and after 1905 produced a new generation of revolutionary leaders inured to violence, committed to conspiratorial methods, and skeptical of moderation. Most revolutionary terrorists of the period 1905–7 threw in their lot with Lenin and the Reds. Many, in fact, found work with the Bolshevik political police, the infamous Cheka. In the early twentieth century, revolutionary terrorism in Russia – as is the norm – destabilized the government, polarized political discourse, and brutalized the population, but failed to generate the liberating revolution its advocates longed for.

More broadly speaking, Russian revolutionary terrorism from the 1860s to the 1900s produced the tactics, the strategies, the justifications, and the rhetoric that became commonplace in the twentieth century. In fact, the revolutionary terrorists of 1905–7 anticipated in important ways the apocalyptic terrorists of almost a century later. What unites these two groups is not their theoretical justifications or political orientations, but their commitment to provocative and indiscriminate violence and their nihilistic worship of terror as an end in itself. In a sense, there is a common ideology at work here, but it is an apolitical ideology of anger, rejection, empowerment, and mayhem. This is a peculiarly modern phenomenon: a revolt *against* modernity that could only exist because of the modern era's paradoxical encouragement of individualism and statism. This is a theme that will dominate the next chapter as well.

Bibliography

Good general surveys of Russian revolutionary terrorism are Philip Pomper, "Russian Revolutionary Terrorism," in *Terrorism in Context*, ed. Martha Crenshaw (cited in the introduction); Adam Ulam, *In the Name of the People: Prophets and Conspirators in Prerevolutionary Russia* (Viking Press, 1977); and the relevant chapter in Steven G. Marks, *How Russia Shaped the Modern World: From Art to Anti-Semitism, Ballet to Bolshevism* (Princeton University Press, 2003).

The classic and comprehensive study of populism and populist terror in the nineteenth century (ending with the assassination of Alexander II) is Franco Venturi, *The Roots of Revolution: A History of the Populist and Socialist Movements in Nineteenth-Century Russia* (University of Chicago Press, 1960). For the generation of the nihilists, see Abbot Gleason, *Young Russia: The Genesis of Russian Radicalism in the 1860s* (Viking Press, 1980). Nechaev's "Catechism of a Revolutionary" (along with other documents) is reprinted in Michael Confino, ed., *Daughter of a Revolutionary: Natalie Herzen and the Bakunin-Nechayev Circle*, (Library Press, 1974). A brief but illuminating study of Nechaev is Paul Avrich, *Bakunin and Nechaev*, 2nd edn. (Freedom Press, 1974). For the direct precursor to the People's Will, see Deborah Hardy, *Land and Freedom: The Origins of Russian Terrorism, 1876–1879* (Greenwood Press, 1987). Vera Zasulich's autobiography is included in Barbara Alpern Engel and Clifford N. Rosenthal, eds., *Five Sisters: Women Against the Tsar* (Knopf, 1975). For another eyewitness account, see Sergei Stepniak-Kravchinsky, *Underground Russia* (Charles Scribner's Sons, 1883).

For a classic study of the subject, see Paul Avrich, *The Russian Anarchists* (Princeton University Press, 1967). The best works on the two towering figures of Russian anarchism are E. H. Carr, *Michael Bakunin* (Vintage, 1961 [1937]); and Martin A. Miller, *Kropotkin* (University of Chicago Press, 1976).

The best study of the Russian Revolution of 1905 is Abraham Ascher, *The Revolution of 1905*, 2 vols., (Stanford University Press, 1988, 1994). For terrorism during this period, the absolutely indispensable study is Anna Geifman, *Thou Shalt Kill: Revolutionary Terrorism in Russia, 1894–1917* (Princeton, 1993). Also see Geifman, *Entangled in Terror: The Azef Affair and the Russian Revolution* (Scholarly Resources, 2000).

On the Okhrana, the Russian secret police, see Jonathan Daly, "The Security Police and Politics in Late Imperial Russia," in Anna Geifman, ed., *Russia under the Last Tsar* (Blackwell, 1999).

A valuable article that addresses, in part, intellectuals' responses to terrorism is Aileen Kelly, "Self-Censorship and the Russian Intelligentsia, 1905–1914," *Slavic Review*, vol. 46, no. 2 (summer 1987), 193–213.

A good work on the SRs' terror boss is Richard B. Spence, *Boris Savinkov: Renegade on the Left* (Eastern European Monographs, 1991). Savinkov's most important works are all available in English: *The Pale Horse* (1919 [1909]); *What Never Happened: A Novel of the Revolution* (1917 [1912]); *Memoirs of a Terrorist* (Kraus Reprint, 1972 [1917, 1932]); and *The Black Horse* (1924 [1923]).

6

The Era of the European *Attentat*

Terrorism first appeared fully in its modern guise in Russia from the 1860s to the 1900s, but the use of terrorism in Europe only barely lagged behind. To trace the development of terrorism there, we must return to the mid nineteenth century, when political and social pressures continued to build across the continent: in fragmented Germany and Italy, the multinational empire of Austria, the comparatively moderate monarchy of Restoration France, and the dynamic, constitutional monarchy of the United Kingdom. Two great fault lines had developed and continued to deepen. On the one hand, liberals, nationalists, and republicans seethed under the rule of conservative, even reactionary dynasties; while on the other, the new industrial workforce and its socialist champions grew bitter at bourgeois industrialists. In the 1840s, communists and anarchists added their voices to the cacophony of anti-conservative frustration. The storm broke in 1848 with a series of revolutions that left few monarchies untouched. But by 1851, the *status quo ante* had largely been restored. Conservative governments had learned important lessons, however, and were becoming increasingly adept at finding ways to co-opt the forces of nationalism and liberalism. Limited parliaments and constitutions defused some anger, while governments and their growing bureaucracies increasingly replaced families, churches, and local communities as record-keepers, educators, and protectors. But European states still faced angry and frustrated populations. Liberals continued to demand more freedom and genuine representation; nationalists protested where peoples still had not achieved independence; socialists and communists cried out for economic justice; and anarchists decried ever-expanding statism. Terrorism came to be seen as a viable option by the radical fringes of each of these four aggrieved segments of the population.

Propaganda of the Deed and Terrorism

Three factors led some anarchists to endorse terrorism – not just insurrection and demonstration – as a legitimate form of propaganda of the deed in the 1870s. The first was the collapse of the International Workingmen's Association, an umbrella organization of socialist and anarchist groups. The second was the failure of a number of comically inept anarchist insurrections. The third, and most decisive, factor was that across much of Europe, governments, even conservative ones, had introduced a number of social reforms meant to improve the lives of workers. This development – a process sometimes called by historians "liberal paternalism" or "paternalistic reform" – led many workers and their advocates to abandon anarchism and radical socialism in favor of trade unions and legitimate political parties. In essence, the anarchist violence that was to horrify the governments and bourgeoisie of Europe for the next thirty years was – as terrorism so often is – an act of desperation by a minority that feared it was losing its audience and its relevance.

Appearances seemed to indicate the reverse. In 1878 anarchist violence – frequently referred to by the French and German word *attentat* (attempt) – came into its own. In Italy, an anarchist attacked the new king and prime minister of Italy with a knife, wounding both. Other attacks that year in Italy indicated the willingness of anarchists to broaden their range of targets to include civilians deemed guilty because of their association with the architecture of oppression. Bombs were thrown at a parade honoring the late king, Victor Emanuel II; a monarchist rally; and a crowd celebrating the queen's birthday.

Anarchists were active that year in Germany as well. Two separate attempts on the life of Kaiser Wilhelm I by Max Hödel and Karl Nobiling in 1878 failed to kill their target, but precipitated a reaction from the government that, in the words of one historian, "turned Berlin into a city that was garrisoned as though it were in a state of siege" (Carlson, "Anarchism and Individual Terror," 178). The ensuing police campaign netted over five hundred people, most of whom were found guilty of nothing more than insulting the dignity of the emperor or expressing sympathy for the would-be assassins. The real target of the German government's wrath were the socialists of the Social Democratic Party, and it was determined to use these incidents to crack down on it, despite the fact that the Social Democrats had no connection to the assassins and had devoted themselves to legal work within the parliamentary system. To this end, the government issued a press release suggesting that the second assassin was, in fact, a member of the Social Democrats. The accusation had the desired effect. The outraged members of the Reichstag quickly passed a sweeping Socialist Law that gave the authorities the power to arrest radicals, shut down their organizations and presses, and drastically curtail free speech – moves that drove the Social Democrats into the underground for twelve years.

In the eyes of some radicals, such stiffening resistance from the author-ities – whether directed at socialists, anarchists, or simply the entire left – demanded an escalation in kind. The result was new found support for terrorism as warfare for a new age. An 1881 gathering in London that launched a new anarchist International, for example, endorsed all illegal acts committed in the name of revolution and encouraged the study of chemistry in order to produce better bombs. Although he was himself never involved in violent work, Peter Kropotkin came out in support of propaganda of the deed, claiming that "one such act may, in a few days, make more propaganda than thousands of pamphlets" (quoted in Laqueur, *Voices*, 98).

Johann Most and Anarcho-Terrorism

The era's most notorious theoretician of terror was Johann Most (d. 1906), the illegitimate son of a low-level Bavarian bureaucrat, who, thanks to a botched surgical procedure, was caricatured as the "ugly, little, mad anar-chist" (quoted in Trautmann, *The Voice of Terror*, 5). After a brief stint in Germany's Reichstag as a Social Democratic deputy, Most grew frustrated with Germany's social democratic leadership and eventually abandoned all hope in the political process. He gravitated toward Bakuninist anar-chism under the influence of the twin failed attempts on Kaiser Wilhelm I in 1878 and the assassination of Alexander II in 1881. Fully under the spell of "direct action," he began a newspaper, *Die Freiheit* (*Freedom*), which he continued to publish when he moved to New York in 1882. Throughout the 1880s, *Die Freiheit* was Most's principal vehicle for communicating to the world his shocking recipe for "[rescuing] mankind through blood, iron, poison, and dynamite." Terrorism, he maintained, should be used, above all, to "stoke the fire of revolution and incite people to revolt in any way we can" (quoted in Miller, *Kropotkin*, 44–5). Most was very sensitive to the effect that revolutionary acts of violence could have on friend and foe alike. What is the use of offing

> blackguards . . . in a dark corner so that no one knows the why and the wherefore of what happened? It would be a form of action, certainly, but not action as propaganda. The great thing about anarchist vengeance is

that it proclaims loud and clear for everyone to hear that this man or that man must die for this and this reason.

The choice of target, the drama of the attack, the perfection of the execution – all these elements could educate the masses. If the meaning of the act was not clear enough, he recommended that the terrorists should place posters explaining the operation "in such a way as to [produce] the best possible benefit" (quoted in Laqueur, *Voices*, 109). Never before had an advocate of terrorism so clearly described the theatrical value of killing and mayhem. Most specialized in offering technical advice to anarcho-terrorists. The most notorious example was his pamphlet, *The Science of Revolutionary Warfare*, which gave step-by-step instructions in the creation and use of disappearing ink, poisons, letter bombs, hand grenades, and dynamite. To ensure the accuracy of his recipes, Most gained experience by working for a short time in a munitions factory.

Most's agents smuggled large quantities of every issue of *Freiheit* into Germany where a strange and unintentional symbiosis emerged between the extremists and the authorities. On the one hand, the occasional bouts of heightened censorship ironically meant that Most achieved even more prominence among radicals and anarchists, since his distributors and correspondents knew how to survive and even thrive in the underground, while more moderate voices were shut down. On the other, when the police managed to infiltrate Most's German network, they used this access not to cripple the paper, but rather to insert even more inflammatory articles into *Freiheit*! These pieces, written by a German police commissioner, proved instrumental in engineering periodic renewals of the Socialist Law.

In the early and mid 1880s German anarchists, egged on by Most, succeeded in carrying out several dramatic "direct actions," including the murder of a police chief, the fatal stabbing of a factory owner, and bombings of restaurants and police and train stations. The crowning achievement was to be an attack on Germany's leading princes, aristocrats, and government officials at the dedication in 1883 of the Niederwald monument memorializing the unification of the German Empire. The botched attempt led to the arrest of August Reinsdorf and his cell, the most accomplished anarcho-terrorists operating in Germany.

Elsewhere in Europe, anarchist attacks likewise succeeded in causing few casualties, but attracted enormous attention because of the nature of the targets and the daring of the execution. A bomb was thrown in a Lyons music hall frequented by the bourgeoisie in 1882, and four years later a mentally unstable anarchist threw a container of hydrocyanic acid (an insecticide later used by the Nazis under the trademark Zyklon B) and fired several shots at traders on the floor of the Paris stock exchange.

Police and Terrorists

With every violent outrage or discovery of Most's newspaper in a hideout, many European governments grew more convinced that these terrorist acts were coordinated by an international organization – this despite the failure of socialists and anarchists alike to organize an effective replacement for the International Workingmen's Association. What were always rather paltry numbers were sometimes inflated by direct governmental involvement as well. A frequent police technique for attracting and arresting anarchists was to create fake cells. The French police even ran advertisements in Parisian newspapers. Sometimes secret agents inflated the threat or embellished the facts to exaggerate their own importance or justify their expenses. Two Italian police spies around the turn of the century, for instance, specialized in reporting on unlikely plots and detailing anarchist counter culture practices, such as free love. And the possibility cannot be discounted that police efforts to entrap anarchists went as far as the use of *agents provocateurs*.

In Germany, police activity, public revulsion, and Bismarck's enactment of some reforms directed toward the working class eroded the popularity and activity of Germany's anarchists. But Bismarck appreciated them as a bogeyman and used various means to help keep alive the anarchist movement, going so far as to send an agent to an international anarchist convention in 1889 when it became evident that Germany's anarchists were unable to do so themselves.

In some instances, police involvement and/or obfuscation was so great that historians doubt the very existence of highly touted terrorist groups and plots. For example, in the late 1870s and 1880s the Spanish government blamed a spate of violence against large landowners and their managers on a shadowy "secret association of kidnappers, murderers, and arsonists," known as *la Mano Negra* – the Black Hand (quoted in Bernecker, "The Strategies of 'Direct Action'," 105). Despite a complete lack of evidence, the government used the alleged existence of the group to crack down on the poor agrarian population, going so far as to publicly execute seven supposed members of the Black Hand in the town of Jerez de la Frontera in 1883.

The Peak of Anarcho-Terrorism

Another reason that European governments believed in such an international plot was the fact that when anarcho-terrorism reached its climax in the 1890s, the perpetrators were convinced of it themselves and demonstrated their beliefs through their terrorist acts. This was the era of what French anarchists called *reprise individuelle* – "the individual exaction" – when individual, even nihilistic, terrorism took on the appearance to the authorities of a vast conspiracy. Such an impression was also conveyed by the European press, which provided extensive coverage of anarcho-terrorist attacks in the 1890s. Two French periodicals in particular, *Le Petit Parisien* and *Le Petit Journal* (whose circulation reached one million), frequently featured visceral yet exquisite drawings of terrorist attacks on their covers.

It began with two bombs set by François-Claudins Ravachol. With a long history of burglary, grave robbing, and murder, Ravachol has been dismissed by many as nothing more than a criminal. His written legacy, however, suggests that he was a sincere anarchist with a highly developed, albeit very personal, ideology. Ravachol, who was born into a very poor family and developed an intense hatred of the bourgeoisie and capitalism, turned toward terrorism to answer the arrest, beating, and sentencing of two French anarchists who had taken part in a May Day parade in 1891. In March 1892, Ravachol bombed the homes of the trial's judge and prosecutor, killing neither, but wounding six others. Arrested after some ill-advised boasts to a waiter tipped off the authorities, Ravachol told the police that his attacks were intended to inform those who would impose harsh sentences on anarchists "that in the future they should be more lenient" (quoted in Maitron, *Histoire*, 198). Ravachol, who did not personally know the arrested anarchists, declared that he similarly expected others to avenge him. And avenged he was. On the day of his trial, an anarchist named Meunier and three accomplices exploded a bomb at the café that had been Ravachol's undoing, killing two. Ravachol was quickly memorialized by popular songs. One linked Ravachol's exploits to the protection of "the miserable ones with their empty stomachs" and contained the refrain, "Let's dance the Ravachol / Long live the sound of the explosion!" Another song declared, "We remember our martyrs / They died to protect us / We hope to make them great / Yes, Ravachol, we know to avenge you" (both quoted from Maitron, *Histoire*, 205). His name even turned into a verb: *ravacholiser*, "to bomb."

The other three principal French terrorists in the period 1892–4 were linked together and similarly motivated. In November 1892, the anarchist Emile Henry left a bomb at the offices of the Carmaux Mining Company in retaliation for the company's brutal suppression of a miners' strike the previous summer. The bomb was removed and taken to a police headquarters where it detonated, killing six. When arrested a year and a half later, Henry offered the odd justification that he "had resolved to prove

Figure 6.1: Meunier avenges Ravachol, as illustrated in a contemporary French newspaper
(© Roger Viollet/Getty Images)

to the miners . . . that only the anarchists were capable of devotion [to them]" (quoted in Maitron, *Ravachol et les Anarchistes*, 87).

In December 1893, the anarchist Auguste Vaillant tossed a crude homemade bomb into the French Chamber of Deputies, slightly wounding several legislators and onlookers. In contemporary accounts, the impoverished Vaillant was depicted as a dreamy and sensitive victim of society whose desperate act was an attempt to strike back before his own death. Poorly versed in anarchist theory he could still play his role well at his execution, crying out "Death to bourgeois society and long live anarchy!" (quoted in Joll, *The Anarchists*, 113).

Clearly Vaillant's lack of theoretical sophistication did not hurt him in the eyes of fellow anarchists, for his execution in February 1894 prompted two spectacular acts of revenge. The first was Henry's second and last terrorist attack, the bombing of a café at the Hotel Terminus at the Gare Saint Lazare, which killed one and wounded twenty. When caught and condemned for killing civilians, Henry replied with the chilling words, "There are no innocents" (quoted in Joll, *The Anarchists*, 118). In June 1894 the popular French president, Sadi Carnot, was stabbed to death by the Italian anarchist Santo-Geronimo Caserio. At his trial, Caserio explicitly stated that his act was meant to avenge the execution of Vaillant. While awaiting his own execution in prison, Caserio received a letter partially written in blood, promising he would be avenged. This promise went unfulfilled; the anarchist tit-for-tat in France was over.

It was this spate of bombings that did the most to produce in the public imagination the image of the anarchist that has survived until today: the crazed fanatic clutching revolver and bomb under his trench coat, hiding in the shadows. Writers of fiction did their part to cement this image. The classic example is the Professor from Joseph Conrad's novel, *The Secret Agent* (1907), who never leaves home without a bomb in his pocket.

Throughout this era, the governments of Europe and North America were convinced that terrorism and anarchism were international threats that demanded international responses. The first attempts at this were made under Bismarck's leadership in the 1870s and were principally directed against the International. The violence of the 1890s led to stepped-up measures. The Rome Conference of 1898 required that signatory states apply the death penalty for all assassination attempts on heads of state, whether successful or not. The St. Petersburg Protocol of 1904 added new measures for tracking radical groups. The effectiveness of these agreements was limited, however, because of the general resistance of the United Kingdom, Switzerland, and the United States to limit free speech or track radical groups from other countries.

Such efforts missed the point, in any case. Despite the plot lines of many contemporary novels (to which we will return shortly), French terrorists of the 1890s acted independently of each other. There clearly existed, however, a sense of collective responsibility that bound them together into a self-conscious movement. Early in 1892, when Ravachol was thought to be a criminal masquerading as an anarchist, Henry denounced him for "dishonor[ing] our party . . . [People like him] do not dream of sacrificing their life for ideas" (quoted in Maitron, *Histoire*, 220–1). What a strange "party" Henry described: no meetings, no rolls, and no dues! And yet there was an undeniable feeling of brotherhood, as Emile Henry insisted to the court in the concluding speech at this trial: "You have hung men in Chicago, cut off their heads in Germany, strangled them in Jerez, shot them in Barcelona, guillotined them in Montbrison and Paris, but what you will never destroy is anarchism" (quoted in Maitron, *Histoire*, 534).

In the days following Vaillant's attack on the Chamber of Deputies in 1893, that body passed two laws that revealed how much the authorities had come to appreciate and fear the doctrine of propaganda of the deed. The laws, which came to be known derisively as *les lois scélérates* ("the villainous laws"), made it a crime to celebrate or justify terrorist acts, a measure which allowed the state to shut down most anarchist newspapers and journals. The laws also mandated harsh sentences for participation in propaganda of the deed, even if there were no human casualties.

Spanish Anarcho-Terrorism

The European city hit hardest by anarcho-terrorism during this period was Barcelona, beginning in the late 1880s, when the attacks were many, but minor. Dynamite was the favorite tool, much beloved for its symbolism as a weapon of the oppressed, but most of the bombs failed to detonate. The motivation of the anarchists behind these bombings is hard to pinpoint. Above all, they were devoted to the cult of violence and the principle of propaganda of the deed. Two Barcelona groups, for instance, claimed the slogan "The ends justify the means," but made little effort to clarify what were their "ends" (Esenwein, *Anarchist Ideology*, 170). After 1892, Ravachol became a particularly popular figure among Spanish anarchists, much acclaimed and idolized for his revolutionary derring-do. Certainly another factor that contributed to the emergence of Spanish terrorism was the anarchists' frustration at their declining popularity vis-à-vis socialism and the trade unions.

Outwardly, the attacks were linked, as in France and elsewhere, by the anarchists' desire for revenge. In 1891, four anarchists were executed for taking part in the failed Jerez uprising, which led Paulino Pallás to throw a bomb at the captain general of catalonia a year later. The general escaped, but two were killed and twelve wounded among the nearby soldiers and bystanders. The attack was hailed by anarchist periodicals as a powerful example of propaganda of the deed. A Valencia newspaper proclaimed, "By throwing the bomb, Pallás was attacking all that society and its institutions stand for; his act was an immense protest against all the social crimes, infamies, and stupidities." Before his execution, Pallás predicted revenge. It was exacted by an acquaintance, Santiago Salvador French, who claimed his intent was to "terrorize those who had enjoyed killing [Pallás]" (quoted in Esenwein, *Anarchist Ideology*, 186). Salvador threw two bombs in Barcelona's opera house during the performance of *William Tell*. Fifteen died and perhaps fifty were wounded. Although Salvador had acted alone, the authorities executed six others as accomplices in a grand anarchist conspiracy.

A year and a half later, an unknown terrorist attacked the city's annual Corpus Christi parade with a bomb that killed six and wounded about forty-five. When no one was caught or claimed credit for the attack, many accused the police's anti-terrorism "Social Brigade" of staging it as the excuse for the brutal crackdown that followed. About four hundred alleged radicals were swept up and imprisoned in the local fortress of Montjuich, where the systematic use of torture elicited much talk of the revival of the Spanish Inquisition. Using testimony gleaned this way, the courts condemned five to death. Hundreds were deported to a Spanish colony in West Africa without trial on orders of the Spanish Prime Minister, Antonio Cánovas del Castillo. The "Montjuich repression," as it became known, temporarily brought an end to anarchist violence in Barcelona, with the exception of the assassination of Cánovas himself in 1897, and crippled for a time the activity of all anarchist groups. Police brutality, however, focused attention on the Spanish government's corruption, inefficiency, and poor oversight of the police. A campaign organized by middle-class professionals led to some reforms, as well as the pardoning of all the deported radicals in 1900. And when a young anarchist tried but failed to kill Lieutenant Portas, the principal torturer of the Montjuich radicals, he was acquitted by a jury of his peers.

Explaining Terrorism

With few exceptions, anarcho-terrorists did little to explain their actions or motives, so thoroughly had they absorbed the essence of propaganda of the deed. The throwing of a bomb, the ritualistic cry of "Vive l'anarchie!" at the guillotine, and the writing of a letter to a newspaper were equally revolutionary in their eyes. They understood their propaganda – whether violent terrorism or non-violent dramatic action – to be significant because of its very nature and immediate impact. Such an event needed no interpretation; it was a complete gesture in and of itself. In the minds of anarchists, terrorism no longer had to obey the laws of logic or linearity, for the terrorist strike was entirely reduced to the provocative symbolic act. In the words of philosophers and literary critics, the terrorist act was aestheticized – that is, self-consciously engaged in by the practitioner as if he were an actor on a stage. In this sense, terrorism became the prototypical modernist exercise: an act of will meant to be understood by viewer and participant as a self-evidently significant piece of art.

At the time, few sought to explain the nature of terrorism itself, choosing instead to focus simply on the turn toward violence. Apologists within anarchism's ranks explained the violent acts as the result of a wicked system. Most notably, Kropotkin eventually discounted the value of individual terrorism but nonetheless held blameless those terrorists "driven mad by horrible conditions" (quoted in Miller, *Kropotkin*, 174). By this he meant not only the wretched social conditions brought on by industrialization and urbanization, but also the values that the state inculcated in the lower classes in order to condition them for a lifetime of mental and physical slavery. Likewise, the anarchist Emma Goldman (d. 1940) argued that most anarchists were peaceful. As for those anarchists who actually engaged in "violent protest," she claimed that it was "their supersensitiveness to the wrong and injustice surrounding them which compels them to pay the toll of our social crimes" (Goldman, *Anarchism*, 80). Johann Most simply considered the anarchist and criminal alike "a product of his age" (quoted in Joll, *The Anarchists*, 127).

From outside the ranks of the anarchists, more "scientific" explanations emerged. A good example comes from the Italian, Cesare Lombroso (d. 1909), one of the founders of the modern school of criminology, the science of studying criminal behavior and causes. During his day, he was most famous for linking certain physical traits, such as a large jaw, a sharply curved nose, and high cheek bones, to a criminal nature. According to Lombroso, Johann Most's cone-shaped head and asymmetric face marked him as naturally prone to criminal behavior. These ideas have fallen by the wayside, but his basic method of investigating the causes of crime through the compilation of social and economic data remains influential. This technique led him to some typically conservative conclusions, for he reasoned that those predisposed toward terrorist violence in the past were usually restrained by the respect and obedience they held toward religious and monarchical authorities. With the destruction of those forces and the failure of any new ones to emerge, individual violence was on the rise.

Literary Responses to Terrorism

European concern with political violence and anarchism was also reflected in the omnipresence of literary terrorists. Russian terrorists were especially attractive, appearing in Émile Zola's *Germinal* (1885), Alphonse Daudet's *Tartarin in the Alps* (1885), and Arthur Conan Doyle's "The Adventure of the Golden Pince-Nez" (1904). In Oscar Wilde's first and rarely performed play, *Vera; or, The Nihilist* (1881), a female Russian terrorist falls in love with the tsarevich. These works of literature fed the public's fascination for a form of violence that seemed to have reached apocalyptic proportions, but they added little to the reader's understanding of the phenomenon. In these stories, the presence of terrorists merely added a note of color or provided a plot device, in much the same way that Soviet spies did for much Cold War popular culture. If anything, the increasing presence of incidental terrorists helped amplify the threat and scale of anarcho-terrorism by encouraging the sense that such purveyors of violence were truly everywhere.

In other instances, novels, plays, and short stories explored the meaning and significance of terrorism for a public desperate to understand *why?* In novels by Henry James, Joseph Conrad, and G. K. Chesterton, terrorism becomes the great metaphor for the age, as it was for Dostoevsky in *The Devils*. In these later instances the understanding of terrorism does not spring from conservatism per se, as was the case with Dostoevsky, who saw terrorism and revolution as the result of the modern era's spiritual decay and hyper-rationalism. At the same time, James, Conrad, and Chesterton were not progressives who praised revolutionary terrorists as the vanguard of a new and better age; rather, in their hands the terrorists and the repressive governments are equally villainous, nearly mirror images of each other.

In *The Princess Casamassima* (1885) by James, the working-class bookbinder Hyacinth Robinson is driven to radical politics and terrorism by his anger at a system that is only capable of creating wealth and happiness for some by virtually enslaving others. When the order comes from his superiors to carry out an assassination, he hesitates. The realization that he is caught between the government and his fellow terrorists produces the final crisis. In the end, he commits suicide rather than kill or be destroyed by another.

The accidental death of an anarchist bomber on the grounds of the Greenwich Observatory furnished Conrad with the seed idea for his classic tale of *agents provocateurs*. In *The Secret Agent*, a Russian official in the London embassy instructs an agent posing as an anarchist to carry out a terrorist "outrage" against the Observatory. The official's hope is that the attack will scare the British public and government into cracking down on the anarchists and revolutionaries – many of them Russian – living in exile in the UK. In Conrad's world, governments and terrorists are morally bankrupt, each wholly deserving of the other.

The most extraordinary novel of terrorism from this period is Chesterton's *The Man Who Was Thursday* (1907), a farcical tale set in London. This novel one-ups those of James and Conrad in that the anarcho-terrorists and government agents are not merely mirror images of each other – they are, in fact, one and the same! One by one, every member of the shadowy Central Council of Anarchists is revealed to be a secret agent recruited by Scotland Yard. As in *The Secret Agent*, terrorists pose little threat. The danger comes from the state, whose pretzel logic leaves it conspiring against itself and its civilians.

In all three novels the true culprit can be said to be progress or modernity itself. Terrorism is seen as primarily a symptom or flash point, a convenient means of illustrating the dilemma. All three writers saw a paradox at the heart of the modern age. On the one hand, developments in the West had elevated the individual to a position of preeminence never before seen in history. The Enlightenment – and its nineteenth-century spin-offs, capitalism, democracy, and scientific positivism – emphasized the worth of the individual, particularly his "inalienable rights" and ability to shape history through the power of rational thought. Even Romanticism, often described as a backlash against the Enlightenment and objectivity, idolized iconoclastic heroes and found "true" meaning in the subjective mind and its understanding of the world. On the other hand, the forces of nationalism and technological development produced enormous bureaucratic states with more coercive power than ever before. Governments increasingly replaced families, churches, and local communities as record-keepers, educators, and providers. The nation-state became not only the fundamental organizing principle for Western society, but the critical shaper of one's identity. Hyper-individualism and hyper-statism created an intractable dilemma, in that individuals *felt* empowered but found themselves stifled and constrained. From this conflict, terrorism emerged, according to these writers, as the ultimate act of individual protest against not just the state, but the modern condition.

The Decline of Anarcho-Terrorism

How should we explain the general decline of anarcho-terrorism that had set in by the 1910s? Certainly the "liberal paternalism" of many European governments took its toll when most radicals came to the conclusion that legal, parliamentary efforts could actually bear fruit. Liberal paternalism also contributed to growing nationalism – that was certainly the intent – as citizens came to see the state as their benefactor and national identity as the natural default. Anarchists and their hatred of the nation-state simply made no sense to most Europeans and Americans, even workers, farmers, and others supposedly oppressed by their governments. The rising international tensions that were to burst into war in the summer of 1914 contributed immensely to this development, as well.

And in Italy, Spain, and France, many anarchists and radical socialists graduated to syndicalism and its emphasis on the trade union-orchestrated general strike as the proper lever for effecting change. This certainly did not entail a renunciation of violence – large-scale strikes were almost always accompanied by clashes between workers and the police, army, or mercenaries hired by factory owners – but it did mean the general rejection of individual terror, which was seen as unproductive, even counterproductive.

The *reprise individuelle*, after all, could alienate as well as attract. A good example was the case of the Bonnot Auto gang, who robbed banks and homes in France in 1911 and 1912, murdering several people in the process so as to leave no witnesses. They fashioned themselves anarchists, but carried out their robberies under the banner of "illegalism," a sort of economic terrorism that delighted in symbolic acts and claimed descent from the infamous Ravachol. This was different from the Russian practice of "revolutionary expropriation" in that no attempt was made by the "illegalists" to justify banditry as a means of funding the revolution. The act of theft was itself deemed revolutionary. Anarchists of nearly all stripes renounced this interpretation of their doctrine, correctly sensing that such criminality would gain no support from either bourgeoisie or workers.

Long before the Bonnot Gang, many leading anarchists had begun to fear that indiscriminate violence done in the name of anarchism would drive away adherents. The French anarcho-syndicalist Fernand Pelloutier stated in 1895 that many workers who would otherwise support anarchism now rejected it since it "simply implies the individualistic use of the bomb." The result was that anarchists increasingly distanced themselves from the doctrine of propaganda of the deed. As Pelloutier announced, anarchists could fully succeed without the services of the "individual dynamiter" (quoted in Linse, "'Propaganda by Deed'," 215).

By the late 1890s, Kropotkin himself began carefully to qualify his endorsement of violent propaganda of the deed, having come to believe that individual acts of terrorism – such as assassination – were largely useless. Rejecting his glorification of propaganda by the deed articulated two decades earlier, he declared that a "structure based on centuries of history cannot be destroyed with a few kilos of explosives" (quoted in

Miller, *Kropotkin*, 174). Purposeful violence, he maintained, was usually collective, spontaneous, and temporary. In other words, it was the violence of insurrection, not that of either the individual assassin or Jacobin state terror. In his last decades, Kropotkin placed his hope in syndicalism. In a similar vein, Kropotkin's follower, Vladimir Zabrezhnev, denounced the violence of both the Russian anarcho-terrorists of 1905–7 and the French anarcho-terrorists of the early 1890s as unprincipled "anger and indignation" that would change nothing (quoted in Avrich, *The Russian Terrorists*, 59–60).

Perhaps anarchist violence changed nothing, but it reflected much. At the turn of the century, Europeans and North Americans believed they stood at the pinnacle of civilization, poised for even greater triumphs – all the result of democracy, capitalism, and the scientific method. But the writings of Nietzsche, Freud, and Einstein undermined the certainties of the Gilded Age. The Dreyfus Affair revealed the corrosive, divisive power of nationalism. And demands from suffragettes threatened the insular values of Victorian Europe. Anarchist terrorism was itself another symptom of the turn-of-the-century crisis of modernity. Pundits and social critics, such as Lombroso and Conrad, certainly interpreted it that way. Everyone expected unrealizable levels of political, economic, and social liberty, and the ensuing tensions produced a new type of violence: individualistic, ideological, and theatrical. In other words, modern, democratic states had produced modern, democratic violence. In an uneasy age defined by an emphasis on the individual, but also the presence of overwhelming state force, terrorist violence was perhaps inevitable.

Bibliography

The indispensable work on anarchism and anarcho-terror is James Joll, *The Anarchists,* 2nd edn. (Harvard University Press, 1980). A number of excellent chapters on these subjects can be found in Wolfgang J. Mommsen and Gerhard Hirschfeld, eds., *Social Protest, Violence and Terror in Nineteenth- and Twentieth-Century Europe* (St. Martin's Press, 1982). Another excellent survey of nineteenth-century anarchist violence can be found in Martin A. Miller, "The Intellectual Origins of Modern Terrorism in Europe," in Martha Crenshaw, ed., *Terrorism in Context* (Pennsylvania State University Press, 2001 [1995]). On different varieties of anarcho-terror, see Ulrich Linse, "'Propaganda by Deed' and 'Direct Action': Two Concepts of Anarchist Violence," in *Social Protest*.

On German anarcho-terror, see Andrew R. Carlson, "Anarchism and Individual Terror in the German Empire, 1870–90," in *Social Protest*.

For French anarchism, the most valuable works are by Jean Maitron: *Histoire du mouvemente anarchiste en France (1880–1914)* (Paris, 1951); and *Ravachol et les anarchistes* (Paris, 1964). The former is the classic study on the subject; the latter is a fine collection of primary sources. The best study of Italian anarchism is Nunzio Pernicone, *Italian Anarchism, 1864–1892* (Princeton University Press, 1993).

On anarchist violence in Spain, see George Richard Esenwein, *Anarchist Ideology and the Working-Class Movement in Spain, 1868–1898* (University of California Press, 1989); Walther L. Bernecker, "The Strategies of 'Direct Action' and Violence in Spanish Anarchism," in Mommsen and Hirschfeld, eds, *Social Protest*; J. Romero Maura, "Terrorism in Barcelona and Its Impact on Spanish Politics 1904–1909," *Past and Present*, no. 41. (Dec., 1968), 130–83.

A valuable biography of one of the most significant trans-Atlantic anarchists is Frederic Trautmann, *The Voice of Terror: A Biography of Johann Most* (Greenwood Press, 1980). For the essays of one of anarchism's most influential figures, see Emma Goldman, *Anarchism and Other Essays* (Dover Publications, 1969 [1910]).

7

Labor, Anarchy, and Terror in America

Modern terrorism first appeared in Europe and Russia but also made its presence felt – as both a real and imagined threat – in the United States during the late nineteenth and early twentieth centuries. During the era of Reconstruction following the Civil War, opponents of Northern occupation and the newly won rights of former slaves waged an extraordinary campaign of terror, which will be the subject of the next chapter. Nearly all other episodes of terrorism in the United States were the result of the economic and social tensions created by rapid industrialization, the focus of this chapter. A significant factor was the extraordinary influx of European immigrants who came to work the mines, railroads, and factories of the New World. They brought with them two distinct elements that figured heavily in the development of terrorism on American soil: the tribalism of old Europe and the radical movements, particularly anarchism, of the new Europe.

The Molly Maguires

The most notorious outburst of violence and terror associated with the labor movement before the 1880s was the famous case of the Molly Maguires. The setting was the anthracite coal fields of Eastern Pennsylvania, where thousands of Irish immigrants worked. Conditions were brutal – a fire in 1869, for example, killed 110 miners – the pay was low, and the authority of the mining bosses and their minions was nearly absolute. An additional source of friction was the fact that the mine owners, foremen, and skilled workers were mostly English or Welsh, thus reproducing the economic, ethnic, and religious antagonisms that back in Ireland had spawned Whiteboy terror and rumors of a similar new rural secret society known as the Molly Maguires. When anti-draft anger and labor unrest led to the murder of sixteen mine bosses in Pennsylvania coal territory in the early 1860s, local officials quickly assumed, despite a complete lack of evidence, that it was the work of a Molly Maguire organization imported from the Old World.

In 1868, mine workers formed a union, which soon attracted 85 percent of the region's miners. Labor unrest and violence soon grew. The region's most powerful mine and railroad owner, Franklin B. Gowen – who also happened to be the local district attorney – vowed to destroy the union, which he alleged was riddled with Mollies. To prove it, he eventually hired James McParlan of the famous Pinkerton detective agency to infiltrate the secret society. For two and a half years, McParlan lived undercover, working his way into what he described as the inner sanctum of the Molly Maguires. After Gowen goaded the miners' union into a self-destructive strike in 1875, there was indeed a smattering of violence against mine authorities, probably carried out by individuals or hastily organized small groups. But according to the uncorroborated testimony of McParlan and a few well-paid turncoats, the violence had been a campaign of terror orchestrated by the Mollies. Today, historians generally doubt whether the group existed at all.

Regardless, Gowen made sure that newspapers were full of stories of supposed Molly atrocities, accounts which helped turn the public and the courts against the miners' union. These crimes achieved national attention, as did the trials orchestrated and prosecuted by none other than Gowen himself. From 1876 to 1879, twenty men were executed, in most instances on the basis of flimsy evidence or purchased testimony. Even though the miners' union denounced "Maguireism," violence and labor activism became synonymous in the public's mind. As a result, unions ceased to be a significant factor in the Pennsylvania coalfields for a generation.

Violence and Labor Organizations

American labor leaders understood that bloodshed could erupt spontaneously during strikes, lockouts, and other tense encounters with management. No major American union or labor organization, however, ever embraced violence as a matter of policy, at least in part because they were so acutely aware of the need to court public opinion. Owners, on the other hand, routinely relied on the police or state militias or employed their own gangs of mercenaries to break up strikes or protect locked out factories. Also mindful of public opinion, industrialists regularly sought to portray labor unions and individual activists as shadowy organizations dedicated to the sowing of violence, the thwarting of industrial progress, and the destruction of private property – charges which owners and the middle class believed to a great degree.

The behavior of the Knights of Labor, one of the first national labor groups in the United States, unintentionally encouraged such a characterization. Earlier activists had learned that open and centrally operated organizations, such as the National Labor Union (founded in 1866), were highly susceptible to infiltration and self-destructive internal disagreements, such as over race. In response, the Knights, founded three years later, kept its proceedings and organizational details secret. Having imagined itself as a fraternal society rather than an open union, it borrowed extensively from Masonic ritual for its initiations and practices. For this reason, the Commissioner of the US Bureau of Labor decried the Knights as a "purely and deeply secret organization," a charge that linked the Knights in the minds of many Americans to a long history of subversive European movements thought to be dedicated to the destruction of civilization.

Anarchy in the USA

By the 1870s in America, this meant radical socialism and anarchism, whose adherents congregated in small, but noisy "revolutionary clubs" in every city that had large working-class populations. Anarcho-socialism particularly thrived among immigrant communities, where there were vivid memories of the 1848 revolutions and the 1871 Paris Commune; intimate knowledge of the writings of Marx, Bakunin, and Most; and practical experience gained in the International Workingmen's Association and anarchist congresses.

Most's arrival in the US in 1882 directly contributed to the spread of anarchism and the doctrine of propaganda of the deed, for he conducted a nationwide tour that left revolutionary clubs springing up in his wake. His speech in Chicago drew six thousand who wildly cheered his theatrics. Before long Most's German-language anarchist newspaper *Freiheit* was joined by revolutionary periodicals espousing propaganda of the deed in French, Italian, Yiddish, Spanish, and English. Many papers focused their efforts on agitation and propaganda in trade unions, a development that helped to cement in the imaginations of many Americans the belief that labor organizations of all stripes nurtured anarchists bent on the destruction of the US government and the property of the bourgeoisie.

Another factor that contributed to the fear and hatred directed toward union organizers and revolutionary activists was the rising tide of anti-immigrant nativism sweeping the country. In the minds of most Americans, anarchism – more often than not espoused in a foreign tongue – ceased to be a legitimate political philosophy; instead, it evoked images of whiskered and unwashed foreigners with unpronounceable names and pockets full of bombs. Anarchists were never more than a tiny minority of the labor force or labor activists – at the movement's peak in 1885, there were perhaps seven thousand active anarchists – but they contributed significantly to how Americans viewed labor and the left. And although anarchists were actually linked to only a few acts of terror, their reputation was such that every bombing or shooting associated with labor disputes was blamed on anarchist immigrants.

This was in large part because the rhetoric of the anarchists was indeed inflammatory. In 1885, Most published his handbook, *The Science of Revolutionary Warfare*, which contained the exhortation, "Proletarians of all countries, arm yourselves! . . . The hour of battle is near." The fingerprints of Heinzen, Nechaev, and Most covered other screeds. One contributor to a Chicago anarchist newspaper wrote, "One man armed with a dynamite bomb is equal to one regiment of militia, when it is used at the right time and place." Another contributor offered the cheery cry, "Dynamite! . . . it brings terror and fear to the robbers . . . A pound of this good stuff beats a bushel of ballots hollow – and don't you forget it!" (quoted in Avrich, *Haymarket*, 165, 166, 170).

The Haymarket Riot

Such incendiary talk, alongside labor tensions, anti-immigrant fear, and the reputed presence of anarchists in every union, created the backdrop for the eruption of America's first red scare. All it took was a match to light the fuse. The prelude was a scattering of bombings during labor disputes in 1885. The real explosion came in 1886 in Chicago where escalating tensions between management and striking workers at the McCormick Harvesting Machine plant led to the shooting death of two unarmed picketers by police on May 3. Labor leaders and anarchists called for a demonstration at Haymarket Square the next day to protest the police violence. At the gathering, Chicago anarchist and labor leader August Spies peppered his speech with the usual vitriol but cautioned his audience that the time for violence had "not yet come." It seemed as if the demonstration would simply peter out.

Figure 7.1: A fanciful contemporary drawing of the Haymarket Riot from
Harper's Weekly
(Wikimedia Commons)

But as things wound down, the rhetoric heated up. Alarmed by
the last speaker who urged listeners to "throttle the law," the police
marched forward to break up the small crowd that remained. As the
people dispersed peacefully, someone – it has never been established
who – threw a bomb which exploded over the heads of the police, killing
one. The police opened fire and kept it up for several minutes, killing and
injuring scores of workers. As the *Chicago Tribune* reported, the police
"were blinded by passion and unable to distinguish between the peace-
able citizen and the Nihilist assassin" (quoted in Avrich, *Haymarket*,
207). Six more policemen died in the tumult, most from shots fired by
other policemen. In the confusion, most accounts assigned blame to the
anarchists for the bullets as well as the bomb.

Panic gripped the nation as reports of the so-called Haymarket Riot
spread. Citizens and authorities alike widely believed that the massacre
was a call to start the "social revolution" long demanded by radicals. The
result was a witch hunt with the police quickly rounding up anarchists,
radicals, and labor leaders across the country. Chicago operated under *de
facto* martial law. The terrified city and the furious police fed each other's
siege mentality. So great was the hysteria that red, the color of socialism

and revolution, was banned in public advertisements. A Chicago grand jury charged ten anarchists, including Spies, with the murder of the policeman who died in the bomb blast. When it quickly became apparent that the authorities had no evidence implicating the accused in the bomb attack, the prosecutor's strategy turned to depicting the defendants as having incited the unknown bomber to act. Even the presiding judge blatantly admitted that the defendants were, for all intents and purposes, on trial for being anarchists and not for the murder of the policeman. Nevertheless, eight were found guilty of murder (one defendant fled the country and another turned state's evidence). Spies and three others were executed by hanging, while a fifth committed suicide in jail before his execution. The last three received prison sentences. Most Americans and the newspapers that spoke for and to them nodded approval. When the anticipated anarchist retaliation never came, the hysteria began to abate and awareness of the authorities' misconduct began to spread. In 1893, the governor of Illinois pardoned all eight defendants and released the three still in prison, announcing that, indeed, the trial had been a gross miscarriage of justice.

Most Americans continued to equate anarchism and terrorism and associated both with unions. Samuel Gompers, the founder of the American Federation of Labor, lamented that the Haymarket Riot wiped out middle-class sympathy for organized labor and temporarily "demolished the eight-hour movement" (quoted in Avrich, *Haymarket*, 429). Unions tried to distance themselves from anarchism and violence. The Chicago branch of the Knights of Labor, for instance, denounced anarchists as "cowardly murderers, cut-throats and robbers, . . . midnight assassins . . . [and] human monstrosities" (quoted in Avrich, *Haymarket*, 220). Nonetheless, across the country membership in the Knights quickly plunged from about 725,000 to around 100,000.

For all practical purposes, anarchism was dead as a political movement, killed by the arrest of its leaders and the backlash from labor in the wake of Haymarket. The great irony, as in Europe, was that as anarchism's political influence faded, society's fear of anarchism only grew. On the one hand, this was because the shrinking anarchist movement increasingly attracted the bitter and desperate radicals who glorified and engaged in propaganda of the deed. They did so as a means of keeping alive the message of revolution, even as the prospects for revolution dimmed. On the other hand, the vilification of anarchism became increasingly useful as a political tactic against the left, labor, and immigrants. From a distance, it is this symbiosis between the agents of revolution and reaction that is particularly striking. The terrorists and the authorities relied on each other's actions and rhetoric to justify and define their existence.

The Spread of Anarcho-Terrorism

Haymarket certainly created symbols – the Chicago Martyrs, as supporters called them – around whom labor activists and radicals could rally. The Riot even attracted some converts to anarchism, such as the Russian immigrants Emma Goldman and Alexander Berkman. Goldman (d. 1940), who became one of the most important anarchist leaders of the first half of the twentieth century, spent a year in prison in the 1890s for "incitement to riot." Berkman, who was much more committed to the theoretical need for violence, staged a famous effort at propaganda of the deed in 1892 when he attempted to kill Henry Clay Frick, chairman of the board of Carnegie Corporation, in retaliation for his company's violent confrontations with steel workers in Homestead, Pennsylvania.

The practice of anarchist assassination climaxed at the turn of the century. Italian anarchists who had lived and planned their attack in Paterson, New Jersey, assassinated the Italian king, Umberto I, in 1900. A Polish-American anarchist, Leon Czolgosz, was so inspired by the Italian terrorists' act that he shot US President William McKinley at the Pan-American Exposition in Buffalo, New York, in September 1901. McKinley died eight days later. Although she disapproved of violence, Goldman went on a speaking tour to encourage leniency for Czolgosz. She was naturally accused of being an apologist for murder and was, in fact, arrested and charged with conspiracy to murder the President. After a short stint in jail, she was released when it became clear she had nothing to do with the shooting, except as partial inspiration for the assassin, to whom she had innocently suggested readings on anarchism when they had met three weeks earlier. The public was seized by a panic nearly the equal of that following the Haymarket Riot. Congress quickly reacted by passing a law forbidding the immigration of anarchists and other radicals, despite the fact that Czolgosz would not have been subject to exclusion or deportation since he was, in fact, born in the United States.

Luigi Galleani and the Galleanists

The occasional anarchist continued to enter the United States. The most notorious was Luigi Galleani, an Italian anarchist who became the Johann Most of his generation. His newsletter, *Cronaca Sovversiva* (*The Subversive Chronicle*), which he started shorted after his arrival from Italy in 1901, promoted propaganda of the deed and praised the actions of anarcho-terrorists such as Ravachol. Galleani's newspaper quickly became the most popular anarchist periodical in America, with a circulation of about five thousand (Avrich, *Sacco and Vanzetti*, 50). In 1905, Galleani published a pamphlet with explicit instructions on how to make bombs – complete with a fatal error in the formula for nitroglycerine that he helpfully corrected in the pages of his newsletter three years later.

Galleani also became the center of an extended group of anarcho-terrorists devoted to the cult of dynamite. His followers carried out their first foray in July 1914, when three Galleanists linked to Alexander Berkman plotted to assassinate John D. Rockefeller, Jr., over his brutal suppression of strikes in Colorado mines. The bomb they were going to use went off prematurely – perhaps they never received Galleani's bomb-making errata – in their Harlem apartment, killing the three along with an innocent neighbor. That fall, bombs were planted across New York. Most were disarmed before they went off, while those that did explode caused minimal damage.

Labor, Terrorism, and Immigration

But there were more effective terrorists out there. Some were union activists, driven to desperation by a new round of success by owners in breaking up or limiting unions. Bombers from the International Association of Bridge and Structural Iron Workers, for example, set off explosions in over one hundred separate incidents aimed at property, not humans. That is, until October 1910, when a bomb seriously damaged the headquarters of the *Los Angeles Times*, which was locked in a debilitating dispute with its union. The blast killed twenty-one non-union employees. Two union leaders were eventually arrested and admitted their guilt, although under questionable circumstances.

The association in the public's mind between terrorism and the radical left was a powerful weapon in the hands of those prepared to use under-handed tactics in the struggle against unions. Such was the case in July 1916, when a bomb exploded in the midst of a San Francisco parade organized by local business leaders to lobby for a defense buildup. Ten people died and over forty were wounded. The authorities arrested a local union leader long considered a thorn in the side of the business community. He and a worker were found guilty, but in such compromised legal proceedings that the US Secretary of Labor successfully pleaded on their behalf to prevent their execution. After several decades of imprisonment they were pardoned, and it is now believed that they were framed by local authorities. The true bombers were never caught.

Continuing unease about foreign and radical elements prompted the Immigration Act of 1917, which made it possible to deport resident aliens who promoted assassination or destruction of property. Many individual states also passed laws that criminalized the endorsement of violence as a means of promoting social change. Over two hundred activists associated with the International Workers of the World (better known as the Wobblies) were imprisoned under such laws for endorsing the use of non-violent "direct action" against corporations and management. After America entered the First World War, Congress passed the Sedition Act of 1918, which went further by prohibiting all anti-government speech. This draconian law was primarily used against anarchists, socialists, and other anti-capitalists, like the Wobblies.

The Terrorist Scare of 1919–20

The Bolshevik Revolution in October 1917 ramped up the fear even more, for now the unthinkable had happened: socialists finally had their own state and they vowed to spread revolution throughout Europe and the world. In the US, all leftists – no matter whether they were socialists, communists, anarchists, or merely union activists – were lumped into the same category: Bolshies bent on bringing the revolution to American shores. This seething mixture of fear and loathing overshadowed the celebration of the end of the Great War and led to America's second Red Scare. All that was needed at this point was a spark.

After the US authorities began to use the Immigration and Sedition Acts to deport Galleani, an anonymous leaflet circulated around New England that cried, "Deport us! We will dynamite you" (quoted in Avrich, *Sacco and Vanzetti*, 139). In April 1919, unknown terrorists sent thirty bombs through the US mail, addressed to federal agents, prominent industrialists, and congressmen, most of whom had been intimately involved in the creation or passage of the Sedition Act. None was killed, and only one person, the housekeeper of a senator, was seriously injured. In fact, most of the packages never detonated: a postal clerk halted the shipment of half the bombs because of insufficient postage, and most of the rest were intercepted before they were opened.

A month and a half later, the terrorists struck again when bombs were set off outside the homes of eight officials, all of whom were associated with the anti-sedition legislation. Investigators found anarchist pamphlets in the vicinity of every explosion that claimed "there will have to be murder: we will kill, because it is necessary; there will have to be destruction; we will destroy to rid the world of your tyrannical institutions."

The pamphlets were signed "The Anarchist Fighters" (quoted in Avrich, *Sacco and Vanzetti*, 149). The bombs killed three people: a guard, a bystander, and one of the bombers. The latter's body, mangled beyond all recognition, was found on the lawn of US Attorney General A. Mitchell Palmer's devastated home. Detectives found a bloody piece of scalp on a nearby roof that was used to identify – somewhat improbably – the bomber as Carlo Valdinoci, a colleague of Galleani.

Public officials and newspapers denounced the bombs of April and June 1919 as evidence of a widespread revolutionary conspiracy, but in all likelihood the culprits were a handful of Galleanists, perhaps fifty or sixty at the most. The US Congress demanded immediate and widespread action, and the still-shaken Attorney General was quick to oblige. Claiming that the United States was under assault by "alien anarchists" and socialists bent on overthrowing the country, Palmer asked and was given money to beef up the Bureau of Investigation – the forerunner of the FBI. Ignored in the hysteria were two facts: (1) international anarchists and Soviet-style communists despised each other and were incapable of cooperation; and (2) in any case, the number of people from the two camps devoted to the use of violence was only in the low thousands. But then the so-called Palmer Raids, during which a young J. Edgar Hoover first made his mark, were never really focused on finding the bombers. The goal was the destruction of the left. To that end, agents arrested ten thousand people, including four thousand in a single night in January 1920. Targets included anarchists, a Russian labor group, Wobblies, and other radicals. Hundreds were deported, including Emma Goldman, Alexander Berkman, Luigi Galleani, and eight of the latter's supporters. Palmer and Hoover gathered information through warrantless taps and seizures, heavy-handed interrogation, informers, and coerced confessions made without access to a lawyer. When civil libertarians and other government officials protested, Palmer denounced them as "friends of the anarchists" (quoted in Avrich, *Sacco and Vanzetti*, 177). The media and most Americans approved of his crackdown. Palmer's zeal was due in part to his belief that he could ride his law-and-order stance to the Democratic nomination in the 1920 presidential elections. By the summer of that year a backlash had emerged. The pundit H. L. Mencken wrote that Palmer was "perhaps the most eminent living exponent of cruelty, dishonesty, and injustice," a stance echoed by enough people to torpedo Palmer's run (quoted in Morgan, *Reds*, 83).

The Immigration Act and the Palmer Raids took care of many Galleanists, but enough remained at large to carry out a spectacular act of revenge against the system. On September 16, 1920, a bomb carried by a horse-drawn cart exploded in front of J. P. Morgan's bank on Wall Street in New York. The blast, the most destructive terrorist event on

US soil until the 1995 Oklahoma City bombing, killed forty, wounded over two hundred, and caused more than $2 million in property damage. One of the few clues was a note from the American Anarchist Fighters, presumably the same band of anarchists responsible for the attacks of the previous year. The note, placed in a nearby mail box and found after the explosion, seemed to refer to those arrested in the preceding months: "Remember we will not tolerate any longer. Free the political prisoners or it will be sure death for all of you" (quoted in McCann, *Terrorism on American Soil*, 64). Suspicion naturally fell on the followers of Galleani. Despite an intensive manhunt, the Wall Street bomber was never caught. Historians and later investigators have determined that the most likely culprit was Mario Buda, a colleague of Galleani and Valdinoci. It is worth noting that the wrath of the Galleanists had ironically fallen on their fellow workers, since almost all of the victims of the bombing were laborers or low-level white-collar employees. No Wall Street financiers were seriously injured in the street blast. But this was a result that the bombers could have predicted. Presumably, they valued the symbolism of the act more than the guilt or innocence of their likely victims.

The anarchists' terror binge and the irrational reactions to it contributed greatly to the era's xenophobia. This anti-foreigner zeal expressed itself primarily in two ways. First, the Immigration Act of 1924 expanded the ban on immigrants from Asia and imposed quotas that dramatically decreased immigration from Southern and Eastern Europe, the perceived home of the terrorist scourge. Second, the increasing backlash against immigrants was manifested in specific judicial misfires. The most famous was the trial of Nicola Sacco and Bartolomeo Vanzetti for two murders and a robbery in Massachusetts in 1920. The two Italian immigrants had well established connections to Galleani and might have been involved in the terrorist attacks of 1919, but most historians doubt whether they were responsible for the crimes with which they were charged and found guilty. Before and after their executions in 1927, unknown assailants used bombs against a number of people associated with the trial, but none was killed. This was the dying gasp of the broader anarchist movement, brought low by suppression, deportation, and internal fragmentation.

Bibliography

The two best books on the Molly Maguires, a subject about which more is guessed than known, are Kevin Kenny, *Making Sense of the Molly Maguires* (Oxford University Press, 1998); and Wayne G. Broehl, Jr., *The Molly Maguires* (Harvard University Press, 1965).

The classic study of the Haymarket Riot is by the acknowledged expert on anarchism: Paul Avrich, *The Haymarket Tragedy* (Princeton University Press, 1984). Also useful is James Green, *Death in the Haymarket* (Pantheon Books, 2006).

The second Red Scare of the 1910s and 1920s is addressed in a number of books: Paul Avrich, *Sacco and Vanzetti: The Anarchist Background* (Princeton University Press, 1991); William Preston, Jr., *Aliens and Dissenters: Federal Suppression of Radicals, 1903–1923* (University of Illinois Press, 1994 [1964]); Ted Morgan, *Reds: McCarthyism in Twentieth-Century America* (Random House, 2003). Terrorism during this period is briefly surveyed in many books: Mike Davis, *Buda's Wagon: A Brief History of the Car Bomb* (Verso, 2007); Joseph T. McCann, *Terrorism on American Soil* (Sentient Publications, 2006); and Jeffrey D. Simon, *The Terrorist Trap: America's Experience with Terrorism* (Indiana University Press, 1994).

8

White Supremacy and American Racial Terrorism

Even as the United States was experiencing the first stirrings of labor-related violence in the 1860s, an even greater source of terror – white supremacy – was emerging from the ashes of the American Civil War. What followed was an unprecedented wave of American domestic terrorism primarily carried out by the Ku Klux Klan (KKK) and directed against former slaves and their allies.

Reconstruction and White Supremacy

It has now become common among historians to refer to Reconstruction – the period from 1865 to 1877 during which the Union sought to "reconstruct" the defeated South as an egalitarian society – as a revolution. Therefore the violence of the Klan and other white supremacists was essentially a counter-revolution, one of the best historical examples of terrorism used in a fundamentally "conservative" cause, that is, with the goal of halting radical change and reverting to the *status quo ante*. Most disturbingly, Reconstruction-era terrorism contributed significantly to its perpetrators' success in attaining their goals.

The sustained pursuit of white supremacist terrorism was made possible by the peculiar circumstances that afflicted the region: the South was an emotionally, economically, and physically devastated region in the wake of the Civil War, and the pervasive racism of most white Southerners left them culturally and intellectually unequipped to handle the emancipation of blacks. This sadly led to the widely held belief that white supremacist terrorism was simply self-defense against corruption, aggression, and "unnatural" race relations. Although few Southerners directly participated in acts of terrorism, they attracted the widespread sympathy and benevolent neutrality of much of the Southern public.

Immediately after the war's end, Southern states passed so-called Black Codes, which were essentially slave codes in another guise. As if to make fully clear their intentions, most Southern states dragged their feet in ratifying the Thirteenth Amendment, which abolished slavery, and outright refused to endorse the Fourteenth Amendment, which extended the rights of full citizenship to former slaves. Nowhere in the South were laws passed that gave blacks the vote.

During these years – 1865 and 1866 – white-on-black racial violence was mostly an expression of white anger and the new social, cultural, and economic tensions that pervaded the decimated South. Blacks were often attacked by bands of ruffians or former Confederate soldiers, who beat, whipped (a replay of slavery-era violence), and sometimes killed the former slaves. There are no overall tallies of black casualties for this period, but the anecdotal evidence is chilling. Whites torched a black village near Pine Bluff, Arkansas, in 1866, for example, and lynched twenty-four men, women, and children. But while ghastly and extensive, this violence was not orchestrated.

Radical Reconstruction and White Southern Resistance

Such violence, coupled with Southern resistance to the Thirteenth and Fourteenth Amendments, led to the sweeping triumph in the North of self-styled "Radical" Republicans in the Congressional elections of 1866. During the next year, they passed three Reconstruction Acts which imposed martial law on most of the South and called for the reintroduction of large numbers of federal troops. The ostensible goal was the imposition of a new egalitarian political and social order, but Radical Reconstruction also carried the unmistakable odor of vengeance against a treasonous and unrepentant South. Southern governments were disbanded, and constitutional congresses and new elections were called for the fall of 1867. Former Confederates were disfranchised, and blacks were given the vote. As a result, Republicans were swept into office throughout the region at every level of government. Some officeholders were black, but most were white. White Republicans from the North were decried as "carpetbaggers," while those from the South became known as "scalawags." The recently established Freedmen's Bureau set up schools and hospitals for blacks. In the minds of most of the white Southern establishment, this was indeed a revolution – one bent on nothing less than the radical empowerment of the black over the white.

The passage of the Reconstruction Acts transformed racial violence in the South and led to the emergence of an outright political struggle and a terrorist campaign of rarely rivaled ferocity. Conservative whites turned to white power groups to help them resist the imposition of a new order on the South by a coalition of Southern blacks and white Republicans. The matter was stated bluntly, if still quite romantically, in a South Carolinian white supremacist manifesto in 1870: "Defeated on the battle-field, defrauded at the ballot box, we have but one remedy – the dagger that was made illustrious in the hands of Brutus" (quoted in Martinez, *Carpetbaggers*, 119). The group most associated with this resistance movement was the Ku Klux Klan, but it actually predated Reconstruction by more than a year.

The Ku Klux Klan

The Klan was founded in Pulaski, Tennessee, in late 1865 or early 1866 by six Confederate veterans who, it is speculated, took its name from the Greek *kuklos*, meaning circle, and modified the word "clan" to suggest their own romanticized Scottish–Irish background. The organization, complete with ornate and intentionally farcical initiations, oaths, rituals, and practices, was probably first intended as a secret fraternal organization for bored and disgruntled former soldiers. The earliest incarnation of the Klan seemed to be inclined toward practical jokes, although even then they were usually at the expense of recently emancipated blacks. Soon the Klan turned to violence, quickly spawning chapters, known as "dens," throughout Tennessee, Mississippi, and Alabama. But it was hardly a paragon of tight organization: Klansmen operated under other names, and other groups of night riders freely adopted the Klan moniker as it suited them. To reassert control over the organization, Tennessee Klan leaders held a national meeting in April 1867, where they imposed on the so-called Invisible Empire a hierarchical structure and elected Nathan Bedford Forrest, a former slave dealer and Confederate cavalry officer, as its Grand Wizard. The Klan meant many things to its members, but first and foremost they were dedicated to "the maintenance of the supremacy of the White Race in this Republic" (quoted in Dobratz and Shanks-Meile, *The White Separatist Movement*, 36). The timing of the Klan's reorganization was critical. The US Congress had just passed the Reconstruction Acts, a development which provided the Klan with a mission and a mandate.

Throughout much of 1867, Klansmen and Southern white conservatives often resorted to the use of economic pressure: vote and you will be fired. But this was not much of a lever, since cheap black labor was essential to the Southern economy. The Klan also held marches and parades – a way for its members to exercise their penchant for ritual and theatrics, as well as an attempt to intimidate blacks and Republicans with the threat of numbers and implied violence.

It was only in late 1867, leading up to the elections in which black men would go to the polls for the first time, that the first manifestations appeared of what was to become a broad campaign of terrorism. Masked riders rode at night and attacked at will. Almost always in numbers that made certain the outcome, Klansmen administered beatings and whippings, raped women, burned down houses and schools, and shot, burned, or lynched hundreds of victims. The targets were Republicans black and white. Sometimes Klansmen simply assaulted people they encountered in their nightly rides; other times victims were painstakingly chosen. According to a Mississippi Klansman, "when a leading negro would make himself particularly obnoxious . . . and was considered dangerous, he was selected as an example" (quoted in Trelease, *White Terror*, xliii). Freedom, like a fever, was understood to be infectious. Former Confederates understood that their way of life could only be preserved if blacks chose not to pursue their rights or make use of their substantial numbers, particularly in the Deep South. Therefore those blacks were targeted who registered or voted, who acquired parcels of land, who taught or attended school, who armed themselves or formed local militias out of self-defense. Any black gathering – even prayer groups – could become the target of Klan terrorism. White Republicans were also attacked when they acted in concert with blacks or supported them as teachers, business partners, tax collectors, election officials, sheriffs, or politicians. In 1868, the newly elected governor of Louisiana, the Northern Republican Henry Clay Warmoth, received the following typical warning in the mail: "Villain, beware. Your doom is sealed. *Death* now awaits you. The midnight owl screams: Revenge! Revenge!! Revenge!!! *Ku Klux Klan*" (quoted in Current, *Those Terrible Carpetbaggers*, 122).

The Klan probably reached its greatest extent, in terms of both membership and degree of organization, in the spring and summer of 1868. In August of that year, Forrest claimed there were over a half-million Klansmen throughout the South. On the other hand, it is impossible to know how many victims there were of white supremacist terrorism in the late 1860s. Records of such violence were often not kept, for the simple reason that it was not regarded as criminal by many authorities, and many victims of Klan violence refused to lodge formal complaints for fear of retribution. What information exists is fragmentary, largely anecdotal, and often difficult to authenticate. But what emerges from the confusion is a truly horrifying picture. For example, between June and October 1867 alone, there were a reported twenty-five murders and 115 assaults on "innocents" in Tennessee (Wade, *The Fiery Cross*, 46). There were two hundred murders in Arkansas between July and October 1868 (Rable, *But There Was No Peace*, 105). Local authorities either supported the Klan or were too terrified to act against it. Republican officials repeatedly complained to military commanders that federal troops were needed to combat Klan terrorism; no significant deployments of US troops were sent.

Forms and Functions of White Supremacist Terrorism

As the Klan and other white supremacists turned to the more explicit use of violence, they drew on the long history of frontier or vigilante justice which was a part of the US' western expansion and had remained an essential feature of Southern life. Leading local townsfolk or self-selected groups had long supplied their communities with law and order, even when it did not comport with constitutionally mandated legal standards. Private disputes were frequently settled by private means – and violently. This was the flip side of that much discussed and usually highly celebrated quality of frontier self-sufficiency. Another contributor to the form and content of Klan violence was the pre-war practice of night patrols. These groups of legal, deputized citizens patrolled the countryside looking for runaway slaves. Moreover, they were seen as protection against what Southerners feared above all else: slave revolts, such as that of Nat Turner in Virginia in 1831. After the war, the specter of uncontrolled black men continued to cast a long shadow over the South, frequently providing justification for the white terror that stalked the land.

Time and time again, white supremacist violence was portrayed as primarily reactive and in the interest of self-defense. One Louisiana paper commented on the murder in 1868 of two Republican officials thus:

> It is, indeed, unfortunate that . . . any portion of any community should be compelled to have recourse to measures of violence and blood to do away with lawless tyrants and wrong-doers in their midst. But who is to blame? . . . Assuredly not we people of the South, who have suffered wrongs beyond endurance. Radicalism and negroism, which in the South are one and the same thing, are alone to blame . . . . We can well pity a people forced to use such harsh means, but we have not the courage to blame them. (Quoted in Trelease, *White Terror*, xlv)

Such intellectual and rhetorical gymnastics were common. It is, in fact, an age-old tactic and common to terrorist movements. This justification even serves to increase the anger and willingness to use violence, for through this tactic the perceived victimizer is responsible for the humiliation and degradation of the victim.

One of the most frequent and devastating charges leveled against blacks was the rape of white women. Sexual contact between black males and white females was the ultimate taboo in the South, and whites widely believed that emancipation would unleash the previously – and only barely – suppressed animalistic sexual hunger of the black man. Although the accusation was nearly always false, the bare whisper of rape was often enough to set in motion Klan violence. The punishment meted out to black men accused of rape or sexual contact was particularly brutal. Beatings and lynching were often accompanied by castration or genital mutilation – a ghastly reminder of the highly symbolic nature of terrorism. Sexualized terrorism, in fact, was a tool commonly used against blacks whatever the putative reason for the violence, and it was understood by Klansmen to have a particularly pronounced effect on the African-American population. In the words of the Tuscaloosa (Alabama) *Independent Monitor*, "The cutting [that is, castration]" of a local black "in [the] presence of crowds of his fellow niggers, has had a salutary influence over the whole of niggerdom hereabout. They now feel their inferiority, in every particular, to the white men" (quoted in Cardyn, "Sexual Terror in the Reconstruction South," 148). Probably just as frequent was the use of rape – euphemistically called "ravaging" or "ravishing" in contemporary accounts – by white Klansmen against black women as a vivid means of making manifest white supremacy.

Another common charge leveled against Reconstruction by conservative white Southerners was that Republican governments were corrupt and/or incompetent. In fact, Republican officialdom was probably deficient at about the same rate as its Democratic cousin. White Southern opinion, however, was quick to be inflamed by any story of Republican chicanery. Newspapers and speechmakers inflated isolated events into a broad, conspiratorial movement aimed at the complete subversion of the Caucasian race by Republicans, especially black Republicans: an oft-repeated justification of white supremacist vigilantism and terrorism.

Membership in White Supremacist Organizations

Who became a white supremacist terrorist? Since the Klan was a secret society, we do not know the identities of most members. But we do have some idea. One steady source was Confederate veterans, many of whom returned to their communities after the war to find themselves unemployed or sorely underemployed. Humiliation and boredom often drove them to don the hood of the Klan. At the same time, though, the Klan drew its membership from every stratum of white Southern society, including the wealthy, the educated, professionals, politicians, and lawmen. After all, it was understood to be in everyone's interest "to keep the Negro in his place." Where the Klan was the most violent, the elite typically withdrew from direct participation in white supremacist terrorism, although they often continued to support it passively or through benign neglect. Therefore, the most violent white supremacists did tend to hail from the poorer ranks, that part of the Southern population that relied on repression of the blacks to preserve the poor whites' place one step up from the bottom of the socio-economic-racial ladder. One characteristic shared by nearly all Klansmen and white supremacists was an unbreakable affiliation, whether formal or informal, with the Democratic Party. In fact, historians routinely call the Klan the "terrorist wing of the Democratic Party."

Klan terrorism became a way to continue the Civil War by other means, but it also sheltered – as terrorist groups often have – criminals and sadists who engaged in violence for all manner of personal reasons. This was exacerbated by the anonymity provided by Klan uniforms and the degree to which local dens and ad hoc bands operated independently of the national organization. Many autonomous groups were connected to the Klan only in the sense that they borrowed its terminology – such as in the case of the Knights of the White Camellia and the Knights of the Rising Sun. Klan leaders, including Forrest, loudly and frequently urged their followers to desist from violence, claiming that such grotesque brutality tainted the honor of the Lost Cause. His pleas fell on deaf ears, certainly in part because Klansmen understood just how disingenuous his protests were. Forrest's eventual response was to disband the Klan officially in 1869, a move proclaimed by apologists as proof that he never supported Klan violence and criminality. It is much likelier that Forrest had lost control over the secret organization and hoped to insulate himself from federal charges of promoting Klan terrorism. Not surprisingly, Forrest's "official" action did nothing to stop Klan violence; if anything, it increased over the next two years, peaking around the 1870 general elections. The military governor of Texas reported, for instance, that the killing of blacks was "so common as to render it impossible to keep an accurate record of them" (quoted in Wade, *The Fiery Cross*, 79).

The Federal Response

Increasingly desperate Republican pleas to the federal government to aid them in their struggle against the Klan yielded negligible results. Finally, in 1871, Congress held hearings on white supremacist violence in the South. One of the highlights was the bloodcurdling testimony of James E. Boyd, an ex-Klansmen who told Congress what many already knew: that Klan terrorism amounted to the continued waging of the Civil War, the goal of which was the return of blacks to a state of virtual slavery. A letter from terrified blacks in Frankfort, Kentucky, put the matter bluntly: " . . . we ask how long is this state of things to last? We appeal to you as law-abiding citizens to *enact some laws that will protect us*" (quoted in Wade, *The Fiery Cross*, 89). Congress was duly horrified and followed up with the Ku Klux Klan Act of 1871, which transferred authority to federal courts for the prosecution of murder, assault, and other crimes committed as part of a conspiracy to deny a citizen his or her civil rights. The law also authorized the declaration of martial law even in the presence of fully constituted Republican governments.

President U. S. Grant's attorney general at the time was dedicated to the establishment of black civil rights and was prepared to use the new law's provisions to achieve it. The most noteworthy of these efforts occurred in York County, South Carolina, where units of the Seventh US Cavalry under Major Lewis Merrill were sent to subdue the Klan in 1871. At first dismissive of the need for his mission, Merrill said four months after his arrival, "I never conceived of such a state of social disorganization being possible in any civilized community as exists in this country now" (quoted in Trelease, *White Terror*, 370). Merrill soon learned that the Klan had murdered at least eleven people and assaulted six hundred during ten months in 1870 and 1871 in York County and that 1,800 of 2,300 adult white males in the county were thought to belong to the group (Trelease, *White Terror*, 363–5). President Grant was persuaded by Merrill's work to suspend habeas corpus temporarily. Hundreds of Klansmen were arrested and hundreds more fled, thus crippling the organization in the state. Congress allocated so little money to the Department of Justice to prosecute indicted Klansmen, however, that only fifty-four were sentenced to prison; the rest were simply released.

But the thuggishness and crude criminality of Klan violence could not be ignored, and the threat of more federal intervention did coax many influential Southerners into renouncing the Klan, if only to avoid the loathsome presence of Northern troops. Over the next several years, national anti-Klan laws were defanged by Congress' repeated failure to fund civil rights trials. Eventually another Attorney General announced that only a few of the worst offenders would be prosecuted, in the hope that white Southerners could be persuaded to maintain law and order on their own. The outline of an implicit compact aimed to bind the nation's wounds at the expense of black freedom was taking shape.

The End of Radical Reconstruction

The end of Reconstruction came nearer with each passing year. Black and white Republicans were kept away from the voting booths by white supremacist terrorism in sufficient numbers that by 1871, four Southern states had returned to the Democratic fold. The pattern for transferring control from Republican to Democratic hands was set in Mississippi. The end of Republican rule was presaged in local elections in Vicksburg in 1874, where armed gangs, known as White Lines, kept blacks away from the polls and, some months later, a small and poorly armed black demonstration triggered a white rampage that killed up to three hundred African-Americans. As statewide elections approached in 1875, Democratic newspapers and politicians artfully constructed the specter of black militia activity and federal intervention; meanwhile, white "rifle clubs" intimidated Republican gatherings and made it clear that blacks would be beaten or killed if they were seen near polling stations. The white scalawag vote almost completely disappeared, and blacks kept away in sufficient numbers to throw the state legislature into Democratic hands. The so-called Mississippi Plan became the template for concerted efforts in much of the rest of the South to use propaganda, coercion, and terrorism to gain what colloquially came to be called white Redemption, that is, rescue from the perfidies of "Negro rule" and Reconstruction. By 1876, four more Southern states had gone Democratic.

That year's contested presidential election reputedly produced a deal in which Southern Democrats provided enough Electoral College votes to elect the Republican candidate to the presidency in exchange for a pledge to formally end Reconstruction. Less than two months after being seated as president, Rutherford B. Hayes ordered federal troops protecting the Louisiana and South Carolina statehouses – the last in the South still tenuously controlled by Republicans – to stand down. One former slave summed up the situation: "The whole South – every State in the South – had got into the hands of the very men who held us as slaves" (quoted in Foner, *Forever Free*, 198–9).

Jim Crow and the Institutionalization of Terrorism

The basic outlines of white Southern Redemption quickly emerged after the end of Reconstruction in 1877. Funding for education of mostly black schools was dramatically cut, and laws regarding employment, vagrancy, and petty crime were enforced so as to create a vast horde of black penal laborers. In Southern cities, blacks often remained better off but increasingly sequestered into menial jobs and black ghettos. In the 1890s, the situation for African-Americans dramatically worsened when Southern states responded to populist campaigns to mobilize poor blacks and whites by systematically disenfranchising all blacks and poor whites using various ruses, such as poll taxes and literacy tests. And given the green light to segregate all aspects of public and private life in the infamous Supreme Court case of *Plessy v. Ferguson* (which made famous the disingenuous expression "separate but equal"), Southern states erected what can only be called American apartheid. Known under the catchall of "Jim Crow," this system of laws ensured the preservation of a strict racial hierarchy.

Some historians suggest or openly state that the Klan was suppressed in the 1870s or somehow brought to heel, but a more accurate explanation is that it slowly melted away (with the rare exception, such as Yorkville, South Carolina). With Reconstruction dead, black emancipation effectively stymied, and white supremacy entrenched in law and everyday practice, the Klan and other similar terrorist organizations no longer had a reason to exist. In essence, the terrorism of Reconstruction-era white supremacists was legitimized – elevated and formalized into a system of thinly veiled state terror. The terror of the apartheid South and Jim Crow was mostly bloodless in that it survived through legal, institutionalized forms. Terror was internalized and widely accepted by Southern blacks who largely understood that they faced a coordinated system of oppression that brooked no opposition.

Lynching

Lynching was the means of providing occasional overt reminders of white power, the implicit threat made explicit and bloody. The message was not lost on blacks. The noted African-American author Richard Wright wrote in his autobiography, *Black Boy*, "The things that influenced my conduct as a Negro did not have to happen to me directly; I needed but to hear of them to feel their full effects in the deepest layers of my consciousness. Indeed, the white brutality that I had not seen was a more effective control of my behavior than that which I knew" (172).

Lynching is defined by the NAACP and the Tuskegee Institute, two of its principal cataloguers, as an illegal killing carried out by a mob (defined as a group of three or more people) which acts "under the pretext of service to justice or tradition." According to the best current calculations, mobs lynched approximately three thousand people, almost all of them black men, in the Southern United States between 1882 and 1930 (Tolnay and Beck, *A Festival of Violence*, 260). An important difference between white supremacist terrorism during Reconstruction and the lynching-cum-state-terror that replaced it was that while practitioners of the former sought anonymity, frequently operated at night, and killed in an atmosphere of lawlessness, lynching was generally carried out by crowds of unmasked individuals who otherwise imagined their world as one of peace and order. Whereas the Klan and other terrorists took advantage of the chaos they sowed in order to work at the edges of respectability, lynchers operated openly as respected members of society and were almost never punished by the state. One of the most disturbing relics of this era are the photos that were taken to commemorate such murders. Often these photos were turned into postcards and proudly sent to friends and relatives. One such postcard is of the charred body of William Stanley, lynched in Temple, Texas, in August 1915. A crowd surrounds the post from which his corpse hangs; a mark, now smudged, has been placed next to one of the onlookers. On the reverse of the post-

Figure 8.1: The Klan prepares to lynch its victim in *The Birth of a Nation* (1915)
(© EPIC / THE KOBAL COLLECTION)

card: "This is the Barbecue we had last night my picture is to the left with a cross over it your son Joe" (quoted in Allen, *Without Sanctuary*, 174).

The Klan Returns

It was within this context of deeply entrenched racism and racial violence that interest in the Klan began to revive. Much of the impetus came from the romantic vision of Reconstruction presented by Thomas Dixon in his novel *The Clansman* (1905). In 1915, the pioneering director D. W. Griffith turned the novel into *The Birth of a Nation*, one of the country's first feature films and one of the world's most disturbing apologies for terrorism. The film was a tremendous success, viewed by perhaps five million moviegoers upon its release. One of the film's key scenes depicted the Klan lynching a black man who, intent on raping a virtuous white woman, had driven her to her death. In the cinematically brilliant climax of the movie, robed Klansmen ride to the rescue of a white woman besieged in a remote cabin by ravenous blacks.

That year, Methodist minister William Simmons, resurrected the Klan, kicking off its second life with a stirring ceremony atop Stone Mountain, Georgia. The swearing in of a new generation of Klansmen was accompanied by one of the first known cross burnings, so enormous that it was supposedly visible in Atlanta, sixteen miles away. Simmons' Klan did not confine its hatred to blacks, expressing its blunt willingness to use violence against all who threatened the prosperity of white, Northern Europeans in America. This meant Catholics, Jews, labor organizers, communists, and immigrants, particularly from China and Eastern and Southern Europe. The new Klan presented itself as a patriotic organization clothed in moral righteousness, and the group briefly flourished as a mass political organization. Membership in the Klan peaked at between three and six million in 1925, and that year, forty thousand Klansmen marched down Pennsylvania Avenue in Washington, DC. The Klan's rolls swelled above the Mason-Dixon line, proving that racism, nativism, and hate were not confined to one region of the country. Five senators and four governors were Klan members, and Indiana officialdom was dominated by the Klan for several years.

The Klan began to lose support quickly when leaders' own moral lapses concerning money, sex, and alcohol were widely publicized. Just as important was the group's tendency to stray into violence against morally wayward whites, which helped puncture the illusion that the Klan was simply a patriotic fraternal organization. By 1930, the Klan had once again fallen into irrelevance in most regions of the country, aided by the fact that lynchings and Jim Crow laws still proved sufficient at limiting challenges to white rule in the South. Membership dropped off dramatically, followed by a run-in with the Internal Revenue Service during the Second World War that led to national but not complete local disbandment.

The Klan in the Post-War Era and the Civil Rights Movement

White supremacists correctly anticipated that blacks who served in the military in the Second World War would naturally demand their rights as citizens, a fear that fueled a second return of the Klan. Klansmen and ad hoc groups of white supremacists, particularly in Alabama, carried out beatings and bombings intended to keep blacks from voting in local and national elections or from joining newly formed trade unions. Violence was rarely punished by the authorities, because there was little public pressure and police forces were riddled with Klan members or sympathizers. The rash of violence and the suppression of black rights brought attention from the national media and fear that the federal government would likely enact civil rights laws if Southern states refused to do so themselves. The implicit threat quickly got the attention of politicians, businessmen, and newspaper editors across Alabama and the South. This led to what one historian has called a campaign of "soft opposition" against white supremacy, a movement motivated more by fear of national attention and federal intrusion than moral revulsion at Klan violence (Feldman, "Soft Opposition," 753). A spate of local anti-Klan legislation followed, and the threat of federal intervention passed. But few Klansmen were prosecuted under the new laws, and almost none served jail time. The Klan lived on, encouraged that "soft opposition" essentially amounted to passive public support for white supremacist terrorism.

In its 1954 ruling in the landmark case of *Brown v. the Board of Education* (of Topeka, Kansas), the Supreme Court ended nearly sixty years of support for the doctrine of "separate but equal." Much of white Southern society in general and white supremacists in particular recognized and feared that American apartheid was under assault. Denounced by some as a second Reconstruction, the Civil Rights Movement led to a revived Klan. In the 1950s and 1960s, membership in competing national Klan organizations and independent local chapters probably topped out at around 35–50,000 people, a figure far below that of the late 1860s or 1920s but deceiving in that a great deal of racist terrorism of the Civil

Rights era was committed by unaffiliated white supremacists (Dobratz and Shanks-Meile, *The White Separatist Movement*, 43).

Violence during the Civil Rights Movement took many forms. Buses carrying Freedom Riders testing the Supreme Court's order to integrate interstate travel were twice attacked in 1961 by white supremacists in Alabama who had coordinated their violence with the police, who agreed not to be present. In 1963 and 1964, civil rights activists involved in voter registration drives and other activities were beaten and murdered in Mississippi; their killers were not found guilty of the crimes for decades, as local juries refused to convict them. Even as public opinion in the South turned against racist terrorism, many whites remained fearful of Klan retaliation and refused to cooperate with federal and local officials working to suppress the Klan. Many more probably succumbed to fatalism and kept to the sidelines, an attitude interpreted by white supremacists as continuing approval and thus a green light for more violence.

Birmingham, Alabama, was a focal point of the Civil Rights Movement and thus a center of white supremacist violence. From 1945 to 1963, dozens of African-American homes were bombed in a bid to intimidate activists and discourage blacks from moving into white neighborhoods; one neighborhood became known as "Dynamite Hill" in a city that became known across the United States as Bombingham. The violence reached its crescendo in the city in 1963 when Klansmen dynamited the Sixteenth Street Baptist Church, a center of civil rights activism, killing four young black girls. Photos of the carnage splashed all over American newspapers helped turn Americans against segregation and forced the direct intervention of the federal government, which passed landmark civil rights legislation in 1964 and 1965. Another critical factor in the success of the Civil Rights Movement was the non-violent protests led by black leaders such as the Revd. Martin Luther King, Jr., Ralph David Abernathy, and Fred Shuttlesworth. Non-violence threw the terrorist violence of the Klan and white supremacists into stark relief and attracted widespread sympathy for civil rights.

In the twentieth century, the fortunes of the Klan and other white supremacist groups have ebbed and flowed in response to some clearly discernable factors. Their activity has increased when whites, regionally or nationally, have felt threatened by blacks and other "dangerous" groups, coupled with a belief that the usual institutions could not protect "traditional" racial and socio-economic hierarchies. Each time this has happened, fanatics in these groups have turned to terrorism and systematic violence, a development that brought much desired publicity to their cause but eventually backfired. Attention from law enforcement, the press, and the broader public led each time to a decline in popularity as the cause – tainted by brutality – lost its legitimacy.

Bibliography

Two surveys of the Ku Klux Klan are Sara Bullard, ed., *The Ku Klux Klan: A History of Racism and Violence*, 4th edn. (Klanwatch, 1991); and Wyn Craig Wade, *The Fiery Cross: The Ku Klux Klan in America* (Oxford, 1998 [1987]). The first is the best of the lot but quite brief; the second is rather sensationalistic. Better works on specific periods of Klan activity are listed below. A useful study that briefly addresses the early history of the Klan and places it in its broader context is Betty A. Dobratz and Stephanie L. Shanks-Meile, *The White Separatist Movement in the United States* (The Johns Hopkins University Press, 2000 [1997]).

Eric Foner has written two exceptional books on Reconstruction: *Reconstruction: America's Unfinished Revolution, 1863–1877* (Harper & Row, 1988); and *Forever Free: The Story of Emancipation and Reconstruction* (Alfred A. Knopf, 2006). The two best studies of Klan and white supremacist violence during Reconstruction are George C. Rable, *But There Was No Peace: The Role of Violence in the Politics of Reconstruction* (University of Georgia Press, 1984); and Allen W. Trelease, *White Terror: The Ku Klux Klan Conspiracy and Southern Reconstruction* (Louisiana State University, 1995 [1971]). Other useful works on terrorism and violence during Reconstruction are Richard Nelson Current, *Those Terrible Carpetbaggers* (Oxford University Press, 1988); Nicholas Lemann, *Redemption: The Last Battle of the Civil War* (Farrar, Straus and Giroux, 2007); J. Michael Martinez, *Carpetbaggers, Cavalry, and the Ku Klux Klan: Exposing the Invisible Empire During Reconstruction* (Rowman & Littlefield, 2007); and Lisa Cardyn, "Sexual Terror in the Reconstruction South," in Catherine Clinton and Nina Silber, eds., *Battle Scars: Gender and Sexuality in the American Civil War* (Oxford University Press, 2006). A valuable eyewitness account is Albion Winegar Tourgée, *The Invisible Empire* (Louisiana State University Press, 1989 [1880]).

There are a number of very good books on lynching. Two of the best are Stewart E. Tolnay and E. M. Beck, *A Festival of Violence: An Analysis of Southern Lynchings, 1882–1930* (University of Illinois Press, 1995); and Christopher Waldrep, *The Many Faces of Judge Lynch: Extralegal Violence and Punishment in America* (Palgrave Macmillan, 2002). Two contemporary accounts, one in words and the other primarily in pictures, are intensely disturbing, but illuminating: Jacqueline Jones Royster, ed., *Southern Horrors and Other Writings: The Anti-Lynching Campaign of Ida B. Wells, 1892–1900* (Bedford/St. Martin's, 1997); and James Allen, ed., *Without Sanctuary: Lynching Photography in America* (Twin Palms, 2000).

Useful information on the Klan in the immediate post-Second World War period is provided in Glenn Feldman, "Soft Opposition: Elite Acquiescence and Klan-Sponsored Terrorism in Alabama, 1946–1950," *The Historical Journal*, vol. 40, no. 3 (Sept. 1997), 753–77.

9

The Dawn of Ethno-Nationalist Terrorism

The Sicarii in first-century Judea were responsible for many firsts, not the least of which was the use of terrorism to pursue the dream of ethnic or national independence. Not until the French Revolution were the ideas of nation and terror so closely linked. Yet for most of the next century, ideological concerns – such as liberalism and socialism – overshadowed the ethno-nationalist impulse. It was not until the late nineteenth century that terrorism began to be widely used in campaigns of national liberation.

Ireland and England

The modern origins of ethno-nationalist terrorism can be found in Ireland, whose residents have been locked in a struggle with the English for most of the island's recorded history. The pope granted the English overlordship of the Irish in the twelfth century, but it was not until the sixteenth and seventeenth centuries that England's rulers settled large numbers of colonists on the best land in northeast Ireland, which became known as the Plantation of Ulster. To make matters worse, the new colonists were Protestants, while the native Irish who were driven from their land or forced into penurious tenant farming remained loyal Catholics. The result was a tangled web of national, religious, and economic hatreds. Actual ethnic differences receded by the nineteenth century, however, since English and Scottish colonists had come to regard themselves as native-born Irish. Political divisions hardened when the United Kingdom of England and Scotland directly incorporated Ireland, thus dividing the Irish into two political blocs. Unionists were Northerners who regarded union with Britain as the best guarantor of their Protestantism and economic superiority, while republicans were Southerners and Northern Catholics who hoped for Irish independence. This created two overlapping conflicts: one between Irish republicans and the British, and one between Irish unionists and Irish republicans.

Whiteboy violence in the eighteenth and nineteenth centuries was one manifestation of these conflicts, although it was far more an expression of anger over economic displacement than religious or ethnic enmity. There was also the more overtly sectarian violence of the Ribbonmen, members of a secret society of Irish Catholics who opposed the Orange Order. The latter was – and remains to this day – an association of Irish Protestants who every year celebrate the victory of England's King William III (of the Dutch House of Orange) over Catholic rebels. A significant republican commitment to the use of violence in pursuit of national independence first surfaced in the late 1850s. That was when two closely linked organizations were formed: the Irish Republican Brotherhood in Dublin and the Fenian Brotherhood (soon to be renamed Clan na Gael) in New York City, home to a large community of Catholic Irish immigrants.

Irish Ethno-Nationalist Terrorism and Assassination

Although republicanism enjoyed a certain sympathy among Irish Catholics, most were inclined toward peace and accommodation and not likely to be roused to open rebellion, in part because they feared British reprisals. In these circumstances, terrorism, particularly the sort associated with propaganda of the deed, became a natural weapon of the Fenians, as Irish republicans on both sides of the Atlantic were often called. But except for the failed effort to spring Irish nationalists from the New Prison in London in 1867, in which twelve people died and more than a hundred were injured, Fenian terrorism amounted to little more than rumors of plots to kidnap or assassinate British officials or Queen Victoria.

That is, until May 1882, when a group of Fenians calling themselves the Irish National Invincibles carried out one of the nineteenth century's most notorious assassinations. Their principal target was Thomas Burke, the third-ranking British official in Ireland and Irish by birth – thus a treasonous collaborator in the eyes of nationalists. Burke was killed in Dublin's Phoenix Park along with his walking companion, the newly arrived second-in-command of Ireland who also happened to be the nephew by marriage of the British prime minister. The murders were roundly denounced in both Ireland and Britain, but did briefly derail efforts at conciliation, a development appreciated by the Fenians who subscribed to the philosophy that the worse things were for the Irish, the more likely they were to rebel. The Dublin authorities eventually arrested the two assassins, as well as twenty-four conspirators. Five were hanged, and several received life sentences. All joined the community of Irish martyrs. Another result of the Phoenix Park murders was the formation of the Special Irish Branch of the London Metropolitan Police, an elite force whose initial mission of countering the Fenians soon expanded to include all efforts against anarchism and terrorism.

The Special Irish Branch had great success, particularly during the so-called "dynamite campaign" of the mid-1880s. This was the first coordinated effort by republicans to use terrorism on English soil. Although it was reported that they possessed enough explosives to blow up "every house and street in London," the bombs they managed to plant caused no casualties and little damage. A rather comical plan to steal the Stone of Scone from Westminster Abbey also came to naught. The authorities convicted twenty-five Fenian dynamiters, of whom sixteen were given life sentences.

For the next three decades, Fenians continued a ramped-up campaign of assassinations and bombings that, for all its attraction to romantic nationalists reared on tales of martyrs and rebellions, actually gained few adherents among the Irish masses. Aided by the gradual dismantlement of anti-Catholic laws and attitudes, most in Southern Ireland slowly assimilated into Great Britain's political and economic orbit and looked forward to what all assumed was inevitable: the granting of home rule, which would lead to heightened Irish autonomy but continued membership in the United Kingdom. Republicans and unionists seemed destined to haunt the fringes of Irish politics. Shortly after the start of the First World War, opposition to home rule in the British parliament finally collapsed, and the government announced that autonomy would be granted upon the successful completion of the war.

The Easter Uprising

The Fenians became desperate, sure that home rule would destroy what remained of the Irish public's interest in independence. This was the inspiration for the Easter Uprising of 1916, whose leaders, such as Padraig Pearse and James Connolly, understood the value of creating martyrs to keep alive the spirit of revolt. Thus, although it was planned and carried out as a military operation, the Easter Uprising had all the trappings of classic anarchist propaganda of the deed. The uprising consisted of only a few thousand poorly armed men, but the British quickly responded in force. All told, fewer than two hundred soldiers died between the two sides, but casualties among the civilians trapped in their homes reached into the thousands, while the property damage exceeded £2.5 million. Even under these conditions, Irish sentiment tended to blame the rebels – who had adopted the name Irish Republican Army (IRA) during the fighting – for the carnage. The British authorities, enraged by what they considered an act of grave wartime treason, carried out a wave of repression that in hindsight almost seemed calculated to radicalize the uncommitted. The British executed ninety Fenians, including some not directly connected to the uprising. The wounded IRA leader Connolly – too weak to stand and, according to some reports, already stricken with gangrene – was strapped into a chair to be shot. Thirty-five hundred Fenians were sentenced to prison terms. The British beefed up the Royal Irish Constabulary, the mostly Protestant police force which was loaded with unionists, and enhanced their powers. London also dispatched tens of thousands of new troops. Home rule returned to the back burner. To make matters worse, Britain threatened mass conscription just two years after the uprising, a move that encouraged the newly ascendant republican cause. In short, the Easter Rebellion and the British response created neither republicanism, Irish national consciousness, nor Fenian violence, but it did crystallize a new commitment to each through powerful symbols and images.

Michael Collins and the Black and Tan War

Moderate elements on both sides of the Irish Sea remained committed to the goal of home rule, but the republican cause emerged from the Easter Rebellion debacle and its aftermath energized and larger than ever. The United Kingdom's first post-war elections in December 1918 confirmed this when the party closest to the IRA, Sinn Féin ("Ourselves" in Gaelic), won just under half of Ireland's seats in Parliament. Soon after, Sinn Féin declared independence for all of Ireland and set up a government led by Eamon de Valera and Michael Collins, veterans of the Easter Uprising. Collins, in charge of the IRA's military forces, knew that the Irish Republican Army was an army in name only and could not beat the British in open battle. The IRA probably consisted of at most fifteen thousand members, but could only muster an effective fighting strength, Collins estimated, of about three thousand (Asprey, *War in the Shadows*, I:274). His solution, in part, was to organize most Irish troops into "flying columns," semi-autonomous bands of one or two dozen fighters that could use hit-and-run tactics against the enemy. Even then, Collins understood that "something more was necessary than a guerrilla war" (quoted in Dwyer, 36). Thus was born Collins' strategy, modeled on that of the People's Will and other late nineteenth-century groups, of mounting a comprehensive terrorist campaign against the British, particularly its police agents in Ireland. His goal was twofold. First, he claimed that terrorism would make "regular government impossible, and the cost of holding the country so great that the British would be compelled to withdraw" (quoted in Asprey, *War in the Shadows*, I:274). The second goal was to blind the British by depriving them of their eyes and ears. Robbed of their ability to gather intelligence on the IRA, Collins surmised, the British would lash out at the broader population sheltering the Fenians, thus turning neutral civilians against British rule.

The result was not a typical war, but rather an escalating exchange of tit-for-tat assassinations and terrorist strikes. When the violence quickly grew beyond the Royal Irish Constabulary's ability to contain, the British responded by reinforcing it with two units composed of recently demobilized veterans; the larger of them – eventually numbering about twelve thousand – became known as the Black and Tans because of their hastily assembled and thus mismatched uniforms. They lent their name to what became known as the Black and Tan War, otherwise called the Irish War of Independence.

In this struggle, Collins' trump card was his prodigious skill at collecting intelligence that usually put the Fenians one step ahead of the British and the Constabulary. This intelligence was then used by the Squad, Collins' handpicked team of assassins, who were popularly known as the Twelve Apostles. They primarily targeted Constabulary policemen, of whom over 450 were killed or wounded in 1920, often in their own homes. The IRA covered the walls of Dublin with clever messages, such as "Join the RAF [Royal Air Force] and See the World. Join the RIC [Royal Irish Constabulary] and See the Next" (quoted in Asprey, *War in the Shadows*, I:275). The Twelve Apostles also killed spies, informers, and unionists, but rarely British servicemen. In a move meant to serve notice to the British that the republicans could strike when and where they liked, Collins had IRA terrorists carry out simultaneous attacks on 315 police stations just before Easter 1920. Collins managed an even greater coup on November 21 of that year – the first of many Irish "Bloody Sundays" – when members of the Squad and other IRA Volunteers crippled British undercover intelligence operations by killing twelve officers and two police cadets across Dublin. Later that day, furious Constabulary auxiliaries killed fourteen people at a soccer match while looking for suspects.

The British strategy during the war was based on the self-defeating hope that the Fenians could be cowed into submission by executing two captured republicans for every soldier or policeman murdered. Before long, the Black and Tans and the auxiliary units, utterly untrained in the delicate art of counterinsurgency, acquired the habit of carrying out mass reprisals against Irish civilians, which naturally drove many of them into the arms of the IRA. Both sides openly pursued campaigns of terror and traded accusations of "terrorism." A contemporary Irish writer, for example, drew the conclusion that "a war of conquest, such as England's war against Ireland, develops, inevitably, into a campaign of terrorism against the people" (quoted in English, 17).

Terror and Counter-Terror: the British and "Small Wars"

There was a larger truth at work here. Although the British and Irish frequently turned to the same tactic – namely terror – they understood them in vastly different ways. The Irish used it consciously as a way of leveling the playing field against a superior foe and as part of a larger strategy of provocation. The British, on the other hand, initially used the Constabulary to respond to what they regarded as a criminal threat. When the Constabulary was overwhelmed, the British then fought using conventional military means. Finally, out of desperation, they lapsed into matching the Fenians terror for terror.

The British should have known better. After all, they had dealt with colonial uprisings since the eighteenth century. From those, the main lesson learned was the necessity of overwhelming firepower and strong unit cohesion. Major Charles Callwell made a breakthrough of sorts, however, with the publication of his seminal work, *Small Wars – Their Principles and Practice*, in 1896. By "small wars," Callwell meant campaigns against guerrillas, expeditions against "savages and semi-civilized races," and all wars against foes who did not use conventional troops in conventional ways. Based on his experience fighting in India, Afghanistan, and the Transvaal, he explained that success in small wars required enhanced flexibility, improved intelligence gathering, and greater initiative. And yet a critical observation eluded Callwell: the struggles he described were primarily political, not military, and as such favored the combatant who could establish political legitimacy in the eyes of the populace. The deployment of regular troops using overwhelming firepower could never provide that, for when fighting a native foe who used guerrilla tactics or terrorist campaigns, such firepower would largely fall on civilians, thus driving the population into the arms of the insurgents. And historically, it has been civilian support – in the form of new recruits, money, supplies, intelligence, safe houses, passive resistance, or even just benign indifference – that allows for the continuation of guerrilla or terrorist operations and thus the slow wearing away of the opponent's will to fight. In the case of the Black and Tan War, strong civilian support for the IRA was the decisive factor. So although Callwell's insights began to have an impact on the British military establishment, the British remained ill-suited and unprepared for small wars. Only in the 1950s when fighting a communist insurgency in Malaya did the British come to realize that a better goal was to establish their legitimacy in the eyes of the native populace, a strategy that has become known as "winning hearts and minds." During the Black and Tan War, the British appealed to neither.

All credit to British Prime Minister David Lloyd George and his cabinet for realizing the futility of their actions. By the spring of 1921, the British came to suspect that they could only defeat the Irish republicans if they brought troop totals to about 150,000 and used concentration camps on the Boer War model. This they were not prepared to do. More to the point, they knew that the British voting public would not go along.

In the summer of 1921, the British began to negotiate an end to the fighting. The result was the creation of the Irish Free State – a self-governing state within the British Commonwealth – but only in the South. Largely Protestant and unionist Ulster remained part of the UK. Collins and the bulk of the IRA were willing to accept this as a provisional victory, while de Valera and his followers refused to settle for anything less than independence for the entire island. A civil war erupted between the pro- and anti-treaty factions, and Ireland experienced a brief reprise of the brutal terror campaigns of the Black and Tan War – but now it was Irish republican killing Irish republican. The most famous casualty of the civil war was Collins, assassinated in an ambush in August 1922, perhaps on the orders of his former comrade in arms, de Valera. Before long, the Irish accepted the de facto division of their island, and the violence abated – at least until a reborn IRA began a new terrorist campaign in Northern Ireland in the 1950s, setting off a new era of "Troubles." But that story is for a bit later.

The Russian Method

In terms of the use of terrorism, the Fenian struggle for Irish independence became – for historians and revolutionaries alike – the prototype for twentieth-century ethno-nationalist movements. But for the Irish and other contemporary national liberation movements, it was the Russian example that proved to be the most influential. In fact, revolutionary terrorism became colloquially known as "the Russian method" throughout much of the world. Knowledge of it was spread by Russian exiles, favorable newspaper accounts, and books. Except for Western Europe, where terrorists were motivated by anarchism or socialism, most who embraced "the Russian Method" adopted it in the name of national independence. The reason was nearly uniform: the presence of a zealously committed group that otherwise lacked sufficient soldiers, resources, and popular support to have any hope of success against the occupying power on the open battlefield. The stated goals were surprisingly alike: to keep alive the spirit of resistance, to inspire the masses to revolt, and to serve notice to the ruling powers that their time in power was limited. The words of Nikolai Morozov (of the People's Will) could be applied over and over – terrorism "should make the struggle popular, historical, and grandiose."

Ethno-Nationalist Terrorism in India

Organized in 1885, the Indian National Congress was the main organization through which moderate, Westernized, middle-class Indians sought more autonomy from Britain, which had been India's colonial master since the eighteenth century. There were others, however, who found inspiration in the Russian Method. These more confrontational nationalists – dubbed Extremists by contemporaries after they formally left the Congress Party – advocated "direct action" against the British. After some false starts, the first serious efforts at this were made in Bengal, a region in Eastern British India where Extremists congregated in youth clubs that served up a heady brew of Hindu mysticism, anti-British hatred, and intense physical exercise. In 1905, Britain partitioned Bengal, an action interpreted by Extremists as an effort to deliver much Hindu territory into the hands of the region's Muslim minority. "Protests are of no avail," wrote Bal Gangadhar Tilak (d. 1920), an activist celebrated as the "father of Indian unrest." "Days of prayer have gone . . . Look to the examples of Ireland, Japan and Russia and follow their methods" (quoted in Wolpert, *Tilak and Gokhale*, 180). Tilak's contemporaries understood this to mean that violence was an appropriate response. They drew on the numerous youth clubs to form secret societies devoted to the use of terrorism to radicalize the masses, defend Hinduism, agitate for national independence, and exact revenge upon the oppressors. Their collective mouthpiece was the newspaper *Jugantar* ("The New Age"). One editorial preached, "Force must be opposed by force, deceit by deceit" (quoted in Heehs, *The Bomb in Bengal*, 84). Conspiratorial groups inspired by *Jugantar* made several assassination attempts in 1906 and 1907. They were unsuccessful but, in turn, inspired the formation of other terrorist groups, similar in rhetoric and purpose, elsewhere in India. Some Indians even traveled to Paris to learn from Russian revolutionaries how to make bombs. Back in India, police raids revealed large quantities of Russian bomb-making manuals and revolutionary literature.

Finally in April 1908, two followers of *Jugantar* drew blood in the Bengali town of Muzzafarpur. Their victims were a British woman and her daughter, whose carriage was mistaken for that of a local British judge, notorious for his heavy-handed punishment of Indians involved in the independence movement. One of the two Indian terrorists immediately committed suicide when he realized his error. The other was promptly arrested, tried, and executed. In the course of the investigation, the British authorities discovered a bomb-making facility and links to *Jugantar* and other secret societies. The so-called Alipore Bomb Conspiracy attracted enormous press attention and led the unnerved British to pass a series of extraordinary decrees meant to nip Indian terrorism in the bud. Tilak and other activists – none of whom were directly linked to the Muzzafarpur attack – were arrested and found guilty of sedition. Tilak disassociated himself from the bombing but blamed the violence on the British for having left Indians with no hope for gaining concessions through peaceful means. The result of this strategy, tales of the bombers' bravery, and British overreaction across all of India did more to publicize the cause of Indian independence than years of peaceful agitation had done. In fact, right after the bombing, another prominent Extremist declared that terrorism was "a means to educate the people up for facing death and doing anything for their country's sake" (quoted in Heehs, *The Bomb in Bengal*, 253). Britain's top Indian official in London recognized this, even in the months preceding the Alipore Bomb Conspiracy. In a letter to the viceroy and governor-general of India, he cautioned, "We must keep order but excess of severity is not the path to order. On the contrary, it is the path to the bomb" (quoted in Vajpeyi, *The Extremist Movement in India*, 125).

This warning proved altogether too prescient. The British clamped down hard on the Extremists and their political agitation, but violence increased. Between 1909 and 1914, assassins carried out twenty-two political murders, mostly of Indian "collaborators." The independence movement quieted down during the First World War, when thousands of Indians volunteered for service in the British Army, but returned with peace in 1918. In April 1919, thousands of Indians peacefully demonstrating were gunned down in the Jallianwala Bagh Massacre. This was the catalyst for the development of contradictory but mutually reinforcing movements. The first was Mahatma Gandhi's Non-Cooperation Movement, which demanded full independence but preached non-violence. In 1921, Gandhi became the face of the Congress Party.

Meanwhile, one of his followers who had grown tired of the commitment to non-violence founded the Hindustan Socialist Republican

Association (HSRA). This was ostensibly a Marxist organization, but its real goal was Indian independence through the use of terrorism. In 1929, HSRA terrorists attacked a session of the Legislative Assembly in Delhi and attempted to blow up a train carrying the British viceroy and other officials. The HSRA and other Indian terrorist groups belonged to the extreme fringe of Indian politics, but their impact was significant. A writer for the English-language daily newspaper of the Extremists summed it up succinctly: "Peaceful means can succeed only when these imply the ugly alternative of more troublesome and fearful methods, recourse to which the failure of peaceful attempts must inevitably lead" (quoted in Heehs, *The Bomb in Bengal*, 254–5). Although it claimed few lives, Indian terrorism maintained enough of a presence to suggest the possibility of such an "ugly alternative." No less a figure than Gandhi himself understood this perfectly. Speaking to British officials in 1931, he stated, "If you will work [with] the Congress for all it is worth you will say good-bye to terrorism; then [Indians] will not need terrorism" (quoted in Heehs, *The Bomb in Bengal*, 255). Gandhi was right in asserting that Indian nationalist terrorism undoubtedly provided him a certain moral and political leverage. As for his claim that Indians would no longer need terrorism once the Congress was empowered, he was, unfortunately, mistaken, as illustrated by his assassination in 1948 at the hands of a Hindu nationalist angered by Gandhi's supposed concessions to Pakistan.

Europe and the Balkans and the Coming of the Great War

Back in Europe, the use of the Russian Method produced even more dramatic results. Europe's leaders and armies were on a hair trigger by the summer of 1914. There were many factors, chief among them an international arms race, rising tensions over international standing and imperial possessions, and soaring nationalism. Two factors that increased the likelihood of even a minor crisis plunging Europe into war were, first, the division of the continent into competing alliances, which meant that a conflict that involved at first only two powers would likely draw in the rest. The second was every state's need to mobilize their armies before sending them into action, a cumbersome process that could not be reversed easily, and one which practically demanded reciprocal action.

Prescient observers understood that the Balkans were a particular source of danger to Europe's uneasy peace. At the center of the volatile region was Serbia, a small, recently independent kingdom of Orthodox Christian Slavs who had developed an intense sense of national identity in the face of their much larger neighbors, the Habsburg Austro-Hungarian

Empire and the Muslim Ottoman Turkish Empire. Large numbers of Serbs remained outside the country's borders in the early twentieth century, particularly in the Habsburg province of Bosnia and Herzegovina. Serb leaders and citizens dreamed of the creation of a Greater Serbia, knowing full well that it could only happen at Austria-Hungary's expense. Such ambitions threatened Great Power relations, because the Russians saw themselves as the protectors of their fellow Orthodox Slavs.

Serbia and the Assassination of Franz Ferdinand

A number of secret societies were devoted to the cause of Serbian irredentism and enjoyed strong support in the Serbian army's officer corps. Thus, although they were technically illegal organizations, they were rarely harassed. The most active of these secret societies operated under not one, but two evocative names: Union or Death, as it was known to its supporters, and the Black Hand, the name bestowed upon it by its enemies. Its constitution, seal – which included a skull-and-crossbones flag, a dagger, a bomb, and a vial of poison – and its initiation rites strongly resembled that most famous of secret societies, the Carbonari. The Black Hand had carried out a number of terrorist strikes against Austro-Hungarian targets along the border, including several attempts on provincial governors, and its members constantly agitated against Habsburg tyranny. The group also attacked targets within its own country out of frustration with Serbian Prime Minister Nikola Pašić insufficient efforts to unify Serbia. Extraordinarily, one of the leaders of the Black Hand was Colonel Dragutin Dimitrijevich (known as Apis), the head of Serbian military intelligence. It was most likely Colonel Dimitrijevich who decided that the Black Hand should assassinate Franz Ferdinand, the heir to the Habsburg throne. In all likelihood, the reason was that Franz Ferdinand supported increased autonomy for the Habsburg Empire's Slavic minorities, a policy that threatened to undercut the appeal of pan-Serbism.

Meanwhile during the spring of 1914, a Bosnian secret society known as Young Bosnia was hatching plans of its own. The group was devoted to the destruction of the Habsburg Empire and the liberation of the South Slavs, but not necessarily under the banner of Serbian irredentism. When some of its members learned that the heir apparent and his wife, the Duchess Sophie, would be visiting the Bosnian capital, Sarajevo, in the summer, they resolved to assassinate him. Their motives are unclear. They seem not to have been terribly interested in his political stances, but rather saw him as simply part of a repressive dynasty that had subjugated their people. One member of the plot to kill Franz Ferdinand said much later, "There was a general belief that *attentats* were the quickest means to revolutionize the people" (quoted in Feuerlicht, *The Desperate Act*, 65). In fact, Young Bosnia was steeped in the rhetoric of tyrannicide, a tradition its members traced back to the Battle of Kosovo Field, where in 1389 the Ottoman Turks inflicted a catastrophic defeat on the Serbs, who partially redeemed themselves at the end of the day when a Serbian hero assassinated the Ottoman sultan. The anniversary of the battle had long been celebrated as the decisive emergence of Serbian and South Slav national identity. And it was on that very day, June 28, that the Archduke's visit to Sarajevo was to take place. For the tyrannicides of Young Bosnia, the stars had aligned. All they needed were the means to carry out the assassination.

Here the two plots intersected in the person of a Black Hand operative, Vojin Tankosich, who had contact with Young Bosnia. When he learned of its plot, he decided to provide three of its terrorists with training, firearms, and hand-held bombs. The assassins – who eventually reached seven in number – learned of Franz Ferdinand's itinerary when it was published in the newspaper. It is almost certain that members of the Serbian cabinet knew of the Black Hand plot to assassinate a Habsburg luminary. They might have even tried to stop it at the last minute, as did Colonel Apis, after he grasped the possible ramifications of a quasi-state-sponsored assassination of the Austro-Hungarian heir to the throne (Feuerlicht, *The Desperate Act*, 85–6). But the job had long been entrusted to free agents beyond the control of the Black Hand's leadership. The wheels were in motion and could not be easily stopped.

On June 28, 1914, the seven Bosnian Serb terrorists placed themselves along the route. As the Archduke's carriage rolled by, one of the conspirators threw a bomb that wounded two officers accompanying the imperial couple. Immediately seized and interrogated by the police, he declared, "I am a Serbian hero" (quoted in Dedijer, *The Road to Sarajevo*, 319). Surprisingly, Franz Ferdinand stuck to his itinerary, but added a visit to the wounded officers in the hospital, thus throwing off other assassins. While sitting in a café, the nineteen-year-old Gavrilo Princip spotted the Archduke's car, which had mistakenly turned into a narrow street. As the driver slowly backed up, Princip wildly fired two shots into the car, killing Franz Ferdinand and Sophie. Princip was quickly captured, as were most of his co-conspirators.

The initial investigation into the assassination swiftly concluded that the Serbian government was uninvolved in the conspiracy, but Austria-Hungary, egged on by Germany, its primary ally, eventually issued a ten-point ultimatum that accused Serbia of allowing its nationals to "incite . . . hatred of the [Habsburg] Monarchy" and to hatch a plot to assassinate its heir (quoted in Lafore, *The Long Fuse*, 225). The ultimatum demanded drastic infringements on Serbian sovereignty. Serbia, rightly concerned about the consequences of war with its vastly larger and more powerful neighbor, agreed to all ten points with only minor caveats. But the Habsburg urge to punish Serbia was strong. The resultant Habsburg declaration of war inexorably drew in Russia, Germany, France, and the UK. A member of the British prime minister's cabinet bluntly confessed in his diary what no one seemed to state publicly: "Why four great powers should fight over Serbia no fellow can understand" (quoted in Gilbert, *The First World War*, 23). But fight they did, producing the most destructive war of the modern era to that point.

A word is in order concerning the oft-stated belief that the assassination of the Archduke started the Great War or, in the most common turn of phrase, was the match that lit the fuse. What has always intrigued historians – and gave hope to contemporaries – was the nearly month-long pause between the assassination and the Austrian ultimatum. What has become clear in hindsight is that the Austrians and Germans alike were keen to find a justification for flexing Austrian muscles in the region and thus reasserting its status as a Great Power. Thus, it was not the murder of Franz Ferdinand that began the war, but the political ends to which the murder was put that drove Europe over the precipice. Yet we can readily imagine other acts of provocation that might not have been as startling and which would not have provided the requisite *cassus belli*. War was not guaranteed, and thus the assassination in Sarajevo takes its place in the annals of terrorism as perhaps the costliest murder ever.

The Internal Macedonian Revolutionary Organization

The Balkans birthed two other terrorist organizations – the Internal Macedonian Revolutionary Organization (the IMRO) and the Croatian Ustaša – with an intertwined history that merits attention for many reasons. The forerunner of the IMRO was established around 1893 by a schoolteacher, Goce Delchev. His goal was independence for Macedonia, a Slavic and Orthodox Christian people whose territory was claimed by Bulgaria, Serbia, and Greece, but mostly ruled at the time by the rapidly receding Ottoman Empire. The small circle of Macedonian intelligentsia had long regarded Bulgaria as its natural ally, so most of the IMRO's leadership relied on Bulgaria for safe haven and support, although they still demanded full independence, not simply unification with Bulgaria. The IMRO's paramilitary wing soon came to overshadow the mother organization and its interest in education, propaganda, and peaceful agitation.

IMRO's military leaders believed that the European powers would inter-vene to protect a Christian people from the Turks if only they could be made aware of the plight of Macedonians. Therefore, IMRO cells carried out terrorist strikes against European targets throughout the region. Two of the most notorious incidents were the seizure of an American mission-ary as a hostage and the sinking of a French ship in the port of Salonika. When European interest was barely aroused, IMRO embraced a new strategy. Perhaps terrorism against Ottoman targets would lead to vio-lence against the Macedonian masses which, in turn, would finally trigger European intervention. IMRO was halfway successful: the Ottomans engaged in bloody reprisals that claimed thousands of Macedonian victims, but Christian Europe remained aloof, in part because Russia and Austria-Hungary had recently come to an unofficial agreement to preserve the status quo in the Balkans, lest an uncontrollable conflict be set off. Meanwhile, IMRO waged a struggle against a splinter group, the External Macedonian Revolutionary Organization, which used terrorism in pursuit of annexation by Bulgaria, which cynically maintained support for both groups. Russian revolutionary terrorism exercised a considerable influ-ence on IMRO and its various factions whose members read the works of Chernyshevsky and Stepniak-Kravchinsky and studied bomb-making with Russian-trained Armenian terrorists.

Following the dismantlement of the Habsburg and Ottoman Empires after the First World War, Macedonia found itself divided between Greece and the Kingdom of Serbs, Croats, and Slovenians (known as Yugoslavia from 1929 onward). IMRO hardly skipped a beat, turning its terrorist cells against those states. If anything, the violence was ratch-eted up several notches, but for a time it was largely transformed into a guerrilla struggle against the police and army of Greece and Yugoslavia. In the 1920s, IMRO was supported by three states at cross purposes. Bulgaria, a constitutional monarchy, had lost most of its Macedonian territory to Yugoslavia and thus supported IMRO with safe haven and money. Mussolini's fascist Italy offered its patronage, as well, hoping to use IMRO to destabilize Yugoslavia so it could acquire territory along the Dalmatian coast. IMRO also developed close ties with the Soviet Union, who hoped to use the group as a means of gaining influence and spreading revolution throughout the Balkans. Leadership struggles and a disagreement over tactics – guerrilla warfare versus terrorism and assas-sination – led to tit-for-tat murders between IMRO factions and the near gutting of the organization. It was kept afloat, however, by its patrons, each of whom conspired to use the IMRO to wage shadow foreign policy. IMRO responded to this state of affairs by increasingly losing sight of its own patriotic origins and turning to criminal enterprises, harkening back to Russia's era of "revolutionary expropriations." In the most startling development, IMRO essentially turned into a free-lance terrorist operation that offered its services to the highest bidder, usually the Bulgarian government. In the 1930s, IMRO also became involved in extortion and narcotics smuggling.

The Ustaše of Croatia

IMRO also became the early patrons of another anti-Serb and anti-Yugoslav organization, the Croatian nationalists of the Ustaše (meaning "insurgents" in their native tongue). The Ustaše were founded in 1929 by Ante Pavelić, who also managed to secure support from Austria, Italy, Hungary, and Bulgaria, all of which bore historical, political, or territorial grudges against the Serbs and Yugoslavia. At a training facility in Hungary, IMRO terrorists trained Ustaše operatives in bomb-making and conspiratorial activity. The Ustaše put the knowledge to immediate use, carrying out about a half-dozen assassinations of Yugoslavian officials or pro-Serb civilians and a dozen bombings of trains – including the Orient Express – and other public targets during the first four years of its existence (Trifkovic, *Ustaša*, 45). The Ustaše received the most funds from Mussolini, who also supplied the group with an Italian headquarters that changed location whenever Yugoslavia managed to track it down. In October 1934, a joint Ustaše-IMRO conspiracy led to the assassination of the Serbian ruler of Yugoslavia, Alexander I, while on a state visit to Marseilles. The French foreign minister, Louis Barthou, died in the attack as well, the victim of a stray bullet from his police escort. In the wake of the assassination, Mussolini renounced the Ustaše, and the group went deeply underground, resurfacing to proclaim an independent Croatia allied to the Nazis after the German invasion of Yugoslavia in 1941.

Widespread outrage at the assassination of Alexander and Barthou led to the first international efforts to combat terrorism since the St. Petersburg Protocol of 1904. The issue was taken up by the League of Nations, which passed the Convention on the Prevention and Punishment of Terrorism in 1937. Initially signed by twenty-five countries, only one – India – ever ratified the document (Gross, "International Terrorism," 508). Plans to set up an international court to try terrorism suspects fared even more poorly when no states ratified that proposal. These halting steps toward international cooperation failed for two main reasons: states reacted strongly against any perceived loss of national sovereignty, and many, in fact, were committed to the use of state-sponsored terrorism.

The Ustaše and the Internal Macedonian Revolutionary Organization illustrated the strong allure and the typically poor results gained from the use of independent terrorist organizations as covert agents of foreign policy. IMRO's involvement in attacks inside Bulgaria showed how terrorist groups have been quite willing to bite the hand that feeds them, and the indirect involvement of the Serbian government in the assassination of Franz Ferdinand demonstrated how state-sponsored terrorism could yield self-defeating results. Nonetheless, state-sponsored terrorism has remained a popular tool for unsavory authoritarian states and even the occasional democratic nation.

Another feature of terrorism amply demonstrated by the history of IMRO is the tendency toward self-destruction. Revolutionaries by their nature tend to be committed to maximal programs that view compromise as anathema (note the frequent use of permutations of the phrase "liberty or death" in such groups' propaganda). Such tendencies are usually exacerbated by the use of violence – the goal of which is the elimination of opposition – and by life in conspiratorial groups that remove the revolutionaries from contact with virtually all moderates. The underground life often heightens the sense of encirclement, induces paranoia, and increasingly focuses attention on the struggle to defend against spies and provocateurs. The frequent result is bewildering splits and violent internal conflicts. IMRO exhibited a particularly odd twist on the age-old tendency of revolutionary commitment to devolve into nihilistic violence for the sake of violence when its agents became terrorists for hire. This bizarre turn of events did not remain historically unique, however. In the 1970s and 1980s, ethno-nationalist and left-wing revolutionary terrorists in the Middle East and Japan became terrorist free-agents available to the highest bidder.

The Uses of Ethno-Nationalist Terrorism

One of the defining features of the twentieth century was the prevalence of ethno-nationalist independence movements, of which the Easter Uprising and the Irish War for Independence were the first widely emulated examples. Leaders of later movements rarely worked toward outright military victories, but rather thought in terms of the symbolic uses of violence and its impact on various observers. The three most relevant audiences have typically been the small core of committed nationalists, who need to be reminded at regular intervals that the movement is still alive and victory is attainable; the larger, uncommitted public, which can be radicalized by the zeal of the nationalists or the brutality of the imperial power; and the imperial homeland's public and government, who might come to believe in time that victory is not worth the cost. According to this startling new calculus, military defeat could produce political triumph. This is essentially the form and function of modern terrorism, even when movements, such as those culminating in the Easter Uprising, do not borrow its specific content, such as assassination, attacks on civilians, and the bombing of buildings and other physical targets. Not surprisingly, ethno-nationalist movements have often in the end resorted to exactly these tactics, since they are well suited to forces operating against technologically and numerically superior enemies in a media-saturated age.

During the era of the world wars the incidence of ethno-nationalist terrorism declined, as did all varieties of terrorism from below. They were often replaced with state terror from above. But the Second World War dealt a tremendous blow to the power and prestige of the great European states and weakened their holds on their imperial possessions. Before long, national movements in the third world turned to terrorism as one of the principal means of pursuing independence from their European overlords. And in their struggles, the examples of the Irish, Indians, Bosnians, Macedonians, and other early ethno-nationalist movements loomed large.

Bibliography

The literature on the IRA and Irish republicanism is full of polemical landmines. Three excellent surveys are J. Bowyer Bell, *The Secret Army: The IRA*, rev. 3rd edn. (Transaction, 2003 [1997]); Tim Pat Coogan, *The IRA*, rev. edn. (Palgrave, 2002); and Richard English, *Armed Struggle: The History of the IRA* (Oxford University Press, 2003). The best work on the Phoenix Park Murders and the pre-history of the IRA is Tom Corfe, *The Phoenix Park Murders: Conflict, Compromise and Tragedy in Ireland, 1879–1882* (Hodder and Stoughton, 1968). For the Easter Uprising, the Black and Tan War, and the early history of the IRA, see Tim Pat Coogan, *Michael Collins: A Biography* (Hutchinson, 1990); T. Ryle Dwyer, *The Squad and the Intelligence Operations of Michael Collins* (Mercier Press, 2005); James Gleeson, *Bloody Sunday* (Lyons Press, 2004 [1962]); and two books by Peter Hart, *The I.R.A. and Its Enemies: Violence and Community in Cork, 1916–1923* (Clarendon Press, 1998), and *The I.R.A. at War 1916–1923* (Oxford University Press, 2005).

Charles Callwell's work is readily available: *Small Wars – Their Principles and Practice* (University of Nebraska Press, 1996 [1896]).

The literature on the assassination of Franz Ferdinand and the start of the First World War is plentiful. The best work on the assassination is Vladimir Dedijer, *The Road to Sarajevo* (Simon and Schuster, 1966). Two other valuable works are Roberta Strauss Feuerlicht, *The Desperate Act: The Assassination of Franz Ferdinand at Sarajevo* (McGraw-Hill, 1968); and Henri Pozzi, *Black Hand Over Europe* (Francis Mott, 1935). An excellent account of the long and short-term causes of the First World War is Laurence Lafore, *The Long Fuse: An Interpretation of the Origins of World War I*, 2nd edn. (Waveland Press, 1971). A standard work on the war is Martin Gilbert, *The First World War: A Complete History* (Henry Holt, 1994).

The best book on extremism and terrorism in pre-independence India is J. N. Vajpeyi, *The Extremist Movement in India* (Chugh Publications, 1974). Other helpful works include Peter Heehs, *The Bomb in Bengal: The Rise of Revolutionary Terrorism in India, 1900–1910* (Oxford University Press, 1993); David M. Laushey, *Bengal Terrorism and the Marxist Left: Aspects of Regional Nationalism in India, 1905–1942* (Firma K. L. Mukhopadhyay, 1975); and Stanley A. Wolpert, *Tilak and Gokhale: Revolution and Reform in the Making of Modern India* (University of California Press, 1962). For the influence of Russia and the Russian Method on the Indian revolutionary movement, see Steven G. Marks, *How Russia Shaped the Modern World* (Princeton University Press, 2003); and P. Sinha, *Indian National Liberation Movement and Russia (1905–1917)* (New Delhi, 1975).

A valuable article on early international efforts to combat terrorism is Leo Gross, "International Terrorism and International Criminal Jurisdiction," *American Journal of International Law*, vol. 67, no. 3 (1973), 508–11.

On IMRO, see Duncan M. Perry, *The Politics of Terror: The Macedonian Liberation Movements 1893–1903* (Duke University Press, 1988).

An excellent work on the Ustaša is Srdja Trifkovic, *Ustaša: Croatian Separatism and European Politics, 1929–1945* (Lord Byron Foundation for Balkan Studies, 1998).

10

The Era of State Terror

Judged by the standards of the day, individual and small-group terrorism around the turn of the century in Russia, Europe, the United States, Ireland, India, and elsewhere seemed to have reached enormous proportions. Two world wars, Nazi genocide, and the creation of totalitarian regimes from 1914 to 1945 reminded Europeans, however, that states were still the primary sources of organized terror, violence, and death. In the Soviet Union alone, an estimated fifty million people died in political purges, man-made famines, and war. The terror unleashed during these years left permanent marks on the maps and psyches of Europeans, marks that continue to exert great influence today.

As for the history of terrorism, there are two principal lessons: that acts carried out by subversive groups provide a treasure trove of tactics and strategies that are as murderously useful to repressive regimes; and that a regime's accusation of terrorism against its opponents can also be useful in manufacturing support and consensus.

Russia's Revolutions

Despite the assassinations carried out by the Combat Organization and the random bombings of the anarchists, it was not terrorism that directly brought down the Russian Empire. That was accomplished in February 1917 by hungry protesters in St. Petersburg demonstrating against an incompetent government's prosecution of a hopeless war, and by the soldiers and police who refused to fire on them. Theirs was a people's revolution. Not so the Bolsheviks' armed coup d'état ten months later against the Provisional Government, which led to a quick Russian exit from the war, the rapid construction of a one-party dictatorship, and the enactment of a radical socialist program.

Lenin's Bolsheviks had in theory rejected individual terror as ahistorical. And yet they bore the imprint of their predecessors: they practiced banditry and economic terrorism under the designation of "revolutionary expropriations"; preserved their underground movement thanks to the conspiratorial methods pioneered by the People's Will and other groups; and walked in the footsteps of Nechaev who demanded a revolution *in the name of* the people. Lastly, Lenin's older brother had been executed for his part in a failed attempt on the life of Alexander III in 1887, a personal loss that made a deep impression on the young Vladimir.

Ultimately there was no question for Lenin about the usefulness of terror in support of the dictatorship of the proletariat *after* the seizure of power. In this regard, he and the Bolsheviks looked to the French Revolution for inspiration and justification. Whereas the Jacobins slowly developed a policy of terror after taking power that was in part a response to unforeseen exigencies, Lenin imagined it as a cornerstone of the new order. In 1908, for example, he noted that the Paris Commune had failed in 1871 because of its "excessive generosity – it should have exterminated its enemies" (quoted in Pipes, *The Russian Revolution*, 790).

The Bolsheviks, therefore, wasted no time in setting up a police organization – the Extraordinary Commission, known by its Russian acronym, the Cheka – that could defend the Revolution by force. It was given sweeping authority to investigate, detain, try, and execute enemies of the new socialist state. Its leader was Felix Dzerzhinsky, a Polish revolutionary who had spent half his life in tsarist prisons and deserved his nickname – "Iron Felix." At first, the Cheka was poorly organized and focused mostly on combating counterfeiters, speculators, and anarchist gangs. Lenin encouraged populist terror under the banner of "looting the looters," claiming that every town should devise its own means of waging "a war to the death against the rich, the idlers, and the parasites" (quoted in Figes, *A People's Tragedy*, 524–5). The Bolsheviks also called for the creation of spontaneous "revolutionary tribunals" modeled after their namesakes in the French Revolution that could mete out justice on the spot. The violence was widespread and brutal, but hardly systematic.

The Civil War and the Red Terror

Things changed dramatically during the summer of 1918 when the Bolsheviks' political opponents – an uncoordinated "White" hodgepodge of

monarchists, moderate socialists, democrats, anarchists, and national separatists – began to field armies. This was the start of the Russian Civil War.

Just as bad was a new Socialist–Revolutionaries terrorist campaign.
The first Soviet official to fall was the commissar of the press, on June
20. Two weeks later, Left SRs – radical SRs who had briefly supported
the Bolsheviks – assassinated Count Mirbach, the German ambassador
to Soviet Russia, in the hopes that it would spark a popular rebellion
and enrage Germany to the point of recommencing offensive operations.
The Left SR plot failed on both counts. Instead, the Bolsheviks clamped
down on their erstwhile allies, creating a true one-party dictatorship.
Newly formed SR terrorist teams continued to stalk leading Bolsheviks.
One narrowly missed its chance at Trotsky, the head of the Red Army
and Lenin's right-hand man, when he abruptly switched trains. On
August 30, an SR assassinated Moisei Uritsky, a leading Cheka official,
and another SR team shot Lenin after he gave a speech. He narrowly
survived, but the bullet that remained lodged in his neck probably contributed to his early death less than six years later.

The Bolsheviks were convinced that they were surrounded by enemies,
their Revolution imperiled. Since they understood Marx to say that
socialism and capitalism could never live side by side, they interpreted
these terrorist strikes as the opening blow in a campaign carried out
by internal counter-revolutionaries who were financed and organized
by foreign imperialists eager to destroy the first socialist state. The
panicking Bolsheviks responded by unleashing a coordinated campaign
against all enemies of the state, officially enacting "The Red Terror" on
September 5, 1918, with a decree authorizing the shooting of all "White
Guard" and counter-revolutionary enemies. "For the blood of Lenin
and Uritsky," announced a leading government newspaper, "let there be
floods of bourgeois blood – more blood, as much as possible" (quoted in
Figes, *A People's Tragedy*, 630).

The term "counter-revolution" was never clearly defined, so nearly
anyone could be arrested or executed under that rubric. The Bolsheviks
used the Cheka to destroy figureheads around whom resistance might
form, most notably the deposed Romanov family in July 1918. Cheka
officers carried out mass executions of those who actively opposed the
state or were suspected of supporting White armies. The Bolsheviks seized
thousands of "bourgeois hostages," releasing some upon payment of a
ransom and killing others. As in the Jacobin Reign of Terror, people were
arrested for wearing the clothes or using the language of the previously
privileged. A stray negative word about the Bolsheviks could land one in
prison, but many of the arrests and executions were simply random. Not
surprisingly, the Cheka used techniques learned from both nineteenth-
century revolutionaries and their jailers, but often with far greater cruelty.

Indeed, the terrorist violence committed by the Left SRs and others
paled in comparison to the violence of the Civil War and the actions of

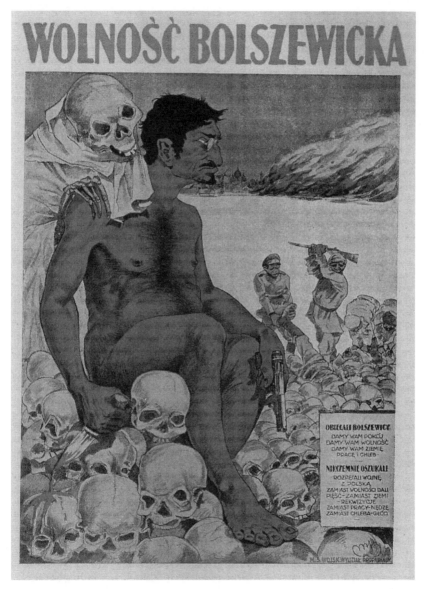

Figure 10.1: "Bolshevik Freedom": A Polish poster featuring Trotsky and
denouncing the Red Terror, ca. 1920
(Wikimedia Commons)

the Cheka. Most Cheka violence was proactive, in the sense that people were arrested for their potential opposition to Soviet power. Violence was thus both targeted and symbolic, meant to destroy active enemies and cow the broad population. Isaac Steinberg, a Left SR who briefly held the position of commissar of justice after the Revolution, fully appreciated what the Bolsheviks were constructing. In 1920, he wrote, "Terror is a *system* . . . a legalized plan of the regime for the purpose of mass intimidation, mass compulsion, mass extermination." Steinberg's Bolshevik successor understood this when he advised his colleagues, "We must execute not only the guilty. Execution of the innocent will impress the masses even more" (quoted in Pipes, *The Russian Revolution*, 793 and 822). In this regard, the Soviets went well beyond what the Jacobins practiced in the French Reign of Terror. This was propaganda of the deed used on behalf of the state, rather than against it. The Cheka remained a power unto itself, virtually a state within a state, taking directions from a handful of hardcore Bolsheviks at the top. Experts have estimated that the Bolsheviks, primarily the Cheka, executed from 50,000 to 200,000 people from the start of the Red Terror into the early 1920s (Leggett, *The Cheka*, 466–7).

Bolshevik victory over the Whites in 1920 led to a lessening of terror, but did not end it. Targeted violence and terror remained an indispensable tool of the state and Party. Just as importantly, the terror of the civil war years left an indelible mark on Soviet Russia's leaders: violence had brutalized society and become fixed in the minds of the Party faithful as the probable midwife of any "great leap forward" to communism. This continued even during the years of relative social and political peace in the 1920s when a truce – under the banner of the New Economic Policy – was declared between the battered Soviet state and its entrepreneurs and technical experts in an attempt to rebuild the economy after six years of war, revolution, and civil conflict.

Stalin and Stalinism

Meanwhile, Lenin's first stroke in 1922 and death in 1924 set off a scramble to succeed him. Trotsky – the man who orchestrated the seizure of power in October and then organized the Red Army during the Civil War – seemed the most likely candidate. His primary rivals drummed Trotsky out of the Party and forced him into exile, eventually in Mexico City. Although Joseph Stalin was never more than a supporting player in these feuds, he soon emerged as the leader of the Communist Party. He began to put his stamp on the Soviet Union in 1929, initiating a series of measures meant to turn the USSR into a modern industrial society in a matter of years.

In order to coerce the public's obedience, Stalin and his cronies organized state terror, ironically, by engineering and inflating a terrorist threat *against* the state. On December 1, 1934, a disgruntled Communist, Leonid Nikolaev, assassinated Sergei Kirov, the popular head of the Leningrad branch of the Party. Historians are reasonably sure that Nikolaev acted on his own, but it seems that he was nudged toward targeting Kirov by Stalin's agents. Stalin's probable motive was twofold: to rid himself of a current rival and to provide a pretext for the elimination of old ones.

In the immediate wake of Kirov's death, Stalin directed the police and courts to target those involved in "acts of terror" (quoted in Conquest, *The Great Terror*, 41). Perpetrators were to be investigated, arrested, "tried" before a three-person tribunal, and executed within a matter of days – all without access to counsel or the possibility of appeals. On the surface, nothing about this decree was particularly new. Such "justice" had been the order of the day during the Civil War and at times since. What was different about this decree and the wave of arrests and executions that followed was that the targets of these investigations were primarily members of the Communist Party. Previously, the worst punishment typically given to any Party member was expulsion from the organization.

Within weeks of Kirov's death, fourteen low-level Party members were tried and executed for participating in a "terrorist conspiracy" to murder him. All fourteen, linked through faked evidence and coerced confessions to shadowy foreign elements, were former followers of Stalin's rivals. Within a year and a half, all of Stalin's principal opponents from the 1920s were linked to the arch-villain Trotsky and put on trial for having planned Kirov's assassination and a terrorist campaign to kill other leading Bolsheviks, including Stalin. The charges of terrorism were absurd lies, but the men confessed in carefully orchestrated show trials designed to demonstrate to Soviet citizens and the world the extent of the threat facing the Soviet Union. One after another, Stalin's rivals were found guilty and executed.

Terrorism became a particularly useful danger around which to build false accusations because it mobilized the public. The result was ever-widening circles of denunciations. From fall 1936 to fall 1938, arrests climbed into the thousands and then millions, with every victim linked through a chain of friendly, familial, or professional associations back to the conspiracy to kill Kirov, assassinate Stalin, or sabotage the economy. Stalinist terror thrived on paranoia, the belief that even your closest colleague or loved one could be a terrorist in hiding, waiting to be activated by a secret message from the devil himself, Trotsky. Each new unmasking ratcheted up the panic and reinforced the impression that the country was under siege from a hidden foe. So great became the need for victims that Stalin and the head of the political police took to issuing specific quotas for arrests and executions, with the names worked out by police agents on the ground. For a campaign beginning July 31, 1937, the quota was 268,950 arrested, of whom 75,950 were to be shot (Service, *Stalin*, 350–1).

As in France in the 1790s, terror was a system intended to fragment society and reshape it according to new goals and standards. Terror was violence, symbolic as well as physical, and was meant to educate people about the necessity of vigilance, obedience, and self-sacrifice. But terror and mass violence also had many practical uses. It provided motivation in a system that had abolished private property and profit. It cleared out all traces of managers and technical experts trained before the Revolution, making room for a new generation loyal to the Party and Stalin. It destroyed entrenched regional and local Party functionaries. The Terror filled the Gulag, which became a valuable source of slave labor. Accusations of terrorism and sabotage also provided a scapegoat for the myriad problems created in the haste to industrialize and collectivize. When the long-promised socialist utopia did not materialize, it became possible to believe that hidden "wreckers, saboteurs, double-dealers, and terrorists" were conspiring with the Soviet Union's international enemies to stall progress. By these means, the rhetorical construction of terrorism from above was reinforced, even amplified from below as the term "terrorism" was drained of all real-world content and filled up with socially and politically expedient messages.

What became known as the Great Terror was finally reined in during the fall of 1938, but Stalin engineered new bouts of terror, complete with new accusations of terrorism and foreign collaboration, on several occasions after the Second World War. According to information from the Soviet archives, the state sentenced to death 786,098 people for counter-revolutionary crimes from 1930 to 1953. Of these, 681,692 were executed during the worst of the violence, in 1937–8. Other estimates run much higher. As for how many who were arrested and sentenced to stints in the Gulag, the numbers are even murkier. Nikita Khrushchev, the Soviet leader following Stalin, estimated that seventeen million people spent time in the penal system from 1937 to 1953. Probably two million were arrested and tried in the years 1934–8. A recent Western writer on the Gulag used the work of post-Soviet historians and statisticians to come up with an even more staggering, but reasonable guesstimate of 28.7 million "forced laborers" in the USSR from the 1920s to the 1950s (Applebaum, *Gulag*, 578–84).

Germany after the First World War

Though they were the masters of the form, the Soviet Union's leaders were not alone in their use of terror as an instrument of coercing obedience from their civilians. Their only true rival in terms of scale and sheer brutality were the Nazis, who made much more explicit use of terrorism than the Bolsheviks did during their rise to power. Once in power, state terror became a cornerstone of the Nazi regime, a policy that flowered into genocide during the Second World War.

Germany paid dearly, in both lives and treasure, during the First World War, but those costs were only the beginning of Germany's woes. As military and civilian authority collapsed in November 1918, Germany's socialist party, the SPD, stepped into the void and declared a republic. In order to defend itself against enemies on both the left and right, the SPD-dominated government encouraged the creation of Freikorps (Free Corps), local militias drawn from the ranks of recently demobilized war veterans.

The Freikorps proved to be a breeding ground for dangerous new movements. Many veterans found it difficult to re-enter peacetime society and desperately searched for the camaraderie and excitement of the *Fronterlebnis* ("front life") they had shared in the trenches. Such veterans were also susceptible to right-wing propaganda that blamed "soft" civilians – particularly socialists, communists, and Jews – for Germany's defeat in the war. This was the birth of the myth that Germany had been felled by a traitorous "stab in the back." To make matters worse, the first duty of the Weimar government – so named after the city in which the founding constitution was drawn up – was to sign the Treaty of Versailles ending the First World War. This document stripped the county of valuable territory, dramatically reduced the size of the formal military, burdened the state with crippling reparations payments to the Allies, and forced Germany to accept all responsibility for starting the war. Before long, a host of right-wing groups emerged, spouting a hatred of democracy, liberalism, socialism, and monopoly capitalism. Members of these groups pined for a past long gone, one of agriculture and small business, a world untouched by electoral divisions, Marxism, and organized labor. They hoped not merely for national regeneration; they sought an alternative – and imagined – history in which the nation was united in organic wholeness. Their nostalgia for *Fronterlebnis* was pervasive. Anti-Semitism crept into the mix, as well.

Some Freikorps veterans naturally gravitated toward political violence and a program of assassination. In the first years following the establishment of Weimar Germany, right-wing death squads linked to the Freikorps assassinated the socialist leader Hugo Haase, the Catholic Center Party politician and Weimar minister, Matthias Erzberger, and Walther Rathenau, the moderate (and Jewish) minister of foreign affairs. Many other lesser political figures in the center or on the left fell victim to these death squads. In March 1920, the government officially disbanded the Freikorps, an act that drove many veterans into underground paramilitary groups, collectively dubbed "the Black Reichswehr."

Political violence was not confined to the underground, because nearly every political party formed an associated paramilitary group. The nationalists founded an array of "Fighting Leagues." The Communist Party of Germany (the KPD) had the Red Front Fighter's League. Even the relatively moderate and mild SPD had the Reichsbanner Black-Red-Gold (named after the colors of the Weimar flag). These groups provided security at party rallies, marched to persuade the unaffiliated of their strength, and engaged in street brawls with their rivals. The more extreme the political party or ideology behind the paramilitary association, the more likely it was to engage in covert violence, including terrorism and assassination.

A real difference between far-left and far-right-wing violence in Weimar Germany was the popular attitude toward them. Those on the right, center, and the moderate left feared the idea of a Soviet-style revolution and therefore saw groups on the far left, particularly the KPD, as existential threats to state and nation. Otherwise discordant voices in the legislature, civil service, military, judiciary, and police could agree on this, and they made sure that left-wing violence was not tolerated. Right-wing violence, on the other hand, enjoyed quiet support or benevolent neutrality from these groups. Authorities condemned Black Reichswehr violence with surprisingly tepid language and handed down sentences that matched. In the case of the Rathenau assassination, for example, the court gave the organizer of the killing a five-year sentence, then released him early. In those instances in which far-right assassins and terrorists received severe punishments, their cases became right-wing cause-célèbres.

Of course, the most significant right-wing beneficiary of public sympathy and indifference was Adolf Hitler's organization, the National Socialist Worker's Party of Germany – the Nazis. The Nazi Party, founded in 1920, was not the most violent of Germany's many right-wing groups. What set the Nazis apart was, first of all, their advocacy of nationalism, but rather an intense Aryan racism and anti-Semitism. The second feature was an abiding faith in the need for an all-powerful dictator – the so-called "leadership principle" – which the Nazis drew, in part, from Benito Mussolini and the Italian fascists. The Nazis called for Germany's revival, but their program was mostly based on hatred for Weimar democracy, communism, the November criminals, and

Versailles. The primary focus of Hitler's wrath was reserved for "Judeo-Bolshevism," the alleged plot by Jews to control Germany and the world through Soviet communism.

Italian Fascism

Although the Italians had fought on the victorious side in the Great War, post-war Italy bore a striking similarity to vanquished Germany. Italy had been promised much by the Allies, but gained little in the Treaty of Versailles. The result was a profound sense of national humiliation, particularly among nationalists and veterans, some of whom formed post-war paramilitary bodies similar to the Freikorps. As in Germany, socialism was a powerful and polarizing force that attracted many workers and horrified middle- and upper-class Italians. In 1919 and 1920, a wave of strikes and the weak government response to it raised the specter of a socialist uprising and became the backdrop for Benito Mussolini's rapid rise to prominence. In 1919 Mussolini formed the Fascio Italiani di Combattimento, the Italian Combat League, and drew on the veterans' groups to form armed squads, whose members became known as *squadristi* or Blackshirts, on account of their garb. The *squadristi* did not embrace a political stance as much as an ethos in which violence and terror was elevated to a way of life. By all accounts, the allure of violence, excitement, and camaraderie attracted far more *squadristi* than did fascist ideology.

The *squadristi* terrorized those on the left through arson, kidnapping, beatings, and even murder. The socialists responded by forming their own paramilitary groups that frequently fought street battles with the fascists. Mussolini's position was cynical and manipulative in the extreme; even as his Blackshirts carried out a campaign of almost unchallenged violence, he repeatedly claimed to be Italy's best candidate to restore law and order. When the unions and parties of the left carried out an anti-fascist general strike in August 1922, Mussolini sent the *squadristi* in as strike-breakers. This spasm of Blackshirt terror was enthusiastically supported by the bourgeoisie, who feared socialism and the unions so much that Mussolini's fascists and the *squadristi* seemed legitimate. The Italian government agreed: for every two fascists arrested for an act of violence, the police collared seven socialists (Petersen, "Violence in Italian Fascism," 280–2).

That October, the Italian fascists staged their "March on Rome" in which 25,000 Blackshirts converged on the capital in a show of force far more theatrical than militarily meaningful. This was not a coup d'état, nor was it intended to be one. King Victor Emmanuel III asked Mussolini to become prime minister because the king believed the fascists would be easier to control as part of the government; moreover, the fascists had showed that they were tough enough to take on Italy's internal enemies. In the history of terrorism, this was a significant development. Whereas Russian revolutionary terrorists struck at the state, fascist terrorists overwhelmingly struck at rival political and social groups. In fact, Italian fascists sought to co-opt the state more than overturn it.

Hitler's Brownshirts

The path followed by Hitler and his Nazis was remarkably similar. For most of the 1920s, they were a tiny party occupying the fringes of German politics. Hitler's hate-filled rants to small, rapturous audiences led most Germans to regard the Nazis as cartoonish and Hitler as an embarrassing lunatic. But they were deadly serious, particularly the Storm Division, the Nazi Party's paramilitary body. The Storm Division – also known as the SA or the Brownshirts because of the members' uniforms – became a haven for many of Germany's ex-Freikorps soldiers and nationalists. Driven by an intense *Fronterlebnis* mentality, the Brownshirts took every opportunity to pick a fight, often fatal, with members of the SPD's Reichsbanner or the KPD's Red Front. The Brownshirts cultivated a sense of victimization, both at the hands of the government and leftists. One Brownshirt wrote, "There isn't a night in which SA men don't lie in the streets as victims of the Communist terror" (quoted in Merkl, "Approaches to Political Violence," 374). This perception was reflected in the disturbing Brownshirt slogan, "terror must be broken by terror." Stormtroopers were led to believe that to be hated and feared by the government was a high calling, indeed.

Hitler and the Nazis continued to rail at Versailles and the Jewish and communist threats, but those issues gained them few converts. It was the economic devastation of the Great Depression, beginning in 1929, and the consequent perception that democracy had failed that caused many Germans to turn to the Nazis out of desperation. By 1932, economic output had dropped by 40 percent since 1929, and roughly one-third of all workers were unemployed. The Reichstag was paralyzed, unable or unwilling to act to halt its slide into irrelevance. And in the streets, the Brownshirts went on the offensive, instigating confrontations that they nicknamed "collisions." A more appropriate name would be terrorism, or even civil war. In 1932, police recorded – but were unable to stop – 461 battles between the Red Front and the Brownshirts in the state of

Prussia alone between June 1 and 20. The casualties were horrendous: eighty-two killed and four hundred wounded. During the next month, thirty-eight Nazis, thirty Communists, and eighteen others were the victims of politically motivated attacks. One street battle in the Hamburg suburb of Altona on July 17 claimed seventeen lives (Shirer, *The Rise and Fall of the Third Reich*, 231; Kershaw, *Hitler*, 368).

The street terror served many purposes, but one was paramount: to provoke the KPD's Red Front fighters to respond in self-defense. The head of the Communist Party obliged them early in 1931 when he declared, "There must no longer be a single act of terror by the Nazi murderers without the workers everywhere reacting immediately with the most aggressive physical mass-struggle" (quoted in Rosenhaft, "The KPD in the Weimar Republic," 349). Nazi terror was also meant to egg the communists on in their own confrontation with the police and government. Nazi leaders knew this would be easy; after all, the Communists were every bit as contemptuous of bourgeois democracy as were the fascists. Sure enough, KPD violence quickly escalated during the summer of 1931, when Communist street battles with the authorities led to the death of four police officers. The violence reached a crescendo in August with the assassination of two police captains. Nazi strategists also understood popular attitudes well enough to know that most civilians would overlook right-wing provocation and blame the Communists for Germany's descent into terror-plagued lawlessness. In particular, the Nazis correctly guessed the impact on the public consciousness of the specter of a left-wing revolution, which grew in the public's imagination with the KPD's increasingly belligerent rhetoric and violence.

Brownshirt terrorism and street violence served another purpose, though. The marches, uniforms, blood, and glory – in sum, the conscious evocation of *Fronterlebnis* – reinforced the collective identity of the stormtroopers, even though by 1933 only about a quarter of their number were actual veterans of the Great War (Merkl, "Approaches to Political Violence," 379). Such was the power of a romantic image. This image also appealed to the politically uncommitted workers who would otherwise have gravitated toward the KPD. Finally, Nazi terrorism was intended to provoke the government into undermining democracy itself, by using harsh, authoritarian measures that would cripple the Reichstag and the Weimar constitution. This was street theatre at its most manipulative and comprehensive, for the Nazis thought in terms of at least four audiences: the far left, the broad public, the unaffiliated worker, and governmental authorities.

Nazi strategy did not need to be embraced or even recognized by the Brownshirts' leaders or storm troopers to be effective. Like anarchist terrorism in Russia and Europe at the turn of the century, hatred and violence had become the means and ends of the SA's worldview. This meant that the Brownshirts were particularly prone to manipulation at the hands of Hitler, who, for all his rhetoric, remained fixated on the seizure of power above all else.

In an important way, Nazi leaders and Brownshirt thugs shared the belief that any incident that struck down the possibility of democratic normalcy was a positive development. Nazi-initiated street terror – and the inevitable communist rejoinder – did just that. By late 1930, the horrified SPD accepted the leadership of what became a string of conservative chancellors who promised to re-establish law and order. That December, Chancellor Heinrich Brüning issued the first of what became many emergency decrees that marked a steady advance to authoritarian rule. Socialist support – tepid as it was – was not returned in kind. After the enormous street-fighting casualties of July 1932, Chancellor Fritz von Papen unilaterally unseated the SPD-run Prussian state government and arrested its members as Communist sympathizers unwilling to crack down on the violence. During the Papen Coup, the chancellor – a conservative opposed to the Nazis – had simultaneously undermined Weimar constitutionalism and validated the Nazis' claim to be defending the "true" Germany.

In a desperate bid to draw on the Nazis' sizable support and simultaneously defang Hitler by making him a part of the system, von Papen and other conservatives convinced Weimar President Paul von Hindenburg to name Hitler as chancellor in January 1933. Overnight, gangs of Brownshirts lost all semblance of restraint and attacked meetings, offices, and homes associated with the SPD, KPD, and trade unions. On February 5, a Nazi murdered the SPD mayor of Stassfurt. Two weeks later, the Brownshirts were declared to be auxiliary police in Prussia and could thus act with impunity. The ensuing wave of terror was the best indicator yet of the sort of state the Nazis would establish.

The Nazi State

Hitler's initial victory was far from total, however. Most of his cabinet ministers were from other parties, and the Nazis did not have a majority in the Reichstag. What Hitler needed was a dramatic event to mobilize his supporters, terrify his opponents, and stampede those in the middle into his arms. It was provided for him by Marinus van der Lubbe, a young Dutch immigrant who had rejected communist revolution in favor of anarcho-syndicalist propaganda of the deed. Despondent at the recent success of the nationalists, van der Lubbe set fire to the Reichstag on

February 27, 1933. He was quickly captured by the police who easily determined that van der Lubbe had acted alone.

Figure 10.2: The German Reichstag on fire, February 1933
(© Roger-Viollet/Rex Features)

The Nazis reacted as if it was entirely otherwise. Hermann Göring, later Hitler's second-in-command, hysterically claimed that it was the start of a communist campaign of terrorism that would destroy public buildings and electrical works, "poison public kitchens," and take hostages (quoted in Evans, *The Coming of the Third Reich*, 333). Hitler himself screeched, "This is a God-given signal . . . ! If this fire, as I believe, is the work of the Communists, then we must crush out this murderous pest with an iron fist!" (quoted in Kershaw, *Hubris*, 458). The next day, Hitler issued an emergency decree – a power given him by the Weimar constitution – that suspended all civil liberties and dramatically expanded the police's powers. The authorities quickly arrested thousands of communists, socialists, and trade-union activists, many of whom disappeared into the Brownshirts' torture cellars. The emergency decree and the terrorism scare helped the Nazis come close to winning an absolute majority in March's parliamentary elections. Weimar's end and the beginning of Hitler's dictatorship came later in the month when the cowed Reichstag, made compliant through the expulsion of all KPD deputies in the wake of the Reichstag fire, handed over all legislative authority to the chancellor in the co-called Enabling Act. The Nazis' claim that the nation was threatened by terrorism had temporarily neutralized Hitler's opposition and handed him the keys to the country.

The last impediments to a Hitler dictatorship were soon gone. In June 1934, in what has come to be called "the Night of the Long Knives," Hitler arrested and quickly executed dozens of his opponents, include Brownshirt leaders who posed a threat to his domination of the Party. Membership in the Brownshirts quickly began to ebb, although many of its members most skilled at spreading terror found new work in Nazi Germany's security organizations, particularly the Gestapo, which now used terror against the Nazis' enemies as a matter of state policy. The terrorists had become the enactors of state terror.

Nazi dogma was soon enacted into law. Opposition parties, most quickly those of the left, were abolished and their members declared criminals. Many were arrested and sent to concentration camps, the first of which, Dachau, was established less than two months after Hitler became chancellor. Step by step, laws stripped Jews and other "racial enemies" of their citizenship, civil rights, and professional opportunities. The Gestapo and its sister organization, the Sicherheitsdienst (Security Service), recruited thousands of informers to collect information on the Reich's enemies. Germans soon came to dread the knock on the door in the middle of the night, just as their ideological enemies, the Soviets, did. Street terror was largely replaced by judicial and police terror, although the Nazis still made room for the former. The bloodiest and most notorious occasion was the Night of Broken Glass (*Kristallnacht*) in November 1938, a state-sponsored pogrom carried out by Brownshirts, the police, and civilian mobs against Jews and their property. Dozens were killed and thirty thousand detained at least briefly in concentration camps. Perhaps 7,500 businesses were damaged or destroyed, as were approximately 1,500 synagogues. The pretext for the rampage was the assassination of Ernst vom Rath, an official in Germany's Parisian embassy, by a German-Polish Jew whose family had been forcibly deported from Germany. Ironically, Rath was not a Nazi; yet his death was useful to the Nazis, who characterized his murder as part of an immense Jewish terrorist conspiracy against the German people. *Kristallnacht* was undoubtedly a realization of Hitler's ideological hatred that was, in part, bound up with the political uses of scapegoats and red herrings. But Nazi terror against Jews and other "undesirables" served other purposes. When German Jews were driven to emigrate by state terror – as thousands were – they sold their property to their neighbors at vastly undervalued prices, paid exorbitant sums for exit papers, and cleared the way for business competitors, who gladly gave their support to the Nazis.

The Second World War changed everything by providing the pretext and the cover for far more violent policies. By the time of the German invasion of the Soviet Union in June 1941, the Nazi program of state terror against Jews and communists had grown into something well beyond the symbolism and violence of the terror-drenched 1930s. It had erupted into full-blown genocide. Like the Ukrainian famine of 1932–3 that killed three to four million people, the goal of the Holocaust – which claimed the lives of approximately six million Jews and five million other enemies of Nazism – was no symbolic exercise in terror. Its aim was the complete eradication of entire categories of people. This was something never imagined by the Jacobins – the purported godfathers of twentieth-century totalitarianism.

The start of the Second World War did not put an end to German efforts to use the term "terrorist" to justify the harsh treatment of non-combatants. For example, in June 1942, the Nazi Security Service published a directive authorizing the use of "third degree" methods – that is, torture – against "Communists, Marxists, Jehovah's Witnesses, saboteurs, terrorists, members of resistance movements, parachute agents, anti-social elements, [and] Polish or Soviet Russian loafers or tramps" (*Trial of the Major War Criminals before the International Military Tribunal at Nuremberg*, 42 vols, 1947–9, 1:243). In particular, the Nazis routinely labeled members of the French Resistance "terrorists."

Even in its death throes, the Nazi regime held fast to its use of terror when it developed Operation Werewolf. This was a "stay-behind" force meant to continue the war through guerrilla fighting and terrorist strikes after Germany's official surrender. Perhaps five or six thousand soldiers were trained and armed for this operation, but German officials actually dismantled the program in the weeks between Hitler's suicide and the eventual Nazi surrender, probably out of eagerness to win favor with their captors. Out of perhaps five thousand casualties inflicted by Werewolf agents, almost all came before the war ended. Their highest profile killing was the March 1945 assassination of the American-appointed mayor of Aachen, one of the first cities to be captured by the Allied forces in Western Germany. Stories about Operation Werewolf did generate some fear among the public, but its military importance was trivial. Werewolf is most significant as another reminder of the fanaticism and surreality of the Nazi elite and as inspiration it provided for some post-war neo-Nazi groups.

A powerful example of the extent to which the word "terrorism" has been invested with meaning outside the normally recognized definitions of the term comes to us via the Nuremberg Trials. The Allies had two goals in these proceedings: to hold accountable the most important captured members of the Nazi regime, and to document for posterity the extent of their war crimes and crimes against humanity. "Terrorism" figures prominently in the enumeration of those crimes. Quite appropriately, the Nazis were accused of conspiring "to undermine and overthrow the German Government by 'legal' forms supported by terrorism." This falls in line with Brownshirt "street terror" and Nazi terrorism as a strategy in the party's bid for power. Elsewhere in the indictment and guilty verdicts, however, the word "terrorism" is used interchangeably with the distinct concept "state terror." Concentration camps, for instance, are described "as a fixed part of the terroristic policy and method of the conspirators." Elsewhere, "terrorism" simply becomes a synonym for violence and brutality, such as in the Allies' description of the orders issued to Wehrmacht field commanders that "troops should use terrorism" against "civilians suspected of offenses against troops." The Allied judges at Nuremberg found Nazi leaders guilty of using "terrorism" against civilians in Denmark, Poland, Bohemia and Moravia, and the Netherlands. And as far as the Soviet judge was concerned, the entire "Hitlerian . . . regime" was "terroristic." (*Trial of the Major War Criminals before the International Military Tribunal at Nuremberg*, 42 vols, 1947–9, 1:31–3, 46, 290, 298, 301, 329, 350). This is, in fact, the impression created by the trial record as a whole, so frequent and generic is the use of the word "terrorism." In the opinion of the judges and witnesses, "terrorism" was a fundamental feature of Nazi ideology, practice, and strategy, from the 1920s to the Third Reich's demise in 1945.

Bibliography

The most balanced and comprehensive work on the Russian Revolution is Orlando Figes, *A People's Tragedy: The Russian Revolution: 1891–1924* (Penguin, 1998 [1997]). Also valuable but more polemical is Richard Pipes, *The Russian Revolution* (Vintage, 1990). An excellent volume on the Soviet secret police and its role in political terror is George Leggett, *The Cheka: Lenin's Political Police* (Clarendon Press, 1981). The best biography of Stalin is Robert Service, *Stalin: A Biography* (Harvard University Press, 2004). On the murder of Kirov, see Amy Knight, *Who Killed Kirov?: The Kremlin's Greatest Mystery* (Hill and Wang, 1999). There are many excellent books on the Great Terror. Two of the most valuable are Robert Conquest, *The Great Terror: A Reassessment* (Oxford University Press, 2007); and J. Arch Getty and Oleg V. Naumov, eds., *The Road to Terror: Stalin and the Self-Destruction of the Bolsheviks, 1932–1939* (Yale University Press, 1999). For an accessible and comprehensive history of the Soviet labor camps, see Anne Applebaum, *Gulag: A History* (Doubleday, 2003).

On Mussolini and the Italian fascists, see Denis Mack Smith, *Mussolini* (Vintage, 1983 [1982]); and Jens Petersen, "Violence in Italian Fascism, 1919–25," in Mommsen and Hirschfeld, eds., *Social Protest, Violence and Terror in Nineteenth- and Twentieth-Century Europe*.

Few topics have been written about more than Hitler and Nazi Germany. The best of a rich and ever-growing body of literature is Richard J. Evans' trilogy, *The Coming of the Third Reich*, *The Third Reich in Power*, and *The Third Reich at War* (Penguin, 2003, 2005, 2009); and Ian Kershaw, *Hitler*, 2 vols. (Norton, 1998, 2000). Also valuable are William Sheridan Allen, *The Nazi Seizure of Power: The Experience of a Single German Town, 1922–1945*, rev. edn. (Franklin Watts, 1984); and William L. Shirer, *The Rise and Fall of the Third Reich* (Ballantine Books, 1960 [1950]).

Mommsen and Hirschfeld's edited volume, *Social Protest*, contains three excellent chapters on political violence and terrorism in Weimar Germany: David B. Southern, "Anti-Democratic Terror in the Weimar Republic: the Black *Reichswehr* and the *Feme*-Murders"; Peter H. Merkl, "Approaches to Political Violence: the Stormtroopers, 1925–33"; and Eve Rosenhaft, "The KPD in the Weimar Republic and the Problem of Terror during the 'Third Period', 1929–33." The best single-volume treatment of Weimar Germany is Detlev J. K. Peukert, *The Weimar Republic* (Hill and Wang, 1993 [1987]).

11

Decolonization and Ethno-Nationalist Terrorism from the 1930s to the Early 1960s

Organizations using terrorism in pursuit of ethno-nationalist goals differ in substantial ways from groups whose motivation is primarily religious or ideological. While their appeal might be narrower, depending on the size of the ethnic group, there are usually more opportunities for finding diehard support. This is one reason why such campaigns tend to last longer than those otherwise motivated – witness the longevity of struggles over Palestine, Northern Ireland, the Tamil region of Sri Lanka, and the Basque region of Spain. Another difference is the purpose behind the violent acts. While ethno-nationalist terrorism retains its symbolic character, its message is somewhat different, for every attack is in part meant to communicate the existence and essence of ethnic identity. Provocation remains a goal, as well, but the audience is often different: ethno-nationalists, like ideologically or politically minded terrorists, seek polarizing reactions from governments but are usually more interested in provoking violent responses from other ethnic populations. Such violence tends to destroy the possibility of a negotiated settlement, since it serves to discredit moderates as temporizing politicians uncommitted to real change, while forcing complete ruptures between overlapping or neighboring ethnic groups. On all sides of such ethnic cleavages, violence produces fear which inflames xenophobia, ethnic identity, and radical commitments.

Varieties of Ethno-Nationalist Terrorism

Although there is tremendous variation among ethno-nationalist proponents of terrorism, they nonetheless fall into two groups. The first are groups fighting for an end to their colonial status. A good example was the struggle to eject the French from Algeria. In these cases, terrorist violence is often part of a broader guerrilla war – sometimes characterized as a revolution – but violence is usually confined "over there" to the colonial possession. A frequent complicating factor is the presence of settlers who have come to see the territory as their own native soil and birthright. Nonetheless, anti-colonial struggles often are resolved when the mother country reaches the conclusion that its continued presence is no longer worth the price. The second category includes those organizations fighting for independence or autonomy within a larger state's "home" borders, such as in the case of the Basques of Spain or the Palestinians in Israel and Jordan. Sometimes the fighting can reach the level of full-blown civil or separatist war, but typically terrorism remains the critical means of waging the struggle. These are the most intractable of terrorist crises since independence is usually not regarded as a possible option by the larger country. The troubles in Northern Ireland, one might say, combine the worst elements of both sorts of ethno-nationalist conflict.

The Waning and Waxing of Ethno-Nationalist Terrorism

To understand the impact of the emergence of ethno-nationalist terrorism, we must remind ourselves of the conditions in the 1930s, when such struggles were rare. Mired in depression, teetering on the brink of the Great Purges, the Holocaust, and the Second World War, and awestruck before the might of the era's great states, Europeans should probably be forgiven for thinking that all varieties of small group terrorism had become a thing of the past. In the United States, leftist terrorism and the second Red Scare closely linked to it had become distant memories. The Great Depression triggered massive state intervention and large-scale labor organization, moves that seemed to bid farewell to the fringe individualism associated with terrorism. Academics shared this belief. In an article on terrorism in the 1933 *Encyclopedia of the Social Sciences*, Jacob Hardman argued that terrorism had become "outmoded as a revolutionary method," something "irrelevant and unnecessary" (quoted in Zulaika and Douglass, *Terror and Taboo*, 17).

While this was to prove not the case, a shift was clearly taking place. With the exception of those groups and movements examined in Chapter 9, terrorism had mostly been associated with revolutionary ideological causes, such as democracy, anarchism, and socialism, for a century or more. From the 1930s onward, sub-state terrorism – as opposed to the violence associated with state terror – was largely a tactic adopted by those pursuing the creation of independent nation-states. What had been a minor trend late in the nineteenth century was to become the dominant motive behind the use of terrorism during the middle decades of the twentieth century.

Two developments sparked global anti-colonial activity and "third world" independence movements, trends that were accompanied by much ethno-nationalist terrorism. The first was Japanese success during the Second World War against Britain, Holland, France, and the United States in Southeast Asia and the Pacific. Overwhelming Japanese military victories – even if they were only temporary – destroyed the perception of Western imperial invincibility. The second factor was the United States' increasingly vocal denunciation of European empire-building. During the First World War, President Woodrow Wilson called for national self-determination in his Fourteen Points, a demand echoed by President Franklin Delano Roosevelt in the Atlantic Charter of 1940. The United Nations charter in 1945 came out even more unmistakably in favor of the cultivation of an international community of equals. In the end, this could only highlight the hypocrisy of Western states, which, despite their own belief in human and civil rights and the rule of law, continued to embrace the dream of empire and hold blatantly racist attitudes toward the non-Western world.

In any case, the primary colonial powers, Britain and France, were in no position to retain their African and Asian possessions against determined opposition after the Second World War. Both countries were deeply in debt and faced the daunting task of recovering from the war. In Britain, the Labour Party's victory and its attendant plans for the construction of a welfare state accentuated the emphasis on domestic rebuilding rather than colonial maintenance. French leaders were far less inclined to abandon the concept of a Greater France, but were resigned to at least a reapportioning of resources – witness the ease and lack of protest when France quickly granted independence to Morocco and Tunisia in the mid 1950s, but not until after a lengthy war to preserve its hold on French Indochina and the escalation of the Algerian War for Independence (see below).

Palestine: Arab, Jew, and Briton

The first stirrings of anti-colonial struggle began while the Great Powers still remained committed to empire. There were isolated examples of terrorism against the British and their local collaborators in Egypt in the 1910s and 1920s. The first organized ethno-nationalist terrorists in the area were not Arabs, but Jews motivated by Zionism, a program of Jewish nationalism that imagined the land of Israel as a divinely promised homeland in which Jews could be a majority and thus organize their own state and their own defense. Zionism was a natural response to the rising tide of state-sponsored nationalism in the late nineteenth century, but it was also a reaction to institutionalized anti-Semitism and pogroms against which Jews seemed quite helpless as minority populations.

The Allied dismemberment of the Ottoman Turkish Empire after the First World War and the British government's Balfour Declaration endorsing the creation of a Jewish homeland sparked a new wave of Zionist emigration to Palestine. By the time Palestine began to be directly administered by the United Kingdom in 1923, less than fifteen per cent of the local population was Jewish. Angered by the indefinite delay to their own independence, Arabs found the small but growing Jewish community a convenient target for their wrath. Arab attacks grew in number and ferocity, prompting the formation in 1921 of Haganah ("Defense" in Hebrew), a self-defense militia to protect immigrant Jews from the occasional eruption of Arab violence. Hoping to prevent the escalation of violence, Haganah avoided reprisals against Arab civilians.

Irgun and LEHI

A number of factors led to dramatic changes by the late 1930s. The rapidly increasing number of Jews, in part fed by growing persecution in Europe, led to more Zionist militancy and more tension between Palestine's populations. Prompted by the outbreak of the Arab Revolt in 1936 and more anti-Semitic violence, the Polish militant Ze'ev Jabotinsky and his followers formed Irgun Zvai Le'umi ("the National Military Organization"), better known simply as Irgun. Members were divided over who was the group's true enemy, the British or Arabs. One Irgun leader asserted that "we must create a situation whereby killing an Arab is like killing a rat, where Arabs are dirt, thereby showing that we and not they are the power to be reckoned with" (quoted in Levine, *The Birth of the Irgun Zvai Leumi*, 134). Not surprisingly, Irgun, which represented a tiny minority of opinion within Jewish Palestine, soon began to carry out reprisals against Arab civilians for attacks on Jews. This quickly escalated into a full-fledged campaign of terrorism, peaking in July 1938 with market bombings that killed seventy-two Arabs and wounded 154. The *Palestine Post* presciently editorialized, "What surer way of spreading the seed of inter-racial war than to make every Arab believe that each Jew is his enemy" (quoted in Levine, *The Birth of the*

Irgun Zvai Leumi, 137). But this was, in fact, Irgun's strategy. If, so its leaders thought, enough Arabs could be coaxed into reacting to Zionist terrorism, perhaps the entire Jewish population could be roused to heroic self-defense and Zionist victory.

Keen to preserve one of its strongholds in the oil-rich Middle East, the United Kingdom sought to mollify both sides. In hindsight, a tightrope act between hostile foes was probably doomed to fail. Sure enough, the leadership of Irgun came to believe that Britain was the greatest impediment to the formation of a Jewish state, particularly after the British decided in May 1939 to limit severely Jewish immigration to Palestine for five years and curtail it entirely in 1944. The UK's ill-timed effort to curry Arab favor and punish Irgun terrorism came at just the moment when European Jews were most in need of a safe haven from rising Nazi violence. While still carrying out attacks against Arabs, Irgun began terrorist operations against British infrastructure in an effort to force them to rescind the new quotas. When the Second World War broke out in September 1939, Irgun leaders declared a ceasefire against the British that they said would last as long as the Nazis constituted a danger.

Dissident members of Irgun who refused to end the struggle against Britain formed the splinter group LEHI (from the Hebrew acronym for "Fighters for the Freedom of Israel"). LEHI's charismatic leader was Avraham Stern, and it was as the Stern Gang that the group was known to the British. Stern understood LEHI's struggle as a direct continuation of that waged by the Sicarii almost two millennia earlier – a conviction so great that Stern adopted the new name of Yair after the Sicarii's messianic leader. LEHI carried out attacks against British soldiers, police, and infrastructure, as well as Jewish collaborators throughout the war, killing at least forty Britons, Arabs, and Jews from 1939 to 1944. Although its tactics often bore a closer resemblance to what is normally called guerrilla war, the LEHI leader Yitzhak Shamir, a future prime minister of Israel, openly embraced the word terrorism. "Neither Jewish ethics nor Jewish tradition can disqualify terrorism as a means of combat," he stated in 1943. "[T]errorism is for us a part of the political battle being conducted under the present circumstances, and it has a great part to play: speaking in a clear voice to the whole world, as well as to our wretched brethren outside this land, it proclaims our war against the occupier" (quoted in Lustick, "Terrorism in the Arab–Israeli Conflict," 527). Shamir cited Michael Collins, the IRA's military leader during the Black and Tan War, as a particular influence.

LEHI continued operations against Britain throughout the war and then fought alongside Irgun when that group ended its ceasefire against the United Kingdom in early 1944. There were many reasons for Irgun's decision. The likelihood of Allied victory had become overwhelming, the full monstrosity of the Holocaust was coming to light, and Britain's five-year window for Jewish immigration was about to close. The decision to resume anti-British terrorism was not welcomed by most Jews. Moderate elements within Haganah and the Jews' semi-autonomous government, the Jewish Agency, repeatedly denounced Zionist terrorism as counterproductive. After two LEHI agents assassinated Britain's senior official in Cairo in November 1944, the Jewish Agency even cooperated with the British authorities for six months in hunting down Irgun and LEHI fighters. By the summer of 1945, Irgun operations were once again in full swing under the leadership of Menachem Begin, another future prime minister of Israel. Haganah and the Jewish Agency were playing a double game, in fact, for they occasionally carried out their own raids against the British and for a time worked with Irgun and LEHI, in part to keep the militants in their own ranks from defecting to the groups that openly embraced terrorism.

The Strategy behind Zionist Terror

Irgun was always the driving force behind Zionist terrorism. The group had at most four or five thousand members, but magnified its impact through the savvy use of violence, which Begin learned by closely studying the history of the Russian revolutionary movement and the IRA. By channeling these earlier terrorists, Irgun exercised tremendous influence on later generations of ethno-nationalist freedom fighters, becoming the model for terrorists from Southeast Asia to Africa and the Middle East – including the Palestine Liberation Organization – to the later struggles in Northern Ireland. Begin's memoir detailing his participation in Irgun has even been studied by al-Qaeda (Wright, *The Looming Tower*, 303).

Begin recognized that the British had more soldiers, guns, and money and resolved to take advantage of those categories in which Irgun enjoyed superiority: resolve, knowledge of local terrain, and a well of civilian frustration and anger. The goal was not the military defeat of the United Kingdom, but its ability to govern Palestine effectively. Begin later wrote in his memoir about Irgun, "History and experience taught us that if we are able to destroy the prestige of the British in the land of Israel, the removal of its rule would follow automatically" (quoted in Hoffman, *The Failure of British Military Strategy*, 50). Irgun's leaders understood that the group's mere survival posed a critical danger to the United Kingdom, for it undermined the image of British omnipotence and required the British to appear increasingly as occupiers. Attacks were designed to force the British on to the defensive, so that the basic functioning of government became impossible behind rows of soldiers and barbed wire. LEHI operated on this principle, as well. In 1944, its newspaper announced to its enemy, "This is how you British will walk the streets of Zion from now on: armed to the teeth, prepared for anything and fear in your eyes: fear from every dark corner, in every turn in the road, every sound at night, fear from every Jewish boy, fear day and night because the Jewish youth have become dynamite in this country" (quoted in Taber, *War of the Flea*, 110). Jewish terrorists strove to turn Britain's strengths against it, understanding that a liberal democracy based on the rule of law would find the draconian means necessary to fight terrorism increasingly unpalatable.

Two factors contributed to the success of the Irgun-LEHI strategy and repeatedly gave hope to the movements around the world that it influenced. The first was the development of portable, highly destructive weapons and their easier availability during and after the Second World War. Of particular importance was the development of the submachine gun, a light, short-range weapon capable of automatic fire using pistol ammunition. The outstanding examples were the American "Tommy" gun – beloved of gangsters – and the British Sten. Even in the hands of poorly trained guerrillas and terrorists, submachine guns could produce a withering hail of fire, particularly in close, urban environments. On several occasions, Irgun's revolt was rejuvenated by shipments of cheap handguns, rifles, submachine guns, and explosives from Europe.

The second factor was the creation of the United Nations. Just as important as its mandate – described earlier – was its presence as a new international forum to which every country could gain access. Unlike the League of Nations, which tended to operate like an international old boys' club, this new forum was available to nations great and small, developed and developing. Furthermore, sub-state ethno-nationalist groups quickly grasped that the UN could function as an enormous megaphone, if only its ear could be caught. For Irgun – and countless groups that followed in its wake – violence became the most important and immediate way of doing so. This was nothing new. The Internal Macedonian Revolutionary Organization, for example, had pinned their hopes on drawing the rest of Europe into their struggles many decades earlier. What was different in the 1940s and beyond was the development of more international newsgathering organizations, as well as the emergence of new technologies for recording and disseminating sounds and images to statesmen and civilians around the world. "We knew," Begin wrote, "that [the land of Israel], in consequence of the revolt, resembled a glass house. The world was looking into it with ever-increasing interest and could see most of what was happening inside" (quoted in Hoffman, *The Failure of British Military Strategy*, 52). And the world responded.

The US Congress passed a resolution condemning Britain's behavior, and the newly formed United Nations began to consider self-government for Palestine. The UN body charged with investigating the region even met with Begin twice. And even as Irgun used terrorism to convince the British of the high cost of their continued occupation of Palestine, its leaders appreciated terrorism as a means of communicating the spirit of resistance to Jews. "There are times," Begin wrote, "when everything in you cries out: your very self-respect as a human being lies in your resistance to evil. *We fight, therefore we are!*" (quoted in Lustick, "Terrorism in the Arab–Israeli Conflict," 526). Irgun, therefore, constantly acted with four audiences in mind: Palestinian Jews, the British colonial administration, British public opinion, and international opinion.

The Impact of Zionist Terror

From 1945 to 1948, Irgun fighters attacked police and military outposts, assassinated British officials, destroyed infrastructure, and assaulted the symbols of Britain's presence, including the much-hated immigration, land registry, and tax offices. One attack on an airfield claimed twenty-two RAF planes, while another series of coordinated operations killed or wounded about eighty British soldiers on a single day (Asprey, *War in the Shadows*, II:776, 780). British officials lived in terror, and every other aspect of British administration of the Palestine Mandate took a backseat to the struggle against Irgun and LEHI. The UK's efforts grew increasingly desperate. In January 1946, for example, new emergency laws for Palestine introduced the death penalty for membership in a terrorist group. Such behavior drove some uncommitted Palestinian Jews into the arms of Shamir and Begin, but, in a development reminiscent of the relationship between Gandhi and Indian extremists, primarily bolstered the standing of the Jewish Agency as a less violent political alternative to Zionist terrorism and British occupation.

The peak of violence came in July 1946, when Irgun operatives smuggled seven milk churns full of explosives into the basement of Jerusalem's King David Hotel, the British headquarters in Palestine. A telephone warning to evacuate the building was ignored, and the ensuing explosion killed ninety-one and injured forty-five. Among the victims were British officials, soldiers, and police, as well as Jewish and Arab civilians. As in Ireland thirty years earlier, the British squandered an opportunity to garner good will by engaging in ham-fisted operations that punished the entire population in pursuit of a small minority. In this instance, the British launched a new round of particularly broad cordon and

Figure 11.1: The King David Hotel in Jerusalem, after Irgun bombing, July 1946
(Wikimedia Commons)

search operations that arrested thousands of people but netted only
one terrorist, Yitzhak Shamir. An Irgun attack on the British embassy
in Rome even fueled rumors of assassination plots against London officials and politicians, including the prime minister. Meanwhile, Irgun
and LEHI relentlessly attacked British police and army installations. In
January 1947, LEHI used the world's first true truck bomb, driving one
into a British police outpost, killing four and injuring 140 (Davis, 4).

Zionist Success

The cost of staying in Palestine seemed less and less reasonable to British civilians still on wartime rationing. The idea of becoming forced into waging war against Palestine's civilian population so soon after the Holocaust struck many as particularly repugnant. Winston Churchill, by now the leader of the opposition, lamented in January 1947, "This is a conflict with the terrorists, and no country in the world is less fit for a conflict with terrorists than Great Britain. That is not because of her weakness or cowardice; it is because of her restraint and virtues, and the way of life which we have lived so long in this sheltered island . . . [It would be] impossible for us to imitate the mass extermination methods of the Germans" (quoted in Zadka, *Blood in Zion*, 6). But some British authorities disliked the use of the word terrorism, since it suggested that British military forces could be "terrorized" by a rag-tag band of insurgents. The government tried, in fact, to ban the local administration's use of the word terrorism in 1947, but to no avail.

In July 1947, the British hanged three Irgun gunmen captured during a massive jailbreak of their colleagues in Acre. Irgun immediately retaliated by kidnapping and hanging two British army sergeants. British papers ran photos of the dead soldiers and denounced the Irgun murders as barbarous, with one going so far as to compare it to Nazi atrocities. Anti-Semitic riots broke out in several British towns and cities. In Palestine, the frustration and anger of British police and troops boiled over; five Jews were killed and fifteen wounded when armored cars opened fire on civilians in Tel Aviv. Jewish respect and acceptance of the British was in tatters. The *Manchester Guardian* carried an editorial that pointedly announced "Time to Go" (Bell, *Zion*, 238–9). Given Britain's post-war budgetary pinch, the cost of maintaining a presence in Palestine now seemed hard to justify. By the end of the summer, the British had endorsed UN plans to end the Mandate and were preparing to abandon the territory to its fate.

The Creation of Israel

Palestine's Jews accepted the UN partition plan that would have created two new states, one Jewish and one Arab, but the latter community rejected it. As it became clear that there would be war, Irgun and LEHI increasingly carried out open paramilitary actions and reprisals against Arabs, who themselves were increasingly taking the offensive against both Jewish civilians and soldiers. The result was a spiraling cycle of terror and counter-terror. Meanwhile, the British prepared for their withdrawal from Palestine, which occurred in May 1948, without establishing any official local governmental institutions. The Jewish community declared the creation of the state of Israel, and Palestine's Arab neighbors – Egypt, Jordan, Syria, Iraq, and Lebanon – promptly invaded. For a time, Irgun and LEHI continued to operate as independent units, but they eventually integrated into the state's new army, the Israel Defense Forces (IDF). The war between Israel and the surrounding Arab states ended with a decisive Israeli victory but no peace agreements, only an exhausted ceasefire.

Arabs called their defeat by Israel and the resultant flood of refugees the *Nakba* or "Disaster" – and with good reason, as over 700,000 Palestinians, that is, more than half the pre-war Arab population of Palestine, became refugees in neighboring Arab states, particularly Jordan. Israeli politicians and historians have maintained until recently that the crisis was a result of deliberate Arab efforts to clear the battlefield, while Arabs have argued that it was a consequence of Zionist terrorism and forced evacuations by the IDF. The most likely answer is that Palestinian flight was a product of a number of factors, including the chaos of war, some forced evacuations, and the ineffective Arab military effort. Whatever the truth may be, Palestinian victimhood and Israeli perfidy have become mainstays of pro-Palestinian propaganda and perpetual justifications for Palestinian terrorism against both Israel and those Arab states deemed insufficiently helpful. In fact, the story of Palestinian martyrdom has become so useful in the fierce rivalries among Arab states that it remains an impediment itself to the resolution of the Israeli–Arab struggle. Likewise, the Israelis long made use of Arab violence and the threat of violence. In 1955, Moshe Dayan, the legendary army chief of staff, said to Israeli diplomats, "We have to cry out that the Negev is in danger, so that young men will go there" (quoted in Lustick, "Terrorism in the Arab–Israeli Conflict," 533).

The Cold War, Marxism, and Ethno-Nationalist Movements

Anti-colonialism in the post-war period, like everything else, was heavily influenced by the Cold War, which shaped all international relations during the second half of the twentieth century. During the Cold War most of the developed world was divided into armed camps centered on the United States on the one hand, and the Soviet Union and China (themselves first as uneasy allies and later as enemies) on the other. Terrorism came to play an important, if secondary, role in the Cold War. Previous generations of terrorists had often espoused socialist agendas, but what was new was the frequency with which subject peoples hoping to achieve independence from their colonial overlords embraced Marxism. On the surface, this was an odd pairing, since Marxists typically denounced nationalism as a bourgeois device used to distract workers from their genuine economic interests. However, during the Cold War, both the Soviets and the Chinese preached Marxism as a doctrine of national liberation. Nikita Khrushchev, the Soviet leader from 1953 to 1964, emphasized the rhetorical links between national and economic liberation out of idealism and in order to gain allies in the unaligned "Third" World.

Mao Zedong, the leader of the Chinese Communist Party from the 1930s until his death in 1976, forged a link in practice. He developed a three-stage model for the seizure of power patterned after his Party's own revolutionary trajectory in the 1930s and 1940s, one appropriate to China's largely agrarian population. In a much quoted metaphor, Mao likened the people to water and guerrillas to the fish who swim in it. As he described it, first, small bands of rural fighters would wage guerrilla war against enemy forces in a bid to wear down the opposition and develop a following among the peasantry. Second, larger guerrilla forces set up bases and liberated zones, while more closely coordinating their attacks on government troops. Finally, guerrillas coalesce into more conventional armies, defeat enemy troops and seize the cities, thus capping the revolution. This strategy was widely adopted throughout the world, including in Cuba and Latin America by the infamous revolutionary Che Guevara. While neither Mao nor Che explicitly called for the use of terrorism, many grasped its appropriateness for the first stage of establishing the legitimacy of the cause, attracting adherents, and intimidating the opposition. Even where the Soviets or the Chinese did not directly back communist insurgencies, the era's ideologically charged atmosphere, as well as the growing understanding of the United States and its allies as first and foremost economic powers, led many ethno-nationalist insurgencies to embrace communism, particularly Maoism, as a natural framework for pursuing independence.

Malaya and the Communist Terrorists

This was the case in the Southeast Asian colony of Malaya, where a communist insurgency that erupted in 1947 became significant for two reasons. First, the insurgency demonstrated how terrorism could become the backbone of an ethno-nationalist revolution – even more than in Palestine – and second, it led to the development of highly effective strategies for combating insurgency and terrorism. Malaya, a British colony since the eighteenth century, was one of the United Kingdom's most profitable possessions because of its vast resources of tin and rubber.

It was the fall of its most important city, Singapore, to the Japanese in 1942 that was the watershed blow against the illusion of European colonial invincibility. During the war, the British enlisted the Malayan Communist Party (MCP) in the fight against the Japanese and trained two hundred of its members in the deadly art of irregular warfare. The MCP's leader was the ethnically Chinese Chin Peng, who was regarded as such a valuable asset by the British that he was decorated with the Order of the British Empire. When the British returned at the end of the war, however, the MCP dedicated itself to the creation of an independent, communist Malaya. The MCP was really Malayan in name only, since it agitated almost exclusively among the territory's sizable Chinese community, whose members were typically poorer, less educated, and owned less land than the Malayan ethnic majority.

Chin chose to follow Mao's three-stage strategy, but substituted terrorism for the traditional guerrilla campaign. The distinction, in this case, was twofold: first, the MCP targeted civilians and infrastructure more frequently than it did soldiers or even police; and second, violence served symbolic purposes designed to influence several audiences. In this regard, the MCP's efforts were more similar to Irgun's than the Chinese Communist Party's. The MCP hoped to undermine the economic basis of British colonialism through terror and win support from Malaya's poor Chinese population in preparation for a colony-wide popular uprising. MCP violence was carried out by three different bodies. The Malayan National Liberation Army consisted of three to four thousand jungle-based fighters, but was augmented by a much larger rural civilian paramilitary group and loosely organized bands of urban marauders. Chin's rural insurgents and urban terrorists sabotaged facilities associated with the rubber and tin industries, terrorized the Europeans who managed the plantations and mines, and assassinated Malayan officials and police constables. Paramilitary cells, which were embedded in villages throughout Malaya, supplied the MCP with intelligence, recruits, and supplies and conducted its own nighttime terror raids, primarily against local villagers who cooperated with the authorities. In 1948, the first full year of the insurrection, the MCP killed 315 civilians, most of whom were Chinese; eighty-nine policemen, most of whom were Malayan; and sixty soldiers, most of whom were British.

The Malayan Emergency and the Briggs Plan

The mounting violence led the British authorities in 1948 to declare a "state of emergency" that was to last for twelve years. New laws allowed the British and their Malayan allies to search suspects without warrant, indefinitely detain suspects, impose curfews, and levy harsh sentences against those who aided the insurgents. The initial British strategy for combating the insurgency, however, emphasized a military response. As a result, the UK dramatically increased its military presence, which topped out at about 55,000 British and Commonwealth troops. Hamstrung by a doctrinaire reliance on conventional tactics learned in the victory over the Japanese and Germans in the Second World War, the British sent battalion-sized units into the jungle to sweep wide swaths of territory or surround guerrilla camps. Since the British were typically armed with little or no intelligence, such operations yielded meager results. Likewise, British bombers carpet-bombed jungle targets, causing minimal damage to the MCP's highly mobile military units and bases. All the while, Chin stepped up the MCP's terrorist campaign, claiming over seven hundred victims in 1949. Throughout 1950 and 1951, the rate of carnage climbed even higher as the "Communist Terrorists," as they were known to the British, killed an average of about one hundred police and ninety civilians per month and caused property damage that ran into the tens of millions of dollars. Although the British and Malayan authorities were killing Communist Terrorists at a prodigious rate, the MCP was attracting far more recruits every month. The insurgency was threatening to destroy all confidence in the ability of the government to preserve order.

But the MCP's terrorist campaign had not yet provoked a mass uprising, and the British had not abandoned the colony, even as its profits steeply declined. Most importantly, British counterinsurgency strategy was undergoing a dramatic overhaul. The men responsible were the successive directors of operation in Malaya, General Sir Henry Briggs (who arrived in 1950) and General Sir Gerald Templer (in 1952). Briggs grasped the strategic aims of Maoist insurgency and channeled British resources into driving a wedge between the insurgents and the broader population. His goal was to separate the MCP from its sources of recruits, intelligence, shelter, food, and money – resources, without which, in the words of one contemporary commentator aware of Mao's famous dictum, "the guerrilla fighter, like a fish out of water, gasps helplessly until he dies" (quoted in Barber, *War of the Running Dogs*, 98).

The British generals understood that the struggle was principally one for the allegiance of Malaya's civilians, not its territory. "The answer," Templer wrote in 1952, coining what was to become an overused phrase in the half-century to come, "lies not in pouring more troops into the jungle, but in the hearts and minds of the people" (quoted in Clutterbuck, *The Long, Long War*, 3). This was a struggle for the perception of legitimacy. At the heart of what came to be known as the Briggs Plan was the resettlement of about 425,000 rural inhabitants, mostly landless Chinese, into "new villages." These settlements could be more effectively defended and, more importantly, gave the villagers a stake in the survival of the British and Malayan governments.

Other components of the Briggs Plan sought to preserve and heighten the government's legitimacy by improving the authorities' ability to target Communist Terrorists, while causing minimal damage to civilian populations. Thus, the gradual shift toward the use of small unit tactics rather than unwieldy and ineffective large army operations – ambushes rather than sweeps, for instance. The plan also called for much closer coordination of the activity of the police, army, and civil service. This produced more actionable intelligence, a commodity much in demand, since the information necessary for successful military operations tended to originate in police work or the civil service's contact with the population. Furthermore, while the British and Malayan authorities did make use of emergency decrees, they largely refused the temptation to act outside the law in their effort to combat terrorism. The colony's civil courts continued to function throughout the struggle against the MCP, thus preserving civilian faith in the legitimacy of the government.

A natural outgrowth of this cooperation between imperial and local authorities was the eventual British decision – in line with the UK's new post-war priorities – to grant independence to Malaya in 1957 (additional territories were later added leading to the creation of the Federation of Malaysia, the name by which the country is known today). Chin Peng and what by then was a small band of followers fled to Thailand and eventually China. In 1960, the Malayan government, still closely cooperating with the British, ended the state of emergency. Chin later tried to restart the insurgency, but found few willing to support him.

What led to British and Malayan success in defeating terrorism and insurgency in the 1950s? It certainly depended on the adoption of the new counter-terrorism strategy, which redefined victory against terrorism from exclusively military into primarily civil terms. The essential victories were not won on battlefields or through kill counts, but in the shifting perceptions of Malaya's population, particularly its Chinese component. The British and Malayans had to learn to keep the big picture in mind and stick to their plan, even when it looked as if they were making little headway. For instance, Communist-Terrorist attacks dramatically spiked in 1951. What could have been regarded as an MCP show of strength was instead seen for what it was: a wave of terror fueled by desperation, coming, as it did, in the immediate wake of the first efforts to relocate Chinese Malayans into the "new villages." The British and Malayans won by not seeking the MCP's surrender or elimination. Rather, they understood that the goal was the reduction of violence and terror to reasonable levels that would allow for a return to "normal" civilian rule. A critical factor was the almost exclusive link between the MCP and Malaya's Chinese minority, a landless population that was won over to the existing state authorities. Ethnic Malayans, the country's clear majority, resisted Chinese and MCP aspirations throughout the conflict and provided the United Kingdom with a largely loyal native population. Such caveats meant that the Briggs Plan, while providing insights, had not produced an easily transferrable blueprint for combating ethno-nationalist terrorism and insurgency elsewhere.

Kenya

Shortly after the MCP insurgency began in Malaya, the British faced another challenge to their empire in the East African colony of Kenya. The story of the British colonization of Kenya is a common one in those cases where Europeans decided to create a settler colony, not just a framework for the extraction of resources. The British arrived toward the end of the nineteenth century, seized the most productive land either by brute force or pseudo-legal means, and forced the indigenous peoples onto small "reserves" within their vast ancestral lands. Most Africans were exploited as virtual slave laborers in a system where thirty thousand Europeans effectively ruled five million black Kenyans. British administrators in distant London tried on occasion to moderate the worst aspects of colonial oppression, but were stymied by white settlers in Kenya eager to preserve their established hierarchy. Many white settlers insisted that they were there to civilize the natives, who were routinely celebrated as romantic, but fundamentally primitive savages easily roused to barbaric violence. Some black Kenyans accepted Western ways and Western domination and were richly rewarded with land, wealth, and influence. As a consequence, British-appointed "chiefs" and their retainers became heavily invested in British rule and cooperation with white settlers.

Of the many peoples indigenous to Kenya, the Kikuyu was the largest and the hardest hit by the "reserve" system. In the 1940s, Kikuyu moderates formed the Kenya African Union, which developed a mass organization and set up underground cells for possible use in a civil disobedience campaign. Its most important leader was Jomo Kenyatta, an English-educated clerk and journalist who flirted with communism, going so far as to visit the Soviet Union in the early 1930s. The Union made liberal use of elaborate oaths, which had long been an important Kikuyu practice; they bound together communities and ushered boys and girls into adulthood. Kikuyu widely believed that those who broke or "confessed" oaths – even those forced upon a reluctant individual – were doomed to an early death, a belief exploited by Union organizers. The Union's secretive behavior and use of belligerent, anti-European oaths deeply troubled white settlers and created the impossible-to-dispel belief that the Union was plotting violence.

Although it probably was not, other groups were, particularly in the capital, Nairobi, where in about 1950 radical associations and trade unions grew adept at mobilizing gangs of poor Kikuyu to whom were administered new and more disturbing oaths. Unsubstantiated stories circulated of the presence of human and animal blood, orgies, and even ritual bestiality. In the beginning, leaders of this incipient Kikuyu insurgency mostly encouraged violence against black Africans who collaborated with or tolerated British rule, but in 1952, gangs began to carry out uncoordinated attacks against white settlers. The authorities declared a state of emergency and arrested Kenyatta and other Union leaders, despite their denunciations of the violence. Far from ending the violence, the arrests heightened it, since they ensured that leadership of the entire anti-British opposition passed to Kikuyu radicals who were more committed to the practice of violence. The British answered by dispersing their few troops around the colony and hastily organizing from among native loyalists a Kikuyu Home Guard to defend villages. White settlers joined the Kenya Police Reserve, an auxiliary body later responsible for the worst atrocities against Africans.

Mau Mau Insurrection

For several years, rumors had circulated about a group operating under the name Mau Mau, a secret society bound together by blood oaths, black magic, and pledges of ghastly violence against settlers. But there had been little violence, and it is in fact doubtful whether the Mau Mau existed as a formal organization. Nonetheless, when Kikuyu violence grew to the level of a general insurgency in 1953, the British authorities, press, and the white settler public began to use the name Mau Mau to refer to what they assumed to be a vast, coordinated conspiracy to shed white blood. The insurgents' real aim seems to have been to forge a larger resistance movement across Kenyan tribes, perhaps with the goal of eventually convincing the British of the futility of continued occupation. The rapidly expanding movement – to this day known as Mau Mau although its members never used the term – principally drew its strength from three populations, all of them Kikuyu: the poor sharecroppers (known as "squatters") who worked the white settlers' lands; those black Africans confined to the overcrowded, overfarmed reserves; and the urban poor. Kenya's vast forests sheltered Mau Mau bases, whence bands of armed men, seeking supplies and victims, descended on white farmsteads and black villages in the reserves. Kikuyu villages bore the brunt of the violence, attacked by terrorists who accused them of accepting the British colonial regime. Of approximately 1850 civilians killed during the uprising, only thirty-two were settlers (additionally about six hundred British soldiers died).

But it was stories of violence against whites that captured the world's attention. The most shocking came in January 1953, when Mau Mau terrorists hacked to death the Rucks, a white settler family, including their six-year-old son, Michael. Photos of his blood-soaked body, bed sheets, and teddy bear were carried in papers around the world and mobilized the British government to act. Throughout the Emergency, in fact, white settlers successfully kept stories of grisly but isolated anti-settler brutality uppermost in the conscience of Britain and the world. Authors and journalists contributed to this perception by penning a number of sensationalist novels about Mau Mau – most famously Elspeth Huxley's *A Thing to Love* and Robert Ruark's *Something of Value* – that owed more to overheated imaginations and racism than to any familiarity with the insurgency. London's officials readily accepted these descriptions of savage Africans. Early in the uprising, in fact, the British assembled a team of ostensible experts on Kikuyu language and culture that concluded that Mau Mau was a form of insanity. This echoed the sentiment of a leader of the white settler movement who bluntly decried Mau Mau as a "mind destroying disease" (quoted in Anderson, *Histories of the Hanged*, 279). Most Britons in and out of government simply accepted that Kikuyu rebellion had no rational basis, least of all the conditions associated with British imperialism.

Kenya's military commander convinced London to send more troops, which were massed and employed in extensive forest sweeps. Old American training planes were even used in bombing runs over stretches of forest. Months-long offenses captured few insurgents, however, and threatened to swallow up as many troops as Britain was willing to commit. The most dangerous Mau Mau terrorist, Dedan Kimathi, remained at large and his reputation for gruesome violence grew to epic proportions among white settlers.

British Counterinsurgency in Kenya

British commanders aware of the success of "hearts and minds" operations in Malaya attempted their own versions thereof. In general, British efforts in Kenya were cruder, more violent, and more narrowly militaristic, in large part because white settlers set the tone of the campaign through anti-Mau Mau publicity and through their participation in the Kenya Police Reserve. Beginning in 1954, the British implemented a resettlement program, but one that bore only a passing resemblance to that of the Briggs Plan. Captured Mau Mau, as well as suspects and supporters – perhaps as many as 150,000 Kikuyu all told – were held in scores of detention camps where epidemics of cholera and other diseases killed thousands. As many as one million suspicious Kikuyu, that is, more than half of the entire pre-insurgency population, were moved into "Emergency villages." Supposedly patterned after those in Malaya, these villages were, in fact, simply prison camps. Inmates were surrounded by barbed wire and kept under guard by members of the loyalist Kikuyu Home Guard. Forced labor, rape, and torture were common, and insurgent raids produced reprisals in the form of public executions. When the Anglican Church protested and the House of Commons launched investigations, the colonial authorities responded with detailed descriptions of Mau Mau savagery – sometimes real, often imagined – and the plea that they were doing what they could with limited resources against a bloodthirsty enemy. Why was there such little immediate public outcry? It seems that the British public was sufficiently horrified by the endless procession of gruesome stories of Mau Mau slaughter, cannibalistic, orgiastic oath-taking, and civilization in peril.

The Emergency villages produced the desired effect, cutting Mau Mau terrorists off from supplies and recruits. Meanwhile, British intelligence and police operations in Kenya became more sophisticated. As in Malaya, the authorities found that small detachments of well-trained troops were vastly more successful than large-scale military maneuvers. Another innovation was the use of "counter" or "pseudo gangs" composed of loyal Kikuyu masquerading as terrorists. These counter gangs gathered intelligence and made their own highly disruptive offensive forays. In October 1956 the British and Kikuyu Home Guard netted the ultimate prize when they captured Kimathi, the Mau Mau terrorist mastermind. His ferocious personality had helped hold together the insurgency – in large part through terror – and his capture led to a precipitous decline in the number of attacks. Shortly thereafter, the last of the British troops left. By 1959, the state of emergency was lifted.

Although the Emergency was over, it left a lingering impression on British authorities. Many, including the incoming conservative Prime Minister Harold Macmillan, grasped that colonialism's heyday was past and that Britain's African colonies could only be held if the Empire was willing to wage war against entire peoples. The costs of such a policy in French Algeria were there for everyone to see (described below). The behavior of Kenya's white settlers, moreover, had horrified many.

Macmillan and his advisors believed that with Mau Mau defeated, it was time to be rid of Kenya. Most importantly, they decided that it should be handed over to "responsible" black Africans. But whom? Once Britain's *bête noire*, Jomo Kenyatta was freed from prison in 1961 and publicly rehabilitated. He even managed to convince most white settlers that he was the best guarantor of their continued prosperity and safety. In 1963, Kenya received its independence, with Kenyatta its first president.

Three main factors led to the failure of the Mau Mau uprising and the return of peace. The first was Mau Mau brutality, the perception of which owed more to racism and the Western imagination than it did to the actual extent of Mau Mau violence. Nonetheless, terrorists bent on gaining attention for their cause must walk a fine line: just enough violence to attract the eyes of the world, but not so much that they are then averted. From the beginning, Mau Mau violence alienated the international audience that might otherwise have been sympathetic to the plight of the Kikuyu. In fact, the perception of Mau Mau violence was so extreme that the British public accepted the necessity of extraordinarily brutal counterinsurgency strategies, while Mau Mau insurgents failed to capitalize on the opportunities afforded by British brutality. This was an extension of a second factor, the lack of realistic insurgent goals and the failure to forge links between the violence and clear political outcomes. The Mau Mau and those who spoke on their behalf gave voice to genuine rage, but were unable to convince downtrodden members of those outside the Kikuyu tribe that Mau Mau offered a solution to their troubles. The British, on the other hand, were able to isolate the Kikuyu and limit Mau Mau's access to wider audiences. Mau Mau violence came to be seen as an end in itself, a development that rarely yields positive socio-political results. The third factor was the eventual British decision to embrace the moderate opposition, Kenyatta, and divest the Empire of its colony.

Cyprus and EOKA

At nearly the same time that the United Kingdom was successfully confronting ethno-nationalist terrorism in Malaya and Kenya, trouble was brewing in a third British possession, Cyprus. On this Eastern Mediterranean island approximately forty miles from the Turkish coast, the lessons of the Irgun/LEHI campaign were put to devastating effect. In fact, the situation on Cyprus was not unlike that of Palestine: antagonistic Greeks and Turks found themselves ruled by an imperial power. Greek Cypriots (who comprised about 80 percent of the population) found a determined leader in General George Grivas, a veteran of the anti-Nazi resistance and anti-communist fighting in the Greek Civil War. His hope echoed that of many Greek Cypriots: union (*enosis*) with the mainland. Grivas assessed the strengths of the Greek Cypriot community and quickly concluded that there were insufficient weapons or trained fighters for even a limited guerrilla war against the British. He did identify two advantages: the broad support of the Greek Cypriot population who could shelter and support a terrorist movement; and links to Radio Athens, a broadcast service that could provide Grivas the international attention he believed would lead to *enosis*.

Grivas organized the few fighters he had – perhaps only eighty at first – into the National Organization of Cypriot Fighters (known as EOKA from its Greek acronym) and began operations in April 1955. Grivas strictly limited EOKA's attacks – what he called "executions" or "sabotage" – to British policemen, soldiers, and urban infrastructure, a strategy that preserved public support and produced maximum visibility. EOKA fighters operated at will and frustrated British attempts to govern effectively. Worst of all, the British reacted as they had in Northern Ireland and Palestine, resorting to collective punishment against civilians in the form of harassment, curfews, mass arrests, enormous fines, and indiscriminate beatings and shootings. "The 'security forces,'" Grivas later noted, "set about their work in a manner which might have been deliberately designed to drive the population into our arms" (quoted in Asprey, *War in the Shadows*, II:895). EOKA proved particularly adept at provoking the British into self-defeating outbursts against civilians. One of the most notorious incidents was the detonation of a large bomb at a soccer field used by off-duty soldiers. The blast killed two and wounded five. The British regiment so struck "rushed through the village beating and kicking everyone they met, smashing windows and ransacking shops for anything worth stealing" (Grivas, *Memoirs*, 96). Compounding the problem, the British exiled the relatively moderate Greek Cypriot leader Archbishop Makarios III, thus depriving themselves of a negotiating partner and leaving Greek Cypriots with little option but to back Grivas' radical strategy.

Meanwhile, as Grivas noted, "The British answer to our methods was to flood the island with troops. It was the wrong answer. Numbers have little meaning in guerrilla warfare" (Grivas, *Memoirs*, 46). By 1956, thirty thousand British soldiers and police were hunting down about 275 EOKA fighters and 750 armed village irregulars (Asprey, *War in the Shadows*, II:894). The absurd ratio provided EOKA with plenty of targets, emphasized the population's impression of the British as foreign occupiers, and heightened the cost of failure. As EOKA mounted more and more attacks, the British reputation fell to previously unimaginable lows. At this moment, *enosis*, EOKA's ultimate goal, seemed within sight. The British had tired of their involvement with Cyprus, which they had come to see as an expensive and humiliating albatross that provided little strategic value in return. But several developments thwarted the realization of union with Greece. British attempts to negotiate a solution with Greece repeatedly inflamed Turkish nationalism, as did EOKA attacks against those Turkish Cypriot police and civilians who cooperated with the British. And although EOKA gained the international attention it had sought, United Nations' involvement meant that a unilateral decision by the British was no longer possible. With *enosis* out of the question, Grivas and other Greek Cypriot leaders settled for independence and de facto partition in 1960.

Grivas and Greece's military junta eventually backed a new incarnation of EOKA – known as EOKA B – which revived the struggle for *enosis*. It targeted Greek Cypriot leaders and civilians seen as insufficiently patriotic, particularly those on the left, as well as Turkish Cypriot civilians. While most Greek Cypriots regarded EOKA as freedom fighters, EOKA B was widely denounced as a terrorist organization, due to its use of indiscriminate violence against civilians. EOKA B also helped trigger repeated Greek and Turkish military interventions, which have kept tensions high and the situation unresolved. The UN has maintained a peacekeeping mission on Cyprus since 1964, the third longest-running operation of this sort. The result has been a mixed legacy for Cyprian political violence. Terrorism played an even more pivotal role in the winning of Cyprian independence than it had in the creation of Israel, but the results were less decisive. The example of Cyprian terrorism illuminates two lessons repeatedly demonstrated in the history of terrorism. First, terrorists rarely are the ones to reap whatever victory is eventually gained, and second, terrorists prove more able to destabilize a state than to construct a lasting and peaceful order.

Empire and Counter-Terrorism

No other country has faced terrorism in the twentieth century for as long or on as many fronts as the United Kingdom. During the 1940s and 1950s, Britain confronted terrorist threats in no less than four sectors of its global empire: Palestine, Malaya, Kenya, and Cyprus. Britain's twelve-year experiment in Malayan counterinsurgency demonstrated that the keys to resolving the matter were an understanding of the unique characteristics of terrorist groups, the presence of organizational flexibility, and firm, yet creative leadership on the ground. Devastating proof of this could be found in the fact that even as the British were turning the tide against Malaya's Communist Terrorists, they nearly botched the struggle against a lesser foe in Kenya and failed miserably against a small, but determined one in Cyprus. In the case of the infamous Mau Mau uprising in Kenya, imperial racism and the fears of the enshrined white settler population exaggerated the threat and almost fatally directed British counterinsurgency efforts into self-defeating overreaction. Capable civil and military leadership eventually defeated the foe, but produced lasting scars. Nowhere were the lessons of Malaya adapted to local circumstances. Why? The probable reason is that the United Kingdom never was in a position to afford these crises the attention they deserved. Britain presided over a far-flung empire and was still recovering from the expense and trauma of the Second World War. Moreover, the overriding international concern was the Cold War and the Soviet threat. Thus, relatively speaking, anti-colonial movements in the far-flung corners of Britain's still enormous empire were pin pricks and received piecemeal attention and resources. Management of these crises primarily fell to local leadership. In Malaya, civil and military leaders developed effective counterinsurgent strategies, whereas in Cyprus, local civil and military commanders never appreciated the nature of the insurgent threat, nor did, unsurprisingly, the distant leaders of the overstretched Empire. Although it took place the farthest from Britain, the Malayan Emergency garnered more resources because of the economic importance of the colony and the presence of a communist threat. Neither Kenya nor Cyprus figured prominently in the grand calculus of the age.

France and Algeria

Next to Vietnam's "American War," Algeria was the bloodiest anti-colonial struggle of the twentieth century. It also produced the century's signature terrorist strategy, the use of symbolic acts of violence to provoke the enemy into counterproductive brutality that could undermine its own goals and mobilize the masses. In this, the paramount lesson from Algeria's conflict was that for ethno-nationalist groups pursuing independence, public opinion at home and abroad could be far more valuable assets than military triumphs.

Algeria bore similarities to Kenya in that it was a settler colony, with an entrenched European population that repeatedly stymied the efforts of the mother country to lessen the political, economic, and social inequities. But it was different from Kenya in several ways. In particular, the European population (about half of which was French) was much larger than in Kenya. When war began in 1954, the European population – known as *pieds noirs*, their leaders called *colons* – was about one million, whereas that of the indigenous Muslim population of Berber and Arab descent was about nine million. And the French had been in Algeria since 1830, so that by the time of the war, many French Algerians could claim that their families had been there for four or more generations. Another crucial difference was that Algeria had been directly incorporated into France in 1851, although few Algerians had been granted French citizenship. As in Kenya, the French systematically dispossessed Algerians, limited their educational opportunities, and forced them into economic servitude, except in the case of a small minority of Westernized, French-speaking Algerians. Most Algerians were convinced that resistance to French rule was futile and self-destructive, but a committed minority had become devoted to the cause of independence. Meanwhile, the successful campaign by Vietnamese nationalists to evict France from Indochina made French authorities all the more committed to staying in Algeria

In 1954, the National Liberation Front – known as the FLN from its French acronym – formed and began military operations against the French. Although virtually all of the FLN's leadership and constituency were Muslims, the group's primary goal was the creation of an independent Algeria with a secular government. In the early stages of the war, the FLN hoped to win independence by attracting international attention through the battlefield success of its military wing, the National Liberation Army. Fighting was largely confined to Algeria's arid hinterland, where FLN soldiers held an advantage because of their knowledge of the territory and ability to live off the rural Muslim population. The FLN survived, but made little military headway against the French. To make matters worse, most of the native population remained indifferent to the cause or were actively alienated by the FLN's tendency to terrorize the indigenous Algerian population. FLN representatives regularly shook down villagers for money and killed those who resisted or were suspected of collaborating with the French.

The Battle of Algiers

The FLN's leaders needed a new strategy to attract the international attention that had so far eluded them. Their response was to create a self-contained terrorist organization in Algeria's capital starting in the summer of 1956. The ensuing Battle of Algiers, as it came to be known, was not a complete departure for the FLN in that it had already used terror to drive apart the Algerians and Europeans in a bid to undermine the government's program of achieving the fuller "assimilation" of Algeria into France. Toward this end, FLN fighters targeted white settlers and Muslim loyalists, sometimes killing their victims by axe or machete and then mutilating the corpses to exact ritual vengeance. Women were sometimes raped.

What the FLN leader Ramdane Abane proposed in 1956 was a dramatic escalation in the scale and visibility of symbolic violence. He hoped to use terrorism to recast the war for liberation, previously defined more narrowly as a military contest, as a psychological contest. Terrorism, he believed, would accomplish several specific purposes. First, it would bring the FLN the international attention it so desperately sought. "Is it preferable," Abane asked rhetorically, "for our cause to kill ten enemies in a dry river bed [far from the cities] when no one will talk of it or a single man in Algiers which will be noted the next day by the American press?" (quoted in Hoffman, *The Failure of British Military Strategy*, 61). Another time he noted even more pithily that "one corpse in a [civilian's] jacket is always worth more than twenty in a uniform" (quoted in Horne, *A Savage War of Peace*, 132). Abane also believed that attacks on civilians would end all talk of a negotiated settlement between Muslims and Europeans, encourage an exodus of European settlers, and convince the French that their continued occupation of Algeria was not worth the effort. In this sense, the FLN hoped to follow in the footsteps of Irgun/LEHI and EOKA. Finally, Abane and the FLN hoped that terrorism would more forcefully establish the FLN as the armed representative of the people, the only body capable of meting out vengeance against the French. In this way did the FLN hope to gain the adherents it needed to mount a mass rebellion against France. Terrorism was thus a means of gaining credibility among the Muslim population. There is also evidence that Abane hoped that terrorism would lead the French authorities to increase their own dependence on violence, thus radicalizing more of the Muslim population.

The FLN's campaign of urban terrorism began as retaliation for the French execution of two captured FLN soldiers in June 1956. Abane's military deputy, Saadi Yacef, organized a spree of shootings that killed forty-nine civilians in four days. FLN terrorism called forth a violent response from the French. The source, however, was not the military or police, but rather the *ultras*, extremist *colons* who emerged as a second terrorist force, but one committed to keeping Algeria French. In August, *ultra* terrorists set off an immense bomb in front of the alleged home of FLN terror suspects. Three neighboring houses were also destroyed, and seventy innocent Muslims killed, including many children. The tit-for-tat continued with the terrorists' own first venture into bombing, the most well-known event from the whole bloody war, recreated in exacting detail in *The Battle of Algiers*, Gillo Pontecorvo's 1966 semi-documentary film on the subject. Yacef recruited three young women from the Muslim quarter of Algiers, the Casbah, who were made up and dressed to appear European so that they could more easily slip through French army checkpoints. Each was armed with a small bomb timed to go off nearly simultaneously. The first exploded in a milk-bar frequented by mothers and children; the second targeted a cafeteria near the university; the third, which failed to detonate, was planted in the Air France terminal of the Algiers airport. Altogether there were three fatalities and more than fifty injured, including many children. Yacef continued to build up his network of cells, eventually amassing an army of fourteen hundred terrorists in Algiers alone. In November, FLN terrorists struck a bus station, a department store, the railroad station, and other targets throughout downtown Algiers, killing dozens. That December Abane and Yacef's top terrorist operative in Algiers, the former petty thief and pimp Ali la Pointe, assassinated the prominent *ultra* mayor of a nearby town.

French Counter-Terrorism

Besieged by furious, terrified *pieds noirs* and clearly unable to maintain order with just the police, Algeria's governor-general granted the military *carte blanche* to combat the FLN in Algiers in January 1957. Algeria's military commander handed the mission to General Jacques Massu and his Tenth Parachute Division. Many of the soldiers were veterans of fighting in Indochina; as such, they were battle hardened, fiercely loyal, and well-versed in counterinsurgency fighting. Many, in fact, had participated in the anti-Nazi Resistance and were thus personally familiar with the tactics of insurgency.

Massu's most important underling was Colonel Roger Trinquier, who had fought in Indochina and contributed to the formulation of a counterinsurgency doctrine he termed "revolutionary" or "modern warfare." In short, Trinquier insisted that states and their armies had to mimic insurgents' tactics and strategies. These, he noted, were primarily political and psychological in nature. Drawing from his knowledge of several insurgent movements, Trinquier asserted that the terrorist was a new type of combatant, previously unseen in the history of warfare. He is not a criminal, Trinquier maintained, since "he fights within the framework of his organization, without personal interest, for a cause he considers noble and for a respectable ideal, the same as the soldiers in the armies confronting him." And yet, he is not a soldier, since he fights out of uniform, targets civilians, and hides in their midst. Therefore, Trinquier's revolutionary war doctrine emphasized four features: the implementation of social reforms to blunt the attractiveness of insurgency; the use of small units which could take the battle to the enemy; the pacification and/or relocation of the population in order to deny its resources to insurgents; and the gathering of intelligence through all available means. Although he avoided use of the term, Trinquier endorsed the use of torture, but with what appears to us to be odd caveats. "Specialists" in "interrogations" could use their "techniques," but only in pursuit of information that captured suspects could reasonably be expected to possess, and afterward captive terrorists were to be treated as normal POWs (Trinquier, *Modern Warfare*, 20–3). The scene was set for a broad application of this doctrine, right down to its most unsavory aspects.

Massu and his assistants immediately went to work. The French surrounded the Casbah with barbed wire and checkpoints, effectively turning it into a vast concentration camp, with every native Algerian treated as a suspect. Acknowledging that they were essentially engaged in detective work, the *paras* sifted through every police document and assembled a vast list of suspects. They also assiduously groomed an extensive network of informers and spies. With the suspension of all judicial niceties, such as warrants and *habeas corpus*, Massu then rounded up thousands of Muslims in enormous sweeps of the Casbah. One highly respected journalist estimated that 30 to 40 percent of the male

Figure 11.2: French paratroopers search an Algerian suspect on the outskirts of Algiers, January 1957
(© Bettmann/CORBIS)

population of the Casbah was arrested at some point during the Battle of Algiers. Massu and his intelligence officers understood that the FLN in Algiers was organized in small cells whose lead member knew only the individual who had recruited him. The French goal was to connect the cells by filling in names – using an enormous blackboard in the Division's headquarters – in order to reveal the larger structure, thus allowing the authorities to target the organizers of the campaign. For as one of Massu's lieutenants noted, "the man who places the bomb is but an arm that tomorrow will be replaced by another arm" (quoted in Horne, *A Savage War of Peace*, 194).

When dealing with suspects and simply those caught up in sweeps, Massu and his officers understood that time was of the essence. When the FLN realized that members were caught, safe houses, passwords, and the like could be swiftly changed, often within hours. Information produced through the judicial process and plea bargaining, prolonged questioning, or the cultivation of goodwill would simply not come fast enough to produce "actionable intelligence," the French authorities believed. And they were under intense pressure to end the FLN's reign of terror. *Colons* demonstrated; their *ultras* engaged in vigilante action, sometimes lynching innocent Muslims in the wake of FLN violence; and Paris demanded results. Moreover, once the authorities granted the army complete freedom of action in Algiers, France could not back down. The only possible outcomes were the cessation of terrorism or a French exit from Algiers.

The French used non-violent methods of coercion, but, in accordance with Trinquier's endorsement of revolutionary war doctrine, torture was also commonly applied. In the technique known as waterboarding, interrogators poured water over the face of a suspect while covering his nose and mouth with cloth in order to simulate drowning. Sometimes they pumped water through tubes into victims' mouths or rectums. The method favored by the French was known as the *gégène*, in which interrogators would attach electrodes to the ears or penis of a suspect and then send a shock through them by cranking a field telephone. The French made little effort to hide their use of such methods from the Algerian public; in fact, they relied on tales of its use spreading. Since Muslims seized by the FLN expected torture, interrogators often had to do little more than begin questioning or gesture toward their equipment to bring forth a torrent of information. At first, torture was a matter of convenience and expediency; in time, its use was institutionalized.

Alongside torture, summary execution became a standard practice. According to Paul Aussaresses, who, it was learned much later, led a secret intelligence unit under Trinquier that was responsible for much of the torture used in Algeria, "The justice system would have been paralyzed had it not been for our initiative . . . Summary executions were therefore an inseparable part of the task associated with keeping law and order. . . . It was so obvious that it became unnecessary to spell out such orders at any level. No one ever asked me openly to execute this one or that one. It was simply understood" (Aussaresses, *The Battle of the Casbah*, 127). Aussaresses' men executed and buried suspects in mass graves outside Algiers or dropped them from helicopters into the Mediterranean. Afterward, the secretary-general of the Algiers police, Paul Teitgen, would sign an order exempting the suspect from the judicial process. Teitgen later admitted that he signed 24,000 such orders before his resignation in October 1957; of those, 3,024 suspects "disappeared." Most were certainly executed, probably after torture (Morgan, 236).

French Success in the Battle of Algiers and Beyond

For a short time after the arrival of Massu, Yacef's cells continued to terrorize Algiers, but soon the general's tactics began to bear fruit. Bombers were caught in immense dragnets, and the French even seized Yacef's chief bomb transporter and the FLN's political chief in Algiers. Although much of the intelligence gained through torture was unusable, inaccurate, or completely fabricated, the French quickly filled in their blackboard diagram of the FLN's structure of cells in Algiers. By the end of March 1957, Algiers was quiet. And none too soon, since the first stories of the widespread use of torture were finally reaching metropolitan France. After less than three months of unhindered activity, the *paras* were withdrawn from Algiers and sent to continue counterinsurgency in the countryside.

But Yacef's terrorist cells were not entirely destroyed. In June, teams led by Ali la Pointe set bombs in street lights near trolley stops and blew up a dance club; seventeen died and almost two hundred were wounded. The city's *colons* exploded in anger. Mobs rampaged through a Muslim market, looting and destroying shops and murdering five shopkeepers and customers. The police and regular army present watched passively. Horrified by FLN terror and concerned that the city might slip into lawlessness, Massu and the governor-general of Algeria agreed to recall the *paras* to finish off the FLN in Algiers. All resources were directed against Yacef, who was captured in July 1957. (Yacef was later sentenced to death but eventually pardoned. After Algerian independence, he entered politics, eventually serving as a senator. His memoirs became the basis of Pontecorvo's film *The Battle of Algiers*; he even played himself in the film.) Ali la Pointe's hiding place in the Casbah was surrounded in October and blown up, killing him, two colleagues, and seventeen innocent Muslims. The Battle of Algiers was over, although the *paras* continued to round up and torture suspects for months.

In the short term, the Battle of Algiers was a rousing success for the French and a disastrous loss for the FLN. The latter had lost nearly all of its strength in Algiers, including several important leaders, and alienated much of the population of the city through its use of terrorism against French and Muslim alike. The United Nations remained aloof from the conflict, sensitive to French claims that the Algerian crisis was an internal matter. The FLN adapted to the new circumstances by moving its leadership and much of its military strength to neighboring Tunisia and the countryside, whence FLN fighters staged hit and run attacks against French military and civilian targets. The FLN aspired to establish "liberated zones," but usually had to settle for exacting taxes and supplies from the population. The FLN frequently carried out its own regimen of terror against collaborators and peasants. Despite *colon* descriptions of Algerian violence as simply anti-settler, most deaths caused by the FLN were Muslim, and in ways deemed equally horrid by Muslims as Europeans.

French success in the Battle of Algiers cemented an alliance between the *colons* and the military establishment in Algeria. Military commanders in Algeria had a habit of adopting the *colons'* worldview, which hinged on Algeria's irreducible Frenchness, the primitiveness and savagery of the Muslims, and the complete illegitimacy of the Algerian nationalist cause. Political instability in metropolitan France drove the two camps even closer together. *Colons* and the military alike suspected that "soft," defeatist Parisian bureaucrats would "give up" in Algeria as they were perceived to have done in Indochina. Thus, *colons* and the military together pressed for the most extreme program of keeping Algeria French and dominated by the *colons*. The *colons'* strong lobby in Paris kept up a steady stream of troops and resources for the war.

The result of this was the Challe Plan, which built on previous military successes and brought France as close as it would ever come to outright victory. Under the Plan, France stationed substantial troops throughout Algeria to guard the settler population and began to use helicopter-mobile troops to achieve decisive victories in the event of contact with FLN soldiers. By 1959, the FLN was on the run or confined to a few outposts in the mountains. And by 1962, less than a few thousand poorly armed fighters remained.

Another French advantage was the presence of capable, imaginative officers well versed in counterinsurgency doctrine. The most celebrated of these was David Galula, who later authored several classic volumes on counterinsurgency doctrine. Galula understood that the FLN engaged in urban terrorism and rural guerrilla war in order to publicize its cause and provoke the French authorities, and he appreciated this strategy's potential for success. He also grasped that the terrorist insurgents could not be destroyed at the expense of alienating the community to whom they appealed. This he expressed in his "first law" of counterinsurgent warfare: "the objective is the population. The population is at the same time the real terrain of the war" (Galula, *Pacification in Algeria*, 246).

The French Win the Battle, but Lose the War

To the detriment of the French cause, however, the ideas of Galula and others like him were never adopted on a grand scale, in large part because of the deeply ingrained French attitude that Muslim Algerians were a population to be controlled rather than courted. And such a belief was continuously encouraged by the FLN, who had become masters at manipulating the public perception of the struggle. Long after the Battle of Algiers, the FLN continued to engage in provocative acts of terrorism in order to enrage the French *colons* and military. The result was that even as the French were achieving military successes under the Challe Plan, the authorities engaged in a massive resettlement program that moved over two million Muslims (nearly one-quarter of the pre-war population) into virtual concentration camps (Ruedy, *Modern Algeria*, 189). The French also stepped up their use of reprisals against uncooperative Muslim villages and continued to make systematic use of torture and extralegal execution, tactics that had proven so effective in the Battle of Algiers.

In the broader war against Algerian independence, these efforts began to prove self-defeating, because French policies increasingly alienated the government and the population of metropolitan France. Rumors about the use of torture had raised eyebrows during the Battle of Algiers in the spring of 1957, but it was stories about French nationals in Algeria who ran afoul of the *paras* that particularly roused the French public against the war. One case was that of the communist Henri Alleg, who survived detention and repeated torture at the hands of the French to write a book denouncing French practices in 1958. By this point, the political left, including some of its most famous members, such as Jean-Paul Sartre and Simone de Beauvoir, was uniformly against the war.

A particularly devastating witness to the *paras'* brutality was General Jacques de Bollardière, who warned of "los[ing] sight, under the fallacious pretext of immediate expediency, of [our] moral values" (quoted in Horne, *A Savage War of Peace*, 203). Bollardière also recognized the cancerous effect of torture on military professionalism and morale, a fact attested to by many soldiers returning from Algeria. And the stories continued to appear. In 1960, readers in France and around the world were horrified by news of Djamila Boupacha, an FLN terrorist who was captured after throwing a bomb and then allegedly tortured and raped with a bottle by French soldiers. Those who denounced torture in Algeria frequently compared French behavior to that of the Gestapo during the Second World War. On their own, however, revelations of torture and execution would not have definitively swayed public opinion in metropolitan France. When added, however, to the mounting cost of the war and the unpopularity of conscription, such stories helped galvanize opposition to the war.

Just as French methods of counter-terrorism in Algiers led many in metropolitan France to turn against continued French occupation of Algeria, it drove many Muslims in Algeria directly into the arms of the FLN. In fact, as it evolved, the FLN's strategy in Algiers came to depend on France's brutal reaction to terrorism. This meant that the FLN accepted as necessary not only the torture and death of its activists, but also the French imprisonment, torture, and killing of innocent Algerians. This was not the first time that a revolutionary movement was willing to seek misery for one's own population as part of an overall strategy. This sort of cold-blooded calculation was central to the strategy of Russian revolutionary terrorists in the nineteenth century, for instance. But never before had such a strategy been so openly and successfully applied. FLN behavior was Nechaevism raised to a horribly fine art. It was dangerous, but paid off in the end. As late as 1958, the beginning of the high point of French success in Algeria, the overwhelming majority of Muslims had voted in support of a referendum that promised far-reaching reforms for Muslims but kept Algeria French. But under the onslaught of French torture, summary execution, and resettlement, Algerian Muslims in increasing numbers abandoned all hope of accommodation with France and openly embraced the nationalist cause. The FLN was the beneficiary of such sentiment, having neutralized its moderate rivals through its own campaign of assassination and intimidation. In 1960, during a critical phase of negotiations between France and the FLN, thousands of Muslims took to the streets in public demonstrations for independence – a scene that would have been unthinkable five years earlier. FLN terrorism and the French response had succeeded in bringing about what the FLN had long hoped for, a decisive break between the European and Muslim populations of Algeria, with the latter finally backing the call for independence. In the end, French methods of counter-terrorism proved self-defeating, and the French proved, once again, a fundamental law of counterinsurgency: successful military operations are futile if not accompanied by successful efforts to establish legitimacy through productive partnerships with the indigenous peoples.

In fact, the violence of the Algerian War of Independence provides one of the most illustrative cases concerning the public contestation of legitimacy in a time of war or terrorism. This begins with the recognition that French activity in Algeria encompasses both meanings inherent in the ambiguous term "counter-terrorism": the French authorities sought to suppress FLN terrorism even as they engaged in their own campaign to terrorize the FLN and its supporters. Rarely had a government's contention that state-sponsored violence is legally and morally more legitimate than that of sub-state rivals been more problematic. Although Algerians appreciated that the FLN did not always act in their best interest, in the end it was counted as preferable to the French. As much as typical Algerians and continental French alike were repulsed by FLN bombings and shootings – and they were most certainly repulsed – they were more angered and disgusted by the stories of French cruelty. FLN violence came to be regarded as necessary, whereas French violence was beyond the pale. FLN violence was seen as just, defensive, and purposeful, whereas French violence was immoral, provocative, and arbitrary. In the end, it was the French who were roundly denounced as the purveyors of terror and, thus, labeled colloquially as the terrorists. This was cogently distilled by the FLN leader Abane, who, when challenged in the wake of the September 1956 bombings by the horrified FLN sympathizer who sheltered him, famously remarked, "I see hardly any difference between the girl who places a bomb in the Milk-Bar and the French aviator who bombards a village or who drops napalm on a prohibited area" (quoted in Horne, *A Savage War of Peace*, 186). When significant numbers of Algerians and French agreed with him, the war was, in effect, over. In the end, it became impossible for the French to continue the war against a larger foe in Algeria and without domestic support back home.

A similar drama played out on the international stage, as well. By 1958, the United Nations was pressing hard to debate the Algerian question and had become the target of intense propaganda efforts from both the French government and the FLN. Over time, the competing arguments and images acquired a certain mirror-like sameness – both sides terrorized, tortured, and killed, but maintained they were motivated by legitimate, moral causes. In October 1957, the American network CBS broadcast a special on Algeria in which the French and native positions were described in parallel, lending them a moral equivalence. Terrorism had brought the Algerians' cause to an international audience, but, to the great chagrin of the French, the presence of terrorism and violence no longer provided a *prima facie* case for dismissing either antagonists' argument. After some time, most people outside France – and eventually within, as well – came to support the cause of the oppressed.

What finally made Algerian victory possible was the political ill health of metropolitan France and the return to power in 1958 of the charismatic realist, Charles de Gaulle, the leader of Free French troops in the

Second World War. The *colons* were convinced he would never abandon Algeria, but de Gaulle was becoming increasingly convinced that the FLN would never cease fighting. After de Gaulle began to speak of "self-determination" for Muslim Algerians, the *colon* population began to look for salvation to the military, which, in the crises of 1956–7, had come to be Algeria's virtual rulers. *Colons* made the first step toward open military opposition to the French state when they staged an uprising in January 1960 and called for the support of the military. Only a direct appeal from de Gaulle carried the day. One year later, French voters, via a referendum, endorsed de Gaulle's vision of "self-determination" for Algeria.

French Terrorism and the OAS

Around this time, disgruntled military officers in Algeria formed the Secret Army Organization (OAS) – a body dedicated to the preservation of Algeria as French at all costs. The OAS, which drew much of its strength from army deserters and *colon ultras*, also attracted many *paras*, heroes of the Battle of Algiers. The OAS formed urban "commando" squads patterned after the FLN's structure in Algiers and unleashed them in January 1961 in a ferocious campaign of terrorism against Muslim civilians, intellectuals, and FLN leaders. It assassinated French policemen, bureaucrats, undercover officers, and FLN sympathizers. It also mounted dozens of unsuccessful assassination attempts on the life of the arch traitor himself, de Gaulle. At its peak, the OAS numbered only about one thousand militants, but garnered strong support from Algeria's *pied noir* population. For this reason, it managed to virtually rule Algiers and Oran in its heyday. OAS goals were vague, even to its members. It seems to have hoped that terrorism might lead to open civil war between the European and Muslim communities and then a full-scale revolt by the *pieds noirs*. It is more likely, however, that most members of the OAS were motivated by their base emotional attachment to *Algérie française* and fear over its imminent demise. Ever more distressed by continuing secret negotiations between de Gaulle and the FLN, the OAS staged a failed military coup in April 1961 led by Algeria's former military commanders, as well as two other retired generals. De Gaulle once again had to appeal directly to the nation and the army to end the threat. OAS treason and ever increasing *colon* stridency by now had pushed de Gaulle toward more explicit support of Algerian independence.

Throughout this period the FLN kept up its attacks against French targets and Muslim loyalists in order to keep *colon* fury at a peak and to prevent de Gaulle from going to the Algerian people through referenda or negotiating with other organizations. FLN pressure succeeded, for in spring 1962, the government arranged a ceasefire and signed the Evian Accords with the FLN, granting Algeria independence. The OAS stepped up its campaign of bombings and assassinations, trying to goad the FLN into compensatory violence that would derail the implementation of the Evian Accords. According to one member of the OAS, "We began by hitting low-level Muslim employees – those who most likely belonged to the FLN. . . . Orders were given to hit all Muslims standing at bus stops who were wearing ties. We killed them. The next day we would go after Muslim pharmaceutical employees. . . . The lads were very efficient. . . . [The objective was to] empty the European quarters of Muslims" (quoted in Harrison, *Challenging De Gaulle*, 116). In May, the OAS killed 230 Muslims, with a single bomb killing over sixty Muslim longshoremen on Algiers' docks.

Nonetheless, French and Algerian leaders agreed on a ceasefire in 1962 and full independence for Algeria, a decision endorsed by overwhelming majorities in referenda in both France and Algeria. Despite a last burst of anti-Muslim terrorist activity from the OAS, Algeria became independent in July 1962 amid a panicked exodus of Europeans. The French had won the battle for Algiers but lost the war for Algeria, five years after the destruction of the FLN's terrorist cells. The cost of war was incredibly high, somewhere between 500,000 and one million killed, most of whom were Algerian Muslims. Terrorism had claimed the lives of nearly 2,800 French civilians; more than 7,500 were wounded. Equally significant but vastly underreported was the death of perhaps ten thousand Muslim Algerians at the hands of the FLN and its rivals. Algerian physical and administrative infrastructure – the most notable achievements of French colonialism – were in tatters. And the prospects for future Algerian national success were likewise critically damaged. The FLN, which emerged from the war as the only possible Algerian ruling party, had learned how to govern while waging a fantastically brutal campaign of terrorism. Coarsened by violence, riven with factions, weaned on extremism, antagonistic toward the concepts of tolerance, compromise, and the rule of law – this was the profile of Algeria's new government. The use of terrorism is indeed poor preparation for effective, democratic governance.

Frantz Fanon and Anti-Colonial Violence

The violence of the Algerian War cast a long shadow over the rest of the twentieth century and later anti-colonial struggles. Other ethno-nationalist and anti-colonial movements understood the pivotal role of terrorism in provoking the *colons* and the French military establishment into an ultimately counterproductive fight to preserve French rule in Algeria. Black South Africans, Palestinians, Tamil Tigers, Irish Republicans, and others have stated that the FLN's strategy heavily influenced their own fights for independence. But many in the developing world came to appreciate the impact of violence on the indigenous population even more. In this, one interpreter bears the most responsibility for spreading the gospel of violence – and indirectly terrorism. His name is Frantz Fanon.

Fanon was born in 1925 into a mixed-race family on the French Caribbean island of Martinique. During his childhood, later service with the Free French Forces during the Second World War, and attendance at a medical school in Lyons, France, Fanon directly experienced French racism. From 1953 to 1956, he worked as a psychiatrist in hospitals in Algeria, where he treated victims of the war, including many who were tortured by French troops. Fanon became well known through his books on colonialism and its consequences. In *Black Skin and White Masks*, Fanon theorized that colonial rule is perpetuated in large part by inculcating in the indigenous population a sense of dependency, passivity, and self-loathing. With their own culture depicted as primitive, violent, and uncivilized, many "natives," particularly the urban, intellectual middle classes, internalize the culture of the colonial power, thus helping to perpetuate colonial rule.

In *The Wretched of the Earth*, Fanon continued to outline this set of relationships, emphasizing the impact of war and colonial violence on the indigenous population. Drawing on his psychiatric training and personal experience treating patients in Algeria, Fanon explored the mental trauma associated with colonialism, essentially treating it as a cause of mental illness. The most famous sections of the book, however, addressed the role of violence in counteracting passivity and throwing off colonial rule. "At the level of individuals, violence is a cleansing force," Fanon asserted. "It frees the native from his inferiority complex and from his despair and inaction; it makes him fearless and restores his self-respect" (Fanon, *The Wretched of the Earth*, 94). Later, he amplified the message: "Violence alone, violence committed by the people, violence organized and educated by its leaders, makes it possible for the masses to understand social truths and gives the key to them" (Fanon, *The Wretched of the Earth*, 147). Although he never speaks directly of terrorism, one can only assume that he understood indigenous violence would most likely take that form. He was a witness to its use in Algeria, and he must have appreciated the limited means natives had to wage "war" against the colonial power. If terrorism is a matter of violence committed for the benefit of various "audiences," then to Fanon, the most important audience is understood almost entirely to be the terrorists' own people, not the colonizers. One scholar has even termed this variety of terrorism "solipsistic" since it barely considers the impact of the violence on the targets themselves (Lustick, "Terrorism in the Arab–Israeli Conflict," 516–17). A rarely noted shortcoming of the text is Fanon's rather cursory treatment of the toll that violence and terrorism might eventually take on the moral, emotional, and social health of an indigenous people emerging from colonial status. Many supporters of Algerian independence, however, accepted violence as not just necessary but positive. According to the philosopher Jean-Paul Sartre, who wrote a preface to *The Wretched of the Earth*, "violence, like Achilles' lance, can heal the wounds that it has inflicted" (30).

Fanon's prescriptions have been widely read and applied. In fact, his rationale for violence has figured prominently in most terrorist movements of the last fifty years. But Fanon's stance was revolutionary only to those unfamiliar with the history of terrorism, for it was simply the most widely read and clearly put articulation of a strand within the history of terrorism stretching back almost two centuries. The first to address the educational role of terror and violence was Robespierre at the time of the French Reign of Terror. He spoke, if somewhat elliptically, of terror, albeit state-directed terror, as serving two purposes: to rid the body politic of its enemies, and to teach citizens about their obligations and appropriate attitudes as members of the nation. And Russian revolutionary terrorists such as Morozov, Tikhomirov, and Kravchinsky wrote quite clearly of the usefulness of terrorism in supplying heroes for the movement, quite apart from any specific impact on the enemy. Kropotkin's "propaganda of the deed" is the direct predecessor to Fanon's therapeutic violence since the former emphasized the ability of "direct action" to rouse a population from passivity, to communicate to them the possibility of change, and to debunk the myth of the enemy's invincibility. Zionist violence in Palestine in the 1930s and 1940s had a similar tone since the first self-defense groups celebrated their break from the past's stereotypes of the quietly suffering Jew. But it was through Fanon that the idea of terrorism as a cleansing, liberating force would reach an enormous audience.

Bibliography

A good introduction to the subject of ethno-nationalist terrorism is Daniel Byman, "The Logic of Ethnic Terrorism," *Studies in Conflict and Terrorism*, vol. 21, no. 2 (1998),149–69. Two excellent works on Britain and its many counter-terrorism and counterinsurgency campaigns during this period are Susan L. Carruthers, *Winning Hearts and Minds: British*

Governments, the Media and Colonial Counter-Insurgency, 1944–1960 (Leicester University Press, 1995); and Charles Townshend, *Britain's Civil Wars: Counterinsurgency in the Twentieth Century* (Faber and Faber, 1986). An extraordinarily comprehensive survey is Robert B. Asprey, *War in the Shadows: The Guerrilla in History*, 2 vols. (Doubleday, 1975). Robert Taber, *The War of the Flea* (Potomac Books, 2002 [1965]), is both a good survey and a valuable document of 1960s' attitudes.

There are many excellent works on the history of conflict, including terrorism, in the Middle East. A particularly insightful survey is J. Bowyer Bell, *Murders on the Nile, The World Trade Center and Global Terror* (Encounter Books, 2002). Others that are helpful include Shlomo Ben-Ami, *Scars of War, Wounds of Peace: The Israeli–Arab Tragedy* (Oxford University Press, 2006); Ian J. Bickerton and Carla L. Klausner, *A Concise History of the Arab–Israeli Conflict*, 3rd edn. (Prentice Hall, 1998); William L. Cleveland, *A History of the Modern Middle East*, 2nd edn. (Westview, 2000); and Ian S. Lustick, "Terrorism in the Arab–Israeli Conflict: Targets and Audiences," in Crenshaw, ed., *Terrorism in Context* (cited earlier). A useful collection of documents is Walter Laqueur, ed., *The Israel–Arab Reader* (Bantam, 1969).

For Irgun/LEHI's campaign against the British, the most comprehensive and illuminating work is J. Bowyer Bell, *Terror Out of Zion: Irgun Zvai Leumi, Lehi and the Palestine Underground, 1929–1949* (Transaction, 1996 [1985]). Other useful works include Joseph Heller, *The Stern Gang: Ideology, Politics and Terror, 1940–1949* (Routledge, 1995); Bruce Hoffman, *The Failure of British Military Strategy within Palestine, 1939–1947* (Bar-Ilan University Press, 1983); Ze'ev Iviansky, "Individual Terror: Concept and Typology," *Journal of Contemporary History*, vol. 12, no. 1 (Jan. 1977), 43–63; Danny Levine, *The Birth of the Irgun Zvai Leumi: The Jewish Resistance Movement* (Gefen, 1996); and Saul Zadka, *Blood in Zion: How the Jewish Guerrillas Drove the British Out of Palestine* (Brassey's UK, 2003). Two books by participants in Irgun's struggle are Menachem Begin (a future prime minister), *The Revolt* (Nash, 1977 [1948]); and Samuel [Shmuel] Katz (an historian), *Days of Fire* (Doubleday, 1968).

Two excellent studies of the Malayan Emergency are Noel Barber, *War of the Running Dogs: Malaya, 1948–1960* (Cassell, 2007 [1971]); and Kumar Ramakrishna, *Emergency Propaganda: The Winning of Malayan Hearts and Minds, 1948–1958* (Taylor and Francis, 2002). Many studies pair the Malayan and Vietnam conflicts. The best of the bunch are John A. Nagl, *Learning to Eat Soup with a Knife: Counterinsurgency Lessons from Malaya and Vietnam* (University of Chicago Press, 2005 [2002]); Sam C. Sarkesian, *Unconventional Conflicts in a New Security Era: Lessons from Malaya and Vietnam* (Greenwood Press, 1993); and

Robert Thompson, *Defeating Communist Insurgency: The Lessons of Malaya and Vietnam* (Praeger, 1966). On a side note, Nagl participated in the writing of the US Army and Marine's new field manual on counter-insurgency. For an insider's view on the Malayan conflict, see Brigadier Richard L. Clutterbuck, *The Long, Long War: Counterinsurgency in Malaya and Vietnam* (Praeger, 1966).

On the Mau Mau uprising in Kenya, see David Anderson, *Histories of the Hanged: The Dirty War in Kenya and the End of Empire* (Norton, 2005); Robert B. Edgerton, *Mau Mau: An African Crucible* (The Free Press, 1989); and Caroline Elkins, *Imperial Reckoning: The Untold Story of Britain's Gulag in Kenya* (Owl Books, 2005).

An excellent study of EOKA's campaign against the British in Cyprus is Charles Foley and W. I. Scobie, *The Struggle for Cyprus* (Hoover Institution, 1975). Two works by George Grivas, the leader of EOKA, are *Guerrilla Warfare and EOKA's Struggle: A Politico-Military Study* (Longmans, 1964 [1962]) and *The Memoirs of General Grivas*, ed. (Charles Foley Praeger, 1965 [1964]).

The bibliography on the Algerian War of Independence is extensive. The classic study is Alistair Horne, *A Savage War of Peace: Algeria 1954–1962* (NYRB, 2006 [1977]). Another excellent work is Martha Crenshaw [Hutchinson], *Revolutionary Terrorism: The FLN in Algeria, 1954–62* (Hoover Institution Press, 1978). Other useful studies include Matthew Connelly, *A Diplomatic Revolution: Algeria's Fight for Independence and the Origins of the Post-Cold War Era* (Oxford University Press, 2002); Crenshaw's chapter, "The Effectiveness of Terrorism in the Algerian War," in her edited volume, *Terrorism in Context*; Martin Evans, *The Memory of Resistance: French Opposition to the Algerian War (1954–1962)* (Berg, 1997); Alexander Harrison, *Challenging De Gaulle: The O.A.S. and the Counterrevolution in Algeria, 1954–1962* (Praeger, 1989); and John Ruedy, *Modern Algeria: The Origins and Development of a Nation* (Indiana University Press, 1992). A fine comparative study is Gil Merom, *How Democracies Lose Small Wars: State, Society, and the Failures of France in Algeria, Israel in Lebanon, and the United States in Vietnam* (Cambridge, 2003).

Illuminating works by participants and contemporaries include Paul Aussaresses, *The Battle of the Casbah: Terrorism and Counterterrorism in Algeria 1955–1957* (Enigma, 2002); Frantz Fanon, *The Wretched of the Earth* (Grove Press, 2005 [first published in French in 1961]); Mouloud Feraoun, *Journal, 1955–1962: Reflections on the French–Algerian War* (University of Nebraska Press, 2000); David Galula, *Pacification in Algeria, 1956–1958* (RAND, 2006 [1963]); Ted Morgan, *My Battle of Algiers: A Memoir* (Collins, 2006); and Roger Trinquier, *Modern Warfare: A French View of Counterinsurgency* (Praeger, 1964).

12

Decolonization and Ethno-Nationalist Terrorism
from the Late 1960s to the Present

A host of ethno-nationalist struggles have spawned terrorist campaigns in the half century since the Battle of Algiers. In fact, two such conflicts produced the groups that became virtually synonymous (before 9/11) with terrorism in the modern imagination, the Palestine Liberation Organization and the Irish Republican Army. These groups, in turn, inspired a new wave of ethno-nationalist terrorism in the last several decades.

Palestinians, the Palestinian Cause, and Intra-Arab Rivalries

After the 1948 Arab–Israeli War, most Palestinians ended up in dirty and crowded refugee camps, particularly in a narrow piece of land along the Mediterranean known as the Gaza Strip (then held by Egypt) and between the new Israeli border and the Jordan River, the so-called West Bank (seized by the new Hashemite Kingdom of Jordan), as well as in southern Lebanon and southwestern Syria. Refugees generally believed that the Arab states would soon attack Israel again and make possible their return to their homes, a belief encouraged by the loud and threatening proclamations of Arab states against the Jews. The Arab defeat had been so devastating, however, that months of exile turned into years. Meanwhile, Palestinian refugees became an increasing economic burden to their hosts, who also clamped down on disruptive expressions of Palestinian nationalism.

Most Arab states loudly supported the Palestinians, but the primary reason was hardly altruism or true moral outrage. Rather, this public support for the hard-luck Palestinians – and its corollary, blind anti-Israeli rage – was and continues to be an effective means of distracting Arab populations from their own demands for political and economic reform. In fact, the Palestinian cause became so useful to Arab governments in maintaining their nakedly authoritarian states that Arab statesmen came to understand that they were better served by Palestinian misery than Palestinian victory.

The first Palestinian patron was Gamal Abdul Nasser, who came to power in Egypt shortly after a 1952 military coup that overthrew a British puppet. Nasser was a secularist who wanted to make Egypt a modern, self-sufficient state. He was also an apostle of pan-Arab nationalism, an agenda that was well-served by encouraging the first post-1948 Palestinian terrorists. In 1955, Egypt armed and trained militants known as *fedayeen* – the term used eight centuries earlier by the Assassins – who engaged in hit-and-run attacks across the border, killing or wounding several dozen Israeli civilians. These attacks helped precipitate an Israeli invasion during the Suez Crisis of 1956, after which Israeli troops briefly occupied the Sinai Peninsula and destroyed Egypt's *fedayeen* training camps, effectively ending for some time Egyptian sponsorship of Palestinian terrorism.

In 1964, Arab states sponsored the creation of the Palestine Liberation Organization (PLO), an umbrella organization for the many groups representing the refugees. The driving forces behind the creation of the PLO were Egypt's Nasser, who hoped to use the group to restrain the sort of Palestinian militancy that had led to the Israeli invasion, and Jordan's King Hussein, who hoped to mollify Palestinians within his borders and solidify his claim on the West Bank seized by Jordan in 1948. The PLO remained a propaganda tool of the Arabs for several years, confining itself to unleashing harsh words but few bullets against Israel.

Fatah and Yasser Arafat

Things might have stayed like this for a while, but for the addition of three ingredients: a new Palestinian champion, a new reason for exploiting the Palestinian cause, and a new Arab humiliation. The champion was Yasser Arafat, a young Palestinian studying engineering in Cairo. In 1959, Arafat and a close colleague formed Fatah, the aim of which was to wage war against Israel by any means possible. (The name "Fatah" is a reverse acronym of "Harakat al-Tahrir al-Filastini" – literally, "Palestinian National Liberation Movement." "Fatah" colloquially means "conquest" in Arabic and is also used to refer to the period of Arab expansion in the first centuries after the foundation of Islam.) Fatah existed in name only for its first few years, eventually carrying out a few dozen ineffectual attacks against the Israeli military and infrastructure in 1965 and 1966.

The second ingredient was sponsorship from Syria, whose deeply unpopular leaders came to power in a coup in 1966, whereupon they quickly realized that sympathy for the Palestinians and hatred of Israel were perhaps the sole issues that they could use to rally their citizens. Syria became the most important patron of Arafat and Fatah, who, now well armed and funded, stepped up *fedayeen* operations against Israel.

But among the Palestinians there was little support and few recruits for such militancy – that is, until war once again erupted between Israel and its Arab neighbors in the summer of 1967. Israel's devastating victory in the so-called Six Day War changed much. Israel seized the Sinai Peninsula and the Gaza Strip; the West Bank, including all of Jerusalem; and the Golan Heights from, respectively, Egypt, Jordan, and Syria. In so doing, the Israelis came to occupy once-foreign territory where 1.3 million Palestinian refugees lived. Upon the anger, frustration, and humiliation of 1948's *Nakba* (disaster) was heaped the experience of daily encounters with a now direct Israeli occupation. Compounding the problem was the rapid appearance of Jewish settlements in the Occupied Territories carried out officially and unofficially by those keen to make permanent the addition of the land to the state of Israel.

Arafat and Terrorism

As a result, Yasser Arafat and his *fedayeen* became the virtual leaders of Palestinian Arabs, for he seemed to be the only leader willing to stand up to the Israelis. He was also increasingly the only option, since the Israelis methodically expelled or suppressed those indigenous Palestinian nationalist leaders who might have eventually emerged as more moderate negotiating partners. Armed resistance from within and beyond the Occupied Territories thus became the basis for the construction of Palestinian national identity, a development well illustrated in "Returning to Haifa," a short story by the prominent Palestinian author Ghassan Kanafani. In the weeks following the Six Day War, Said and his wife visit Haifa, the city from which they were forced to flee during the *Nakba*. They find that their old house is now occupied by a Jewish woman who adopted the infant son from whom they were separated in the chaos of their flight. As they leave their former home, Said fervently prays that their other son, whom Said had recently forbidden from joining the *fedayeen*, has now done so in their absence. Kanafani suggests, like Frantz Fanon before him, that only violence can counter twenty years of passivity, humiliation, and victimhood.

Arafat studied the FLN's strategy in Algeria and became convinced that terrorism could achieve for the Palestinians what it had for the Algerians. Fatah's first efforts at carrying out terrorist attacks against Israeli civilians in the wake of the Six Day War quickly petered out, however, when Israeli neighborhood watch groups led to the arrest of many of Fatah's inexperienced terrorists. Arafat's response was to set up the group's primary bases across the border in Jordan. The Israeli Defense Forces launched a raid against Fatah headquarters in the Karameh refugee camp in March 1968 but were forced to retreat by Fatah fighters supported by Jordanian artillery – a rare instance in which Arabs had turned back Israelis. Boosted by this psychological victory, Arafat was soon leading a mini-state within the refugee camps of Jordan – what Israeli Prime Minister Golda Meir called "Fatahland" – and effectively commandeered the PLO early in 1969 (he remained chairman of the PLO until his death in 2004). The PLO's governing charter was amended to state that Arafat's *fedayeen* of Fatah were to be the core of the armed struggle against Israel. The PLO's new charter reiterated that its primary goals were the destruction of the state of Israel and the creation of a Palestinian state encompassing all pre-1948 Palestinian territory.

PLO Factions and International Terrorism

The PLO, however, was a fractious coalition, with its constituent organizations divided on matters of personal leadership, ideology, rival Arab backing, and the acceptability of a two-state solution. The latter, first proposed by the UN in 1947, would mean that Palestinians would gain an independent homeland alongside a Jewish state whose existence would be regarded as legitimate. Fatah, the PLO's largest and most influential organization, occupied the center, maintaining a delicate but successful balance among competing ideological concerns and the region's various Arab backers. The PLO's second-largest group was the Popular Front for the Liberation of Palestine, a doctrinaire Marxist group led by the Palestinian Christian George Habash and committed to a modern, secular state. There were many smaller groups as well, several of which were front organizations for other Arab countries. What bound the PLO together during the late 1960s and made possible Arafat's claim to head a united Palestinian front was agreement on the current necessity of armed struggle against Israel.

PLO factionalism gave the lie to any notion of a united front. Other leaders resented Arafat's position atop the PLO and hoped that they could outflank him via more spectacular acts of violence. Many of the

PLO's other factions also wanted to wage the fight against Israel on a larger field, striking Israelis and Israeli interests wherever they could be engaged. After 1967, Palestinian terrorists were soon carrying out attacks outside the Middle East against targets that often had scant connection to Israel, Jews, or Zionism, giving birth to the phenomenon known as international terrorism. Although the new strategy made little military sense, it proved to be an incredibly effective means of publicizing the Palestinian cause, far more than anything pursued by Arafat or Fatah. The champion of this new approach was the Popular Front's George Habash, whose favorite means was airliner hijackings. Habash defended his novel tactic in words that consciously echoed those of the FLN's terrorist mastermind, Ramdane Abane, bluntly asserting, "When we hijack a plane it has more effect than if we killed a hundred Israelis in battle. For decades world opinion has been neither for nor against the Palestinians. It simply ignored us. At least the world is talking about us now" (quoted in Hoffman, *Inside Terrorism*, 70–1).

The Popular Front's first try at "publicity terrorism" was against Israel's national airline, El Al, in July 1968, when a Rome-to-Tel Aviv flight was diverted to Algiers. The hijackers demanded that Israel release sixteen captured guerrillas, which it did after forty days of negotiations. No passengers were harmed, as per Habash's strict instructions. Before long the zeal of young hijackers began to overwhelm Habash's concern about the dangers of bad publicity. Popular Front terrorists stormed an El Al jet several months later on the ground in Athens, screaming "We want to kill the Jews!" (quoted in Wallach and Wallach, *Arafat*, 210). One person was killed and two others were injured. In response, Israel attacked the Beirut airport, destroying thirteen jets belonging to Arab airlines. This act of counter-terror merely attracted more attention to the Palestinian cause.

It also encouraged more hijackings. In August 1969, a Popular Front team including the beautiful and charming female terrorist Leila Khaled hijacked a TWA flight leaving Rome and diverted it to Damascus, where they evacuated the plane and blew it up on the tarmac. The attack drew extraordinary attention, even though there was not a single human casualty. Palestinians also gained their first international celebrity in Khaled, who soon became the darling of revolutionaries everywhere. Leftists around the world decorated their walls with posters of a smiling Khaled in a head scarf, clutching an AK-47, an iconic image second only, perhaps, to that of Che Guevara. Just over a year later, Popular Front hijackers simultaneously tried to seize four planes in Europe. When one attempt failed and Khaled was captured, a fifth flight was hijacked, which successfully secured her release. The lack of governmental preparedness amplified the impact of these hijackings, lending credence to the terrorists' claims that states were at their mercy.

Figure 12.1: Leila Khaled, photographed shortly after hijacking an international flight, 1969
(© Bettmann/CORBIS)

Black September, from Jordan to Munich and Beyond

The flagrant use of Fatahland as an autonomous base for attacking Israeli interests humiliated and angered Jordan's King Hussein, a situation certainly exacerbated by repeated Popular Front attempts to assassinate him. The king finally struck back in September 1970, when the Jordanian army attacked the PLO's camps, killing at least three thousand guerrillas and supporters. The last formal vestiges of PLO's presence in Jordan were soon gone, Arafat, Fatah, and much of the rest of the PLO having fled to new camps in southern Lebanon.

According to some accounts, Arafat had been opposed to the use beyond Israel of what he and his closest associates called the "terror weapon." But humiliated by the destruction of the Fatah mini-state and overshadowed by Habash and the Popular Front's attention-grabbing exploits, Arafat was now courting one indignity he could never suffer: irrelevance. He therefore desperately embraced the "terror weapon" to reclaim authority over Fatah and the PLO. The result was his sponsorship of Black September, a new terrorist organization that took its name from the month of Hussein's humiliating destruction of PLO operations in Jordan. Its first attack, appropriately enough, was the assassination of Jordan's prime minister. Other Fatah terrorist teams struck outside the Middle East against Jewish and third-party targets calculated to generate publicity. Not to be outdone, Habash and the Popular Front carried out a massacre of travelers at Israel's Lod airport. In minutes, twenty-four people were dead and seventy-eight wounded, most of them Puerto Rican pilgrims. Arafat was reportedly horrified, aware of the possible backlash against the Palestinian cause, but he felt constrained to keep pace with the Popular Front.

The result was Black September's most infamous attack, perhaps the most famous in the history of terrorism before 9/11. The goal was maximum visibility for the Palestinian cause; therefore the attack took place against the largest backdrop imaginable, the 1972 Summer Olympics in Munich, West Germany. One of the organizers of the attack bluntly described its rationale: "Bombing attacks on El Al do not serve our cause. We have to kill their most important and most famous people. Since we cannot come close to their statesmen, we have to kill artists and sportsmen" (quoted in Hoffman, *Inside Terrorism*, 71). The Black September team took advantage of lax West German security to gain easy access to the Olympic Village in the early morning hours of September 5. They immediately killed two members of the Israeli Olympic team and took another nine hostage. When Olympics officials suspended all competition for the day, Black September, Arafat, and the PLO achieved what would have been thought impossible before: an estimated international audience of 900 million viewers focused on the demands of the Palestinians. Television commentators, including Jim McKay of ABC Sports, narrated the drama throughout the day, while cameras beamed iconic images around the world of Black September terrorists wearing balaclavas, bearing AK-47s, and peering around doorways and over balconies.

Figure 12.2: Black September terrorists at the Munich Olympics, September 1972. In the lower photo, an International Olympic Committee official negotiates with the terrorists' spokesman
(© Bettmann/CORBIS)

Although international exposure was their real goal, the hostage-takers eventually presented demands: free passage and the release of 236 Palestinians held by the Israelis, as well as several members of ostensibly fraternal revolutionary organizations. The Israelis repeated their by now categorical refusal to negotiate with terrorists. West German officials – horrified at the idea of a massacre of Jewish men on German soil only thirty years after the Holocaust – felt bound to discuss terms with Black September. The West Germans eventually feigned acquiescence, agreeing to transport the terrorists and the hostages via helicopter to the military airbase at Fürstenfeldbruck, whence they were supposedly to be taken to Cairo where prisoners would be exchanged. At the airbase, West

German police botched the hastily arranged rescue attempt. The final list of victims included all nine of the hostages, five of the eight terrorists, and one policeman. The West Germans captured three hostage-takers, all of whom were released less than two months later when a Lufthansa plane was hijacked. The members of Black September were widely praised as martyrs or heroes by Arab radicals for having taken the battle to the enemy in a distant land. Almost everywhere else, there was revulsion.

On the one hand, the Munich attack was a tremendous success, for Black September had attracted international attention to the Palestinian cause on a scale never achieved by earlier ethno-nationalist terrorist organizations. On the other hand, one high-ranking Fatah leader admitted that Munich was a disaster because the deadly outcome escalated the violent tit-for-tat between Israel and the PLO (Hart, *Arafat*, 352). Israel's response took place on two fronts. The Israeli Defense Forces immediately carried out a series of punishing air strikes and incursions against PLO positions in south Lebanon. This marked the beginning of Israel's decades-long pattern of using limited, but devastating attacks against Palestinian communities and suspected PLO bases as retaliation for terrorist strikes. The results became increasingly predictable: the PLO found it more difficult to mount raids against Israel, but sizable Palestinian civilian casualties – there were several hundred in the fall of 1972 – further eroded Israeli legitimacy in the eyes of its neighbors and provided fodder to those who chose to characterize Israel as the true terrorist enterprise.

Israel also carried out a more targeted hunt for the Black September agents who planned the Munich operation, as well as PLO and Fatah officials involved in terrorism. Over the next seven years Operation Wrath of God tracked down and assassinated over a dozen Palestinians, including Ali Hassan Salameh, purportedly Munich's master planner, and two of the Black September hostage takers who had survived the shootout at Fürstenfeldbruck. Israeli hit squads used handguns, car bombs, land mines, and bombs planted in telephones. A separate operation, Spring of Youth, used a team of Israeli commandos to assassinate PLO officials in Lebanon. These Israeli operations created as many problems as they solved, however, particularly when an Israeli assassination squad killed a Moroccan waiter in Lillehammer, Norway, by mistake.

Arafat: Terrorist or Statesman?

Arafat had come to recognize international terrorism's utility in gaining attention in a way that wars, humanitarian nightmares in refugee camps, and classic insurgency never had. He began to cash in on such attention in the years after Munich. In 1974, Arafat was invited to address the United Nations' General Assembly. There he presented himself as a revolutionary and a seeker of justice, stating, "Today I have come bearing an olive branch and a freedom fighter's gun. Do not let the olive branch fall from my hand" (quoted in Hart, *Arafat*, 409). The UN recognized Arafat and the PLO as the sole representatives of the Palestinian people. Arafat, the PLO, and the failure of the Arab states to militarily oppose Israel had essentially turned the Israeli–Arab conflict into an Israeli–Palestinian one; no resolution of the former was now possible without the resolution of the latter, and probably first.

Arafat tried his hand at a statesman's approach to the Israeli–Palestinian conflict less than two years after the Munich massacre. He proposed a plan for a Palestinian "national authority" in the Occupied Territories, which was welcomed by many Palestinians as the first step toward normalization of daily life. But such a plan also implied that Arafat was willing to renounce a Palestinian right of return to the land lost to Israel in the 1948 war, as well as recognize Israel's right to exist within its 1948 borders.

Rejectionism: Abu Nidal and Carlos the Jackal

At this point, the PLO's internal tensions emerged full blown. Arafat barely fought off a coup attempt by several Fatah leaders, and several hard-line groups, including the Popular Front and its splinter factions, defected from the PLO, pledging their opposition to any reconciliation with Israel. The so-called Rejectionist Front was backed by the leaders of Iraq, Syria, and Libya, who feared the impact of the resolution of the Israeli–Palestinian struggle on their ability to control their own populations. Syria continued to fund mutually hostile factions of the Popular Front throughout this period, a good indication of the cynicism of Arab leaders and the political utility of the Palestinian cause.

The most notable product of the PLO's rupture in 1974 was the emergence of two notorious – some would say psychopathic – terrorists who rose to prominence first as Palestinian nationalists and later mercenaries. The first was Sabri Khalil al-Banna, who adopted the *nom de guerre* Abu Nidal ("father of the struggle"). As leader of the Rejectionist organization known as the Fatah Revolutionary Council or simply the Abu Nidal group, his platform was absolute opposition to negotiations with Israel and any Palestinian who engaged in such. Between 1978 and 1983, Abu Nidal's group assassinated more than twenty PLO/Fatah representatives involved in establishing contact with Israeli and Mossad officials throughout Europe and the Middle East. Fatah tried to kill Abu Nidal several times but failed because he was sheltered by the government of Iraq. As an Iraqi agent, Abu Nidal worked to counter Syrian influence in the Palestinian movement, later becoming closely involved in the Lebanese Civil War as a representative of Iraqi interest. Syria later pried him away from Iraq with promises of safe havens and money; on behalf of Damascus he carried out assassinations of Jordanian officials. For a long while in the 1980s, Abu Nidal worked for Libya, organizing terrorism as covert foreign policy for Muammar al-Gaddaf.

The other Palestinian advocate-turned-terrorist-mercenary was the Venezuelan-born revolutionary Ilich Ramírez Sánchez, who became known by the media-bequeathed nickname Carlos the Jackal. In December 1975, Carlos led a Popular Front team in storming a summit of the Organization of the Petroleum Exporting Countries held in Vienna, taking about sixty hostages. All the hostages were eventually released after an international flying odyssey. The goal had been to intimidate those Arab powers contemplating negotiating with Israel or supporting Arafat and the PLO in their efforts to do the same. In the late 1970s Carlos formed the Organization of the Armed Arab Struggle, which in the 1980s carried out assassinations and terrorist attacks on behalf of Cuba, some of the Soviet Union's Eastern European satellites, and several Arab states, including Syria, Iraq, and Libya. It is impossible to create a definitive list of the terrorist attacks for which Carlos was responsible, since he repeatedly claimed credit for strikes that he almost certainly was not involved in, so devoted had he become to the international media attention granted to terrorists. "The more I'm talked about," Carlos declared to a colleague, "the more dangerous I appear. That's all the better for me" (quoted in Richardson, *Paradise Poisoned*, 96).

From the mid 1970s onward, Arafat became more and more a prisoner of terrorism, a tool that he had helped unleash in the Israeli–Palestinian conflict. He wanted to be viewed as a statesman and the father of his country, but had become addicted to terrorism as the primary source of funding, influence, legitimacy, and respect. He repeatedly turned to terrorism in order to assert control or leadership over the PLO, to outflank his rivals in the PLO and Arab states, and to restore morale after repeated disappointments, such as the Jordanian disaster. For instance, Arafat ordered a 1974 raid against the northern Israeli city of Nahariya primarily in order to preserve Fatah's *bona fides* in the wake of recent attacks by Rejectionist groups that killed and wounded dozens of adults and schoolchildren. When it came to the use of terror against Israel, Arafat and Fatah believed that to be outpaced by their rivals was the most dangerous path of all.

The PLO in Lebanon and Israeli Counter-Terrorism

The move to southern Lebanon in 1970 further hemmed in Arafat who, not having learned his lesson in Jordan, proceeded to construct another Fatah mini-state. In Lebanon, this possibility was all the more tempting given the civil war that broke out in 1975, a war brought on in part by the destabilizing presence of PLO militias. The chaos of the Lebanese Civil War provided opportunities to Arafat but failed to materially advance the cause of Palestinian independence or alleviate the condition of the great numbers of Palestinian refugees. The virtual disintegration of central Lebanese authority produced a vacuum filled by a new generation of militias and terror organizations. It also provoked even more intervention and sponsorship of terrorism by foreign powers, particularly Syria, which harbored dreams of greater influence or even territorial expansion at the expense of Lebanon and Jordan. During this period, PLO factionalism seemed to increase daily. Even as he tried to carve out a new Fatahland, Arafat continued to carry out attacks against Israel, often using elaborate shell games to allow him to claim to his inner circle that he was still fighting against the Zionist enemy while establishing plausible deniability with Israel and its allies. One such attack took place in March 1978 when a shootout with Israeli troops near Haifa ended with a Fatah massacre of at least thirty-five civilians. This raid prompted the first of several Israeli incursions into southern Lebanon.

Arafat's house of cards came tumbling down around him when Israel launched a full-fledged invasion of Lebanon in 1982. Ariel Sharon, the Israeli defense minister and principal architect of the plan, hoped to destroy the PLO and secure Israel's northern border against Palestinian insurgents and terrorists. The invasion set in motion a chain of events that deepened Lebanese factionalism and increased the role of Syria, thus ensuring more violence and chaos on Israel's northern border, particularly after Israel withdrew from central and eastern Lebanon in 1985. The Israeli invasion also failed to eliminate Arafat and the PLO. Early in the invasion, Israeli troops surrounded Arafat and his Fatah guerrillas in West Beirut, but house-to-house fighting and intense shelling killed thousands of civilians without destroying the *fedayeen*. When Arafat could hold out no longer, he prepared to flee. His international standing was so great that he was ushered out of Lebanon – first to Tripoli, north of the city, and then to Tunisia, his third place of exile – with a US Marine escort. Infuriated at Arafat's escape and convinced that he still had an opportunity to inflict severe damage on the PLO's "terrorist nests," Sharon allowed Israeli-allied Christian militias to enter Palestinian refugee camps at Sabra and Shatila, which were ringed with Israeli troops. The Christian militias went on a rampage, killing over a thousand Palestinian and Lebanese Muslim civilians as Israeli soldiers and tanks illuminated the camps with flares and prevented anyone from fleeing. The massacre stoked grassroots Palestinian hatred of the Jewish state and doubts about Arafat's ability to materially advance Palestinian civilian interests. Israeli public sentiment also turned against the invasion, with Sharon soon forced out of office. The Lebanese Civil War and the Israeli invasion were counter productive on another front, as well, triggering the costly US Marine intervention and the emergence of new militias and foreign-backed organizations, such as Islamic Jihad and Hezbollah, which were determined to punish the West and take the war to Israel. This was a critical moment in the development of Islamism and the targeting of Americans, a subject to which we will return in Chapter 14.

The results of Israeli intervention in the Lebanese Civil War highlighted the difficulties inherent in Israel's efforts to deal with Arafat, the PLO, and terrorism. Several decades of Israeli military success ironically forced the Palestinians into believing that terrorism was the only way to continue their struggle against the Jewish state. Israel became locked into tit-for-tat violence with the most militant segments of the Palestinian cause, a process that sidelined moderates on both sides, creating a self-sustaining logic of confrontation. Each side justified its hard-edged policies in reference to their foe's radical violence, in essence coming to depend on the cycles of terror and violence. And without a doubt, Israel's myriad military and intelligence agencies became adept at counter-terror (in both senses of the word) not only through its use of infiltrators, efficient intelligence gathering, and targeted assassination but also through the use of collective punishment. In the case of Lebanon, the Israeli decision to maintain a presence in the South as a defensive bulwark against Hezbollah and other militias aided Palestinian and Lebanese groups in their efforts to raise money and recruit fighters in their struggle for national liberation. Not until 2000 did Israeli troops fully withdraw from southern Lebanon.

Complicating matters further, Israel has long maintained a double standard when identifying terrorism in its history. Until very recently, new conscripts were welcomed into Israeli armored units with a dramatic night-time oath atop Masada that invoked the Sicarii as heroic freedom fighters, not the terrorists-cum-bandits they were. Two pro-Zionist terrorists during and after the Second World War, Yitzhak Shamir and Menachem Begin, became Israeli prime ministers. And to this day, Israeli cities and towns are full of streets named after members and units of Irgun and LEHI. Stamps and medals have been issued honoring them, as well. If anything, Israeli memorialization of Irgun *et al* stepped up after Begin became prime minister in 1977, thus ushering in a new era of respect and prominence for the old Zionist/Israeli right.

Arafat in Tunisia, Rejectionist Terror, and Gaddafi of Libya

Arafat was even more locked into a mindset keyed to cycles of terror and counter-terror. Once again chastened and now with his forces more fragmented than ever, Arafat responded in what had become his characteristic ways. On the one hand, Arafat the statesman explored a peace initiative introduced by US President Ronald Reagan that would have created a "self-governing," but not independent, Palestinian entity in the West Bank to be jointly administered by Jordan. On the other hand, Arafat the terrorist fought to regain the initiative against his Rejectionist rivals. In order to keep his statesman's hands clean, Arafat continued to operate behind a multitude of other organizations. The most prominent example in this period was the seajacking of the Italian cruise ship *Achille Lauro* in October 1985 by a small PLO faction backed by Iraq but led by a member of Fatah. The seajacking went awry, and the terrorists abandoned the ship after killing the wheelchair-bound Jewish-American Leon Klinghoffer. So great was the PLO's notoriety by this point that even terror operations with only one casualty served to reinforce the image of Arafat and his henchmen as the era's most bloodthirsty purveyors of terrorist violence. In this, one could say that the PLO had become a victim of its own success.

Arafat, who always claimed to be the sole leader of the Palestinian diaspora, increasingly reaped the whirlwind, since Israel blamed him for every terrorist atrocity carried out by Palestinian Rejectionist groups. Rejectionist groups were aware of this and carried out some terrorist attacks in order to discredit – even frame – Arafat and derail Israeli–Jordanian negotiations.

Those dictators in the region who maintained their hold on power in part by denouncing Israel and exploiting anger over the plight of the Palestinians also sponsored such terrorism. Enter Muammar al-Gaddafi, Libya's secular, pan-Arabist leader since coming to power in a coup in 1969. Gaddafi eventually became the principal employer of the Abu Nidal group, which, presumably on orders from Gaddafi, carried out simultaneous attacks on El Al ticket counters in Vienna and Rome in 1985, killing eighteen civilians and wounding 120. Arafat immediately denounced the massacres, sensing there was little to be gained in such attacks anymore. After President Reagan denounced Gaddafi as the "mad dog of the Middle East" for his backing of international terrorism, the United States began a campaign to intimidate and limit Libya, in particular challenging the extent of Libya's reach into territorial waters in the Mediterranean. In response, Gaddafi used Abu Nidal to wage a covert campaign of revenge against US interests. In 1986, a bomb attack on a Berlin night club killed two US soldiers and a civilian and injured nearly three hundred others. The US traced the attacks to Gaddafi as Abu Nidal's backer and retaliated later that year by bombing Gaddafi's headquarters in Tripoli, killing about sixty military officials, governmental personnel, and civilians, including Gaddafi's adopted daughter. The feud escalated even further when Libyan officials, presumably acting on Gaddafi's orders, planted a bomb on board Pan Am Flight 103 in December 1988. The plane exploded over Lockerbie, Scotland, killing 270, including eleven on the ground.

The First Intifada

Back in the Occupied Territories, Palestinians – feeling betrayed by the Israelis and the PLO alike – took matters into their own hands with what became known as the first Intifada ("shaking off") in December 1987. Civilians in Gaza and the West Bank mounted enormous demonstrations, engaged in passive resistance, staged strikes, and stoned Israeli checkpoints, settlers, troops, and tanks. The Israeli military, long used to dealing with terrorists and guerrillas, responded to rock-throwing teenagers with deadly force. By mid 1990, over eight hundred Palestinians had died in the violence, at least one-quarter of them boys and girls under the age of sixteen. International opinion had never been more on the side of the Palestinians.

Arafat was caught off guard by the uprising but within a year had managed to impose considerable control over the Intifada. In the meantime, a new organization was also exercising influence, particularly in the Gaza Strip. This was Hamas, an armed branch of Egypt's Sunni Muslim Brotherhood. Recently, evidence has emerged that the Israeli authorities funneled intelligence and funds to Hamas in an effort to produce a counterweight to Arafat and the PLO, a move that later became one of the twentieth century's most notorious backfires. Hamas and its development as part of the modern Islamist movement will be explored in Chapter 14.

Arafat's Hits and Misses

Arafat, meanwhile, sensed that with much international opinion on the side of the Palestinians, this was his moment to make a bold move. In late 1988, Arafat and the PLO declared the creation of an independent

Palestinian state, informally acknowledged the Israeli right to existence, and condemned the use of terrorism (including Israeli "state terrorism"). During a December 14, 1988, press conference, Arafat renounced his own use of terror as a political weapon, stating, "Enough is enough. Enough is enough. Enough is enough" (quoted in Bickerton and Klausner, *Concise History of the Arab–Israeli Conflict*, 234). Meanwhile, Arafat encouraged more protests, which he knew would result in Israeli crackdowns and the deaths of young Palestinians – deaths which were useful in mobilizing significant Israeli public opinion against the Shamir government, the Israeli military's stridency, and new settlements. With the PLO posed to achieve a breakthrough victory, Arafat committed a potentially fatal error when he refused to condemn Saddam Hussein and Iraq's invasion of Kuwait in August 1990. As US troops poured into Saudi Arabia, Arafat called on all Arabs to resist the West. Never had Arafat more lived up to the famous pronouncement by the Israeli diplomat and historian Abba Eban that under Arafat, "The Palestinians never miss an opportunity to miss an opportunity."

The complete breakdown of pan-Arab unity in the wake of the 1991 Gulf War seriously hurt Arafat and the PLO. Those Arab states most responsible for funding Arafat and the PLO's activities, such as Saudi Arabia and Kuwait, slowed their money to a trickle. Inside the Occupied Territories, Hamas took advantage of the PLO's troubles to exert more and more influence over the Intifada. In southern Lebanon, Hezbollah became a regional force to be reckoned with and an uncompromising foe of Israel. Here it is important to note that popular Palestinian and Lebanese support for Hamas and Hezbollah probably owes more to their lack of corruption and their emphasis on social services than because of their use of terror and militancy, a conclusion that sheds much light on the PLO's four-decade crusade for legitimacy.

Arafat as Statesman

Arafat seemed to have been outhustled and the PLO outflanked on every front. Perhaps his loss of control over the Palestinian movement triggered some new thinking on Arafat's part, or perhaps his renunciation of terrorism – always treated by the Israelis as simply a piece of theatre – was actually genuine. In any case, Arafat responded to his position of weakness in dramatically different fashion than he had after the expulsion from Jordan or Lebanon. This time his emissaries carried out secret talks with the Israelis. Circumstances, particularly the success of the Intifada and the rise of Hamas and Hezbollah, had finally cast Arafat, Fatah, and the

PLO in the role of Palestinian moderates, despite all the carnage inflicted by the PLO. Israel and the PLO formally recognized each other in 1993 in the Oslo Accords and pledged to engage in direct talks geared toward the creation of an autonomous – but still not independent – Palestinian entity in Gaza and the West Bank. The next summer, Arafat's transition to full-fledged statesman was complete when he was elected president of the Palestinian Authority and made a triumphant return to newly established headquarters in Gaza City. His triumph was only partial, however, for Arafat had to now contend with Hamas, which increasingly imagined itself as the legitimate voice of the Palestinian people. As negotiations between the PLO and Israel dragged on, caught up on a wide array of thorny issues, Hamas played the role of the new Rejectionist Front. With peace tantalizingly close, but most Palestinians still living in depressingly difficult circumstances, a second Intifida broke out in September 2000, with Hamas and Fatah vying for control of the movement. Some of the PLO's secular factions have continued to use terror against Israel, but recently the source of most terror attacks has been Hamas and Hezbollah.

The Irish Republican Army

The story of the Irish Republican Army and its predecessors is central to the introduction of ethno-nationalist terrorism in the late nineteenth and early twentieth centuries, but it is the IRA of the last third of the twentieth century that has most fascinated and horrified observers. In fact, the IRA is second only to the PLO as the pre-9/11 world's most iconic terrorist organization. Its emergence as such followed an odd route, and the IRA was reduced to near obscurity on more than one occasion. It embraced socialism in the 1930s and began to champion class struggle as equally vital as the national struggle. Flirtation with the Nazis during the Second World War – as common enemies of the United Kingdom – nearly destroyed what status the IRA retained as the banner carriers for Irish republicanism. Its irrelevance was exacerbated by its commitment to abstentionism, the long-standing policy of refusing to occupy seats in Northern Ireland's devolved parliament, even when support for republicanism won it enough votes to do so. In a bid to reassert its importance, the IRA began a terrorism campaign in Northern Ireland in 1956 that eventually claimed the life of eleven Irish "traitors" and six Royal Ulster Constabulary policemen but alienated many republicans. Short on public support in the north and south, the IRA suspended its terrorism campaign in 1962, but did not disband its paramilitary structure. The IRA was biding its time.

Northern Ireland Ignites

Meanwhile, a Catholic civil rights movement in the north (informed by the American campaign led by the Revd. Martin Luther King, Jr.) peacefully agitated for better education, better housing, and more employment opportunities. While the Catholic population generally supported the new civil rights movement as more politically viable and less morally problematic than IRA violence, the romance of the armed struggle deeply resonated with Catholics who felt themselves abandoned and in need of protection. For their part, even moderate Protestants saw their position as highly precarious and suspected that the civil rights movement was simply cover for IRA republicanism. This fear encouraged the Protestant, unionist ruling elite of Northern Ireland to hold fast to its near monopoly on political power and force, particularly through the unionist-only police agency, the well-armed and well-trained Royal Ulster Constabulary, and its reserve force, the so-called B-Specials, itself a highly sectarian but poorly trained civilian militia.

The situation was made worse by the Ulster Volunteer Force (UVF), a unionist terror organization that attacked Catholics in order to provoke violent responses, harden sectarian lines, and encourage observers to conflate the Catholic civil rights movement and militant republicanism. The UVF's hope was to precipitate the civil war between unionists and republicans that it felt had been brewing for years. The group's notorious Malvern Street Murders in the summer of 1966 nearly provoked a general outbreak of violence, a development only averted by the authorities' swift prosecution of the UVF killers. But the situation continued to deteriorate: more unionist paramilitaries formed, egged on by the hardline Protestant politician Ian Paisley; and IRA posters and republican rhetoric ominously spread throughout Catholic neighborhoods.

Things came to a head – and the UVF got its wish – in August 1969 when the Constabulary and the B-Specials beat, tear-gassed, and terrorized a peaceful civil rights march from Londonderry to Belfast and then watched as gangs of unionist Apprentice Boys rioted. A reporter who witnessed a Constabulary unit machine-gunning a Catholic neighborhood summed up the scene: "Anyone who was there that August night in Belfast . . . understood how the revival of the IRA became possible, and why the Royal Ulster Constabulary forfeited for ever the trust of Catholic Ireland" (quoted in Mulholland, *Northern Ireland*, 60). With Belfast in flames, at least six people dead, and hundreds wounded from gunshots, London sent in six thousand British troops to restore order, a number soon to rise to twenty-five thousand.

Catholics and Protestants alike welcomed the British Army, but for different reasons. Catholics – even many republicans – hoped the British would serve as peacekeepers and honest brokers, while the Protestants saw in the British an ally. The British soldiers sent from Germany to Northern Ireland had been trained to counter a Soviet invasion with overwhelming force and unsurprisingly treated demonstrators and agitators as an armed enemy and responded to the threat of shadowy agents operating in the midst of civilians with indiscriminate violence. British troops quickly went to work with the Constabulary and B-Specials quarantining Catholic neighborhoods, beating demonstrators, ferreting out still hidden IRA activists, and alienating the public. In a self-fulfilling prophecy made possible by the UVF, hardline Protestants, and the British Army, the Catholic population – hungry for protection, leadership, and respect – turned to the IRA, which leapt at the opportunity to reclaim its position as the voice of Catholics and eager to channel all disgruntlement into republicanism.

The heightened legitimacy and support accorded the IRA triggered fresh demands for self-defense among Northern Ireland's Protestants, leading to the formation and operation of ever more unionist paramilitary organizations. When the British Army, finally aware of the beast it helped unleash, began to crack down on paramilitary activity, British soldiers found themselves the target of terrorist violence from both sides, an unwitting participant in a tribal war. Developments in Northern Ireland echoed those of a decade earlier in Algeria, where the French Army was drawn into a war not of its choosing, increasingly tethered to the *colons* who always suspected that Paris was about to make unacceptable concessions to the native population. The British made their own position more difficult by tolerating the legal presence of many unionist paramilitaries, such as the Ulster Defence Association and the Ulster Volunteer Force, which carried out assassinations and terror attacks and repeatedly drew the British into the middle of gunfights through their provocative parades and demonstrations in Catholic neighborhoods. As with Algeria's *colon* vigilantism and the eventual outright treason of the OAS, most unionist terrorism was simply meant to exact revenge.

The Provisional Irish Republican Army

In the wake of the return to open struggle in 1969, long-simmering tensions within the IRA came to the fore. Those in the IRA most committed to socialism were uncomfortable with a turn toward open militancy, instead preferring to develop a mass movement embracing the whole island. Dissenters concentrated in the north responded that the republican struggle, now particularly articulated as the defense of the Catholic population, should trump all else. They soon walked out, declaring themselves the Provisional IRA. For the so-called Provos, the armed struggle was paramount and any talk of pursuing political compromises was treasonous. The remaining republicans fashioned themselves the Official IRA. Although it briefly engaged in violence, the OIRA declared a ceasefire in 1972 and repudiated revolutionary violence. The field was left to the Provos – who soon coopted the name IRA – and the inevitable splinter groups it generated. The Provos' endgame was barely more reasonable than the unionists, since Provo demands for unification with the rest of the island were fanciful for at least three reasons. First, the British all along held fast to the position that Northern Ireland's status could only be changed by a majority decision, and Protestant unionists were clearly in the majority. Second, unionists were hardly likely to be compelled to leave for England, since their identity was inextricably bound up with Northern Ireland as their historical homeland. And third, the Republic of Ireland was in no position to absorb Ulster, given that the latter's population had grown accustomed to the inordinately expensive British welfare state. Unfortunately, for decades, any sort of negotiated middle ground itself remained a hopeless fantasy, in light of both sides' entrenched attitudes concerning self-defense and survival.

For the first two years of the new armed struggle, Provo violence was directed solely against unionists and Catholic Irish thought to be spies, informers, and mutineers. Provos killed the first British soldier in 1971, after the UK introduced the policy of internment without trial and stepped up operations to seize IRA weapons and suspects. One such tactic was the use of curfews to clear the streets, followed up with house-to-house searches backed up by helicopters and armored vehicles. Between 1971 and 1976, the Army made about 250,000 such house searches. As far as Catholics were concerned, the British Army had become an occupying army. London's decision in 1972 to disband Northern Ireland's parliament handed the IRA a major propaganda victory, since it could now claim that Ulster was a British colony in word and deed.

New levels of Provo violence were not long in coming, and in 1972 British officials began to describe the Troubles as "war with the IRA" (quoted in Mulholland, *Northern Ireland*, 75). Such talk fed the growing Catholic perception of the IRA as a legitimate army, a sense that was heightened even more by the fact that the British tolerated the organization of IRA prisoners along military lines. Posters and graffiti that aped civil defense propaganda during the Second World War came to dominate public spaces throughout Catholic neighborhoods. All of this served to erode lingering Catholic restraints on the use of political violence and terror. The final step toward the abyss occurred on January 30, 1972, when British troops killed fourteen unarmed civilians during a violent crackdown on an unruly demonstration. The event quickly dubbed "Bloody Sunday" led to a surge of "volunteers," as they were known, into the IRA and the establishment of wide-scale passive support for IRA operations among the Catholic population. Throughout the Troubles, volunteers often revealed that they joined the IRA after they or a family member were victimized by the British or unionist paramilitaries.

IRA gun battles and sniping attacks on British troops soon lent the conflict the air of a guerrilla war. Parallel IRA attacks on civilians made clear that this was also a war of terror. In July 21, 1972 – what unionists came to call "Bloody Friday" – the IRA exploded twenty-two bombs in downtown Belfast, killing nine civilians and wounding over one hundred. Ten days later, three more IRA car bombs killed nine civilians near Derry. Most of these bombs were made out of a mix of ammonium nitrate and fuel oil (ANFO), cheap and readily available ingredients capable of unleashing an amazing amount of devastation for their weight. For this reason, ANFO bombs became staples of IRA's terror campaign, as well as countless others around the globe.

IRA vs. UVF vs. Britain

The IRA directed most of its energy and bile toward its enemy's armed units during the mid-1970s. The majority of the IRA's victims were thus British soldiers, Constabulary policemen, and members of armed paramilitary unionist groups, despite the occasional explosion of violence against civilians as in July 1972. On the other hand, since unionist paramilitaries were no more capable of ferreting IRA gunmen out from the larger population than was the British Army, unionist violence and terror was overwhelmingly directed against the Catholic population. In the words of the UVF's leader, Gusty Spence, "If it wasn't possible to get at the IRA then some thought, 'We'll get those who are harboring them, succoring them, comforting them and supporting them'" (quoted in Mulholland, *Northern Ireland*, 90). Not surprisingly, the majority of the victims of unionist violence were Catholic civilians. Unionists sometimes struck south of the border, as in 1974, when they set off two car bombs in Dublin and Monaghan that killed thirty-three civilians, an attack that helped derail negotiations over a power-sharing agreement between the Republic of Ireland and the UK. Because Protestants, unlike the Catholics, could enlist in an overt military or police force, those who fought the IRA through participation in a paramilitary organization tended to do so because their thuggish, often criminal records precluded joining the military. Unionist terror, as a result, tended to be more flamboyant, provocative, and brutal; it also more frequently involved torture, which was conducted in the so-called "romper rooms" of unionist hangouts.

In 1974, the British began to move away from the sort of overt military behavior that routinely inflamed public opinion and increased Catholic support for the IRA. The UK redirected its efforts in two not entirely reconcilable ways. The first was to try to recast the Troubles as a criminal matter. More emphasis was placed on the courts as the proper vehicle for securing Northern Ireland. The British had some success in this regard, but the strategy also proved counterproductive in that the authorities yielded to the temptation of denouncing as "terrorism" a wide variety of behaviors – including propaganda, arms procurement, fundraising, and guerrilla operations – that many Catholics regarded as part of a legitimate struggle, armed or otherwise.

The second – and far more controversial – manner in which the British redirected the conflict involved the increased use of covert operations that combined intelligence gathering, psychological warfare, and counterterror. The British used teams of commandos from the elite Special Air Service as well as other newly created organizations to tail, capture, and/or kill IRA volunteers. British agents involved in such operations occasionally used assassination and torture and became involved in criminal enterprises, a fact that lent covert operations the air of mafia undertakings. Widespread knowledge – or at least suspicion – about the work of British commandos gave rise to the widely held opinion that London was conducting a "dirty war" against Irish republicanism in Northern Ireland. The result of both efforts – increased use of the courts and covert operations – was negatively and mutually reinforcing and contributed to the further erosion of the legitimacy of the UK's presence in Northern Ireland. As Karl Heinzen had observed in the middle of the previous century, the use of ostensibly legal means as the cover for what was widely perceived as immoral and illegitimate purposes tended to debase the law rather than elevate the purposes. The British, nonetheless, managed to curtail the IRA's overt military behavior and shaved what had been a mass movement down to perhaps five to seven hundred volunteers.

The Provos' "Long War"

British success bred its own problems, for a desperate IRA soon adopted more traditional terror tactics, such as assassinations of officials and more frequent attacks on civilians. It also forced the IRA to organize itself into small cells which were better insulated from infiltration, but also more prone to acts of unsanctioned violence. British insistence on applying the word "terrorist" to all IRA behavior thus once again proved to be a self-fulfilling prophecy.

The IRA had built up enough credibility with the Catholic population of Northern Ireland during the early phases of the Troubles that it was able to sustain operations – despite its far more overt turn toward terrorism – well into the 1990s. The IRA dubbed its new strategy "the long war," and it combined elements of both classic guerrilla warfare and terrorism. *The Green Book*, a manual distributed to all volunteers, stated in its 1977 edition that the IRA was waging a "war of attrition against enemy personnel which is aimed at causing as many casualties and deaths as possible so as to create a demand from their people at home for their withdrawal." The manual also called for a "bombing campaign aimed at making the enemy's financial interest . . . unprofitable" and "to make the Six Counties . . . ungovernable except by colonial military rule" (quoted in Coogan, *The IRA*, 555).

The IRA had always been aware that British heavy-handedness provided the single greatest boost to IRA popularity and legitimacy. The IRA thus took the battle to England on several occasions, hoping to coax the British Army into more self-defeating behavior. In the fall of 1974, the IRA set off bombs in five pubs across England, killing twenty-eight civilians and wounding over two hundred. These bombings called forth much revulsion even in Northern Ireland, but the effects were mitigated and even reversed when the British imprisoned the wrong people (the so-called Guilford Four and the Birmingham Six) for over fifteen years. Nor was this the end of violence outside of Northern Ireland. In 1979, an IRA team pulled off perhaps its most spectacular attack, assassinating the 79-year-old Lord Louis Mountbatten – a war hero, the last viceroy of British India, and Queen Elizabeth's cousin – on his yacht off the northwest coast of the Republic of Ireland. Gerry Adams, soon to be the head of Sinn Féin, the IRA's political arm, declared, "In my opinion, the IRA achieved its objective: people started paying attention to what was happening in Ireland" (quoted in *Time*, November 19, 1979). Five years later, IRA brazenness reached new levels when operatives bombed the Grand Hotel in Brighton, England, during the Conservative Party's conference in 1984. Five people died, and Margaret Thatcher, Britain's prime minister, narrowly escaped injury.

The IRA's terrorism strategy was born of weakness, but it made Britain's task of dealing with Northern Ireland very difficult. While the IRA remained fixated on a number of long-term – but admittedly unreasonable – goals, British attention was distracted away from the creation of a master plan toward more immediate concerns over security. The result was a makeshift policy that exacerbated the situation, for it alienated all, satisfied none, secured little, and rectified nothing. Even when the British Army was adapted to the specifics of the conflict in Northern Ireland, it remained a force ill suited to the primary work at hand, namely police investigation and legitimacy building. All it took was an occasional lapse in British military discipline, and a new generation of martyrs was created to serve the cause of Irish republicanism and IRA militancy.

The IRA Abroad

But martyrs and recruits were not enough to keep the IRA afloat during its long campaign; the IRA relied on money and arms from abroad. The IRA's greatest source of funding was the sizable Irish-American community, whose support had tapered off during the IRA's drift toward Marxism mid-century. With the start of the Troubles in 1969 and the emergence of the Provisional IRA, there was once again a cause and an appropriate object of Irish-American support. One group, the Irish Northern Aid Committee, raised money in bars and through dinners in the 1970s to the tune of nearly $3 million (Geldard and Craig, *IRA, INLA*, 53–4). Such funds were ostensibly for prisoner relief and victims' care, but much of the money was used to purchase weapons. Some sympathetic Irish-Americans simply cut to the chase: one smuggler supposedly supplied the IRA with approximately 250 civilian versions of the standard US Army issue M-I6 every year for most of the 1970s.

Outside of North America, the IRA portrayed itself as a rather different sort of organization, depending on the audience. In Europe, the IRA forged links with revolutionary Marxist groups, such as West Germany's Red Army Faction and Italy's Red Brigades, with whom it played up its own revolutionary and socialist heritages. These groups not only provided the IRA with some weapons and training, but also intelligence and organizational help. The IRA formed its closest and most productive relationships with other ethno-nationalist organizations that saw themselves, as did the Provos, fighting against a colonial occupier. The IRA and the Basque separatist group ETA traded weapons and equipment, and IRA volunteers trained at PLO camps in the Middle East and North Africa in 1968 and throughout the late 1970s.

Gerry Adams and the Provos also studied classic texts and campaigns from the history of terrorism and guerrilla warfare. IRA leadership was strongly influenced by Fanon's works on anti-colonialism and tales of the Greek Cypriots' struggle against the British. Of particular interest was Robert Taber's 1965 study of guerrilla movements, *The War of the Flea*, in which he recounted how the Irgun, EOKA, and other organizations studied the work and writings of the early IRA leader, Michael Collins. For a group so rooted in history, it was odd that the IRA had to rediscover its own past. It becomes understandable when we remember that the IRA's version of its history had been extensively mythologized and Collins' contributions minimized given his willingness to accept partition in 1921.

Alternatives to Terrorism

Irish-American, Red Army Faction, and PLO aid did not produce victory for the IRA; rather it simply kept it afloat. The stalemate between the IRA and British authorities was perhaps best illustrated in 1980–1, when thirty-three IRA volunteers held in the notorious prison known as the Maze launched a hunger strike. Demanding that they be treated as political prisoners, the inmates foreswore all food and welcomed martyrdom, attracting unprecedented international attention to the IRA cause. The central figure in the drama was Bobby Sands, a 26-year-old arrested for a non-violent crime. Seizing on the public relations value of the hunger strike, other volunteers serving sentences for violent crimes were forbidden to engage in the protest. On the verge of death, Sands was even elected to Northern Ireland's parliament (the first of four such hunger strikers). When Sands died, an estimated 100,000 people attended his funeral in Belfast. All told, ten hunger strikers died before the IRA called off the protest. Unable to win on the battlefield or through terrorism, the IRA had reasserted its importance from within the walls of a prison.

A window of opportunity was opening. The first inklings of progress came in 1985, when the British and Irish governments – aided by moderate Northern Catholic leaders – concluded the Anglo-Irish Agreement. The Agreement provided a framework for the two states to discuss policies for Northern Ireland and led to the first clear improvements in Catholic housing and employment in a generation. Just as importantly, Thatcher excluded unionists from the negotiations, an acknowledgment that the UK's patience with Ulster's *colons* was thinning.

Negotiations and Terrorism

The specter of compromise led hardcore republicans and unionists to more violence. Unionists grew alarmed at the prospect of a British sell-out, and the IRA had to demonstrate it was still in possession of its revolutionary *bona fides*. But Catholic tolerance for IRA violence was beginning to wane.

The reasons for this were many. Catholics sensed that IRA provocations jeopardized the possibility of more negotiations and thus more improvements in the Catholic standard of living. With new options for addressing long-held grievances, the population no longer felt backed into a corner, dependent on IRA violence as the sole means of self-defense and self-respect. The Irish government's involvement in the North also implied that the IRA was no longer the sole defender of the nation, a conviction that had always encouraged the IRA's win-at-all-cost rhetoric. Perhaps most importantly, Catholics had grown tired of the funerals and fear. When the IRA killed civilians – such as a Remembrance Day bombing in Enniskillen in 1987 that killed eleven Protestants, a landmine attack in 1992 that killed seven, and a botched effort to target the leadership of a unionist paramilitary group in 1993 that killed nine – Catholic revulsion throughout Northern Ireland was palpable. Catholic hopes unfortunately meant new fears for Ulster's unionist paramilitaries, who repeatedly lashed out at the IRA. When volunteers could not be found, Catholic civilians would do. The Ulster Freedom Fighters and other groups killed dozens of civilians in the late 1980s and early 1990s, particularly after IRA attacks.

But changes were afoot, in Northern Ireland as well as the leadership of the IRA. By the early 1990s Adams and his deputy Martin McGuinness had grown tired of the endless tit-for-tat killing that always threatened to erupt into full-scale sectarian warfare; more importantly, they had come to understand that the armed struggle had failed to achieve its lofty goals. The hunger strikes and associated electoral successes of the early 1980s had demonstrated that Sinn Féin could become a real force in Northern Ireland's political scene, achieving through the ballot box at least some of what seemed further and further out of reach through violence. And now, IRA violence, particularly the Remembrance Day massacre in Enniskillen, threatened that electoral success, alienating Catholics who were increasingly disgusted by the pointless killing. Adams was particularly sensitive to the public's mood and showed himself to be flexible, even reasonable. He was a charismatic leader and as one of the most ardent advocates of the armed struggle was immunized against charges of cowardice or betrayal.

At last motivated by something more realistic than the fanciful dream of all-island nationalism and something more substantive than revenge and self-defense of Northern Irish Catholics, the IRA pursued a different kind of terror campaign in Britain in the early 1990s. The first hint of this came in February 1991 when the IRA carried out a mortar strike on the prime minister's London residence that shocked the British people but, by design or serendipitous accident, caused no casualties. In any case, the attack prefigured a serious change in the IRA's approach, which was increasingly calculated to provoke outrage, attract international attention, and convince the government that the IRA could not be defeated, all while causing a minimum of casualties and thus a minimum of damage to Britain's willingness to engage in talks. This was terrorism meant to push the enemy toward the negotiation table, rather than the more common goal of entrenching differences and polarizing the neutral middle. In the IRA's new British campaign, phoned-in warnings, off-hours bombings, and massive property damage became the norm. In April 1992, the IRA set off an enormous bomb in London's financial center known as the Baltic Exchange that killed three civilians and caused hundreds of millions of pounds' worth of damage – approximately as much financial damage, in fact, as had been inflicted so far in more than twenty years of IRA violence. In April 1993, a car bomb in the London financial area of Bishopsgate went off after hours, killing only one person, a foolhardy photographer who had rushed to where the IRA had warned a bomb would go off. Once again, the IRA caused a spectacular amount of economic damage – some initial estimates, later scaled down, ran to £1 billion.

The British authorities repeatedly denounced the attacks and pledged not to negotiate with their perpetrators, but the outrages helped convince the UK that although the IRA could not achieve a military victory, it could also not be eliminated. Northern Ireland's most reasonable negotiating partner was John Hume, leader of the Social Democratic and Labour Party (SDLP), who had been involved in the Anglo-Irish Agreement of 1985; it was to him that Britain reached out for direct talks. Shortly thereafter, Hume took the next critical step of contacting Adams and Sinn Féin for talks that essentially led to the formation of a united nationalist front in 1993. Also critical was the close involvement of Albert Reynolds, the Prime Minister of Ireland, whom Sinn Féin regarded as a sympathetic and honest broker. Reynolds, in turn, helped gain the backing of US officials and eventually newly elected President Bill Clinton. American visas, long withheld, were granted to Sinn Féin officials, including Gerry Adams and the notorious terrorist Joe Cahill, in January 1994. This granting of recognition to republicans went far in convincing them that negotiation and compromise would indeed be more fruitful than armed struggle. That August, the IRA announced a "complete and unequivocal" ceasefire, which was shortly answered in kind by unionist paramilitaries – an altogether different sort of call-and-response than Northern Ireland was used to.

The Final Spasms of Violence

Direct talks between Britain, Ireland, the SDLP, and the largest Protestant party, the Ulster Unionist Party (UUP), proceeded slowly. A major impediment to progress were British and UUP demands that Sinn Féin be excluded until the IRA decommissioned its weapons. In 1996, the IRA renounced its ceasefire, in part to placate hardliners, and returned to violent activity, the centerpiece of which was the February bombing of Canary Wharf in London's Docklands. Essentially a continuation of the IRA's early 1990s terror campaign, the bomb caused relatively few human casualties (two dead and more than one hundred wounded), but caused enormous economic damage. A nearly simultaneous recommendation from former US Senator George Mitchell to include Sinn Féin in talks without an IRA commitment to decommissioning provided British Prime Minister John Major the cover to recommence talks with Sinn Féin present. In 1997, the IRA declared a new ceasefire. The election of Tony Blair and the transition to Labour Party rule in Britain, as well as the continued involvement of Mitchell, led to renewed progress in talks dominated by the SDLP and the UUP. On Good Friday, April 10, 1998, Britain and Ireland's leaders announced the formation of a new devolved government for Northern Ireland, complete with a complicated but balanced power-sharing agreement. Critical features of the agreement included reform of the Constabulary to include Catholics and the granting of full and equal civil rights for all citizens. Northern Ireland's voters supported the agreement in a plebiscite, and Sinn Féin reluctantly signed off on it, as well.

IRA extremists predictably formed splinter groups, such as the Continuity IRA and the Real IRA. In August, the latter set off a car bomb in the Ulster town of Omagh. The result was twenty-nine civilian dead, one of the largest single-day body counts of the Troubles. The dead included nine children, a pregnant woman, two Spanish tourists, and Catholics as well as Protestants. The Omagh tragedy crystallized support for a renewed commitment to peaceful negotiations, as denunciations of the attack flowed in from every direction. In a striking turn, Gerry Adams condemned the bombing in his most strident language to date and followed in 2000 with a commitment to put the IRA's vast arsenal of weapons "beyond use." Sinn Féin's acceptance of the peace process was duly rewarded in 2001 when it surpassed for the first time the SDLP as the largest recipient of the Catholic vote in Northern Ireland. Talks broke down several times, but in 2005 the IRA renounced the use of violence and terror and committed itself to "exclusively peaceful means" in securing its goals. One year later it announced that all of its weapons had been decommissioned, a claim disputed by some. As of 2007, the recently empowered Northern Ireland Assembly government is headed by Ian Paisley of the Democratic Unionist Party and Martin McGuinness of Sinn Féin – the most unlikely government partners in recent history.

The total number of casualties associated with the Troubles is hard to pin down. It has been estimated that the IRA's principal factions killed more than eighteen hundred people. Other republican groups killed at least two hundred more. Unionist paramilitary groups killed nearly one thousand, while British troops and the Constabulary killed more than 350 people, nearly two hundred of whom were civilians.

Sri Lanka and the Tamil Tigers

While Palestine and Northern Ireland have been the epicenters of the two largest ethno-nationalist terror campaigns of the last forty years, there have been several other notable ones. One of the most vicious and bloody has been the struggle of ethnic Tamils to gain a homeland on Sri Lanka, a large island about twenty miles from the southeastern tip of India. The island's population is about 74 percent Sinhalese (most of whom are Buddhist), 16 percent Tamil (most of whom are Hindu and concentrated in the north and east of the island), with the rest Muslim. The struggle, however, has largely been over ethnic, not religious identity. There are, in fact, both Hindu and Christian Tamils that participate in terror missions. The roots of ethnic conflict lie in the divide-and-conquer tactics of the Portuguese, Dutch, and British colonists in Ceylon (as it was known until 1972). Tensions became much greater after Sri Lanka achieved independence from Britain in 1948 – one year after India did – and the Sinhalese majority began to limit the use of the Tamil language and the influence of Tamil culture, even in the north of the island. The Sinhalese majority refused some Tamils citizenship, systematically disenfranchised others, imposed strict quotas on Tamil university attendance and membership in the civil service, and forcibly repatriated some of the Tamil population to India.

Tamil rebels waged a sporadic campaign of terror and assassination against the Sinhalese-dominated government starting shortly after independence, but to little effect. The Liberation Tigers of Tamil Eelam, better known as the Tamil Tigers, became the primary vehicle for Tamil militancy and terrorism in the mid-1970s, gradually eclipsing other nationalist groups through violence and intimidation. The man who eventually rose to lead the Tamil Tigers, Velupillai Prabhakaran, distinguished himself early by assassinating the moderate Tamil nationalist mayor of Jaffna, the largest city in the Tamil-majority region of Sri Lanka. The Tamil Tigers still seek an independent homeland and have proven their ability to adapt to the opportunities available to them in their struggle. In fact, the Tamil Tigers are most significant in the history of terrorism for two features: (1) their illustration of the typological fluidity that exists among terrorism, guerrilla warfare, and conventional struggles; and (2) their inventiveness in introducing new tactics, particularly suicide bombers and piracy.

The Tamil Tigers: Terrorism, Guerrilla War, and Conventional Struggle

The Tamil Tigers' goal over the last three-plus decades has been to achieve independence through a popularly supported mass movement fielding a conventional army. The early Tigers and their antecedents were Marxists; all that remained by the late 1970s, however, was a certain millenarianism and Mao's proposed revolutionary trajectory. The Tigers have always represented the extremist fringe of the Tamil nationalist movement and as such have found it difficult to generate un-coerced support from the Tamil minority. They have long carried out terrorism against moderate Tamils and their own people to raise money and demand obedience, as well as against the Sinhalese-dominated government and population in pursuit of a homeland. The Tigers have used assassination and attacks on military and police outposts, as well as shootings and bombings of civilian targets, such as shopping centers; passenger planes, commuter trains, and buses; mosques and temples (including the Buddhist temple at Kandy, the country's most revered site); and village and city streets. The total number of casualties of such attacks stretches well into the tens of thousands.

What made the Tamil Tigers particularly able to grow into a potent and deadly force was sizable financial support from the large Tamil population of southeastern India and relatively well-off Tamil expatriate communities in Western Europe, North America, and Australasia. For a time in the 1980s, the Tamil Tigers were also the beneficiaries of intelligence and material aid from elements of the Indian secret services opposed to the Sri Lankan government. The Tamil Tigers have also relied from time to time on bank robberies and other small-scale criminal enterprises to raise funds. The Tamil Tigers have recently expanded into far more lucrative ventures, such as legitimate business, money laundering, extortion, arms and drug smuggling, and forcible taxation of Tamils, particularly as efforts to clamp down on international funding of terrorist activities since 9/11 have grown more successful.

International support and the narrowness of the straits separating Sri Lanka from the mainland made it possible until recently for the Tamil Tigers to continue carrying out operations even when successful Sinhalese counterinsurgency efforts and waning support from Sri Lankan Tamils would otherwise have extinguished the movement. Under those circumstances, the Tamil Tigers have retreated into near total dependency on terror tactics to keep their struggle alive.

When support grew, the Tamil Tigers carried out more extensive guerrilla operations against the Sri Lankan armed forces, making particular use of child soldiers and female-only units. In 1988 and 1994–5, the

Tamil Tigers were able to support small, uniformed conventional forces in the field, essentially creating a Tamil mini-state. Even while on the defensive in 1996, the Tamil Tigers engaged in relatively large-scale military operations with several thousand fighters.

A constant factor has been the presence of a virulent form of nationalism that has entirely replaced the early interest in Marxism. One source of inspiration was early twentieth-century Hindu nationalism in India. Wherever possible, the Tamil Tigers have established schools in base camps in Sri Lanka and abroad designed to indoctrinate young Tamils with a heady mix of nationalism, Hindu mysticism, asceticism, and self-sacrifice. No matter how close or far away success has seemed at any particular moment, Tamil Tiger leaders continue to prepare a new generation of fighters and terrorists for the struggle. As a result, teenagers have consistently made up over half of the membership of the Tamil Tigers.

Another feature of the Tamil Tigers' insurgency has been the repeated involvement of India in the conflict. From 1987 to 1990, Indian peacekeeping troops sought to enforce a ceasefire, in the end becoming directly involved in fighting the Tamil Tigers. Such efforts have been a calculated attempt by the Indians to keep the Tamil Tigers' struggle from spreading to the mainland. As a consequence, the Tamil Tigers have targeted Indian troops in Sri Lanka and have even taken the fight to the Indian sub-continent. The most notable attack was the assassination of Rajiv Gandhi, the prime minister of India, in 1991.

The Tamil Tigers and Suicide Terrorism

The most notable feature of the Tamil Tigers' campaign has been their introduction of new means suited to the particular circumstances of their insurgency. The most striking has been the use of so-called suicide bombers – individual terrorists who carry and detonate bombs alongside their target. The tactic is alarmingly successful in penetrating counter-terror defenses and inflicting either large numbers of casualties or destroying precise targets. Suicide bombers can react to circumstances as they develop and can get much closer to their targets, having dispensed with the need to escape. Hezbollah was the first group in recent memory to employ the tactic, beginning with the 1983 attacks on US and French forces in Lebanon, events that made a strong impression on the Tamil Tiger leader, Prabhakaran. The Tigers began using the tactic in 1987, rapidly becoming, until recently, the most prolific agents of suicidal terror missions. The Tigers carried out more suicide attacks – as many as 200 – from 1987 to 2001 than all other groups using the tactic combined

(Bloom, *Dying to Kill*, 60; Hopgood, "Tamil Tigers,"44). (In recent years, Palestinian and jihadist groups have become the most frequent sponsors of suicide bombings.) The Tamil Tigers, like others before and since, dispatched suicide bombers because the group was desperate to regain the initiative and was rich in but one resource: young, fanatically devoted fighters. Summing up, Prabhakaran stated in a 1998 speech: "In terms of manpower, firepower, and resources, the enemy was strong and the balance of military power was in his favor. Yet we had an extraordinary weapon which was not in the arsenal of the enemy. The courage and commitment of our fighters was our most powerful weapon in the battle" (quoted in Pape, *Dying to Win*, 33). So great became the Tamil Tigers' dependence on the tactic that it created two branches of the organization devoted specifically to suicide bombing, the Black Tigers for men and the Birds of Freedom for women. The Tigers have used suicide missions against their moderate nationalist rivals and the government. From 1991 to 1994, the Tigers engaged in a particularly destructive campaign of violence, eliminating through the use of suicide bombers most of the leadership of one of Sri Lanka's principal parties, the United National Party, including its presidential candidate and more than fifty others. Suicide bombing missions by Tamil Tigers have also been an effective tactic for mitigating Sri Lankan military gains. In 1994, waterborne Black Tigers destroyed the second largest vessel in the Sri Lankan Navy. Four years later, Black Tiger teams assassinated a Sri Lankan general and carried out bloody attacks on army and police columns.

Who would choose such a fate for themselves? The Tamil Tigers have received a steady stream of volunteers, in large part through the group's policy of seizing and rearing children in such a virulently and passionately nationalistic environment. Garlanded photos of young martyrs decorate the walls of Tamil Tiger training camps and Tamil-controlled cities and are regularly featured in Tamil newspapers. Monuments to Black Tiger martyrs dot Tamil cities. Another inducement is that bombers are granted the privilege of eating their last meal with the group's charismatic leader, Prabhakaran. On the other hand, parents of young martyrs are sometimes rewarded materially or are intimidated into relinquishing control over their children. Even for those Tamil Tigers whose missions are not meant to end in their own deaths, the allure of martyrdom and the comfort of death exert a strong hold. Tamil Tiger guerrillas and terrorists alike are required to carry vials bearing cyanide to be used in the event of imminent capture. "We are married to our cyanide," one claimed. "It makes us clear-headed and purposeful" (quoted in Laqueur, *The New Terrorism*, 101). More than six hundred Tamil Tigers have thus committed suicide.

In recent years, the Sri Lankan government has dramatically moderated its stance toward Tamil linguistic, cultural, and political demands. Tamil is now an official language of Sri Lanka, and many ethnic Tamils serve in the Sri Lankan government. Nonetheless, the fanaticism of the Tamil Tigers and their sources of expatriate funding and internal support have kept the cause of Tamil independence alive into the twenty-first century, still accompanied by the concerted use of terror, particularly suicide missions.

ETA: Basque Nation and Liberty

One of the longest running unresolved ethno-nationalist struggles is that of Basque Nation and Liberty (ETA, from its Basque name), which has fought for national independence, often aided by terrorism, for decades. The Basques inhabit the Pyrenees in northern Spain, and although they have not had an independent state for over a millennium, Basque language, culture, and identity has remained distinct. In the 1950s, Spain's fascist dictator and ultra-nationalist Francisco Franco forcibly tried to suppress Basque separatism and assimilate Basques into Spain. Basque nationalists organized opposition to Franco, but made little headway. The most radical formed ETA in order to wage an armed struggle against Spain for independence, consciously emulating other Third World nations' fights against colonial powers. In 1965, ETA leaders adopted the "action-repression-action spiral theory," a strategy for the use of terrorism that built on the experience of other revolutionary ethno-nationalist groups, particularly the FLN in Algeria. The "spiral theory" acknowledged that although there was no broad revolutionary movement, it could be created or, rather, coaxed out of latency. The strategy was, by now, a familiar one, although never articulated as clearly: terrorist or "commando" units would stage attacks against the Spanish government, police, and military who, unable to narrowly target the terrorists, would brutally crack down on the population believed to be sheltering them, thus alienating the population, inflaming Basque separatism, and building a broad revolutionary movement that could compel Spain to cut the Basques free. This plan closely paralleled the ideas simultaneously developed by Carlos Marighella in Brazil (see Chapter 13 for more on Marighella and the Latin American groups he inspired).

In 1968, ETA – as well as a host of splinter groups that typically carried out attacks under the ETA name – began to launch terrorist strikes in accordance with the "spiral theory." ETA agents kidnapped and assassinated government and police officials, as well as prominent Basques who opposed independence or the use of violence. ETA also robbed banks and extorted businesses (charging what it called a "revolutionary tax") to fund their activities, which, besides terrorism, included a substantial propaganda effort. Although most Basques would consider themselves nationalists and have backed independence or at least autonomy throughout this period, relatively few have supported ETA. Probably the high-water mark of ETA's popularity among Basques came in 1970, when sixteen ETA defendants used a trial in the city of Burgos to publicize their cause. Six defendants were condemned to death, but the sentences were reduced in the wake of massive demonstrations that portrayed the Burgos defendants as martyrs. The strategy of the "spiral theory" seemed to be paying off. Support for ETA grew, much of it coming from Spanish opposition groups, such as the socialists and communists, who understood ETA as primarily anti-authoritarian rather than pro-Basque, a reputation enhanced by ETA's assassination in 1973 of Luis Carrero Blanco, Franco's prime minister and heir apparent.

Ironically, ETA's short term success precipitated a long term decline, in that Carrero Blanco's death hastened the collapse of fascism in the wake of Franco's death in 1975. The return of constitutional democracy dramatically undermined ETA's level of support and prospects for victory by removing the enemy that had defined ETA's existence and garnered it support from across Spain. Many Basques, in fact, questioned the need for a revolution given the possibilities for free expression and autonomy within a democratic state. But ETA's terrorist campaign continued and even intensified. Intoxicated by violence and desperate to reclaim attention and momentum, ETA terrorists began to target civilians in Basque lands and across Spain in the late 1970s, the period of the worst bloodletting in ETA's four-decades long campaign. ETA and its sympathizers long maintained that it sought to minimize casualties in favor of highly symbolic targets, all while generally avoiding the killing of innocents. When ETA bombs did, in fact, kill civilians, spokesmen tried to shift blame to the authorities by accusing them of ignoring phoned-in warnings, such as in the bombing of the Hipercor supermarket in Barcelona in 1987 that killed twenty-one civilians, including several small children. Nonetheless, the bottom line has been clear: ETA has killed more than 800 people since the 1960s, and roughly one-third of the victims have been civilians.

ETA has also been strongly rooted in the working-class identity of most of its members for most of its existence. Since the late 1960s, in fact, ETA and several of its splinter groups have been avowedly Marxist in their ideology and goals, a choice linked to ETA's close identification with Third World liberation movements. In the 1980s the Spanish government began to take advantage of this, hoping to peel away moderate middle-class Basques by granting cultural and linguistic equality and virtual political autonomy to the region. ETA effectiveness was also diminished by improved police work and increasing French willingness to extradite ETA terrorists and activists hiding in the French Pyrenees. Despite the fact that

it was gaining ground against ETA in the mid 1980s, the Spanish government became so concerned about ETA terrorism that security officials
conducted a "dirty war" in which secret government hit squads – known
as Anti-terrorist Liberation Groups or GAL – used kidnapping, torture,
and assassination against ETA members and whatever innocent civilians
accidentally fell into their clutches. In the program's four year existence,
GAL teams killed at least twenty-seven people, including at least nine
who have never been connected to ETA. Stories and rumors about GAL
extra-legal brutality did not bring about the realization of ETA's "spiral
theory" – that is, the creation of a Basque popular separatist movement
that forced Spain to grant Basque independence – but they did give ETA
new life, adding substance to its claim of fighting against an authoritarian
state. When asked why ETA retained enough support to keep operating
through the lean years of the 1980s, one former ETA official answered
simply: "the GAL's dirty war" kept ETA popular (quoted in Woodworth,
Dirty War, Clean Hands, 346). In light of GAL violence, many Spaniards
openly questioned how far Spain had traveled toward the creation of a
liberal democratic state since the death of Franco. In the eyes of many
Spaniards, Basques, and international observers, though, the stain of
GAL's "dirty war" was partially lifted in the 1990s by government trials
and convictions of many GAL counter-terrorists, including the interior
minister, the director of State Security, and numerous regional officials.

With the granting of virtual autonomy to the Basques, particularly
the right of self-policing, Basque separatists' goals have been achieved
in all but name. Few, therefore, have been willing to continue a military/
terrorist campaign for independence. As a consequence, ETA has been
reduced to a small core of radical members largely pushed into exile
abroad. Some observers have ironically noted that with the end of GAL
counter-terrorism and with it the belief in the possibility of the complete
eradication of ETA violence, terrorism has returned, but only to what
might be called manageable levels. ETA still engages in terrorism, but at
a much reduced level. Still more than a nuisance, it certainly no longer
represents a threat to the state or the social order. Two factors have
been critical in the decline of what was already marginal Basque support
for ETA terrorism. The first was the popular reaction to the 1997 ETA
kidnapping and murder of a local conservative Basque politician, Miguel
Ángel Blanco. One hundred thousand Basques marched to protest his
murder, as did several million in the rest of Spain. ETA partisans found
themselves on the defensive, routinely harassed within the communities
that they thought were "theirs." The other event that contributed to the
decline of ETA popularity and effectiveness was 9/11, a terrorist act of
such carnage and magnitude that it undermined in Spain, as it did in
much of the West, any organization's justification of terrorism.

Bibliography

For works on the broader Arab–Israeli conflict, see the bibliography at the end of the preceding chapter. The most useful books on Arafat, Fatah, and the PLO include Jillian Becker, *The PLO: The Rise and Fall of the Palestine Liberation Organization* (St. Martin's Press, 1984); Alan Hart, *Arafat: A Political Biography*, 4th edn. (Indiana University Press, 1989 [1984]); Neil C. Livingstone and David Halevy, *Inside the PLO: Covert Units, Secret Funds, and the War against Israel and the United States* (Quill/William Morrow, 1990); and Janet Wallach and John Wallach, *Arafat: In the Eyes of the Beholder*, rev. edn. (Birch Lane Press, 1997).

The three best surveys of the IRA are those cited at the end of Chapter 9: J. Bowyer Bell, *The Secret Army: The IRA*; Tim Pat Coogan, *The IRA*; and Richard English, *Armed Struggle: The History of the IRA*. Particularly valuable works for the period covered in this chapter include Martin Dillon, *The Dirty War* (Routledge, 1999); and Ian Geldard and Keith Craig, *IRA, INLA: Foreign Support and International Connections* (Institute for the Study of Terrorism, 1988). Marc Mulholland provides a useful overview of Northern Irish history in *Northern Ireland: A Very Short Introduction* (Oxford University Press, 2003 [2002]). The IRA's so-called Green Book is available: *Handbook For Volunteers of the Irish Republican Army: Notes On Guerrilla Warfare* (Paladin Press, 1985). An illuminating work by a contemporary is Maria McGuire, *Take Arms: A Year in the Provisional IRA* (Quartet, 1973).

Two excellent works on Sri Lanka's lengthy civil war are John Richardson, *Paradise Poisoned: Learning About Conflict, Terrorism and Development from Sri Lanka's Civil Wars* (International Centre for Ethnic Studies, 2005); and Robert I. Rotberg, ed., *Creating Peace in Sri Lanka: Civil War and Reconciliation* (Brookings Institution Press, 1999). On the Tamil Tigers and suicide terrorism, see Mia Bloom, *Dying to Kill: The Allure of Suicide Terrorism* (Columbia University Press, 2005); and Robert A. Pape, *Dying to Win: The Strategic Logic of Suicide Terrorism* (Random House, 2006). Both are also excellent sources on the suicide terrorism of Hamas and Hezbollah. On the Tigers, also see Stephen Hopgood, "Tamil Tigers, 1987–2002," in Diego Gambetta, ed., *Making Sense of Suicide Missions* (Oxford University Press, 2005).

A comprehensive account of the Basque struggle is Ludger Mees, *Nationalism, Violence, and Democracy: The Basque Clash of Identities* (Palgrave Macmillan, 2003). Two very good studies of ETA (although both are now rather outdated) are Robert Clark, *The Basque Insurgents: ETA, 1952–1980* (University of Wisconsin Press, 1984); and John Sullivan, *ETA and Basque Nationalism: The Fight for Euskadi,*

1890–1986 (London: Routledge, 1988). A more recent but briefer analysis is Goldie Shabad and Francisco José Llera Ramo, "Political Violence in a Democratic State: Basque Terrorism in Spain," in Crenshaw, ed., *Terrorism in Context* (cited earlier). An excellent work on the Dirty War of the mid 1980s is Paddy Woodworth, *Dirty War, Clean Hands: ETA, the GAL, and Spanish Democracy* (Cork: Cork University Press, 2001). A fascinating post-structuralist analysis of Basque terrorism is Joseba Zulaika, *Basque Violence: Metaphor and Sacrament* (University of Nevada Press, 1988).

13

The Era of Leftist and International Terrorism

Leftist-inspired, revolutionary terrorism receded into the background between the 1920s and 1950s, overshadowed first by state and then ethno-nationalist terror. In the 1960s and 1970s, however, leftist terrorism roared back into prominence, eventually provoking fears of a new left-wing international terrorist conspiracy.

The Return of Revolutionary Terrorism

The recrudescence of revolutionary terrorism can be traced to the confluence of a number of factors in the 1960s. The first was the sense of possibility and anger created by the rapidly broadening anti-colonial movement, which had already led to independence for many countries in Africa and Asia. The First World's frequently brutal efforts to oppose these movements, such as in Algeria and Vietnam, fit the Marxists' definition of imperialism, particularly in the ideological hothouse environment spawned by the Cold War. Mao and Soviet leader Nikita Khrushchev contributed to this by peddling Marxism as a strategy for anti-colonial wars of independence. In those countries where a foreign occupier could not be identified as the enemy, Marxists directed their hatred toward the entrenched ruling elite, frequently portraying their local government – whether it be a First World democracy or a Third World dictatorship – as a stooge of the era's greatest military and commercial power, the United States.

A new generation of theorists sought to make Marxism relevant to such circumstances, and they found an eager audience, particularly in the massive student populations created by the expansion of post-secondary education and the growing middle class. Increasing disparities in wealth, often coupled with the conservatism of older generations, helped push young adults toward such highly ideological readings of contemporary developments. These conditions helped shape what was to be a central feature of the new revolutionary terrorist tradition: groups of affluent, educated students hoping to make revolutions on behalf of what they imagined to be the poor (and ignorant) masses.

Latin American Revolutionary Movements

The most influential figure in the budding new revolutionary tradition was the Argentinian Ernesto "Che" Guevara. Together with Fidel Castro, he led an insurrection that toppled the American-backed Batista regime in Cuba in 1959. Shortly thereafter, Guevara wrote *Guerrilla Warfare*, a practical guide to making revolutions. Guevara claimed that in Latin America enlightened "vanguards" should create revolutionary situations in the impoverished countryside that could be exploited through military, rather than political, means.

Whereas Guevara barely mentioned terrorism, describing it as an urban adjunct to a largely rural process, later revolutionaries began to promote terrorism as the primary means of coming to power. The first manifestations of revolutionary terrorism in Latin America in the 1960s occurred in Venezuela, where the Armed Forces of National Liberation carried out attacks on foreign businesses and assassinated police officers, and in Guatemala, where the Rebel Armed Forces kidnapped and assassinated Guatemalan and foreign officials, including the US ambassador, who was killed in 1968. Little came of either campaign, both of which petered out quickly.

Uruguay and the Tupamaros

A far more destructive and influential revolutionary movement emerged in Uruguay. The country – nestled between Brazil and Argentina on the South Atlantic coast – seemed ill-suited to a Guevaran revolution, for it boasted an overwhelmingly urban population, a booming economy, and a surprisingly stable democratic government. By the late 1950s, however, the export-driven economy began to stall. Conditions rapidly deteriorated for both the poor, who fell through the welfare state's safety net in ever greater numbers, and for well-educated young adults, who could not be absorbed into the economy in sufficient numbers. Without long-standing democratic traditions, the state instinctively began to lean on the army, police, courts, and government-controlled media to suppress dissent. Raúl Sendic, a young law student from the capital of Montevideo, tried to organize Uruguay's sugar cane workers, but the movement was suppressed by the army in league with large landowners. Sendic resolved to challenge the state through violence. Moreover, he decided to base the movement in Montevideo – home to half the country's population – where his small number of supporters could more readily attract the attention of impoverished workers. In 1962 or 1963, he formed the National Liberation Movement, better known as the Tupamaros in honor of the Incan leader Tupac Amaru II who had led a rebellion against the Spanish in the late eighteenth century. Essentially a Marxist party, the Tupamaros set as their major goals the destruction of capitalism and sham democracy, the massive redistribution of wealth, and the creation of a decentralized socialist state.

During their first five years, the Tupamaros gathered arms, secured funding, and tried to set up the rudiments of what they dubbed "dual power." They imagined this as a parallel pseudo-government that would satisfy the real needs of the people and undermine faith in Uruguay's official government. Toward this end, the Tupamaros robbed banks and warehouses and hijacked food delivery trucks, distributing the proceeds to the poor like modern-day Robin Hoods. The group itself remained small, confined mostly to young, well-educated, middle- and upper-class urbanites, about a third of whom were students.

Marighella and the Urban Guerrilla

Sendic and the Tupamaros had amassed enough guns, money, and popular support by 1968 to embrace a new strategy, one espoused by Carlos Marighella, a Brazilian legislator turned communist revolutionary who was killed in a shootout with police in 1969. Marighella wrote many short works on revolutionary war, but his best-known work is the *Mini-Manual of the Urban Guerrilla* (published just a few months before his death). Marighella's body of writing remains one of the most influential – perhaps *the* most influential – in the modern history of terrorism, owing to his success in synthesizing a wide array of sources into a coherent and disturbing statement about the tactics, strategy, and ultimate purposes of violence.

Marighella believed that popular support eluded revolutionaries because of the state's success in convincing the masses that they lived in a sufficiently just and benevolent society. His strategy was to overwhelm the government on all fronts with chaotic violence so that the state would "be obliged to transform the political situation into a military one" (Marighella,

Mini-Manual, 38). The resultant brutal police and army crackdowns would reveal, he believed, that the state was, indeed, an oppressive, fascist entity in service to international capital. The scales would drop from the eyes of the masses, and they would inexorably flock to a guerrilla army led by the revolutionary vanguard in quantities sufficient to overthrow the state.

Perhaps the most important element of Marighella's strategy was to proclaim that since the goal of revolutionary violence is to provoke the state, the specific target, form, and casualty count of the violence is irrelevant, as long as the result is chaos. Appropriate targets for revolutionary terrorism could be found everywhere: "banks, industries, armories, military barracks, prisons, public offices, radio and television stations, North American firms, gas storage tanks, oil refineries, ships, airplanes, ports, airports, hospitals, health centers, blood banks, stores, garages, embassies, residences of high-ranking members of the regime such as ministers and generals, police stations, official organizations, etc." (Marighella, *Mini-Manual*, 20). His list of tactics is equally exhaustive: assaults, bank robberies, strikes and work stoppages, desertions, expropriation of weapons, liberation of prisoners, executions, kidnappings, and sabotage. And in his hands all of them amount to terrorism, since the express purpose was provocation through symbolic violence.

Since Marighella's campaign of revolutionary violence required virtually no coordination, just maximum mayhem, he stated that the ideal means of organizing urban guerrilla warfare was in isolated cells or "firing groups" of four or five members. The National Liberation Front of Algeria had pioneered such a structure, with each cell connected to only one other through just the cell's leader. Such a decentralized structure ensured that if one revolutionary were captured, he or she had a limited amount of information about the rest of the organization.

In a single stroke, Marighella brought together almost every strand of innovation by theorists and practitioners in the history of terrorism. What remained was an easily grasped dictate: sow chaos and wait for the government to fall. In all fairness, Marighella's description of his strategy was somewhat more complex than that, but in effect its sophistication was undermined by its seductive simplicity. So widespread has his approach become that most who have adopted it over the last forty years are probably incapable of naming its author.

The Tupamaros and Terrorism

This was not so in the case of Sendic and the Tupamaros of Uruguay, who eagerly devoured Marighella's pamphlets. The Tupamaros remained convinced that a small Guevaran vanguard could create the necessary political crisis, but believed it would be exploited not by a Cuban-style military insurrection, but by a popular revolution sparked by government oppression. Terrorism was indeed the alpha and omega of the Tupamaros' military plans, which they began to put into effect in 1968. Their bank and food store robberies became grander in scale and much more likely to involve the shooting deaths of policemen and even innocent bystanders. The Tupamaros' efforts to humiliate the government also led them to steal the accounting books of the Financiera Monty, a loan company involved in bribery and kick-backs. The Tupamaros mailed the books to a judge, leading to the resignation of several politicians. Tupamaros "firing groups" assassinated police officials and bombed government buildings. What made the Tupamaros most notorious was their practice of kidnapping government officials, foreign dignitaries (including the Brazilian consul and the British ambassador), and businessmen. The victims – fourteen between 1968 and 1972 – were held in Tupamaro hideouts dubbed "people's prisons" until the government released prisoners or someone paid exorbitant ransoms.

In its early stages, Tupamaro urban terrorism achieved its desired effect. The group's well-chosen symbolic attacks, publicity stunts, and welfare operations attracted significant public support. According to one poll, 59 percent of Uruguayans agreed that the Tupamaros were motivated by "a sense of social justice," a fact that helped swell the group's ranks to its high water mark of somewhere between several hundred and several thousand members (Townshend, *Terrorism*, 65). And, indeed, as the situation began to grow more desperate, the state resorted to the sort of tactics Marighella and Sendic ironically hoped it would. The government granted police the use of emergency powers, suspended civil liberties, ramped up censorship, arrested supporters and labor leaders, and subjected terror suspects to lengthy extralegal detentions and torture.

By 1971, the Tupamaros had grown overconfident, convinced that the public was on the verge of passing completely into their camp. As a result, they dramatically overplayed their hand, opting to join a left-wing coalition running in presidential and parliamentary elections late that year. The public, however, had wearied of the Tupamaros' violent antics, particularly after the murder of eight policemen in July 1970 and, one month later, the kidnapping and murder of Dan Mitrione, an American AID worker and alleged CIA agent. Counter to Marighella's predictions, the violence had disgusted Uruguayans and convinced them that they were themselves the targets of terror. Civilians welcomed the government's crackdown on the Tupamaros, even the decision to transfer all anti-terror operations to the army. In the elections of 1971, Uruguayans decisively voted against the leftists and in favor of a hardline right-wing ticket, which turned more and more to the use of emergency powers to combat Tupamaro terror. Aided by more public cooperation and its own use of infiltration, massive searches, and torture, the army gained the upper hand in its fight with the Tupamaros. By the end of 1972, the army had killed scores of Tupamaros in gun battles and captured three thousand suspects, effectively crushing the rebel group. But the damage had been done to Uruguay's constitutional order. The military had grown accustomed to its new-found powers and disgusted at democratic corruption and inefficiency. In 1973, President Juan María Bordaberry dissolved Congress and ruled as a military-backed dictator until the army ousted him in 1976, exercising direct control over the state until 1985. Throughout this twelve-year period, there were widespread human rights abuses by the military.

The Tupamaros had hoped to unmask the Uruguayan government for the fascist, repressive entity they believed it to have always been. Instead, Sendic and his supporters simply encouraged – enabled, even – the rise of a far right movement within the army and security apparatus. The Tupamaros hoped that terror and violence would lead to popular support. Instead, terrorism eventually alienated the populace. By the time the Tupamaros realized their error, it was too late for them and for democracy in Uruguay. The most common errors of those who follow Carlos Marighella's *Mini-Manual of the Urban Guerrilla* – and that, we might say, is most of today's terrorists, whether they consciously realize it or not – are that they overestimate the revolutionary potential of the masses and underestimate the repressive power of the state. Moreover, even under the most favorable circumstances, the strategy requires a finely calibrated quantity and quality of violence that inflames, but does not repel the public. As has so often been the case – most notably in the Russian Empire, Cyprus, and, more recently, Palestine – terrorists are much more likely to destabilize a country than achieve anything resembling their goals. Terrorism is thus a tactic easily adopted – particularly in desperate times by those who preach action – but difficult to convert into victory.

Similar storylines played out in much of Latin America. In Argentina, for instance, two groups – the People's Revolutionary Army and the Montoneros – carried out urban guerrilla warfare that claimed, according to the government, seven hundred victims and created a backlash that included military coups and the emergence of the Argentine Anticommunist Alliance, a state-supported right-wing death squad that is said to have killed over two thousand opponents through the early 1980s. As in Uruguay, the Argentine military's 1976 takeover was justified by the need to combat terrorism, even though the Montoneros and the People's Revolutionary Army had already been suppressed. The military junta's leader, General Jorge Videla, demonstrated that the political uses of anti-terrorism were far more important than definitional rigor when he described a terrorist as "not just someone with a gun or a bomb, but also someone who spreads ideas that are contrary to Western and Christian civilization" (quoted in Townshend, *Terrorism*, 47).

The Revolutionary Armed Forces of Colombia and Narco-Terrorism

Not all Latin American revolutionary groups have adopted the urban guerrilla strategy. In fact, the region's longest-tenured such group, the Revolutionary Armed Forces of Colombia (FARC), has remained somewhat truer to the Cuban pattern. Established in 1964 as the armed wing of the Colombian Communist Party, FARC has from the beginning drawn most of its support and recruits from the countryside. FARC remains mired in the second phase of Maoist or Guevarist revolution in that it has a powerful uniformed guerrilla force of anywhere between six and twelve thousand members that have been used to carve out sizable "liberated zones" but have been unable to seize the cities or force the government to its knees. Like the Tamil Tigers of Sri Lanka, FARC readily slides along the typological range of violent behavior, engaging in terrorism, guerrilla fighting, and conventional warfare as their abilities and opportunities warrant. FARC's terrorist activities have included assassinations, hijackings, and bombings and other attacks on military and civilian targets. Like the Tupamaros, FARC has made liberal use of kidnapping. Victims – perhaps as many as 2,500 since the 1970s – have included politicians (including cabinet ministers, members of congress, and presidential candidates), wealthy landowners, foreign and domestic business people, and tourists. What probably began as a means of propaganda has developed into an important financial prop, with FARC raising millions of dollars through ransoms. Since the 1980s, FARC has become involved in drug trafficking, particularly by providing security for cocaine growers and transporters. FARC also raises funds through extortion, protection rackets, and levying "taxes" and other fees in their liberated zones. While the group claims it is still a revolutionary organization, the truth is that it is closer to a criminal enterprise or, within the territories it controls, a quasi-government. Many recruits join because FARC is essentially the only employment opportunity in impoverished rural regions of Colombia.

The Shining Path

Without a doubt, Latin America's most violent and disruptive terrorist organization has been Peru's Sendero Luminoso – the Shining Path. The group was largely the creation of Abimael Gúzman (b. 1934), a one-time philosophy professor at a provincial university in the central Andes and a member of the Maoist faction of the Peruvian Communist Party. In 1970, the charismatic Gúzman established his own off-shoot, the Shining Path, the goal of which was the establishment of an agrarian communist state essentially pre-colonial in character. Gúzman established a cult-like following among students and fellow professors and used his university's education program to send recruits into the surrounding highlands where they established "people's schools" to indoctrinate peasants. Although Gúzman and his core of supporters were Westernized, middle-class intellectuals, the program of the Shining Path, particularly its emphasis on Incan mythology and anti-white rhetoric, was designed to appeal to Peru's impoverished and underserved indigenous population.

Gúzman took advantage of the state's relative absence in the Andean highlands and built a well disciplined and highly centralized organiza-tion during the 1970s. After ten years of preparation, the Shining Path began its "People's War" in 1980 – ironically at nearly the very moment that Peru was returning to civilian rule after a twelve-year military junta. When the government responded with a series of emergency power dec-larations, the Shining Path dispersed throughout the Andes and began a classic terrorist campaign. Although the state could rightly claim that it had achieved military victory against the Shining Path by the mid-1980s, the organization's leadership core remained intact. The Shining Path's cynical alliance with Peruvian drug lords also meant that the group was awash in money – reportedly up to $30 million a year. These funds were used to bribe officials, purchase weapons, and fund social services for otherwise poorly served indigenous communities in Peru's highlands. The government's worsening human rights record – fed by the transfer of more and more power to military authorities answerable to no one – also drove many into the arms of the Shining Path. The net result was that Gúzman could attract recruits faster than the military could capture or kill them.

Shining Path violence took many forms, with the scale of its assas-sination campaign particularly awe-inspiring. The group targeted rival socialist, labor, and grass roots organizations, but saved its greatest wrath for the political establishment. By 1988, the Shining Path had assassinated more than 250 officials of the dominant political party and then ramped up the pace, killing over one hundred candidates for local offices in 1989 alone. All told, an estimated thirty thousand people died as a result of the Shining Path's violence. The group also carried out an extensive bombing campaign, hitting approximately 3,700 targets from 1980 to 1988. A favorite target was Peru's electricity infrastructure, so much so that power outages in the capital city of Lima were common. During these outages, the Shining Path would burn an enormous hammer and sickle in the hills above the city to remind Lima's residents of the fate that was in store for them.

Peruvian Counter-Terrorism

In response, Peru's army and security organs engaged in a vicious campaign of "disappearances" and extra-judicial killings, frequently attacking villages that they suspected harbored the Shining Path. According to one army commander, "In order for the security forces to be successful, they will have to begin to kill Senderistas [members of the Shining Path] and non-Senderistas alike . . . They will kill 60 people and at best three will be Senderistas, but they will say that all 60 were Senderistas" (quoted in Arena and Arrigo, *The Terrorist Identity*, 156). Thousands of innocent Peruvians died, and the broad population found itself caught between Shining Path terror and governmental counter-terror.

In 1992, the authorities captured Gúzman in one of his safe houses in Lima using surveillance and old-fashioned police methods. Along with the terrorist mastermind, the police were able to seize a computer and other records that laid bare the group's organization. By the fall of 1994, the state had seven thousand Senderistas in custody. This was finally a pace that recruitment could not match. Moreover, the group had been so focused on Gúzman's cult of personality that cutting off the head nearly killed the whole beast. Gúzman was eventually convicted of a number of crimes related to terrorism and is serving a life sentence in prison. In his absence, a few leaders have tried to carry on, occasionally resuming terrorist operations, but at a fraction of the scale achieved in the 1980s and early 1990s.

The United States, the New Left, and the Weathermen

In the United States, student movements and social unrest led to violence, as well, but the radical groups had far less direct impact, while the popular and state-sponsored reactions were decidedly less violent and less anti-democratic. The question remains: why did radical organizations turn to violence at all in a democratic, wealthy, and highly educated society? Moreover, why were the privileged children of middle and upper class families in the forefront of this violence? This was an era of transitions, and its cultural, social, and political ferment crystallized in what came to be known as the New Left. This movement distinguished itself from traditional leftism by concentrating not on labor and economics, but rather on issues of personal freedom and justice such as civil rights and women's rights. Baby boomers were swelling colleges and universities to the bursting point (the US student population quadrupled from 1946 to 1970), and students were at the forefront of the Civil Rights Movement, the sexual revolution, and the burgeoning countercultural world of drugs, music, and alternative lifestyles. But campuses were electrified by one issue in particular: anger over a supposedly imperialistic war in Vietnam and the highly unpopular draft it made necessary.

The nexus of the New Left, student unrest, the counterculture, and opposition to the Vietnam War was Students for a Democratic Society (SDS). Formed in 1960, the organization's goal was nothing less than the transformation of American politics and culture largely through control of the Democratic Party. At its height the group had 100,000 members and was a force to be reckoned with. But by the end of the decade, tensions over the group's identity and mission were at a breaking point.

Marxist analysis had played an important role for those on the radical edge of the New Left from the beginning, for it made sense of the confluence of military, political, and economic behaviors they saw in the United States and abroad. By the late 1960s, SDS' most radical Marxists had turned for inspiration to Third World leaders such as Ho Chi Minh of Vietnam, Guevara, and Marighella. These radicals formed a faction within SDS known as the Weathermen, a name lifted from Bob Dylan's song, "Subterranean Homesick Blues." The Weathermen believed that the path to revolution lay not in the development of a mass movement via America's factories and universities, but rather through a guerrilla alliance of white ultra-radicals, black power activists, and Third World rebels. In order to destroy what they perceived as a police state, the Weathermen advocated "bringing the war in Vietnam home to Amerikkka" – their derisive term for the United States meant to suggest its underlying racist character. In June 1969, the group hijacked SDS, expelling the more traditional socialists and progressives through procedural moves and posturing that would have impressed even Lenin.

In hindsight, the Weathermen's quick slide toward violence and notoriety is rather easily explained. As its radicals became more removed from the New Left mainstream and popular support, they turned toward ever more radical solutions. The Weathermen's first attempt at violent agitation was the so-called "Days of Rage" in October 1969, when street-fighting radicals set fire to cars, smashed store fronts, and baited the police in downtown Chicago. "You hate the pigs [police] so much you want to kill them," one rioting student later claimed. "We may lose militarily, but by smashing pigs we will win in the eyes of the workers" (quoted in Moss, *The War for the Cities*, 71). The Days of Rage repulsed most Americans, who noted the absurdity of privileged middle-class students engaging in revolutionary violence against working-class police.

The Weather Underground

Shortly thereafter, the Weathermen transformed themselves into the Weather Underground and adopted a strategy of sowing "strategic armed chaos" in order to foment "mass public action" against capitalism and bourgeois democracy (quoted in Moss, *The War for the Cities*, 72–3). In this, they were consciously following Marighella and modeling themselves after the Tupamaros. In theory, the American rebels organized themselves into small, decentralized cells in imitation of the Uruguayan group. But this was entirely beside the point; with membership measured in, at most, the dozens, the Weather Underground was numerically incapable of forming more than a few firing teams. Befitting their status as middle-class amateur militants, the group's terror campaign began disastrously. In March 1970, three members of the group died in a Greenwich Village townhouse when a bomb they were constructing went off. Later that year, operatives bombed New York City's police headquarters, the National Guard headquarters in Washington, DC, the Presidio army base in San Francisco, and a facility doing army research at the University of Wisconsin in Madison. The sole fatality was a UW graduate student. Over the next seven years, the Weather Underground set off a number of bombs, most notably in the Senate wing of the US Capitol and the Air Force wing of the Pentagon. Showing off their supposed connections to the international revolutionary movement, the Weather Underground staged attacks to celebrate the anniversary of the Cuban Revolution and in response to the escalation of the war in Vietnam, the overthrow of Chilean President Salvador Allende, and Gulf Oil's operations in Angola. With few exceptions, Weather Underground bombs caused no casualties but extensive property damage. The group's last armed action was the 1981 robbery of a Brinks armored car that killed one guard.

The Weather Underground utterly failed in its mission to radicalize the American public and precipitate a revolution. The group was nonetheless seen as a serious threat to national security by the US government. The Federal Bureau of Investigation, suspecting that the Weathermen were actually – not just rhetorically – in league with foreign communists, mounted a major investigation of the group through COINTELPRO, its counterintelligence program used to surveil and disrupt dissident organizations both legal and illegal, even before the group transformed into a terrorist outfit and began to carry out bombings. This led to a number of arrests, most of which eventually came to naught since incriminating evidence had typically been gathered through illegal means. For this reason, some of the Weather Underground's most prominent members – such as the husband and wife team of Bill Ayers and Bernardine Dorhn – never served jail time and have re-integrated, unrepentant, back into society.

The Symbionese Liberation Army

Another American urban guerrilla outfit, the Symbionese Liberation Army, proved that very small groups – the SLA never had more than fifteen members – could attract disproportionately influential attention. The group's bizarre outlook was rooted in communalism (the group's name is derived from the word symbiosis), anti-capitalism, and devotion to the international revolutionary movement. Active from 1973 to 1975, the SLA is best known for its kidnapping of the newspaper heiress Patty Hearst, who later took part in a bank robbery meant to sow chaos and fund future operations. Hearst's mother later claimed that her daughter had been "brainwashed." Hearst was nonetheless found guilty, although she was released early and later pardoned fully. Most of the members of the SLA, including its cultish leader Donald DeFreeze, were killed when their hideout burned down during a shootout with police. The remaining members committed another bank robbery in which a customer was shot to death and later planted bombs under Los Angeles police cars.

For the middle-class activists and students (usually former students, since revolutionary activities made it difficult to keep up with one's studies) who made up the Weather Underground, the Symbionese Liberation Army, and similar groups, the revolutionary lifestyle was probably more important than participation in revolutionary violence. Members embraced all the trappings of the age's counterculture, rejecting private property, living in communes, swapping sexual partners, and engaging in heavy drug use. Their affluent, educated profiles made their criminal, sometimes even sadistic behavior all the more inexplicable – the Weather Underground's Bernardine Dorhn, for example, famously enthused over the Manson Family's grisly murders.

Their ultra-radical stances and their disavowal of bread-and-butter issues associated with progressivism and socialism made it nearly impossible for them to appeal to anything but the tiniest sliver of the population, although, as their critics on the left repeatedly noted, their violence and outlandish behavior roused moderates and conservatives – what Richard Nixon called the "silent majority" – against the New Left and leftist causes in general. Dedicated to the destruction of capitalism and bourgeois democracy, the only thing that American urban guerrillas destroyed was the SDS. Instead of provoking a popular uprising, the Weather Underground and the SLA created widespread support for COINTELPRO's mild police repression and Nixon's presidential shenanigans.

These groups highlight one of the most noteworthy trends in terrorism since the 1960s: the dramatic increase in the amount of terrorism directed against liberal democratic states. This is true for both left-wing revolutionary groups (including the Tupamaros, to the extent that Uruguay had a moderately liberal democratic government) and ethno-nationalist groups (for instance, the IRA, ETA in post-Franco Spain, and Canada's separatist Québec Liberation Front). Two principal factors explain this development. In liberal democratic societies, constitutionally protected civil liberties – such as judicial due process and freedom of the press and assembly – afford terrorist groups greater cover under which to organize and launch plots. Conversely, authoritarian states and their relatively unrestrained security organs tend to fare better at unearthing and dispatching subversive groups. Secondly, liberal democratic societies and their freer and more developed media networks provide terrorist groups the means to publicize their grievances through violence. In authoritarian states, government-run media can deprive opposition groups, including those that resort to terrorism, most of their access to the public. Under such circumstances, subversive groups usually are geared toward less symbolic forms of violence, such as guerrilla warfare.

The Left in Europe

The dilemmas that democratic societies face in dealing with left-wing revolutionary terror were on even greater display in Europe than the United States. Europe was home to dozens of such groups from the late 1960s through the 1980s, nearly all of which engaged in some combination of Guevaran rebellion and Marighella-style "urban guerrilla" warfare and modeled themselves after the Tupamaros. In France, Action Directe carried out dozens of attacks on governmental buildings, prominent businesses, and military-industrial infrastructure. In Britain, the so-called Angry Brigade planted bombs and robbed banks. Both hoped to create through their actions revolutionary crises that would disable bourgeois society and lead to popular uprisings. When the public responded negatively, if at all, Action Directe and the Angry Brigade descended into criminality, violence for the sake of violence, and eventual oblivion. The two most violent such groups – West Germany's Red Army Faction and Italy's Red Brigades – were more successful on many counts. Although neither triggered the revolution they hoped for, both achieved a disquieting amount of public sympathy and brought their respective countries to the brink of political crises.

Europe experienced the same general circumstances that gave birth to leftist revolutionary movements in the United States. There was also significant opposition to what was perceived as their own government and business community's support of American imperialism. In West Germany and Italy, there was also particular anger at the older generation and its complicity in Nazism and fascism, world war, and genocide. Although liberal democracy had been firmly established in both countries, former Nazis and fascists were still prominent in government, business, and public life, a factor which helped explain why neither country had satisfactorily come to grips with its recent, horrid past.

The Baader-Meinhof Gang/Red Army Faction

The founders of Germany's most notorious terror group of the 1970s shared several characteristics: a middle-class upbringing, an eagerness to reject conventional society in favor of counterculture beliefs, and a deep-seated hunger for radical social justice. The bad-boy and petty criminal Andreas Baader, his lover Gudrun Ensslin, and the radical journalist Ulrike Meinhof met through Frankfurt and West Berlin's radical student circles and got their start in 1968's myriad street fights with police. During one standoff with the police, Meinhof issued a statement that shrilly announced, "This fascist state means to kill us all! We must organize resistance. Violence is the only way to answer violence. This is the Auschwitz Generation, and there's no arguing with them!" (quoted in Leavold, "Baader-Meinhof," 132).

The group began by setting off small bombs in department stores as protests of bourgeois decadence. But it soon graduated to dreams of an urban guerrilla campaign intended to tear the mask off what it saw as a hopelessly fascist West Germany. But these were pampered young men and women with no direct experience of guns, bombs, and violence. To prepare themselves, Baader and his followers went to Jordan in the summer of 1970 in order to train in a PLO-operated camp. The state of unreality surrounding the group was well illustrated by one run-in they had with their hosts. When horrified members of the PLO protested that the German women were sunbathing in the nude, Baader lectured them: "The anti-imperialist struggle and sexual emancipation go hand in hand. Fucking and shooting are the same thing!" (quoted in Vague, *Televisionaries*, 22). Shortly after returning to Germany, Baader and his small band began to rob banks to raise funds for their war against the socio-economic Establishment, soon gaining fame as the Baader-Meinhof Gang. Baader's penchant for carrying out their revolutionary expropriations in high style made the group media darlings among West Germany's left-wing intellectuals and students. Their frequent use of stolen luxury vehicles as their getaway cars led to the popular joke that BMW stood for Baader-Meinhof Wagon.

Shootouts with the police produced deaths on both sides and allowed the Baader-Meinhof Gang to present themselves absurdly as the victims of a fascist state. While this was quite a stretch for most West Germans, a poll revealed that 20 percent of the population had "a certain sympathy" for the group. The group, rechristened the Red Army Faction (RAF) in a nod to the Marxist Japanese Red Army, began to carry out bombings in the spring of 1972 targeting the United States' military presence in West Germany. Four US soldiers died and dozens were wounded. Within months, Baader, Ensslin, Meinhof, and other ringleaders, including Jan-Carl Raspe, were arrested and soon held in a special facility constructed for them at Stammheim prison. It seemed the RAF was finished.

The German Autumn of 1977

In fact, the climax had not come yet. The RAF's imprisoned members began a hunger strike – from which one died – that garnered more public sympathy, as did the suspicious prison suicide of Meinhof. In the meantime, the RAF was almost completely reconstituted with new leaders and members who went into action during Baader, Ensslin, and Raspe's long-delayed trial for murder in 1977. RAF terrorists killed a federal prosecutor and the head of Dresdner Bank and staged a barely foiled rocket attack on a government building. The violence and drama crested in what became known as "the German Autumn" of 1977, when the RAF's second generation kidnapped Hanns-Martin Schleyer and demanded the release of Stammheim's RAF prisoners. Schleyer, a former Nazi and member of the SS, was a member of the board of directors of Daimler-Benz and head of an influential industrialists' association. With the public panicking about RAF terror and the government refusing to negotiate with Schleyer's captors, sympathetic PLO hijackers seized a Lufthansa airliner and demanded the release of the RAF prisoners in return for the plane's passengers. Eventually the hijackers murdered the pilot and took the plane to Mogadishu, Somalia, where it was stormed by the German anti-terrorist group GSG 9 (which had been formed in the wake of the Munich massacre). When it became clear that they were

Figure 13.1: Funeral of Ulrike Meinhof, May 1976
(© Giehr/dpa/Corbis)

not going to be sprung from jail, Baader, Ensslin, and Raspe committed suicide in their prison cells, staging them to appear as if they were murdered by their jailers. Many on the left believed it. With the death of the RAF's imprisoned leaders, Schleyer was killed and left in the trunk of a car in Alsace.

The German Autumn of 1977 failed to produce a revolutionary upheaval or government collapse but did trigger considerable debate about the country's Nazi past. Artists, writers, and filmmakers had already begun to respond to the duel between the RAF and West Germany's security organs with a host of creative efforts that warned about the return of authoritarianism. In his 1974 novel *The Lost Honor of Katharina Blum*, for instance, one of post-war Germany's most popular authors, Heinrich Böll, described how one woman's life is destroyed by the media and the police after a one-night stand with a man who later turns out to be a terrorist. The most compelling depiction of Germany's troubled 1970s was the multi-director semi-documentary, *Germany in Autumn* (1978). The film portrays a deeply divided population, opening with older, conservative West Germans attending the funeral of Schleyer and ending with younger West Germans mourning at the graves of Baader, Ensslin, and Raspe.

Within a year of Schleyer's murder, most of the RAF's second generation of terrorists were arrested. But the RAF restocked its ranks again.
This was a pattern that would repeat itself into the 1990s, with the RAF
destroyed and reconstituted several times. By this point, the group bore
little similarity to its original version, except for its thirst for chaos and
vengeance. Although it was never able to equal the group's earlier political
impact, the RAF continued its campaign of politically motivated killing.
Most notable was a bombing within the US Rhein-Main Air Force Base
in 1985, which killed three civilians. The Red Army Faction was also
accused of the murders of the heads of Deutsche Bank, Siemens, and the
engineering firm MTU. The RAF finally announced its disbandment in a
1998 communiqué, leaving behind a legacy of mayhem, brutality, and
hopelessly misguided idealism.

Italy – Left vs. Right

Italian terrorism of the 1960s, 1970s, and 1980s was a more complicated and violent affair than elsewhere in Europe, involving tremendous
bloodshed from hundreds of left- and right-wing groups. According to
one calculation, there were over 14,500 politically motivated attacks
from 1969 to 1994 producing over 1,800 casualties (Francis, "Brigate
Rosse," 214). Unlike West Germany in the 1970s, where terrorists
entertained fanciful dreams of creating a revolutionary crisis, Italy
during this period was arguably close to one already. Across the
political spectrum, people grew increasingly disenchanted with Italian
liberal democracy and its notorious penchant for corruption and
unstable coalition governments. The Socialist and Communist Parties
attracted considerable support, encouraging, in turn, the emergence
of a plethora of neo-fascist groups. In scenes reminiscent of Italy and
Germany in the 1920s, far-left and far-right gangs waged fierce street
battles to establish their *bona fides*, attract support, and prepare for
the final confrontation.

Fascist street violence was augmented by methodically planned terrorist attacks carried out by groups such as New Order and National
Avant-garde. The worst of the atrocities took place on December 12,
1969, when neo-fascists set off a bomb in Milan's Piazza Fontana. Unlike
some other attacks that were primarily meant to intimidate and propa-
gandize, this was also meant to kill. And kill it did: the bomb left seventeen
dead and eighty-eight wounded. Those on the left grew convinced that
the state – particularly its military and security organs – was in league
with neo-fascists in carrying out what came to be called a "strategy of

tension": a campaign of violence and terror that could be conveniently blamed on communists, socialists, and anarchists in order to discredit the left, justify more repressive measures, and ultimately pave the way for a military coup. While the evidence for the existence of such a conspiratorial strategy is fragmentary, the government's behavior did lend it credence. In the case of the Piazza Fontana bombing, the state arrested two anarchists, one of whom was finally acquitted only in 1987.

The Red Brigades

This sense of siege contributed to the decision by some on the far left in 1969 to form a Marxist-Leninist group, the Red Brigades, dedicated to the use of revolutionary violence. The social composition of the Red Brigades differed somewhat from contemporary leftist revolutionary groups in other countries in that it drew not only from Italy's radical student population, but also from the Communist-affiliated working class. The Red Brigades' plans for using terror were also a bit different. While definitely influenced by Marighella and the Tupamaros, the Red Brigades imagined a much more protracted conflict in which they would gradually render the cities ungovernable, thus creating the ideal circumstances for the development of a politically conscious and armed proletariat aware of its world historical role. To carry this out, the Red Brigades, like the Tupamaros, formed a large, decentralized organization – a terrorist confederation, as it were – in which each city's cell operated independently of others. This made for a terrorist movement that was difficult to penetrate.

Throughout the first half of the 1970s, the Red Brigades hardly registered on the authorities' radar, given the scale of neo-fascist violence and the manic, undisciplined terrorist attacks of a myriad of left-wing groups. Meanwhile, the Red Brigades organized and gathered arms, funds, and recruits. When they carried out operations, they were generally kidnappings in which the victim was held for a short while and then released unharmed. In 1978, however, the Red Brigades began the campaign of violence that was to make them the most notorious terrorist group on the continent. First came the February assassination of a judge, followed shortly after by the kidnapping and murder of Aldo Moro. Moro was a five-time Italian prime minister and the leader of the Christian Democratic Party. Recently he had effected a reconciliation between the Christian Democrats and the Communist Party that was about to make him prime minister again, this time at the head of a center-left coalition. The Red Brigades targeted Moro not only as Italy's best known politician, but also as a warning to the Communists whom the Red Brigades now

Figure 13.2: Aldo Moro in captivity, 1978
(© ARCHVIO /ANSA/Corbis)

regarded as traitors to the true revolution. Through 1980, the Red Brigades carried out dozens of assassinations of policemen, federal and regional government and police officials, judges, and business executives. In 1981, a Red Brigade cell kidnapped US General James Dozier, who was serving with NATO. After being held for a month, during which the

Red Brigades tried to use him as ransom for the release of comrades in prison, a newly formed and specially trained anti-terrorism unit sprang him from captivity.

All the while, other far-left and neo-fascist groups continued to carry out their own terrorist outrages, killing almost eighty people in the year 1978–9 alone. Ominously, organizations on the far right began to adopt the left's strategy of decentralized, long-term armed struggle. The most notorious such group was the Armed Revolutionary Nuclei, which carried out attacks on leftist politicians, labor leaders, and magistrates and governmental officials involved in the hunt for neo-fascist terrorists. Much of the Nuclei's violence, however, was simply meant to disrupt daily life and undermine the normal functioning of state and society. Such was the only explanation possible for the era's worst terrorist attack, which the Nuclei carried out in August 1980. A bomb in the waiting room in Bologna's main train station killed eighty-five people and wounded over two hundred. The conviction of two members of the Nuclei was fifteen years in coming, a delay partially caused by sophisticated efforts by members of Italy's security apparatus to manufacture evidence that pointed to the involvement of foreign terrorists. Such malfeasance lent credence to the left's belief in a neo-fascist "strategy of tension."

Red Brigade terror dramatically declined after 1981. Improved efforts by center and left politicians to address some working-class concerns and general fatigue with the terror campaign led to a drop in passive support for the Red Brigades. A Red Brigade tactical error played no small role as well: in 1979, terrorists killed a member of the Communist Party who had informed the police about Red Brigade operations.

In the case of the Red Brigades as well as the Red Army Faction, the Weather Underground, and the Tupamaros, revolutionary terrorism emerged in democratic states under peculiar and specific circumstances. In each of these cases, the broader society was experiencing tremendous upheavals that produced radical groups with maximalist programs of social and cultural transformation. When these groups recognized that they enjoyed too little popular support to achieve their goals peacefully through democratic processes, they turned to violence. But since these groups were born of broader, radical movements, they became convinced that the revolutionary crisis was only a few bomb blasts away. In none of these cases did terrorism create the hoped-for revolution. This is not to say, however, that terrorism had no effect. In Uruguay, it contributed to the rise of a right-wing dictatorship, while in Germany it touched off extensive soul-searching about contemporary society's links to its Nazi past. In the United States, Italy, France, and Great Britain, left-wing terrorism helped to discredit broader and more moderate leftist movements.

The Rise of International Terrorism

Concurrent with the rise of leftist revolutionary terrorism was the advent and expansion of the phenomenon known as international terrorism. This referred to the behavior of those terrorist organizations that acted well beyond the borders of their own countries when establishing bases and safe havens, raising money, and carrying out attacks. Sometimes this meant staging strikes against citizens of countries uninvolved with the terrorists' struggles. The most prominent practitioners of this sort of terrorist violence were members of the PLO, particularly George Habash's People's Front for the Liberation of Palestine, which was particularly fond of hijacking airliners to attract attention to the Palestinian cause. Later, Black September carried out the Munich Olympics massacre, using a stage far from Palestine to attack Israeli interests. Indeed, international terrorism seemed to dominate headlines around the world from the late 1960s well into the 1980s. In the Western world there was an almost universal sense that this had become the pre-eminent form of terrorism. This was reflected in the rise of Hollywood films that depicted the arrival of terrorism on American shores. The first was 1977's *Black Sunday* about a Palestinian plot to crash the Goodyear blimp into the Super Bowl as punishment for American support of Israel.

What made this brand of violence so frightening was the dawning sense that everyone everywhere had become a potential target. By the mid-1970s, organizations concerned with security began to count incidences of international terrorism. The criteria for counting acts of international terrorism, however, have always been open to broad interpretation, thus producing wildly different results. For instance, where the CIA counted 2,698 international terrorist attacks for the period 1968 to 1977, the more cautious RAND Corporation reported barely one thousand (the majority of which, it emphasized, produced no casualties). Whatever the figures – all of them seemed large to governments and societies alike – there was the implication that international terrorism was monolithic and thus the expression of a worldwide conspiracy.

The security organs of the United States and the rest of the Western world unconsciously began to conflate the overlapping yet distinct phenomena of revolutionary and international terrorism. In practice, this meant a tendency to overlook what truly motivated the organizations that turned to terrorism. There were, of course, such revolutionary groups as the Tupamaros, the Weather Underground, the Red Army Faction, and the Red Brigades who were Marxists and thus internationalists by definition. Moreover, these groups had a penchant for speaking frequently of revolutionary alliances, even if they reflected general sympathies rather than hard and fast links in practice. Complicating matters was the fact that some of the most influential and active terrorist groups of the era – such as George Habash's Popular Front – sometimes draped their fundamentally ethno-nationalist concerns in the language of socialism or Marxism. No matter how much Habash expressed his solidarity with the Red Army Faction, his only real goal was a Palestinian homeland. Many political leaders and security experts failed to recognize that participation in international terrorism often had no ideological component. This was particularly the case for the Provisional IRA, whose acts of violence were often categorized as international terrorism because of their North American fundraising and cross border attacks from the Republic of Ireland. The Provos' links to revolutionary socialism, however, were minimal at best.

The United States: International Terrorism as a Communist Conspiracy

For the United States, the increasing conflation of revolutionary and international terrorism had disastrous consequences because it distorted the way leaders understood and prioritized threats to America's national security. This is a story whose consequences continue to be felt to the present day. In short, key US officials came to two egregiously erroneous conclusions about terrorism: first, that it was an ideological stance, rather than a tactical and strategic decision; and second, that terrorist groups of any substance could only carry out their activities if sponsored by states. The history of terrorism offers few lessons, but one certainly is that terrorism has appeared in many forms and served many purposes over the centuries. Nonetheless, influential Americans in the field of national security defied the historical evidence and committed the United States to policies based on the assumption that terrorism could only exist in certain guises. As a consequence, threats from other quarters, namely trans-national religious and ethno-nationalist groups, were discounted or overlooked.

Much of the explanation for these disastrous decisions lies in the fact that American thinking about national security in the 1970s and 1980s was dominated by the Cold War, as it had been since the late 1940s. Many commentators saw proof of the existence of an international terrorist conspiracy in the anti-imperialist rhetoric and limited connections between violent leftists in the 1970s. The journalist and mystery writer Ovid Demaris warned, for example, of these groups' "determination to replace the few democratic societies left in the world with totalitarian governments" (183). And the political scientist Louis René Beres cautioned that international terrorists had adopted "Trotsky's theory of 'permanent revolution'" (113). The most sensationalistic warnings were delivered by Claire Sterling, a conservative journalist and author. Her 1981 book *The Terror Network* contended that the Soviet Union, unwilling to risk everything on war, had turned to destabilizing the West through terrorism. Her study, however, was based on sketchy evidence, such as European newspaper accounts and government contacts; furthermore, her work lacked any appreciation of the political and historical contexts of the terrorist campaigns she purported to analyze.

Of greater significance was the fact that US leaders had come to assume the existence of geopolitical bipolarity and understood international politics as a zero-sum contest between the United States and the Soviet Union. By the early 1980s, many national security officials had come to see terrorism in this same way. Contributing to the Americans' bipolar view of the world was the fact that some revolutionary groups had begun to target American interests as part of their broad – if, of course, largely symbolic – assault on imperialism. Particularly influential was the Red Army Faction's 1979 assassination attempt on Alexander Haig, an American general and NATO commander. In his first press conference as Ronald Reagan's secretary of state less than two years later, Haig stated that Moscow was "training, funding, and equipping terrorists" and that "international terrorism will take the place of human rights in our concern" (January 28, 1981, *Current Policy* no. 258, US Department of State). This was a dramatic change in direction and a staggering intellectual leap: the United States had conflated all threats against it into one, folding terrorism into the Cold War.

William Casey, head of the Central Intelligence Agency, was another influential member of the Reagan White House who believed that the Soviets were behind nearly all terrorist activity. His principal source of proof – besides his gut instinct that in a black and white world the Soviet Union was a natural backer of terrorism – was the "research" of Claire Sterling. According to the CIA's chief Soviet analyst at the time, "Casey contemptuously told CIA analysts that he had learned more from Sterling than from all of them." What CIA analysts knew, however, was that "much of [Sterling's book] was based on CIA 'black propaganda,' anti-communist allegations planted in the European press" (Parry, *Secrecy and Privilege*, 185). The CIA's disinformation campaign had been so successful that the White House had come to believe the propaganda.

The CIA soon learned that it had something to gain by acquiescing in this fantasy, for the White House successfully worked to boost the CIA's funding and free it from some of the more onerous intelligence-gathering restrictions placed on it during the Watergate era. If the CIA ultimately rejected the fiction that the Soviet Union was terrorism's prime mover, it came to accept the underlying assumption that terrorism was primarily a device sponsored by states to advance covertly their foreign policy agendas. While this was certainly the case with some groups and sponsors in the Middle East – particularly when it came to Syria, Iraq, and the PLO's more obscure factions – such a statement hardly covered the activity of the era's bloodiest and most disruptive groups (the Provisional IRA, Fatah, the Shining Path, ETA, the Tamil Tigers, etc.). American policymakers grew ever more convinced, however, that state sponsorship was the primary form of terrorism in the 1980s, a conviction solidified by the American experience in Lebanon in 1982 and 1983 (see the next chapter for more information on this). Such a conviction was also both a cause and consequence of the United States' feud with Libya and its leader, Colonel Gaddafi. These assumptions about the fundamental character of terrorism blinded the CIA and the United States to the possibility of international terrorists of a rather different type whose transnational concerns were religious and conservative, not secular and Marxist.

At the same time, US officials downplayed the rhetorical and functional similarities between terrorism and state-sponsored terrorism, on the one hand, and state terror, on the other – this, of course, at a time when the United States directly supported a number of right-wing, anti-communist governments, particularly in Latin America, that used death squads, torture, "disappearances," and the systematic suppression of democracy and civil liberties in order to terrify and control their populations. US support was primarily financial, but it also involved the direct training of military personnel through the School of the Americas at Fort Benning in Georgia. In 1996, the Pentagon released seven of the school's training manuals from the 1980s which provided explicit instruction on torture, kidnapping, assassination, and the suppression of civil liberties. At the time, the US government denied allegations of such training and the application of such techniques in Latin American "dirty wars," and strongly endorsed the legitimacy of those governments. Jeane Kirkpatrick, one of President Reagan's most influential national security gurus, provided the justification for such support in the doctrine that was named after her: totalitarian states, such as the Soviet Union and those sought by leftist revolutionaries, were more destructive than authoritarian regimes. Thus, in an imperfect and bipolar world, the United States had little choice but to aid authoritarian states.

Terrorism and Security

A rather different consequence of the obsession with international terrorism was the single-mindedness with which governments around the world concentrated on securing international and then, rather later, domestic air travel. Terrorists, however, are similar to water running downhill – both seek the path of least resistance, sweeping around obstacles to find less obstructed routes. This is why purely defensive counter-terrorism – the hardening of sites, the deployment of more security, etc. – is incredibly expensive and minimally effective. When terrorists find it too difficult to attack one way, they will attack another. In the 1970s, authorities throughout the world came to assume that hijacking was the main danger that terrorists posed to airplanes; the main defensive measure was the massive deployment of metal detectors to screen for handheld weapons. Traveling by airplane soon became significantly safer, until the 1980s, when terrorists began to bomb rather than hijack planes. The newer tactic was a blunter weapon, since it no longer gave terrorists the opportunity to speak directly to their various audiences and, in fact, threatened to overly horrify the target audiences. But it was effective at attracting attention. The authorities' assumptions were destroyed a second time when terrorists graduated from smuggling bombs aboard planes in luggage to bringing bombs aboard on their own bodies. Those in charge of security had never addressed the possibility that some terrorists would be willing to die in order to complete their missions. Meanwhile, much less was done to secure other forms of transportation, such as by rail and sea, or other high-profile targets, such as sporting and entertainment venues, energy infrastructure, large office buildings, and even government buildings.

This development also illustrates the critical relationship that exists between the terrorists' goals, targets, audiences, weapons, and usual scale of violence. Ideologically and politically motivated terrorists with domestic agendas and orientations are usually most interested in communicating values, mobilizing the uninvolved, and building sympathy; therefore, they are more likely to be sensitive to public opinion and thus far more likely to prize drama and visibility over casualties. On the other hand, ethno-nationalist terrorists seeking a complete rupture with an occupying country are more interested in destroying the possibility of compromise, perhaps by provoking a brutal governmental reaction or civil war; thus, this sort of terrorist is more inclined to seek more casualties. Those terrorists, including those whose motive is primarily religious, who have no interest in winning over segments of the "enemy" population are most inclined to use great violence, although even then, until recently, such terrorists were often constrained by the fact that horrendous violence might alienate their own population by humanizing the enemy.

Bibliography

There are several good volumes on leftist terrorism from the 1960s to the 1980s. The two most scholarly are Michael Freeman, *Freedom or Security: The Consequences for Democracies Using Emergency Powers to Fight Terror* (Praeger, 2003); and Jeremy Varon, *Bringing the War Home: The Weather Underground, the Red Army Faction, and Revolutionary Violence in the Sixties and Seventies* (University of California Press, 2004). Jack Sargeant, ed., *Guns, Death, Terror: 1960s and 1970s Revolutionaries, Urban Guerrillas and Terrorists* (Creation Books, 2003) provides some good details and summaries. A contemporary analysis is Robert Moss, *The War for the Cities* (Coward, McCann, & Geoghegan, 1972).

The definitive scholarly treatment of the Tupamaros has yet to be written. In fact, the field is dominated by nearly contemporary accounts, such as Maria Esther Gilio, *The Tupamaro Guerrillas* (Saturday Review Press, 1972); and Alain Labrousse, *Tupamaros* (Pelican, 1973). For an account by a member of the group, see Carlos Wilson, *The Tupamaros: The Unmentionables* (Branden, 1974). Marighella's influential pamphlet, thankfully, is available: Carlos Marighella, *Mini-Manual of the Urban Guerrilla* (Abraham Guillen Press, 2002 [1969]).

The Shining Path of Peru is the subject of three excellent studies: Gustavo Gorriti, *The Shining Path: A History of the Millenarian War in Peru* (University of North Carolina Press, 1999); David Scott Palmer, *The Shining Path of Peru*, 2nd edn. (Palgrave Macmillan, 1994); and Steve Stern, ed., *Shining and Other Paths: War and Society in Peru, 1980–1995* (Duke University Press, 1998). Also useful is the relevant chapter in Michael P. Arena and Bruce A. Arrigo, *The Terrorist Identity: Explaining the Terrorist Threat* (New York University Press, 2006). This work also has valuable chapters on the Provisional IRA, Hamas, and the Tamil Tigers.

On the Weather Underground, see Varon, cited above, and Ron Jacobs, *The Way the Wind Blew: A History of the Weather Underground* (Verso, 1997). The best study of the broader political, social, and cultural ferment that produced the Weather Underground is Allen J. Matusow, *The Unraveling of America: A History of Liberalism in the 1960s* (Harper Torchbooks, 1984). For a participant's perspective, see Bill Ayers, *Fugitive Days: A Memoir* (Beacon Press, 2001).

There are a number of good volumes on the Red Army Faction/Baader-Meinhof Gang, but none of them are definitive: Jillian Becker, *Hitler's Children: The Story of the Baader-Meinhof Terrorist Gang* (Lippincott, 1977); Andrew Leavold, "Baader-Meinhof: Bring Me the Head of Ulrike

Meinhof," in Sargeant, ed., *Guns, Death, Terror*; Peter H. Merkl, "West German Left-Wing Terrorism," in Crenshaw, ed.. *Terrorism in Context*; Tom Vague, *Televisionaries: The Red Army Faction Story, 1963–1993* (AK Press, 1994); and Varon, cited above.

On the Red Brigades, see Donatella Della Porta, "Left-Wing Terrorism in Italy," in Crenshaw, ed., *Terrorism in Context*; Richard Drake, *The Aldo Moro Murder Case* (Harvard University Press, 1995); Peter Francis, "Brigate Rosse: Seeing Red," in Sargeant, ed., *Guns, Death, Terror*; and Robert C. Meade, *The Red Brigades: The Story of Italian Terrorism* (St. Martin's, 1989). For an alleged participant's account, see Giorgio, *Memoirs of an Italian Terrorist* (Carroll & Graf, 2003 [1981]).

For works on the United States and its reactions to international terrorism, see David C. Martin and John Walcott, *Best Laid Plans: The Inside Story of America's War Against Terrorism* (Harper & Row, 1988); Robert Parry, *Secrecy and Privilege: Rise of the Bush Dynasty from Watergate to Iraq* (The Media Consortium, 2004); and Jeffrey D. Simon, *The Terrorist Trap: America's Experience with Terrorism* (Indiana University Press, 1994). For an analysis of the training manuals used at the School of Americas, see Lisa Haugaard, "Declassified Army and CIA Manuals Used in Latin America: An Analysis of Their Content (Latin America Working Group, 18 February 1997, on line at http://www.lawg. org/misc/Publications-manuals.htm). For an intelligent, but polemical denunciation of the US government's efforts in the 1980s to shape the public perception of terrorism and state terror, see Edward Herman, *The Real Terror Network* (South End Press, 1983 [1982]); and Herman and Gerry O'Sullivan, *The "Terrorism" Industry* (Pantheon, 1989).

The classic contemporary account of the international terrorist conspiracy is Claire Sterling, *The Terror Network: The Secret War of International Terrorism* (Holt, Rinehart, & Winston, 1981). Other warnings of an international terrorist conspiracy include Ovid Demaris, *Brothers in Blood* (Scribner, 1977); and L. R. Beres, *Apocalypse* (University of Chicago Press, 1980).

14
The Rise of Jihadist Terrorism

On September 11, 2001, nineteen Arabs hijacked three airliners and flew them into the Pentagon and the two main towers of the World Trade Center. A fourth plane crashed in a field in Pennsylvania when passengers threatened to overpower the hijackers. The attacks killed three thousand people – at least 10 per cent of whom were not American – caused billions of dollars of damage to the US economy, and precipitated invasions of Afghanistan and Iraq as part of the Bush Administration's so-called "War on Terror." The group behind 9/11 was al-Qaeda, a shadowy transnational organization formed in the 1980s by the Arab Muslim extremist Osama bin Laden in order to fight the Soviets in Afghanistan. The doctrine that motivated bin Laden and al-Qaeda is known by many names, most often jihadism. Whatever the appellation, jihadism has replaced both ethno-nationalism and revolutionary leftism as the pre-eminent force behind terrorism today.

Jihadism

As described in Chapter 2, the central tenet of Islam is *tawhid*, the oneness of God. Not only does this demand of Muslims strict monotheism, but it means that God alone is the source of all authority. Strictly speaking, every Muslim is to be guided solely by *sharia*, Allah's all-encompassing will for humanity as expressed in the Quran and the *hadith* (the sayings and actions of the Prophet). Thus the Muslim "political" ideal has always been the early Islamic empire in which a single figure wielded both political and spiritual authority. But barely a generation after Muhammad's death in 632 CE, rival caliphs ("successors" to the Prophet) claimed his political and spiritual mantles. With the collapse of the Ottoman Turkish Empire in the 1920s, Islam lost its last caliph, in whom political and spiritual leadership were theoretically united. Long before that, each of the four primary schools of Sunni Islam had developed its own interpretive framework for applying the Quran and the *hadith* in a world of divided loyalties.

Throughout Islam's fourteen-century history, many spiritual leaders have sought to reinvigorate the idea of the caliphate and return to the mythical purity and ideal existence of the *Salafi* or "predecessors" – the first Muslims of the seventh century. One of the earliest was Ahmad ibn Taymiyya, a fourteenth-century scholar who taught that Islam had always sought the establishment of state power in order that Muslims could live under leaders ruling in full accordance with every teaching of the Prophet. Toward that end, ibn Taymiyya proclaimed jihad a critical component of faith. Jihad, then as now, has two meanings: the so-called greater jihad is the inner struggle to live in accordance with *sharia*, while lesser jihad is war to ensure that all Muslims can live under *sharia*-abiding Muslim rulers. Ibn Taymiyya went further, however, by declaring that those Muslims, particularly rulers, who did not accept the full length and breadth of *sharia* could be declared *takfir* (excommunicated) and killed as enemies of Islam. Much later, Muhammad ibn 'Abd al-Wahhab, an eighteenth-century Arab scholar, denounced Shiites and their idolatrous behavior toward their imams and saints, as well as Sunnis who blindly followed clerics and traditions that had made too many accommodations with the contemporary world. Ibn Taymiyya's and Wahhab's puritanical visions of Sunni Islam gained few adherents during their day.

A note on terminology: the doctrine that begins with ibn Taymiyya and finds expression today in the terrorist violence of al-Qaeda, Hamas, Hezbollah, and similar organizations is known by many names. Jihadism references the focus on lesser, that is, violent jihad, while the terms Islamism or political Islam emphasize the desire to apply *sharia* as a total substitute for secular ideologies. The term salafism refers to those fundamentalist and/or literalist Islamic movements that accept only the Quran and *hadith* as legitimate guides for behavior, while the term takfirism emphasizes the desire to purify Islam by eliminating heretical, particularly secularist, Muslims and their leaders.

Islam and Europe

The anger so prevalent in Muslim societies today cannot be understood without recognizing that for most of their history, the Islamic empires of the Middle East were not just militarily powerful but more intellectually and culturally sophisticated than their European contemporaries. Beginning in the late eighteenth century, however, core Islamic territories began to fall to the advances of the great European powers, whose technological and bureaucratic advances produced more powerful militaries. By the 1920s, only a few states with Muslim populations remained independent. Most of the modern Middle East had become League of Nations mandate territories – essentially imperial colonies – of the British and French. Meanwhile, Egypt was ruled by a British puppet whose autonomy was suffered as long as British military and economic interests were respected. Across the Islamic world, the result was the creation of a small, Westernized elite who generally accepted that the only way forward was along the Western path of secularization, industrialization, and bureaucratization.

Some leaders turned to Islam in hopes of finding a way to counter foreign political domination and cultural erosion. One was Rashid Rida (d. 1935), a Syrian modernizer who came to despair the region's virtual enslavement to the West. In the writings of ibn Taymiyya, Rida found a solution: a return to the values and practices of the righteous predecessors. Rida is responsible for taking a Quranic term, *jahiliyya*, which referred to the spiritual ignorance or darkness of pre-Islamic Arabia, and applying it to the contemporary Middle East, declaring that his fellow Muslims were lapsing into apostasy and selling out their civilization to the West.

Egypt and the Muslim Brotherhood

The man who began to turn such words into deeds was Hasan al-Banna, an Egyptian primary school teacher who in 1928 formed the Muslim Brotherhood, the goal of which was the creation of a spiritually rejuvenated society. "Our task," al-Banna wrote, "is to stand against the flood of modernist civilization overflowing from the swamp of materialistic and sinful desires" (quoted in Habeck, *Knowing the Enemy*, 31). He believed that the Western world was decaying from within and thus on the brink of collapse; all it needed was a push from those acting out the will of Allah. The group's credo summarized its world view perfectly: "God is our objective; the Quran is our constitution; the Prophet is our leader; Struggle is our way; and death for the sake of God is the highest of our aspirations" (quoted in Benjamin and Simon, *The Age of Sacred Terror*, 57). The Muslim Brotherhood published literature, engaged in preaching and missionary work, and established religious schools, medical clinics, welfare societies, and social clubs. By the 1930s, it had three hundred branches.

The Muslim Brotherhood also was successful in infiltrating the military and creating an armed group prepared to fight if the opportunity presented itself. The 1944 assassination of Lord Moyne, Britain's chief official in Cairo, by the Zionist terror organization LEHI exercised a strong influence on the Muslim Brotherhood, as did Irgun and LEHI's role in pushing the British out of Palestine by 1948. That year, in a bid to hasten Britain's departure from Egypt, the group attacked British and Jewish shops and assassinated a judge and other government officials. As a result, the Egyptian prime minister banned the Muslim Brotherhood. Less than three weeks later, a member of the group assassinated the prime minister. When al-Banna was killed in February 1949, everyone assumed that Egypt's police were responsible. The Muslim Brotherhood, which by this time had 75,000 members and many times that many supporters, soon went into hiding in order to plot the destruction of secular Egypt. When British-backed King Farouk was overthrown in 1952, the perpetrators were the Free Officers, modernizing members of the military led by Gamal Abdel Nasser and his protégé Anwar Sadat. Nasser briefly courted the Muslim Brotherhood and lifted the ban on the group, but the Free Officers' secular nationalism was ultimately irreconcilable with the Islamists' vision for Egypt. A violent clash between the two groups grew increasingly inevitable.

Sayyid Qutb

At the center of this clash was Sayyid Qutb, a modernizing school inspector early in life who went on to become the pre-eminent Islamist ideologist of the twentieth century. Qutb seemed destined for a life among Egypt's Westernized political elite, but along the way he grew disenchanted with the West and its influence on Egypt. The critical break came during his stay in the United States from 1948 to 1950, where he studied education at the behest of the Egyptian government. Qutb's disgust at American culture and its influence was total. Everywhere he was struck by materialism and what he regarded as the lax sexual morals of Americans. Not long after he returned to Egypt, Qutb left the Ministry of Education and joined the Muslim Brotherhood.

When a member of the organization carried out an unsuccessful assassination attempt on Nasser in 1954, Qutb was swept up in the wave of arrests. The authorities sentenced him to fifteen years in prison, where he produced the eight-volume exegesis *In the Shade of the Quran*, which was later abridged into the work for which he is best known, *Milestones*. The influence of this book can hardly be overstated, for in it he brought together multiple strains of Islamist thinking into a complete – and disturbing – worldview that has become a guide to thousands of people. The concept of *tawhid*, Qutb wrote, demands not just obedience to Allah, but a commitment to living in a community that follows all of *sharia*, rejecting everything else as sinful and idolatrous. He married this proposition to a broader application of Rida's use of the term *jahiliyyah*, thus conflating all history so that the Arab world's apostate rulers were the "new pharaohs" and Israel was but the most recent "Crusader" state established in the Middle East. And behind everything, Qutb saw the hand of the United States, encouraging the spread of carnal sensuality, materialism, and idolatrous worship of the laws of man, all of which would produce spiritual death if not stopped.

What is necessary, Qutb demanded, is "a full revolt against human rulership in all its shapes and forms, systems and arrangements . . . It means destroying the kingdom of man to establish the kingdom of heaven on earth" (quoted in Benjamin and Simon, *The Age of Sacred Terror*, 65). Although he prescribed no specific program, he made clear that such a campaign of violent jihad had to start at home by ridding the Arab world of those tyrants who rejected Islam. Given Qutb's criteria, this meant virtually every Middle Eastern ruler, including Egypt's Arab nationalists, Lebanon's Western liberals, Syria and Iraq's socialist Baath Party, and Iran's Shite idolaters.

Qutb called for the emergence of a new generation of Muslim leaders whose devotion to *sharia* would allow them to lead by example and through fatwas, explanations of the proper application of the Quran and *hadith* to contemporary issues. What his followers heard was that personal piety trumped the normal scholarly procedures for acquiring the mantle of spiritual leadership.

After nearly a decade in prison, Qutb was released in 1964 in a goodwill gesture by Nasser who believed that the Muslim Brotherhood had been crushed by years of persecution. Less than a year later, Nasser announced the discovery of a new Islamist conspiracy. The state once again arrested Qutb, who was put on trial for treason and sentenced to death. Nasser held out an olive branch to Qutb, who dutifully swatted it away. "My words," he prophesied, "will be stronger if they kill me" (quoted in Wright, *The Looming Tower*, 31). He was hanged in August 1966.

Islamism Finds an Audience

Qutb's vision would not have found much of an audience, but for a number of developments in the late 1960s and 1970s. The first was the failure of

Nasser to deliver on his grandiose promises of prosperity via the command economy and national rejuvenation through pan-Arabism. When Nasser died in 1970, his successor, Anwar Sadat, tried a different path, encouraging the growth of capitalism and closer ties to the West. Neither approach produced an economic breakthrough. Sadat's popularity was particularly undermined by the regime's dependence on the police to suppress dissent and the failure of economic liberalization to provide enough satisfying jobs for the thousands of graduates annually produced by the country's burgeoning educational system. In this way Egypt's program of modernization saddled the country with a well-trained, ambitious, but ultimately frustrated generation that increasingly looked for inspiration beyond the seemingly tired and disappointing "isms" of the West.

A second factor was the twentieth-century retreat of the *ulema*, the Islamic scholars responsible for interpreting and applying *sharia*, into a staid conservatism, a situation exacerbated by the efforts of modernizing governments across the region to diminish the *ulema*'s influence on secondary and university education. The results were dramatic: a new generation was growing up with scant respect for traditional Islamic authorities, little knowledge of the traditional schools of Quranic interpretation, and little faith in the ability of Islam as currently taught to answer the pressing questions of the day. Under these conditions, Qutb's call for a new generation of Islamic leadership unfettered by centuries of scholarly interpretations was particularly well received. The message that many heard was that piety and the Quran could be enough.

Meanwhile, Sadat engaged in US-brokered talks with Israel, producing a full-fledged peace treaty with the Jewish state in 1979 and a substantial infusion of military and financial aid from the United States. The cost of closer ties with America and compromise with Israel was enormous, of course, for it opened up Sadat to charges of becoming another "new pharaoh" willing to allow the further expansion of *jahiliyyah* into Egypt. Sadat heaped insult upon injury when his government provided women the right to divorce and banned the wearing in universities of the Egyptian version of Muslim modesty clothing for women.

A fourth factor were the unintended consequences of the Middle East's new-found oil wealth, particularly after the oil embargo of 1973 caused prices to skyrocket. Unfortunately, given the lack of democracy, this new revenue disproportionately benefited the region's elite. No country grew wealthier or experienced more jarring contradictions than Saudi Arabia, home to approximately one-quarter of the world's petroleum reserves, as well as Islam's two holiest sites, the mosques at Mecca and Medina. As early as the eighteenth century, the House of Saud forged an alliance with puritanical Wahhabist clerics who endorsed the dynasty as the protectors of Islam. Saudi oil wealth drew the regime even closer to the Wahhabist clergy, who were bankrolled and essentially allowed to dictate public morality. This wealth also allowed the kingdom's Wahhabist clerics to expand their influence abroad by establishing schools, training religious leaders, setting up social services, and disseminating literature, including the writings of the jihadist ibn Taymiyya. Ironically, two factors led to widespread discontent among Saudi Arabia's radical Islamists. The first was the very nature of the implicit agreement between Wahhabist religious leaders and the Saudi ruling family: in exchange for being placed on the state's payroll and given extensive control over public morality, Saudi Arabia's clerics have essentially given up any formal claim to political authority. The second has been the behavior of many royal princes, who flout Wahhabist demands for ultra pious behavior through lives of profligacy and dissipation.

In Egypt, President Sadat removed the ban on the Muslim Brotherhood and tolerated its widespread growth in an ill-informed attempt to buy the allegiance of the country's increasingly alienated Islamists. In return, the Muslim Brotherhood renounced violence and settled into uneasy coexistence with the state. The organization, however, continued to preach of the presence of *jahiliyyah*, the evils of secularization, and the pure moral vision of the *Salafi*. If the Muslim Brotherhood were no longer prepared – at least openly – to advocate violence to resolve the situation, others certainly would. And indeed, the spread once again of the Muslim Brotherhood nurtured the emergence of a new crop of leaders and secret organizations in answer to Qutb's call for new leaders whose goal was the establishment of an Islamic state, the elimination of Western influences, and the enforcement of *sharia*.

Egyptian Jihadists Organize

The two most important Egyptian leaders were the blind cleric Omar Ahmad Abdel Rahman (b. 1938) – known widely as Sheikh Omar – and Ayman al-Zawahiri (b. 1951), followers of Qutb who left the Muslim Brotherhood in order to preach and plot violence. Rahman, a theology instructor at a provincial Egyptian university, became widely known as one of the most vocal opponents of Sadat. In private, Rahman grew close to a radical jihadist outfit known as al-Gamaa al-Islamiyya – the Islamic Group – which had cells in nearly every Egyptian university. To fund its activities, the Islamic Group carried out robberies of Christians. Rahman quietly issued fatwas – Quranic justifications – for such activities in the name of Islamic revolution.

Al-Zawahiri, on the other hand, chose the path of dissimulation. Outwardly, he was a respected surgeon and a member of a prominent middle-class family that had produced generations of scholars and professionals. Privately, he formed a revolutionary cell, which, in the mid-1970s, merged with others around Cairo. This umbrella organization was known as Jamaat al-Jihad (the Jihad Group), or simply al-Jihad. Before long, al-Zawahiri was one of its most influential members. Like Rahman, he denounced *jahiliyyah* and embraced jihad, but al-Zawahiri deeply mistrusted the masses whom he believed were incapable of the requisite purity of word and deed. Both believed in conspiratorial violence, but it was al-Zawahiri who would make it the essence of his life's work.

The Iranian Revolution and the Hostage Crisis

During the tumultuous years 1979–83 Islamism and jihadism began to shake the foundations of the Middle East, becoming, in fact, a transnational phenomenon stretching from Algeria to Afghanistan. But dreams of transnational jihad were always threatened by sectarian, ethnic, and cultural differences. The only hope for uniting such a wide-ranging movement was to explain its motives and its goals in terms that transcended regional differences, to look outside the Middle East for the fundamental source of *jahiliyyah* and a target that could draw jihadists together.

The year 1979 began with the Islamist movement's greatest success to date, the Iranian Revolution. Although it occurred in a Shiite society, it inspired Sunni Islamists and radical jihadists, such as al-Zawahiri, throughout the Muslim world. The ruler of Iran, Shah Muhammad Reza Pahlavi, personified *jahiliyyah* to Islamists, for he used oil revenues to develop a modern, industrialized state – as well as to line his deep pockets and those of the state's Westernized elite. As a fierce anti-communist he was a close ally of the United States, which had helped him back into power with a CIA-backed coup against the reforming socialist politician Muhammad Mossadegh in 1953. Worst of all, the Shah ruthlessly crushed dissent using his security police, the infamous SAVAK. In 1978, a popular revolt broke out in which millions of Iranians participated as demonstrators. It came to be directed from abroad by an exiled imam, the Ayatollah Ruhollah Khomeini, who tailored his vague Islamist pronouncements in order to channel all dissent. In January 1979 the Shah fled and Khomeini returned to a rapturous welcome. Three months later, Iranians passed a referendum proclaiming an Islamic republic in which a regime of clerics would enforce *sharia* and establish a true Islamic state. This was widely viewed by Islamists as a victory over the forces of darkness, particularly the United States, dubbed by Khomeini "the Great Satan." What emerged was not wholly without its secular elements, but it still set other jihadists to hoping and dreaming for similar results in their own countries.

The Iranian Revolution produced another precedent: the use of terrorism as a means of striking blows – if only largely symbolic – against the Great Satan. After all, what really brought the Iranian Revolution to the attention of most Americans was the Tehran hostage crisis. In November 1979, young radicals stormed the American embassy and took sixty-three hostages. Although not directly ordered to do so by the Ayatollah, the militants had certainly been encouraged by his rabidly anti-American rhetoric. Eleven hostages were shortly released, but the remaining fifty-two were held for an excruciating 444 days. Recent interviews with the hostage-takers have demonstrated that the motivation was not simple anti-Americanism but fear that US diplomats and moderate elements in Iran were working to develop a post-Shah rapprochement. The hostage crisis effectively scuttled any such developments. American prestige suffered, particularly in the wake of the failed rescue operation of April 1980. The hostage crisis certainly contributed to US President Jimmy Carter's decisive defeat in 1980 by Ronald Reagan, whose conservative credentials and tough-as-nails rhetoric appealed to an embarrassed and insecure electorate. More immediately, the embassy seizure strengthened the hand of Iran's militant Islamists and energized a generation of jihadists who came to realize that a small vanguard of revolutionaries willing to act decisively could garner international attention, humiliate the United States, and even cripple a presidency through terrorism.

Another consequence of the Revolution was the invigoration of an already influential feature of Shiite Islam: the celebration and pursuit of martyrdom. For centuries the most visible manifestation of this were the bouts of bloody self-mutilation during festivities recognizing the martyrdom of Imam Hussein in 680. After 1979, this behavior became a critical component of Iranian national symbology, encouraged by the authorities as a means of uniting the populace, submerging internal differences, and rechanneling otherwise potentially destabilizing political demands.

The Assassination of Sadat

The events of 1979 caused much shock and consternation in Egypt. Peace between Egypt and Israel dismayed Islamists, while the Iranian Revolution horrified Sadat and the modernizing elite. The battle lines were starker than ever, and bloodshed was not long in coming. In October 1981, a small al-Jihad cell within the Egyptian army assassinated President Sadat while he was reviewing troops during a public holiday. "I have killed Pharaoh, and I do not fear death!" the leader of the assassination team shouted before he was wounded and captured by the slain president's security detail (quoted in Bell, *Murders on the Nile*, 60). Although there was little public mourning in the wake of Sadat's death, there was also no popular uprising. Instead, Sadat's successor, Hosni Mubarak, coordinated a swift and far-reaching round-up of thousands of Islamists. Both al-Zawahiri, the al-Jihad leader involved in a coup plot intended to capitalize on the assassination, and Rahman, the religious advisor to the Islamic Group who happened to be uninvolved in the murder, were caught in the dragnet. Suspects were held in the immense twelfth-century fortress in Cairo known as the Citadel. Many, including al-Zawahiri, were tortured over the period of many months while the state prepared for a public trial that it thought would destroy jihadism. Both Rahman and al-Zawahiri used their trials to preach their principles to the broader public. "We owe to God obedience and no obedience is owed to [the president of the Republic] who disobeys God," declared Rahman, who escaped conviction (quoted in Bell, *Murders on the Nile*, 63). Al-Zawahiri was particularly effective at highlighting the state's authoritarian record, at one point reciting the names of those suspects who had died from torture. "So where is democracy?" he shouted. "Where is freedom? Where is human rights? Where is justice? Where is justice? We will never forget! We will never forget!" (quoted in Wright, *The Looming Tower*, 54–5). Eventually convicted on a weapons charge, al-Zawahiri was sentenced to a relatively short three-year term and released from prison in 1985.

Possibilities for jihad in Egypt seemed to recede. Mubarak and Egypt's security organs had dealt severe blows to al-Jihad, the Islamic Group, and the host of other small jihadist groups that had been plotting against the state since the mid-1970s. Although jihadists had killed Sadat the pharaoh, no Islamist popular insurrection had taken place. Throughout the 1980s, Mubarak successfully placated moderate Islamists, including the Muslim Brotherhood, with concessions. Public piety, such as beards for men and veils for women, was encouraged. The conservative, orthodox *ulema* was given new authority. Meanwhile, new state investments in education, housing, and infrastructure blunted some lower-class anger. Police authority was undiminished, however, and close watch was kept on radicals, such as Rahman and al-Zawahiri. What was a jihadi to do?

Jihadists in Saudi Arabia and Syria

In Saudi Arabia, jihadists gathered their strength to strike a blow against *jahiliyyah* and a regime that helped spread Wahhabism, but whose princes lived in profligate splendor, stymied the political ambitions of Islamists, and cozied up to the United States. Jihadist anger took shocking form in November 1979 when four to five hundred insurgents – partially inspired by Iranian militants' capture of the US embassy in Tehran – seized the Grand Mosque in Mecca on the last day of the annual pilgrimage. The leader of the group was Juhayman al-Utaybi, a wild-eyed fundamentalist preacher who recruited followers from the Muslim Brotherhood chapter at the Islamic University of Medina. In sermons that al-Utaybi delivered over the mosque's public address system during the two-week crisis, he decried a litany of sins that would become staples of Osama bin Laden's pronouncements two decades later: Saudi Arabia's close relationship with the United States, its supposed sufferance of Israel, the presence of thousands of Western military and technical advisors in the Kingdom so close to Islam's holiest shrines, the decadent ways of its rulers, and the corruption and passivity of the country's Muslim clerics. It seems that al-Utaybi and his followers hoped to spark an uprising that would force out the al-Saud family and all foreigners and lead to the establishment of a theocratic state. After a number of bungled, bloody efforts to retake the Mosque from the rebels, the Saudi authorities finally managed to seize the holy site and capture al-Utaybi and the bedraggled rebels. A few weeks later, al-Utaybi and sixty-two of his followers were executed by beheading.

The results of jihadist efforts in Syria were similarly disappointing. Beginning in 1979, the Muslim Brotherhood carried out guerrilla attacks and terrorist strikes against the dictatorial regime of Syrian President Hafiz al-Assad, including an assault on a military school that killed over eighty cadets, a series of car bombs in Damascus that killed several hundred civilians, and an insurrection in the provincial city of Hama. Assad's brutal response forced the Muslim Brotherhood in Syria to the brink of extinction but killed tens of thousands of civilians in the process. If Syrian Islamists were to wage jihad against the evils of the modern world, it was not going to be in Syria.

Hezbollah and Iran

The Israeli invasion of Lebanon in 1982 to destroy the PLO (see Chapter 12) took a dangerous situation and made it worse. Although Arafat and the PLO were forced to flee, the Israeli presence created new enemies. This was particularly the case among the poor and marginalized Shiites of southern and eastern Lebanon who had begun to organize in the mid-1970s, often around clerics who turned away from the state in favor of community-based social transformation. The most radical was

Ayatollah Muhammad Hussein Fadlallah, who established a number of schools and other social services in south Lebanon. After 1979, Fadlallah loudly preached the necessity of an Iranian-style revolution in Lebanon, a message that gathered much support after the Israeli invasion and even more after American, French, and Italian peacekeepers arrived in Beirut shortly thereafter. Not surprisingly, Arab Muslims of all stripes resented the Western presence, which they came to see, rightly or wrongly, as simply a force meant to prop up the Christian Maronite presidency and Israel's Christian militia allies.

In 1982, Iran began providing the means for waging jihad against Israel and the West by supplying funds, weapons, and advisors to Fadlallah's group, which soon became known as Hezbollah ("The Party of God"). Iran hoped to spark a Shiite revolution in Lebanon but was also eager to export its radical extremists who were starting to get disenchanted back home. The new group took on several roles. The first was the provision of social services to the area's Shiite population, now made possible on a much grander scale with the infusion of Iranian funds. A second was the creation of a militia, which provided security to Shiite communities and occasionally worked in concert with the Syrians, who dominated eastern Lebanon. The result was a virtual state within a state, made possible by the chaos and deprivation of civil war.

Hezbollah and Terrorism

Hezbollah's role as a terrorist organization, however, brought the group the most attention abroad. The mastermind behind Hezbollah's terror operations was the Lebanese Shiite Imad Mughniyeh who, for many years, was one of Arafat's bodyguards while the PLO operated out of Lebanon. Mughniyeh stayed behind when the PLO fled and eventually became Hezbollah's security chief, eventually receiving military training from members of the Iranian Revolutionary Guard. Mughniyeh remained the principal point of contact between Iran and Hezbollah until his death in a car bombing in February 2008, allegedly at the hands of the Israelis.

Mughniyeh introduced two tactics into the jihadist conflict with the West: the use of suicide bombers and kidnappings. Mughniyeh and his cousin, the explosives expert Mustafa Badreddin, organized a series of attacks starting in late 1982 under the name of Islamic Jihad, itself merely a shadowy front for Hezbollah's first operations. In November 1982, a suicide attack on Israeli military headquarters in Tyre killed ninety Israelis and many Lebanese and Palestinian prisoners. In April 1983, a

Figure 14.1: US Marine barracks bombing, Beirut, October 1983
(© Bettmann/CORBIS)

suicide bomber struck the US embassy in Beirut, killing eighty people, almost half of whom were Lebanese. Among the American casualties was nearly every member of the CIA's Middle East team. On October 23, Hezbollah struck again, with simultaneous suicide car bomb attacks on barracks housing US and French peacekeepers in Beirut. Most of the 241 American fatalities were Marines, the Corps' largest single day loss of life since the Battle of Iwo Jima in the Second World War. Fifty-eight French paratroopers died as well, the gravest military losses suffered by that country since the Algerian War. Although Hezbollah denied involvement, it heaped effusive praise on the "martyrs" who had taken the battle to US forces. Although President Reagan initially pledged that the US would not abandon the peacekeeping operation, the massive losses had made clear how vulnerable American forces were. With more casualties likely for the open-ended mission, popular support in the United States evaporated. Within four months, the Marines were gone, and Lebanon slipped wholly into Syria's sphere of influence. Hezbollah had forced the United States and its allies out of Lebanon, only a few years after the humiliation and paralysis of the Tehran hostage crisis. These were lessons not lost on jihadists across the region.

Meanwhile, Mughniyeh carried out attacks outside Lebanon as part of a shadowy Iranian campaign against its enemies. Iran's rivals soon came to understand that terrorism would follow in the wake of any effort to damage Iranian interests. Indeed, in December 1983, with America and France still mulling over their Lebanon policy, Mughniyeh and another Iranian-backed Shiite group carried out simultaneous suicide bombings of six targets in Kuwait, including the American and French embassies. In April 1984, a Hezbollah attack on a restaurant in Spain killed eighteen members of the US military. Taking a page from the Palestinian playbook of the previous decades, Hezbollah teams hijacked airliners, twice murdering Americans. After Badreddin was arrested and sentenced to death in Kuwait for the December 1983 attacks, Mughniyeh began to kidnap Americans in Beirut, threatening to kill them if his accomplice was not released. All told Hezbollah took thirty Western hostages, including the CIA's station chief in Beirut, several American journalists, two relief workers working for Christian charities, and several administrators and professors from the American University of Beirut. The Americans and Kuwaitis refused to release Badreddin and sixteen others held in the bombings. Eventually Mughniyeh and Islamic Jihad killed four American hostages.

Despite Reagan's very firm and very public pledge not to negotiate with terrorists, US officials sought ways to secure the hostages' release through backdoor channels. US officials eventually sold much-needed anti-tank missiles and other weapons systems to Iran (this, of course, while the US armed its Persian Gulf rival during the Iran–Iraq War of 1980–8) through Israeli intermediaries in exchange for pressure on Mughniyeh and Hezbollah to release American hostages. The profits from the arms sales were then channeled, against the explicit orders of the US Congress, to fund the Contras, an insurgent group fighting the pro-Soviet Sandinista regime of Nicaragua. Reagan justified the scheme to himself, claiming "I did not think of the operation . . . as an 'arms-for-hostage' deal"; but, of course, it was (quoted in Oren, *Power, Faith, and Fantasy*, 559). In any event, Mughniyeh released three hostages, but then quickly took three more Americans hostage, confirming the beliefs of many American and Israeli officials that negotiations with terrorists simply produced more terrorism. The rest of the hostages were eventually released on Iran's orders, some after nearly seven years in captivity.

Mughniyeh remained active well into the 1990s, carrying out operations against Hezbollah's enemies as well as those of Iran. Although the group's rhetoric was still dominated by Islamist pronouncements, in practical terms its behavior was largely motivated by ethno-nationalist concerns and its existence as an Iranian-funded extension of that country's foreign policy. In 1992, in response to the Israeli assassination of a Hezbollah leader, Mughniyeh engineered a suicide truck bomb attack on the Israeli Embassy in Buenos Aires, Argentina, killing twenty-nine people. Two years later, a similar attack leveled a Jewish center in Buenos

Aires, killing eighty-five people. Saudi investigators also suspected that Mughniyeh and Hezbollah were responsible for a massive car bomb in June 1996 that devastated Khobar Towers, a large complex housing US military personnel taking part in the "no-fly" operations over Iraq. Nineteen US soldiers and airmen died in the blast.

The Afghan Mujahideen

While the United States' Middle East policy drifted and veered among competing concerns in the late 1970s and early 1980s, on the fringes of the region an opportunity opened up for American advantage that US intelligence and foreign police officials judged to have little downside. In hindsight, it was, in fact, the most significant development in the emergence of jihadism as an international force. That event was the Soviet invasion of Afghanistan in December 1979, an effort intended to prop up the Afghan communists who had come to power in a bloody coup the previous year. The Afghans' radical Marxist-Leninist agenda was an improbable one since they tried to impose it on a remote and inhospitable country with barely no industrial infrastructure or working class, and barely even any semblance of national identity. Afghanistan's tribal chieftains, who suffered a central government only when it maintained virtually no presence, immediately took up arms against the new communist regime. The rebels who fought the central government quickly became known as mujahideen, a word meaning "those who wage jihad," or, more literally, "those who struggle." In its early stages, the mujahideen were hardly the "holy warriors" they later became. In the first years of their resistance, they fought not for the imposition of *sharia* or as part of a sacramental desire to destroy infidels, but rather to restore the status quo ante of ethno-tribal domination.

The United States immediately seized upon the opportunity to harass and humiliate its Cold War foe. President Carter's national security advisor, the rabidly anti-communist Zbigniew Brzezinski, proposed an indirect intervention via Pakistan, a close American ally and neighbor of Afghanistan. While noting that the US had to avoid direct confrontation with the Soviets which could lead to superpower war, Brzezinski informed Carter that "it is essential that Afghanistan's resistance continues. This means more money as well as arms shipments to the rebels, and some technical advice" (quoted in Coll, *Ghost Wars*, 51). That Pakistan's military dictator, Muhammad Zia-al-Haq, was also an ardent Islamist did not bother Brzezinski, nor did the fact that the largest mujahideen group had a loose affiliation with the Muslim Brotherhood.

Within a year, US arms, cash, and advisors were flowing to Pakistan, as was money from American allies Egypt and Saudi Arabia. Before long, Israel, France, Britain, and even the People's Republic of China were contributing funds in an effort to damage Soviet interests. Most American efforts to support the mujahideen – who quickly organized into a bewildering array of at least seven major armed camps – flowed through Pakistan's main intelligence agency, the Interservices Intelligence (ISI), whose officers received training from American advisors in the US and Pakistan. ISI officials, in turn, passed on to the mujahideen what they had learned: how to use small arms and heavy weapons, sniper rifles, camouflage, explosives, and car bombs. Just as importantly, they taught the mujahideen the conspiratorial habits and skills of successful guerrilla warriors.

In its first year of funding, the US Congress secretly appropriated about $30 million for the mujahideen. By 1987, the annual American appropriation had reached $630 million, boisterously encouraged by Congress' biggest supporter of the mujahideen: Rep. Charlie Wilson, a gung ho, fun-loving, alcoholic Texas Democrat who frequently traveled to Pakistan to indulge his romantic yearning for adventure and attention. In 1986, the United States began shipping one of the military's newest and most sophisticated weapons to the mujahideen: shoulder-launched anti-aircraft Stinger missiles. The mujahideen's skillful deployment of the Stingers forced the Soviets to curtail their use of helicopters and dramatically shifted the advantage to Afghan's anti-communist forces.

Egypt and Saudi Arabia were both keen to establish presences in Pakistan and Afghanistan independent of the US. This meant not only channeling funds through various religious and social agencies to the mujahideen, but also recruiting small contingents of men to fight alongside them. Little official encouragement was really needed. As early as 1979, Islamist clerics throughout the Middle East kept their followers informed about the efforts of their Muslim brethren to kick out the Soviet infidels. Before long, clerics began to preach the necessity of supporting the anti-communist jihad through financial support and personal involvement. For many committed Islamists, the journey to Pakistan to take part in jihad against the Soviets became a passable substitute for the social transformation at home that seemed more than ever out of reach (except in Iran).

The collective effort to support the mujahideen also helped cement America's close ties with Egypt and Saudi Arabia, both of whom were eager to bolster their own militaries with American weapons and training and to counter the Soviet-backed Syrians and the drift toward communism among some of their own intellectuals. Before long, American advisors were training Egyptian and Saudi officers who passed this knowledge along to the few young men recruited to join the fight against the Soviets in Afghanistan.

Osama bin Laden and Afghanistan

The most successful fundraiser and recruiter for the effort in Afghanistan was a young, pious, and impressionable millionaire, Osama bin Laden. His father was Yemeni, but had become the operator of Saudi Arabia's largest construction business and thus a close associate of King Faisal. Born in 1957, bin Laden attended university in the city of Jedda, where he studied under two influential Islamists: Muhammad Qutb, the younger brother of Egypt's Islamist martyr, and Abdullah Azzam, a radical Islamic scholar from Palestine. Azzam traveled frequently to Afghanistan to meet with the mujahideen. Back in Jedda, he was particularly skilled at recruiting fighters for the anti-communist jihad. "You *have* to do this!" Azzam urged his listeners, "It is your duty! You have to leave everything and go!" (quoted in Wright, *The Looming Tower*, 96). The importance of martyrdom grew in his exhortations until it occupied a central place. For the so-called Arab Afghans who went to fight the Soviets and their Afghan puppets, a righteous death in combat was the most sought-after goal. For these Arabs who had come to believe that life was no longer worth living in their home countries, a glorious death and the immediate reward of heaven became the best alternative.

Bin Laden was hooked. In time, he became the jihad's biggest private financier, raising millions of dollars to support the struggle and aid displaced refugees. By 1984 he had visited Afghanistan. Two years later, bin Laden brought his family to Pakistan. That year, he and Azzam established the Services Bureau in order to raise funds, recruit fighters, and operate a training base near Peshawar on the Afghan–Pakistan border. Bin Laden worked exclusively at first as a fundraiser and recruiter, but around 1987 he began venturing into Afghanistan with small bands of guerrillas. After a firefight in 1987, he secured an AK-47, a trophy that can be seeing dangling from his shoulder in his videotaped communiqués from the late 1990s and 2000s.

Azzam was one of the two most critical influences on the intellectual development of bin Laden during his time in Afghanistan, convincing his junior of the need to create an organization capable of fomenting and leading international jihad against non-Muslims. The other major influence on bin Laden was al-Zawahiri, the Egyptian leader of al-Jihad, who first traveled to Pakistan in 1980 to work in a hospital for refugees. What he saw there convinced him that Pakistan and Afghanistan provided far better opportunities for organizing jihad than were available in Egypt. His hope was to develop a battle-tested, conspiratorial group that he could transport to Egypt where it could deliver results otherwise impossible under the tyrant Sadat. In 1981, however, al-Zawahiri was arrested in the wake of Sadat's assassination. He returned to Afghanistan shortly after his release from prison in 1985 and soon embraced the doctrine of *takfir* (the excommunication and even killing of heretical Muslims). Always the conspirator, al-Zawahiri now fully took on the conspirator's arrogance visible in such figures as Nechaev and Lenin: he would decide who was and was not a proper Muslim and dispense justice accordingly.

Azzam and al-Zawahiri fought for access to bin Laden and his wealth. In the end, bin Laden merged their worldviews, committing himself to continuing *takfiri* jihad beyond Afghanistan's borders after the war against the Soviets ended. But where and against whom? That remained to be seen. In the meantime, bin Laden began in 1988 to set up the infrastructure for training and maintaining a band of elite, committed fighters – a private army dedicated to jihad, to be supported by bin Laden's personal wealth and his proven fund-raising abilities. The body's name was al-Qaeda – "the base," that is, the training base where this group would be organized. Besides bin Laden, most of the other leaders of al-Qaeda were Egyptians, including al-Zawahiri.

Most estimates of the number of Arabs who fought in Afghanistan hover around five thousand. Their military influence was minor, and they were often marginalized by the Afghans who considered their jihadist death wish odd – and oddly un-Islamic. Although in general they experienced less combat than their Afghan comrades, the Arabs became immersed in the culture of anti-communist jihad and acquired the means to wage it. The Americans had little control over where weapons, cash, and training ended up, since their transfer was entirely in the hands of Pakistan's intelligence services. Part of the problem was that the Americans cared little about who used the weapons, as long as they were used against the Soviets and their Afghan allies. As Secretary Brzezinski later said, "Which was more important in world history? The Taliban [who succeeded the mujahideen] or the fall of the Soviet empire? A few over-excited Islamists or the liberation of Central Europe and the end of the Cold War?" (quoted in Cooley, *Unholy Wars*, 20). In any event, the CIA was lucky if half of the weapons sent to Pakistan reached its nominal allies. Of the rest, some were purloined or sold on the black market in Afghanistan where they could be bought by anyone, including Arab Afghans.

Like the Americans in Vietnam, the Soviet public had little love for an interminable war that produced mounting casualties and little progress (approximately fifteen thousand Soviet soldiers died in the war). By 1988, the Soviet Union's new leader, Mikhail Gorbachev, was looking for a way out of the war; the last Soviet soldiers left Afghanistan within a year. When it became clear that Afghanistan's communist regime could not hold out long on its own, the barely contained animosities among the various Afghan tribal warlords and Arab fighters erupted into a bitter contest for post-communist supremacy. One of the first casualties of this civil war was bin Laden's chief mentor, Abdullah Azzam, who was killed by an enormous roadside bomb in November 1989. No one claimed credit for the assassination, but much suspicion has fallen on al-Zawahiri, who after the killing was left without competition for bin Laden's support.

Just a few months earlier, bin Laden had returned to Saudi Arabia, giddy with victory against the Soviets and highly respected as the chief architect of the Arab Afghan force, but disillusioned by the rapid disintegration of what was never a united Arab front. Bin Laden pondered what to do with al-Qaeda, his small but well-armed and well-trained private army of holy warriors. After a brief involvement in a civil war between nationalists and Marxists in Yemen (just south of Saudi Arabia), bin Laden began to agitate against the secular, pseudo-socialist dictator of Iraq, Saddam Hussein. When Hussein invaded Kuwait in August 1990, thus threatening the entire region, the Saudis were inclined to turn to the United States for aid. Bin Laden urged the Saudis to let him organize the defense of the kingdom. When asked how he would defend against tanks, chemical weapons, and a million-man army, bin Laden responded, "We will fight him with faith." Unimpressed, the Saudi king implored the US to "come with all you can bring" (quoted in Wright, *The Looming Tower*, 157).

Bin Laden Focuses on the US

Sometime between the Soviet exit and the fall of Kabul to the Afghan warlords in 1992, most of the foreign mujahideen tried to return to their home countries. In many cases, their governments refused them re-entry, knowing how potentially dangerous these armed and trained Afghan Arabs were. Some became stateless warriors, wandering from jihad to jihad. Many made their way to Sudan, where, in the summer of 1989, a coup inspired by a radical Islamist, Hasan al-Turabi, deposed the civilian government. Al-Turabi opened up Sudan to Islamists and jihadists of every stripe, hoping to create a new international center for jihad. One of the first to arrive was bin Laden, who settled in, briefly abandoning jihad.

Three things drew him out of early retirement and turned him from an anti-communist insurgent into an international terrorist. The first was the continuing presence of American troops in Saudi Arabia. It was now 1992, more than a year after the Gulf War had pushed Saddam Hussein out of Kuwait, and the United States seemed to be there to stay. To make matters worse, US soldiers arrived in nearby Somalia in December under a UN mandate to halt fighting in that country's civil war. Bin Laden was horrified about the inroads the United States was making into the Islamic world, aided by leading Muslim states such as Egypt and Saudi Arabia and the Zionist state of Israel, a veritable twentieth-century Crusader kingdom in the Middle East. Like Sayyid Qutb, the towering figure of modern Islamism, bin Laden increasingly saw the influence of the United States behind every manifestation of *jahiliyyah* and in every example of Arab or Muslim impotence. And like Qutb, bin Laden believed the United States was vulnerable. Had not the Marines been chased from Beirut by a few suicide bombers? Bin Laden's confidence in America's lack of willingness to sustain casualties was to be further borne out when Bill Clinton quickly extracted US troops from Somalia in October 1993 after an ambush killed eighteen soldiers.

The second factor in bin Laden's transition to committed international jihadist was his constant mingling in Khartoum with the leaders of Islamist and jihadi groups from every corner of the Muslim world. Contact with representatives of al-Jihad, the Islamic Group, Hamas, the Abu Nidal Organization, Carlos the Jackal, and even the Shiite group Hezbollah convinced bin Laden that the resources and willingness existed for a truly international jihad, and that even a Sunni–Shiite alliance toward this end was possible. It has also been conjectured that bin Laden's possible contact with Hezbollah's terrorist mastermind Mughniyeh led to the conviction that suicide bombings were the most effective and efficient way to strike at a numerically, financially, and technologically superior enemy.

The third factor was a new round of intense study of the Quran and Islamic history, particularly his discovery of the teachings of ibn Taymiyya. By conflating the thirteenth and twentieth centuries – something bin Laden and the *salafis* were always keen to do – ibn Taymiyya's fatwas ostensibly provided all the Quranic support necessary for a campaign of purifying violence against all enemies of true Islam. Bin Laden even went so far as to read into the fatwas permission to kill innocent bystanders if their deaths made it possible to destroy infidels.

But how to proceed with jihad? There were limits to how effective the attacks on heretical Muslim rulers and societies could be, since on the whole these were resilient, authoritarian states with vast police powers. After all, the executed "pharaoh" Sadat had simply been replaced by Mubarak, who continued most of his policies. What propped these states up, bin Laden believed, was the almighty American dollar, given both in foreign aid and as payment to siphon away the region's vast oil wealth. Only by forcing the United States out of the Middle East could Islam truly regenerate itself.

Bin Laden's decision to unleash his venom on the United States was also motivated by his need to find a target that would pull together the disparate elements of the ragtag international jihad who, as bin Laden knew all too well, were at each other's throats in Afghanistan. This was but one more variation on a theme that bin Laden saw everywhere in the Middle East. Anger, jealousy, and suspicion had long prevented Egyptians, Saudis, Syrians, and Iraqis from cooperating, even against the Israelis, a foe they universally despised. Bin Laden himself, until recently, had regarded Shiites as heretics. He became convinced that only a campaign of terror against the United States provided the targets and symbols that could obliterate the sectarian, cultural, and ethno-nationalist barriers that divided the international jihadist movement against itself. Bin Laden believed that he could exploit the Middle East's history of victimization by Crusaders and imperialists, if only the United States could be shown to be the late twentieth-century heir to those traditions. Ultimately, bin Laden centered his plans on the hope that the United States could be coaxed into responding to terrorism with strikes or, better yet, an invasion of an Islamic country. Then the blueprint developed in the mujahideen's struggle against the Soviets could be applied to the sole remaining superpower, the USSR having collapsed in 1991.

Ramzi Yousef and the First World Trade Center Attack

The first jihadist conspiracy to carry out an attack on American soil, however, was not hatched by al-Qaeda. This was the 1993 attack on the World Trade Center, which was carried out by a small, unnamed band of men led by Ramzi Yousef, a Kuwaiti-born, half-Pakistani, half-Palestinian twenty-four-year-old who wished to punish the United States for its backing of Israel. Yousef and his colleagues, although independently organized, were deeply enmeshed in the rapidly developing international jihadist movement. Yousef had been exposed to the teachings of Abdullah Azzam, who preached for a while in Kuwait, and was infuriated by what he saw of the first Intifada on television. Moreover, two of his uncles were killed fighting with the mujahideen in Afghanistan. Rendered homeless by Saddam's invasion of Kuwait in August 1990, Yousef went to Pakistan, where he trained as a guerrilla and a bomb maker with equipment donated by the CIA. During this time, he might have met bin Laden. In September 1992 he came to New York City to scout targets.

There he attended one of two mosques run by Sheikh Omar Rahman, the Egyptian leader of the Islamic Group. Rahman, increasingly frus-trated by the prospects of waging jihad against Egypt, had come to New York in 1990 to spread his gospel of hate and drum up support for taking the war to the real enemy, the United States. From his home in Jersey

City, just across the Hudson from New York, Rahman issued fatwas legitimating the murder of Jews and calling on Muslims to attack the West, to "cut the transportation of their countries, tear it apart, destroy their economy, burn their companies, eliminate their interests, sink their ships, shoot down their planes, kill them on the sea, air, or land" (quoted in Wright, *The Looming Tower*, 177).

Yousef needed little encouragement, but Rahman's urgings apparently led Yousef to advance the date of his plan. His goal was to set off an enormous bomb in the parking garage beneath the World Trade Center, one large enough to topple one of the great towers into another. He hoped to kill a quarter of a million people – roughly equal, he thought, to the amount of pain that US-backed Israel had inflicted on Palestinians. The bomb he constructed was an updated version of the classic ammonium nitrate and fuel oil concoction that had been the staple of terrorist car bombs for several decades. The bomb, packed into a rented Ryder van, was enormous. When it was detonated on February 26, 1993, the explosion created a seven-story deep crater, killed six people in the garage, and injured over a thousand who inhaled the toxic smoke that filled the towers. It was not big enough, however, to bring down the World Trade Center. The bomb that cost at most a few thousand dollars eventually caused over a half billion dollars in damage.

Yousef quickly fled the country, but the other conspirators were quickly captured, in large part because of their sloppiness. One had actually rented the Ryder van in his own name and called after the explosion to report the vehicle stolen so he could get his deposit back! Convinced that they were dealing with rank amateurs, the authorities became overconfident and dismissed the importance of the plentiful evidence that linked the terrorists to an enormous, shadowy international movement. Barely one year after the attack on the World Trade Center, Yousef's four principal co-conspirators were found guilty and given multiple life sentences.

Meanwhile, the FBI-led Joint Terrorism Task Force infiltrated an informer into a Brooklyn jihadist cell associated with one of Rahman's mosques. The authorities were thus fully informed about the plot the cell was hatching to assassinate Egypt's President Mubarak and to simultaneously bomb five New York landmarks, including the United Nations building. In summer 1993, the conspirators were arrested, along with Rahman. The Sheikh received a life sentence for inspiring the conspiracy, and the rest of the plotters received prison sentences of at least twenty-five years.

After fleeing the United States, Yousef went to the Philippines, where he linked up with associates from his days in Afghanistan, now operating as the Abu Sayyaf Group. The Wahhabist organization operated in the remote south Philippine Islands where they used their CIA/ISI training to terrorize and kill those who opposed the establishment of an Islamist state. Yousef trained a few members of the Abu Sayyaf Group in bomb making but concentrated his efforts on designing bombs whose components could be smuggled aboard airplanes, reassembled in the bathroom, and left to detonate after the bomber exited the plane. In a test run in December 1994, Yousef planted a bomb that killed a Japanese passenger aboard a flight from Manila to Tokyo but failed to bring down the aircraft. Yousef made adjustments and proceeded with plans to set off the bombs on twelve near-simultaneous flights bound for the United States via the Pacific. On the eve of the plan's launch, however, Yousef accidentally started a fire while working on the bombs in a Manila apartment. He fled, but was captured one month later by Pakistani police in Peshawar. He was handed over to American officials and returned to the US, where he was put on trial and found guilty for the World Trade Center bombing, as well as his new conspiracies.

Jihad in Egypt

Meanwhile, Egyptian jihadists, particularly Arab Afghans returned from the holy war, once again went on the offensive after years of quietude. From 1992 to 1997, jihadi terrorists killed more than twelve hundred people, including Egypt's speaker of parliament, a government minister, and the head of the country's counter-terror unit. The two main purveyors of this violence were the Islamic Group, which still followed Omar Rahman despite his self-imposed exile and then imprisonment in the United States, and Ayman al-Zawahiri's organization, al-Jihad. Of the two, the Islamic Group was far more active, targeting intellectuals, journalists, Christians, government officials, and foreign tourists. Al-Jihad, however, was the innovator, becoming the first Sunni terror organization to use suicide bombings, a tactic previously used only by Shiites.

Al-Jihad was almost entirely destroyed in the early 1990s when the Egyptian police captured the organization's membership director along with his lists. The public, in any case, was growing increasingly disgusted by indiscriminate Islamist violence, an attitude that crystallized in 1993 when a young girl was accidentally killed during an unsuccessful attempt by al-Jihad on the life of Egypt's prime minister. Civilians took to the streets to denounce violence carried out in the name of Islam; mourners at the girl's funeral cried out, "Terrorism is the enemy of God!" (quoted in Wright, The Looming Tower, 186). Under such circumstances, there was no public protest when another heavy-handed government crackdown gutted al-Zawahiri's organization in Egypt.

The Islamic Group was also suffering from attrition in its war with the security forces – so much so that in 1997 Rahman's followers brokered a truce with the government, to which many in al-Jihad added their voice. Al-Zawahiri, by now back in Afghanistan, was furious and gathered what bitter dissenters he could. The attack they planned was an act of desperation designed, in the style of Marighella and the Tupamaros, to provoke a response from the authorities that would radicalize the masses and return the initiative to the jihadists. In November, a commando team massacred fifty-eight tourists and four Egyptians in a shooting spree at Queen Hatshepsut's temple near Luxor. The killings were particularly grisly, even by the standards of the jihadists. One survivor saw a terrorist behead her father; another shoved an Islamist pamphlet into the body of an eviscerated tourist. All six terrorists immediately committed suicide a short distance from the temple. So great was the Egyptian public's revulsion and anger, that every jihadist group denied involvement. Cut off from funding and recruiting and denied shelter or safe houses, jihadist violence simply evaporated. "We thought we'd never hear from them again," said one Egyptian human rights worker (quoted in Wright, *The Looming Tower*, 258).

The Taliban and bin Laden

Al-Qaeda had built an organization, trained guerrillas, dispersed cash, and hatched plots, but had not yet carried out any operations. In 1996, the Sudanese Islamist and dictator Hasan al-Turabi finally grew tired of bin Laden's troublesome behavior and ordered his expulsion. A stateless castaway, bin Laden decided to return to the scene of his greatest successes, for in Afghanistan there had been a surprising turn of events. After the mujahideen overthrew the communist leader Najibullah in 1992, a vicious new civil war among rival warlords produced a surprising victor. The Taliban's leader, the reclusive Mullah Muhammad Omar, preached an austere version of Islam that made Saudi Arabia's Wahhabists appear downright permissive. But the Taliban and their stern law-and-order program attracted much support from an Afghan population weary from nearly two decades of war. In 1996, the Taliban captured Kabul and immediately began to establish a puritanical regime that forbade women's participation in nearly all sectors of public life and even dictated the lengths of men's beards. A sign on the wall of the Taliban's religious police in Kabul summed it all up: "Throw reason to the dogs. It stinks of corruption" (quoted in Wright, *The Looming Tower*, 231).

In Afghanistan, bin Laden began to lay the groundwork for the campaign of violence that was to make him the world's most wanted terrorist just five years later. But he had nearly been bankrupted by his hasty flight from Sudan, and his organization was scattered. Nonetheless, one of his first acts in Afghanistan was to issue his famous "Declaration of War" against the United States in August 1996. Bin Laden's primary concern was the continuing presence in Saudi Arabia of American troops, to whom he stated, "Terrorizing you, while you carry weapons in our land, is a legitimate right and a moral obligation. . . . These youths [al-Qaeda's members] love death as you love life. . . . They will sing out that there is nothing between us that needs to be explained, there is only killing and neck-smiting" (quoted in Wright, *The Looming Tower*, 4). No operations were mounted to make good on the threats. In 1997, Peter Arnett of CNN conducted an interview with bin Laden in which the al-Qaeda leader declared the entire Saudi royal family to be heretics. When Arnett asked what sort of society bin Laden wanted for his adopted homeland, he answered only in generalities about the enforcement of *sharia*. As has been typical of nearly all radical organizations that resort to terrorism, al-Qaeda had few plans for what would follow "the revolution." Indeed, for those who adhere to maximalist programs, revolution *is* the answer to all the questions.

Figure 14.2: Osama bin Laden and Ayman al-Zawahiri in Afghanistan, November 2001
(© Reuters/CORBIS)

Desperate to remain a relevant force in Islamist circles, al-Zawahiri, now living in Afghanistan as well, merged most of al-Jihad's organization into the far wealthier al-Qaeda and placed his scholarly credentials at the service of bin Laden. One of al-Zawahiri's first actions in this regard was to issue a fatwa declaring that "to kill Americans and their allies – civilians and military – is an individual duty for every Muslim." The declaration cited three specific grievances: the continuing presence of US troops in Saudi Arabia, Iraqi civilians' suffering under the burdens of the anti-Saddam economic boycotts, and US backing of the state of Israel (reprinted in Laqueur, *Voices of Terror*, 410–12). Most jihadist organizations, including the remnants of al-Jihad in Egypt, recoiled in bafflement at bin Laden and al-Zawahiri's stated commitment to attack the United States.

But their call resounded with individual jihadists who began to arrive in Afghanistan, where they formed cells and trained for combat operations. In this regard, al-Qaeda functioned as an umbrella organization, not a traditional terrorist group. Many of bin Laden's followers returned to their homelands, including Chechnya and Kashmir, to fight for an Islamic revolution. Others prepared for operations and simply waited. It is estimated that between ten and twenty thousand men traveled to bin Laden's training facilities in Afghanistan between 1996, the year of the "declaration of war," and 2001, when the camps were destroyed in the wake of 9/11. The volunteers were indoctrinated into al-Qaeda's worldview and received a short course in the use of small arms, bomb-making, and conspiratorial methods. Although they had varied ethnic and national backgrounds, these men typically shared many traits in common. Most were middle-class, educated professionals, who had spent much of their adult life in the West. As such, they felt isolated, suspended between the Muslim and Western worlds, belonging to neither. Mosques across Europe established by Saudi petro-dollars and staffed by Wahhabist clerics often provided these men with their first sense of belonging to a true community. Since many of these men came from secularized families, they had little grounding in Muslim history or theology, thus making them more susceptible to radical teachings. The most important feature they shared in common was a yearning for martyrdom.

American Reactions

A number of factors inhibited the Clinton administration (1993–2001) from acting more forcefully to counter the jihadist threat. Revelations about CIA behavior abroad, particularly in Latin America and Southeast

Asia, had led Congress to impose limits on covert foreign operations and intelligence gathering. On the home front, Watergate and Nixon's criminal misuse of the FBI spurred Congress to pass new laws preventing the routine sharing of information among the country's most important domestic and international intelligence agencies. Moreover, the Cold War had just ended, leading many Americans, including the newly elected president, to believe that the time had finally come to concentrate on issues of domestic importance. In any case, the institutions that had been created to wage the Cold War were geared to the collection and analysis of data from sources that provided little information on terrorist cells. Where there was awareness of terrorism as a national security threat, American thinking was still dominated by the late Cold War belief that terrorism primarily existed as a covert extension of enemy states' military and foreign policy. Among those involved in national security in the early 1990s, the notion of a vast international terrorist conspiracy smacked of the sort of embarrassing leaps of logic entertained by William Casey and Alexander Haig. Another widespread assumption held by Americans in and out of government was that most global terrorism involved hijackings that were largely meant to publicize a cause, not inflict large casualties. And – although it is difficult to remember in hindsight – bin Laden was not directly linked to any terrorist actions until 1998. Before that he was simply a financier and propagandist.

But some Americans were waking up to the threat, including John O'Neil of the FBI and Richard Clarke, America's counter-terrorism czar in the National Security Council. Together these two men began to forge some of the interagency links that would become so critical in the near future. At the moment, however, their demands for more resources and more counter-terrorism planning yielded relatively few results. In January 1996, another farsighted individual, Michael Scheuer, set up a CIA unit known as Alec Station to gather information on bin Laden. Only at the end of 1996 did US officials become aware for the first time of al-Qaeda.

Al-Qaeda Attacks

The first terrorist attacks known to be planned and carried out by al-Qaeda took place on August 7, 1998. On that day, enormous truck bombs simultaneously struck the American embassies in Nairobi, Kenya, and Dar es Salaam, Tanzania. The two blasts killed 224 people and injured over 4,500. Two facts befuddled and outraged the world, including most Muslims: the targets had nothing to do with American "atrocities" in

Palestine, Iraq, or Saudi Arabia, and most of the victims were Africans. Ten days later, the US fired cruise missiles against three targets. The first was a Sudanese pharmaceutical plant mistakenly thought to be making chemical weapons for bin Laden. The other two were al-Qaeda camps in Afghanistan. In the wake of the attacks, bin Laden began to present himself as a battle-tested enemy of the United States, a superpower willing to impersonally lob missiles, many of which went astray, killing civilians. The missile strikes effectively overrode the negative publicity bin Laden gained from the embassy attacks and brought in a new wave of recruits. Al-Qaeda's operational competence was still rather low, however, a fact on display in late 1999 when complicated plots to bomb targets in Los Angeles, Yemen, and Jordan unraveled and led to many arrests. But in October 2000, an al-Qaeda team piloted a small boat alongside the missile destroyer USS Cole refueling in the Yemeni port of Aden; after waving at the ship's crew, the men detonated their explosives, blasting a hole in the side of the vessel and killing seventeen American sailors.

Even as al-Qaeda grew in the late 1980s and 1990s, the international jihad against Western influence was growing on a number of other fronts. One common denominator was the frequent participation by guerrillas who had gained experience in Afghanistan as mujahideen. In most instances, the number of tangible connections between the fronts were few. There were important symbolic connections, however. In particular, these groups used the same vocabulary of *jahiliyyah*, *takfir*, and *salafa* and imagined themselves as part of a single effort to restore true Islam. Second, they promoted each others' struggles, as did the various leftist and ethno-nationalist groups of the 1970s, thereby conflating – or so they hoped – all regional Islamist campaigns into a single all-encompassing one. And third, they sometimes swapped propaganda and promotional materials, including cheap videos and DVDs of grisly executions and martyrdoms.

Hamas

The most prominent Islamist organization in Palestine began life in the 1940s as a branch of the Muslim Brotherhood, but it remained a small organization until the involvement, starting in the late 1970s, of a paraplegic educator, Sheikh Ahmad Yassin. He transformed the organization into a broader Islamic Society whose goals were the provision of Islamic education and social services, as well as preparation for armed resistance to Israel. Some evidence exists that from the late 1970s to the mid-1980s that the Israeli government provided assistance to Yassin's group in the hope that it would undermine Palestinians' attraction to Arafat's largely secular Fatah and PLO.

At the beginning of the first Intifada in December 1987, Yassin reformed the group as Hamas. The name is an acronym meaning the Islamic Resistance Movement and means "zeal" in Arabic. Bin Laden's teacher, Abdullah Azzam, contributed significantly to the writing of Hamas' constitution. That document, as well as subsequent pronouncements, reveal Hamas' dual concerns as both an ethno-nationalist organization devoted to the liberation of Palestine and the destruction of Israel and an Islamist group dedicated to spiritual and social awakening and the establishment of a theocratic state enforcing *sharia*. As far as Hamas is concerned, however, the two concerns are merely flip sides of the same coin, for defense of Islamic land is the duty of every true Muslim. In its charter and subsequent statements, Hamas has declared that all Israelis are enemy combatants and thus legitimate targets.

From the beginning Hamas devoted many of its resources to social and educational programs, which has made it very popular, even among those who are less convinced of the morality of violent resistance. Hamas' influence grew by leaps and bounds in 1990 and '91 at the expense of Arafat and Fatah, who sided with Saddam Hussein and Iraq and subsequently lost much of their funding from Arab states.

Suicide Bombing in Palestine

Hamas became a critical organizer of the Intifada, but for many years carried out few attacks. This changed when the group's paramilitary wing, the al-Qassam Brigades, began to unleash suicide bombers against Israel. From 1993 until 2005, when it declared a temporary truce with Israel, over four hundred Israelis died in such attacks. Other organizations have used suicide bombers in Israel and Palestine since 1993, as well. The two most significant are Palestinian Islamic Jihad, which was originally affiliated with al-Zawahiri's al-Jihad, and the al-Aqsa Martyr Brigades, a military arm of Arafat's Fatah that began operations after the start of the second Intifada in 2000 but then broke away from Fatah to protest Arafat's cooperation with Israel. Together, these two groups have caused more than two hundred fatalities (Pape, *Dying to Win*, 265–81). Targets for suicide attacks have included a full range of places frequented by civilians: restaurants, cafes, shopping centers, markets, pedestrian malls, buses, railway stations, hotels, synagogues, pool halls, and discos.

The al-Qassam Brigades' first attack occurred in 1993 (the same year as al-Zawahiri and al-Jihad's first suicide attack). Two reasons are generally given for Hamas' decision to suddenly start using suicide bombers more than five years after the start of the Intifada. Some have speculated that suicide attacks were specifically intended to undermine the Oslo peace process, which publicly began in September 1993, eventually leading to the creation of the Palestinian Authority and Arafat's renunciation of terrorism and recognition of the right of Israel to exist. Others have conjectured that Palestinians turned to the tactic primarily as a form of retaliation against acts that underlined their sense of helplessness. One of the most devastating occurred in February 1994, when Baruch Goldstein, an Israeli–American member of an extremist religious/nationalist group, massacred twenty-nine Muslims worshipping in the Cave of the Patriarchs mosque in Hebron in the West Bank. Equally demoralizing were Israel's targeted assassinations of militant Palestinian leaders, such as Hamas' principal bomb maker and the leader of the al-Qassam Brigades. Another development that exacerbated Palestinians' sense of futility was the rapid increase in the number of Jewish settlers in the West Bank and Gaza – from 1990 to 2002, the number tripled from 76,000 to 226,000. Just as important was Palestinians' increasing disenchantment with the stagnating Oslo peace process and the ever more apparent corruption and ineffectiveness of Arafat, Fatah, and the Palestinian Authority. Polls reflect this dynamic: as faith in the prospects of peace dropped, support for suicide bombers rose. With few legitimate political or social outlets for Palestinian rage and bitterness, Hamas and other terrorist groups have been able to find plenty of recruits. Sheikh Ahmad Yassin described the use of suicide bombers thusly: "Once we have warplanes and missiles, then we can think of changing our means of legitimate self-defense. But right now, we can only tackle the fire with our bare hands and sacrifice ourselves" (quoted in Bloom, *Dying to Kill*, 3–4).

Palestinian terror and Israeli counter-terror have fed off each other, creating a pattern of violence increasingly difficult to break. For instance, a Hamas terrorist – who had joined the group after his brother was killed by the Israeli army – detonated his bomb on a bus in Tel Aviv in October 1994, killing himself and twenty-two civilians. Israeli authorities almost immediately identified the bomber using DNA evidence. Later that day, Israeli soldiers demolished the family's home after giving them one hour to remove all their possessions.

Even Israeli soldiers observed the futility of such punitive actions. During one operation in 2002, an Israeli soldier lamented, "There's no way to break the system of terror in the West Bank, because the system is now in the minds of the people, in the minds of the teenagers, and what we're doing by this operation is giving them more reasons to build that system" (quoted in Bloom, *Dying to Kill*, 39).

Jihad in Bosnia and Chechnya

In the early 1990s *salafists* failed to transform the civil war between the former Yugoslavia's Serbian Christians and Bosnian Muslims into a jihad, despite the arrival of as many as four thousand veterans of the anti-Soviet war. Images of Arab Afghans posing with the severed heads of their Serbian foes harmed Bosnian attempts to court Western aid, and very few members of the highly secular Bosnian community responded positively to Islamist rhetoric. Bosnian authorities eventually forced the mujahideen to depart. Jihadists' high hopes for spreading the war against *jahiliyyah* into Europe were dashed by Bosnian Muslims' clear preference for liberal democracy and closer association with Europe and America.

The dissolution of the Soviet Union presented an even more attractive opportunity to wage jihad. In 1993, an Islamist group fighting to break away from the newly established Republic of Georgia used Afghan War-era Stinger missiles, now sold on the black market or transferred from one jihadist group to another, to bring down three airliners, killing 126 people.

But the real epicenter of violence in the former USSR has been Chechnya, a small ethnic enclave in the northern Caucasus with a history of opposing Russian and Soviet imperialism since the nineteenth century. In 1991, separatists in Chechnya declared independence from Russia; by 1994, open fighting was raging between Chechen guerrillas and Russian troops, the start of the first of two wars that in less than a decade killed or turned into refugees half of Chechnya's pre-war population of about one million.

Nearly all Chechens are indeed Muslim, but most are highly secularized and have understood the conflict in ethno-nationalist terms. Al-Qaeda, however, saw an opportunity to transform the conflict and began sponsoring a small jihadist enterprise – sometimes operating under the name the Wolves of Islam – led by Shamil Basayev, a Chechen warlord, and his lieutenant, the Saudi-born Wahhabist, Amir al-Khattab. The Wolves' goal was, in the words of the latter, to create "a pure Islamic land wiped clean of infidels" that could serve as a springboard for a "new world Islamic order" (quoted in Murphy, *The Wolves of Islam*, 2). During the first Chechen War, Basayev and Khattab frequently seized and executed hostages, a tactic that helped force the Russian authorities to negotiate a truce ending the first war in early 1996. So great had Basayev's fame grown that he came in second in the region's presidential election two years later.

But the underlying political standoff remained unresolved, and terrorism returned on an even greater scale. Several different groups carried out hijackings, bombings, and attacks on Russians as well as on pro-Kremlin Chechen politicians. Hostages were ransomed for exorbitant amounts of money. Many were beheaded, their deaths filmed and circulated throughout the Muslim world. Suicide bombers targeted public spaces and assassinated officials. In 1999, massive explosions in three Moscow apartment buildings killed 236 people and wounded more than four hundred. Although he did not claim credit for the bombings, al-Khattab declared that the war "had shifted to all Russian cities and would be directed against all Russians" (quoted in Murphy, *The Wolves of Islam*, 105). Russia's new president, Vladimir Putin, renewed open warfare against Chechnya, almost completely leveling the region's capital of Grozny in the process. But the war continued. Putin's habit of refusing to negotiate with any Chechen moderates, save those appointed by the Kremlin as its puppets in the region, meant that, by default, only the jihadist radicals had any standing in the public's eye, despite the population's clear distaste for an Islamist government. Russia's use of overwhelming land and airpower, however, slowly turned the war in its favor. By 2002, guerrillas had been driven out of nearly all the region's urban areas and into the mountains.

Basayev and Khattab's answer was to take the war, once again, to Moscow. In October, a number of bomb blasts hit the city. The centerpiece of the campaign was the seizure of the Dubrovka Theatre in the city center by a commando team, almost half of which was made up of veiled women. The group took more than 750 hostages, rigged the theatre with explosives, and declared that they would execute hostages and/or blow up the building if their confused demands were not met. After several days, the Russian authorities pumped a mysterious gas – variously described as fentanyl, halothane, nerve gas, or BZ, a Vietnam-era US weapon – into the theatre, knocking out many of the hostages and terrorists alike. Russian counter-terror teams efficiently stormed the building, killing most of the terrorists, but at least 130 hostages died from the effects of the gas.

The Dubrovka Theatre debacle did not change the course of the war in Chechnya, however. There, the Russians slowly ground out a military victory; what conflict remained was carried out through occasional guerrilla attacks and terrorist strikes in Chechnya, neighboring regions, and Moscow. Basayev increasingly relied on suicide bombers, many of them women dubbed "black widows." In 2004, Basayev masterminded another hostage-taking operation, this time of a school in the town of Beslan in the neighboring region of North Ossetia. When Russian security forces stormed the building – supposedly fearing that the terrorists were about to blow it up – one-third of the 1,100 hostages died in the gun battle and firestorm that engulfed the school's gymnasium. Basayev was finally killed in 2006, either in a Russian covert operation or by rival guerrillas. Meanwhile, massive Russian expenditures have largely rebuilt downtown Grozny and restored many services, effectively bribing Chechens into backing a pro-Kremlin regional government.

Jihadism in Algeria

Islamism and jihadism exerted the most influence and caused the most bloodshed in those areas where there was already political instability. By far the bloodiest example of this is Algeria, which by the late 1980s had been ruled by the secular, mildly socialist National Liberation Front since independence in 1962. Its one-party rule, however, generated a steadily growing opposition, one sector of which was led by the Islamic Salvation Front, an Islamist party dedicated to the creation of a theocratic state and the enforcement of *sharia*. In a bid to regain legitimacy, the government embarked on some much-needed economic reforms and, more significantly, rewrote the constitution to allow for multi-party elections. Meanwhile, returning veterans of the Afghan war ground their teeth in frustration, looking for a local conflict into which they could pour their rage and rabid desire for radical change. Salvation Front extremists thundered against the spread of *jahiliyyah* and Western influences. In the first round of parliamentary elections in December 1991, the Salvation Front won an astounding 82 percent of available seats, whereupon the government, sure of an impending Islamist sweep of the parliament, declared a state of emergency, banned the Salvation Front, and arrested its leaders, triggering the slide toward all-out war.

At least 160,000 people died during the Algerian Civil War, fought from 1992 to 2000 between the government and several armed factions. One of these factions was the Armed Islamic Group (GIA), whose radical jihadist pronouncements went far beyond what the Islamic Salvation Front had demanded. One of GIA's most important influences was bin Laden, who, in 1993, sent an emissary and a small amount of cash. Anywhere from several hundred to several thousand Algerians who had gained experience fighting in Afghanistan took part in jihad back home. GIA attracted much attention for its terrorist attacks on Algeria's foreign community in 1993 and 1994, but the vast majority of GIA's victims were fellow Muslims. GIA members imagined themselves to be twentieth-century Kharijites, the early Muslim faction that judged it permissible to kill *takfiri*, those Muslims "excommunicated" for their failure to follow every jot and tittle of *sharia*. One GIA communiqué bluntly declared, "There is no neutrality in the war we are waging. With the exception of those who are with us, all others are apostates and deserve to die" (quoted in Wright,

The Looming Tower, 190). GIA terrorists slaughtered entire villages and targeted journalists, veil-less women, politicians, and the leaders and members of rival guerrilla groups. As the civil war ground on, however, GIA lost nearly all public support, and most of its leaders were killed in internecine quarrels or through police infiltration. In 1999, a far-sighted and bold government initiative lured as many as 85 percent of GIA's fighters away from the movement with the promise of amnesty and a return to normalcy. A splinter group, the appropriately named Salafist Group for Preaching and Combat, has carried on the struggle with isolated terror attacks, but Algeria has regained a semblance of peace since 2002.

In the meantime, al-Qaeda's jihad had come to America's shores, a subject to which we will return in the last chapter.

Bibliography

There are many good books on the history of jihadism. The best is Gilles Kepel, *Jihad: The Trail of Political Islam* (Belknap/Harvard University Press, 2002). Other valuable books are Charles Allen, *God's Terrorists: The Wahhabi Cult and the Hidden Roots of Modern Jihad* (Da Capo Press, 2007); J. Bowyer Bell, *Murders on the Nile* (cited previously); Daniel Benjamin and Steven Simon, *The Age of Sacred Terror* (Random House, 2002); Mary Habeck, *Knowing the Enemy: Jihadist Ideology and the War on Terror* (Yale University Press, 2007); and Bernard Lewis, *The Crisis of Islam: Holy War and Unholy Terror* (Modern Library, 2003).

The best work on bin Laden and al-Qaeda is Lawrence Wright, *The Looming Tower: Al-Qaeda and the Road to 9/11* (Knopf, 2006). Others on bin Laden, Afghanistan, and the pre-history of the War on Terror are Peter L. Bergen, *Holy War Inc.: Inside the Secret World of Osama bin Laden* (Free Press, 2002); Steve Coll, *Ghost Wars* (Penguin, 2004); John K. Cooley, *Unholy Wars: Afghanistan, America and International Terrorism*, 2nd edn. (Pluto Press, 2000); Robert Dreyfuss, *Devil's Game: How the United States Helped Unleash Fundamentalist Islam* (Owl Books, 2005); and Michael Scheuer, *Through Our Enemies' Eyes: Osama Bin Laden, Radical Islam and the Future of America*, rev. edn. (Potomac Books, 2006).

On the events of 1979, see David W. Lesch, *1979: The Year That Shaped the Modern Middle East* (Westview Press, 2001); Mark Bowden, *Guests of the Ayatollah* (Grove Press, 2006); and Yaroslav Trofimov, *The Siege of Mecca* (Doubleday, 2007).

Two good books on Hezbollah are Ahmad Nizar Hamzeh, *In the Path of Hizbullah* (Syracuse University Press, 2004); and Augustus Richard

Norton, *Hezbollah: A Short History* (Princeton University Press, 2007).

The best book on Hamas is Zaki Chehab, *Inside Hamas: The Untold Story of the Militant Islamic Movement* (Nation Books, 2007). Also useful are Khaled Hroub, *Hamas: Political Thought and Practice* (Institute for Palestine Studies, 2000); and Samuel Katz, *The Hunt for the Engineer* (Lyons Press, 2002).

For America's interaction with jihadism, see the above cited books on bin Laden and al-Qaeda, as well as David C. Martin and John Walcott, *Best Laid Plans* (previously cited); Richard A. Clarke, *Against All Enemies: Inside America's War on Terror* (Free Press, 2004); and Michael B. Oren, *Power, Faith, and Fantasy: America in the Middle East, 1776 to the Present* (Norton, 2007).

On Chechnya, see Paul Murphy, *The Wolves of Islam: Russia and the Faces of Chechen Terror* (Potomac Books, 2006 [2004]).

For Algeria's civil war in the 1990s, see Martin Stone, *The Agony of Algeria* (Columbia University Press, 1997).

15

Alternative Terrorisms

In the last decades of the twentieth century, terrorism has been adopted as a strategy by a number of groups and movements that do not fit easily into the century's dominant storylines concerning ethno-nationalism, revolutionary leftism, or jihadism. These groups generally fall into one of two categories. The first includes those who tend toward apocalyptic rhetoric and who often use terrorism not as a means of publicizing their causes but as a strategy for waging a private war against their perceived enemies. Examples of this kind of violence include cults, right-wing militias, and lone-wolf vigilantes. The second category includes groups and individuals who embrace relatively mainstream political goals but with an extreme degree of conviction – for example, eco-terrorists and violent anti-abortion activists. Although these forms of terrorism associated with apocalyptic rhetoric or mainstream goals are responsible for much terrorism today, they are, historically speaking, recent developments best understood as variations on earlier themes.

Leaderless Resistance

Two elements common to many of these varieties of terrorism are the presence of a single polarizing issue and an organizational principle that has come to be known as leaderless resistance. The link between these two elements has been made clear by Louis Beam, a white supremacist, former Grand Dragon of the Texas Ku Klux Klan, and perhaps the most influential proponent of leaderless resistance. In a 1983 essay, he called for "like-minded individuals to form independent cells that . . . commit acts of sabotage or terrorism without coordination from above . . . while minimizing communication with other cells. . . . All persons involved have the same general outlook, are acquainted with the same philosophy, and generally react to given situations in similar ways" (quoted in McCann, *Terrorism on American Soil*, 257). In such cases, guidance is not provided by hierarchies; instead, these movements' touchstones are novels, one-off manifestos, individual acts, or seminal events. Communication between the otherwise unconnected adherents of these causes often takes place through the internet or informal associations. Movements that engage in leaderless resistance are generally unable to transform political systems, since they do not hope to stage revolutions, but are sometimes able to pervert mainstream debates or cause tremendous havoc.

American Militias

Several brands of extremism have emerged on the far right of the American political spectrum in the last several decades. The first began with the Posse Comitatus in the late 1960s, which saw itself as part of a long American tradition of anti-federalist agitation and sedition stretching back to the Whiskey Rebellion of the 1790s. The Posse Comitatus is a perfect example of leaderless resistance; in fact, it was the movement's core principle, for its advocates protested the existence of all government institutions above the local or county level. Local Posse Comitatus cells often engaged in symbolic forms of resistance, refusing to pay income taxes, apply for driver's licenses, or comply with virtually any business or social regulation. In the 1980s, this form of anti-tax and anti-federalist resistance began to develop into the militia movement. Militias, of which there were several hundred at one time with a total membership of perhaps several tens of thousands, are paramilitary organizations devoted to survivalism and weapons training. They imagine themselves as heirs to the Minutemen of the 1770s, who protected their rights against an encroaching government. Believing as they do that private gun ownership is the right most critical for the protection of individual freedom, militias believe that federal gun control legislation is the gravest threat to democracy. Every state has been home to a militia group at some point in the last two decades.

Researchers have identified two types of militias. The so-called "talking" or "out-front" militias, constituting the vast bulk of militia membership, are typically composed of anti-gun control activists and weekend warriors who, despite their galvanizing hostility toward Big Government, do little more than slog through the woods and shoot tin cans. On the other hand, the "marching" or "up-front" militias aspire to something much more sinister. They are convinced that war against a gun-confiscating state or a UN-backed one-world government will soon become necessary. Among the dozens of such groups in existence, the largest and most influential have been the Militia of Montana and the Michigan Militia.

White Supremacy, Christian Identity, and Aryan Nations

The second main strain within far right extremism is a more vitriolic and shadowy recrudescence of the white supremacist movement. While Ku Klux Klan klaverns remain, they have been overshadowed by far more dangerous and vituperative organizations linked by gun shows, mail order catalogs, and now the internet. Notable examples are the Covenant, the Sword and the Arm of the Lord; White Aryan Resistance; the World Church of the Creator; and the National Alliance. White supremacy, anti-Semitism, and race hatred constitute the core features of these groups, but they quite often also have a religious component. Although most white supremacists desire most of all to be left alone – to the point sometimes of retreating from society into isolated communes – some have gravitated toward violence and even terrorism.

In recent decades, many white supremacists have gravitated toward a bizarre set of beliefs collectively known as Christian Identity. The movement has its roots in the nineteenth-century doctrine of Anglo-Israelism, a not uncommon belief among the English elite that the Israelites and thus Jesus were Anglo-Saxons, not Jews. The doctrine was embraced in the US in the twentieth century by the carmaker Henry Ford, the occasional evangelist, some members of the Ku Klux Klan, and a few fringe politicians. By the 1970s, the movement had adopted the positions that it continues to emphasize today: that Jewish "parasites and vultures" are intent on enslaving Aryans through domination of world banking and media and are willing to use blacks, immigrants, and other "mongrels" to do their work. The United States is identified as God's chosen country; its mission, to defend and promote Anglo-Saxon heritage and blood.

The Aryan Nations has been the centerpiece organization of the diffuse and secretive Christian Identity movement since the 1970s, despite the fact that the group has never claimed more than a few score official members. In pamphlets available at its web site, the group proclaims that violence is the only way to create a whites-only state that can overcome "the Jew [who] is like a destroying virus that attacks our racial body to destroy our Aryan culture and the purity of our Race." For several decades, the group was headquartered on a huge property near Coeur D'Alene, Idaho, where the Aryan Nations held annual "congresses" that brought together leaders and members of the disparate Christian Identity movement. In 2001, a judge awarded a woman and her son the group's compound as compensation for an attack committed against them by Aryan Nations guards. The man behind the lawsuit was Morris Dees, founder and chief legal counsel for the Southern Poverty Law Center, which had already won multi-million dollar settlements against two Klan groups and the White Aryan Resistance. Although bankrupted, Aryan Nations continues to have an influential web presence.

For the last thirty years, the cultural touchstone and central document of the Christian Identity movement, oddly enough, has been a novel. The neo-Nazi and white supremacist William Pierce – writing under the pseudonym Andrew MacDonald – published *The Turner Diaries* in 1978. The novel describes, ostensibly in retrospect, how a shadowy group known as the Order uses terrorism against the state following the US government's confiscation of all privately owned weapons. The Order's campaign involves assassinating Jews and government officials, poisoning urban water supplies, shooting down airliners, committing economic sabotage, and using a truck bomb to devastate FBI headquarters in Washington. In time, the Order's terrorism sparks a race war that leads to the extermination of all non-whites and the creation of an Aryan utopia.

The Aryan Nations has spawned or influenced a number of paramilitary organizations, the most significant of which was known as the Silent Brotherhood or simply the Order, in emulation of Pierce's novel. Its goal was the creation of a whites-only homeland in the Pacific Northwest via terrorism, although the group never developed a systematic plan for achieving its vision. Many of the Order's members came from the Aryan Nations, having grown impatient at that group's lack of action. Shortly after organizing in 1983, the Order began counterfeiting money and staging robberies and armored car heists; a Brinks robbery near Ukiah, California, netted the group $3.6 million. Some of the money was used to amass a storehouse of weapons and explosives, while the rest was doled out to various individuals and groups, including the Aryan Nations, William Pierce, and Louis Beam (the KKK Grand Dragon and proponent of leaderless resistance). The Order reputedly drew up a hit list that included Dees; Norman Lear, the Jewish TV producer; and Alan Berg, a Jewish liberal radio host in Denver known for his combativeness. In June 1984, members of the Order murdered Berg outside his home. Later that year, the Order's leader died in a gunfight with FBI agents; within a few months, the group was nearly destroyed by arrests.

Christian Patriotism vs. the US Government

Several developments in the early 1990s further radicalized the various components of the extreme far right, in the process producing a broad movement often dubbed Christian Patriotism that created new sympathies and connections between Christian Identity groups and militias. The collapse of the Soviet Union and the end of the Cold War removed the threat of communism, which was for many on the far right the US government's sole *raison d'être*. Now that the United States was the world's only superpower, there was nothing, in their estimation, to prevent the lock-step movement of the US and the United Nations toward a "one world government" that would destroy individual freedom. At roughly the same time, the US Congress enacted laws that imposed mandatory waiting periods for gun purchases and made illegal the sale to civilians of military-style semi-automatic weapons. As far as militia members were concerned, this was merely the start of a campaign to criminalize all private gun ownership and thus the ability of private citizens to defend themselves against the advances of a tyrannical government. The county's most powerful gun rights lobby, the National Rifle Association, fanned the flames of paranoia and fear, making anti-government rhetoric virtually mainstream.

At the same time, two deadly confrontations between federal agents and survivalists led militia groups to believe that government crackdowns on all forms of dissent were imminent. The first occurred in August 1992, when US Marshals investigating gun violations by Randy Weaver, who was linked to Aryan Nations and Christian Identity, engaged in a firefight and lengthy standoff at the family's cabin in Ruby Ridge, Idaho. Weaver's wife and son died, as did a marshal. Six months later, agents from the Bureau of Alcohol, Tobacco, and Firearms (ATF) fought a bloody gun battle with a weapons-hoarding apocalyptic cult at its compound outside Waco, Texas. The shootout with the Branch Davidians led to a fifty-one-day siege by the FBI that ended in fire and more gunshots. By the end of the debacle, more than seventy-five people died, at least twenty of whom were children. Although the Branch Davidians were not associated with Christian Identity or anti-government resistance, far right groups adopted the Davidians as martyrs.

The Oklahoma City Bombing

Two years to the day after the deadly climax to the Branch Davidian standoff – and 220 years after the Battles of Lexington and Concord began the American Revolutionary War – a Gulf War veteran named Timothy McVeigh carried out the deadliest domestic terrorist attack in US history. McVeigh had extensive ties to Christian Identity and several militias, although he never actually belonged to a group espousing either philosophy. *The Turner Diaries* was reputedly "his bible," according to some acquaintances. A close friend of McVeigh later said, "We both believed that the United Nations was actively trying to form a one-world government, disarm the American public, take away our weapons" (quoted in Hoffman, *Inside Terrorism*, 106). With the help of another friend and army buddy, Terry Nichols, McVeigh gathered the materials for what would be a 4,800-pound ammonium nitrate/fuel oil bomb.

The day of the attack, April 19, 1995, McVeigh donned a t-shirt emblazoned with the phrase *Sic simper tyranis* – "Thus always to tyrants," the words shouted out by John Wilkes Booth after he assassinated Abraham Lincoln. On the back was a quote from Thomas Jefferson: "The tree of liberty must be refreshed from time to time with the blood of patriots and tyrants." McVeigh drove the bomb in a rented Ryder truck to Oklahoma City, leaving it in front of the Alfred P. Murrah Federal Building, which housed regional offices of the FBI and ATF, two federal agencies he deemed responsible for the Waco tragedy. The entire operation was closely patterned after the climactic strike against the FBI building described in *The Turner Diaries*. The explosion, timed to go off after the start of the workday in order to inflict maximum casualties, caused the northern third of the building to collapse and shattered windows in hundreds of buildings across downtown Oklahoma City. One hundred and sixty eight people died in the blast, including fifteen children in a daycare facility in the Murrah Building. McVeigh was arrested less than an hour from the city by a trooper who had pulled him over for a minor traffic violation. Two days later, McVeigh was connected to the bombing. He was eventually found guilty and executed for the attack. Nichols received a life sentence without parole. Many questions still remain, including the identity of the mysterious "John Doe #2" who was with McVeigh when he rented the Ryder truck. Some investigators have produced evidence ostensibly linking McVeigh and Nichols to the Philippines-based al-Qaeda partner, the Abu Sayyaf Group, as well as to Ramzi Yousef, the terrorist who masterminded the 1993 World Trade Center Bombing. The US government, however, considers the case closed.

Even before the Oklahoma City bombing, officials had awakened to the real danger of the militia movement in the US and become zealous – perhaps too zealous – in their hunt for groups poised to carry out violence. In 1996 alone, the FBI, ATF, and state and local police uncovered at least four plots. The first – and most questionable – was the arrest of three members of the single-cell Militia-at-Large for the Republic of

Georgia. The group had built at least ten pipe bombs that, according to the media's first reports, were to be set off during that summer's Olympic Games in Atlanta. The accused maintained that the bombs were simply meant for self-defense in the event of a government raid. The other three plots involved militia groups in Arizona, Washington state, and West Virginia. There is little or no evidence that any of these groups were actually planning to carry out terrorist attacks, yet the arrests and the media's coverage of the plots suggested otherwise. Nonetheless, Christian Patriot groups continue to exhibit a level of hate that is hard to fathom, and many of them possess an extensive knowledge of weapons, demolitions, and survival skills. They will continue to constitute a simmering threat to the United States for the foreseeable future.

Anti-Abortion Terrorism

Abortion has been one of the most controversial issues in the United States for several decades. Advocates on both sides of the issue have turned it into a litmus test in political contests, often carrying their stance well beyond the electoral realm. While almost all who are involved in advocacy on either side would never think to commit violence to further their cause, the passion and bitterness aroused by the issue has created a climate in which violence seems but the next in a sequence of small steps. A case in point is Operation Rescue, founded by Randall Terry in the late 1980s. The group has long engaged in civil disobedience outside abortion clinics; in the 1990s, it began to harass abortion providers and potential abortion recipients, some of whom successfully sued the group for physical intimidation and financial losses. Convinced that they are working to prevent the murder of unborn babies, Operation Rescue has steadily grown more sympathetic toward – without ever actually participating in – violence against abortion providers. Terry's successor has publicly supported those who have attacked or murdered abortionists. With good reason, those who have crossed the line to use violence believe that they enjoy broad support, a situation reminiscent of Russia in the 1870s or the southern United States during Reconstruction, when significant segments of educated society sympathized with populist terrorism.

Although abortion had been legal under certain circumstances in the United States since 1973, the violent anti-abortion movement really got its start in 1984, when Michael Bray, one of the movement's figureheads, and two others destroyed by fire seven abortion clinics in the mid-Atlantic region. Bray is affiliated with the leaderless umbrella organization the Army of God, whose on-line manifesto proclaims "the justice of taking all godly action necessary, including the use of force, to defend innocent human life (born and unborn)" (ArmyofGod.com). Though Bray has focused his activism against abortion providers, his framework is a generalized opposition to America's modern secular society. He despises the US government for the Waco tragedy, but more generally for presiding over a society that has rejected God and tolerates depravity (homosexuality, fornication, and abortion). His hope has been that Americans could be shocked out of their lethargy into taking up arms against the government in order to establish a state guided by fundamentalist Christian principles. The parallels with jihadist thinking are significant, right down to the fact that violence against "baby killers" is characterized as essentially defensive and that it is justified by selective citation from scripture, such as Jesus' proclamation, "I have come not to bring peace but a sword" (Matthew 10:34). Bray and his ilk hold to a post-millennial understanding of the New Testament, meaning they believe that Jesus will return to Earth only after humans have established Christian rule for a thousand years. Religiously inspired political and social activism thus hastens the second coming of Christ.

Beginning in 1993, violent anti-abortion radicals – sometimes ironically proclaiming themselves to be "pro-life" – actually began to target humans, killing seven people over the next five years. More than a year before he killed a doctor and his volunteer bodyguard, Paul Hill published an essay in which he compared abortion to slavery, arguing that although the latter was legal for a long time, it was always immoral and ungodly. Hill and the others who killed doctors, nurses, and security guards associated with abortion clinics between 1993 and 1998 all acted alone but enjoyed the support of Operation Rescue and other anti-abortion groups. Bray, for instance, served as an unsolicited spokesman for Hill. The internet also provided disembodied support, publicizing the cause and celebrating its victories. The website "The Nuremberg Files," for instance, promoted the murder of abortion providers and included a list of targets, such as Dr. Barnett Slepian, whose name was crossed out on the day he was murdered in 1998.

There is some crossover between anti-abortion violence and Christian Patriotism. The most significant example is the case of Eric Rudolph, who carried out four bombings from 1996 to 1998, including one during the Atlanta Summer Olympics and two against abortion clinics. Two people died and many were injured. Rudolph was an Army veteran and had ties to a Christian Identity group. Moreover, three of the bombings involved secondary explosions, the intent of which was to cause casualties among first responders and law enforcement personnel. In letters to media outlets, he made clear his hatred of abortion providers and homosexuals. Rudolph was identified after his last attack, but made use of his survival training to elude capture for over five years. Authorities suspect he was assisted in this by some people sympathetic to his anti-government agenda.

Cults and Terrorism

Another sort of alternative terrorism is that carried out by contemporary religious cults, who often attract little attention in Western societies because of their secretiveness and right to worship in freedom. There are pre-modern antecedents to such violence, the most famous of which was the Thuggees, an Indian group active in the seventeenth to nineteenth centuries. The Thuggees killed and robbed travelers in a bid to propitiate the Hindu goddess Kali; reportedly they believed that each ritual murder they committed delayed her vengeful return another thousand years. Some scholars argue that the Thuggees' primary goal was actually robbery and that their religious practices were not that different from those of peaceful worshipers of Kali. In fact, most groups that claim – or have been claimed – to terrorize or commit murder as a sacramental act of worship had other equally important motivations. The medieval Assassins are a good example. Although individual members of the Ismaili sect might have killed in the conviction that their holy deeds would earn them instant access to paradise, others, particularly their leaders, carried out terror and violence in a bid to eliminate their ethnic and sectarian enemies, carve out a state, and spread their faith – religious motivation, perhaps, but not necessarily sacramental acts.

The same is true of some recent acts of cult violence, the most notorious of which were carried out by followers of the Indian mystic Bhagwan Shree Rajneesh, who had established a religious commune near the town of Dalles, Oregon. In 1984, they carried out the world's first known act of bioterrorism, spreading salmonella via the salad bars of local restaurants. The attack was part of an effort to keep voters away during local elections so that Rajneesh's followers could gain control of the county. Over 750 people became sick, but no one died in the incident. During the ensuing criminal investigation, detectives discovered on the commune's property extensive literature on biological weapons and explosives and a sophisticated laboratory for producing salmonella. Although Rajneesh's followers killed no one and failed in their goal of seizing political control, the apparent ease with which they planned and carried out their attack alarmed authorities who had previously discounted the danger posed by terrorists using so-called NRBC weapons – those using nuclear, radiological, biological, or chemical means.

Aum Shinrikyo

The danger of NRBC weapons was real and to date best realized by a Japanese cult known as Aum Shinrikyo (Aum Supreme Truth), which was led by the charismatic Shoko Asahara. The group's first three operations in 1990, twice using botulinus toxin and once using anthrax, failed to cause any casualties. In 1994 Aum Shinrikyo gained its first success, dispersing sarin nerve gas throughout a resort town neighborhood inhabited by three judges presiding over a lawsuit involving the group. Seven people – but none of the judges – died in the attack and at least 200 became ill. At the time, investigators homed in on one of those injured in the attack. The real culprits were not discovered until after the cult's most infamous attack in March 1995 when the group's agents unleashed sarin gas on five Tokyo subway trains during morning rush hour. The operation was timed so that the trains would arrive almost simultaneously in a central station, thereby hopefully releasing a huge cloud of poisonous gas into downtown Tokyo just blocks from parliament, the imperial palace, and a host of government offices. Twelve people died from the fumes and as many as 5,500 were injured. Asahara, his aides, and those involved in the development and dispersal of the sarin were quickly arrested by the

Figure 15.1: Japanese authorities clad in chem-suits respond to sarin nerve gas attack in Tokyo subway, March 1995
(© TOKYO SHIMBUN/CORBIS SYGMA)

Japanese authorities, but the cult still has several thousand members in Japan and abroad.

What would lead a religious group to carry out such a devastating attack? The organization's history provides some, but not enough, clues. Aum Shinrikyo was founded in the mid-1980s by Asahara, who drew on Buddhism, Taoism, Hinduism, Christianity, and even astrology and the predictions of Nostradamus. In the end, Aum Shinrikyo had little to do with sacred texts or established religious traditions. The centerpiece of the cult was Asahara himself, a partially blind mystic who claimed to have experienced visions in which God anointed him as his prophet or perhaps even the world's messiah. Asahara prophesied that the end of the world via a world war was near at hand, with his predictions ranging from 1997 to 2003; he specifically spoke of a poison gas attack as one of the possible signs of the coming Armageddon. Asahara also claimed that only his followers would survive the catastrophe and that they alone would be prepared to rebuild the world. Astonishingly, Asahara had ten thousand followers in Japan by the mid-1990s, with several tens of thousands more in other countries. In Japan, most members of Aum Shinrikyo were not the poor and disenfranchised but rather came from the highly educated elite, particularly its scientific and technological communities. Some scholars explain this phenomenon by noting that modern Japanese society's emphasis on material success and rapid change have alienated many who are left to find comfort, community, and spiritual succor wherever they can.

Having raised hundreds of millions of dollars through membership dues, legitimate businesses, and donations from wealthy followers, Aum Shinrikyo began to stockpile weapons in order to safeguard the group during the difficult days that they expected would come. Its arsenal of conventional weapons included small arms and heavy weapons – even a surplus Soviet military helicopter. Asahara was most interested in building a nuclear weapon, but was stymied. Aum Shinrikyo's scientists had more success developing chemical weapons, such as sarin nerve gas, and biological agents, including anthrax and possibly Ebola virus. Scholars and Japanese authorities are still not sure why Asahara decided to unleash his weapons on the world. Some have conjectured that the violence was Asahara's sincere attempt to hasten the coming of Armageddon. Others have guessed that Asahara cynically carried out the subway attack to lend credence to his prophecies of doom and thus maintain the loyalty of his followers. Still others have surmised that the violence was meant to distract the authorities, who had begun to investigate Aum Shinrikyo. As a result, it is not possible to definitively orient the group within the history of religious or cult terrorism. There seems to have been no direct political agenda behind the Tokyo subway attack, but earlier operations do show that Aum Shinrikyo was willing to use chemical and biological agents to disrupt the justice system or exact revenge.

Eco-terror or Eco-defense?

One of the best examples of a mainstream cause whose radical fringe has turned to "leaderless resistance" is the environmental movement. Violence in the name of environmental protection also offers one of the clearest examples of the rhetorical contest for legitimacy. Proponents of such violence refer to their acts as "eco-defense" or "eco-tage," whereas its critics have dubbed it eco-terror. Advocates of "eco-tage" turn the term "terrorist" on its head, charging that the word best fits those individuals, countries, and corporations that damage the environment. The modern touchstone of the movement is Edward Abbey's 1975 novel, *The Monkey Wrench Gang*, in which a group of four outsiders roam the American Southwest, sabotaging bulldozers and burning billboards, all in an attempt to halt the despoilment of pristine wilderness. In the novel's climax, the gang plots the destruction of the Glen Canyon Dam on the Colorado River in Arizona. So great is the influence of the novel that the term "monkeywrenching" has been adopted by the movement to mean the use of sabotage and other illegal forms of violence to protect the environment. According to the website of Earth First!, a prominent eco-terrorist/eco-defense group, "Monkeywrenching is a step beyond civil disobedience . . . aimed only at inanimate objects . . . when almost all other measures have failed." Eco-defenders usually target projects in or near wilderness areas, such as housing developments, construction sites, resource mining, new road construction, etc. One highly controversial tactic is tree spiking, a practice intended to deter logging. Perhaps the best known eco-defense group is the Earth Liberation Front (ELF), itself simply a banner employed by autonomous, decentralized cells engaged in eco-terror. A cell acting in the name of ELF set seven fires on a single night in October 1998, doing $12 million in damage to the Vail Ski Resort in Colorado. The cell's announced goal was to prevent new construction that would have threatened a prime lynx habitat.

A related phenomenon is the radical animal rights movement, whose proponents target a whole range of practices, including the food industry, fur farming, hunting, and product testing and medical research on animals. Typical tactics include "liberation" of penned animals, harassment, sabotage, and arson. Prominent groups include the Animal Liberation Front (ALF), the Band of Mercy, and the Animal Rights Militia. In 2004, FBI testimony to Congress claimed that "ALF/ELF and related groups have committed more than 1,100 criminal acts in the United States since 1976, resulting in damages conservatively estimated at approximately $110 million" (FBI website). One study by *The Portland Oregonian* valued the property damage between 1995 and 1999 alone at $28.8 million. In the wake of the torching of a luxury housing development in Washington state in March 2008, an FBI agent declared that "[Eco-terror] remains what we would probably consider the No. 1 domestic terrorism threat, because they have successfully continued to conduct different types of attacks in and around the country" (FoxNews.com, 3/31/08).

The Unabomber

A different sort of anger at the modern world motivated Theodore Kaczynski, a former Berkeley mathematics professor who carried out a seventeen-year campaign of violence. The FBI, which spent millions of dollars and thousands of hours investigating him, dubbed Kaczynski the "Unabomber" because of his early targeting of people affiliated with universities and airlines. After killing three and wounding twenty-three with his simple but effective mail bombs, he mailed a 35,000-word manifesto to several newspapers in 1995, offering "to desist from terrorism" if it was published. After much deliberation, *The New York Times* and *The Washington Post* ran the document in its entirety. The rambling philosophical discourse, in which Kaczynski referred to himself as "The Freedom Club," was essentially a Rousseauian denunciation of technology and modern civilization. Kaczynski's brother recognized the language of the manifesto and contacted the authorities, who promptly arrested, tried, and convicted the Unabomber. Since Kaczynski acted alone and with such obscure motives, not unlike some nineteenth-century anarcho-terrorists, his actions are often not considered terrorism. Yet his reign of violence is highly relevant to the history of the subject for two reasons. First, Kaczynski demonstrated how much damage could be done and how many investigative resources could be engaged by a single determined individual using relatively primitive materials. Second, he also demonstrated how terrorists can easily be undone by the very publicity they seek.

Bibliography

The best book on the history of white separatism in the US is Dobratz and Shanks-Meile, *The White Separatist Movement in the United States* (previously cited). Other valuable books on white separatism and the militia movement include James Coates, *Armed and Dangerous: The Rise of the Survivalist Right* (Hill and Wang, 1995 [1987]); Morris Dees, with James Corcoran, *Gathering Storm: America's Militia Threat* (HarperPerennial, 1997 [1996]); and Robert L. Snow, *Terrorists Among Us: The Militia Threat* (Perseus, 2002 [1999]). A good survey of the principal terrorist acts in the US is Joseph T. McCann, *Terrorism on American Soil* (Sentient Publications, 2006).

An excellent study of the recent resurgence in religious violence, including Christian Patriot and cult terrorism, as well as jihadism, is Mark Juergensmeyer, *Terror in the Mind of God: The Global Rise of Religious Violence*, 3rd edn. (University of California Press, 2003). Two good books on Aum Shinrikyo are David E. Kaplan and Andrew Marshall, *The Cult at the End of the World* (Crown, 1996); and Robert Jay Lifton, *Destroying the World to Save It: Aum Shinrikyo, Apocalyptic Violence, and the New Global Terrorism* (Holt, 2000).

On ELF and eco-terrorism, see Donald R. Liddick, *Eco-Terrorism: Radical Environmental and Animal Liberation Movements* (Praeger, 2006). One of eco-tage's foremost proponents presents his case in Dave Foreman, *Ecodefense: A Field Guide to Monkeywrenching*, 3rd edn. (Abbzug, 1993). The book that remains the touchstone of the movement is Edward Abbey, *The Monkey Wrench Gang* (Avon Books, 1976 [1975]).

16

9/11, the War on Terror, and Recent Trends in Terrorism

There is nothing new about humanity's eagerness to ignore the proclaimed motives of arch-villains in favor of psychological musings. Such has recently been the case with Osama bin Laden, who is routinely decried as a madman or summed up as murderously jealous or angry at American freedoms. If al-Qaeda carried out its attacks on the United States simply because of its members' pathological hatred of Western freedoms and values, "Why," in Osama bin Laden's own words, "did we not attack Sweden?" (quoted by Fallows, Introduction to Robb, *Brave New War*, vii). In fact, bin Laden and al-Qaeda have provided a plethora of statements indicating their goals and reasoning. Although many might protest, these statements are models of logic and reason – within the history of terrorism, that is.

Planning 9/11

Al-Qaeda's bombing of US embassies in Kenya and Tanzania in 1998 triggered US cruise missile strikes against targets in Sudan and Afghanistan but no full-on American military intervention in Afghanistan. Paradoxically, the latter had been bin Laden's hope, for only such an invasion, he believed, would force Muslims around the world – in a replay of the anti-Soviet jihad of the 1980s – to set aside their myriad differences and come together in a great campaign to expel US forces and their allies completely from the Middle East. And only then, shorn of their American support, could local "pharaohs" such as President

Mubarak of Egypt and King Abdullah of Saudi Arabia be expelled and Islamic theocracies established.

Therefore, in 1999, bin Laden turned to a plan first devised by the jihadist Khalid Sheikh Muhammad three years earlier. Muhammad is the uncle of Ramzi Yousef, the first World Trade Center bomber, whose grandiose plans for blowing up trans-Pacific flights might have provided the first seeds of the scheme that came to pass. Muhammad approached bin Laden with the idea of flying hijacked planes into symbolic landmarks, not long after bin Laden arrived in Afghanistan. Bin Laden demurred at the time but seized on it sometime after the embassy bombings failed to provoke the American reaction he sought. One of the cells that bin Laden tapped to carry out the plan had been formed several years earlier in Hamburg, Germany, and was led by the eventual chief hijacker of 9/11, Muhammad Atta. He and several others already fluent in English and Western ways began to arrive in the United States in spring 2000 received rudimentary flight training from private teachers. The so-called "muscle hijackers" arrived in spring and summer 2001.

American Intelligence Failures

The operation that al-Qaeda planned was exponentially larger and more complicated than anything the group had done in the past. Almost inevitably, the planners made countless mistakes – some as a result of ignorance, some out of sloppiness. The constant travel, the extensive communication, and the transfer of significant sums of money gained the notice of many in the American and international intelligence communities. The National Security Agency's vast arrays of antennae picked up "chatter" from cell phones and other sorts of communications that spoke of an impending major attack that would be "spectacular" and "another Hiroshima." An Afghan commander still fighting the Taliban warned US officials that al-Qaeda was plotting something bigger than the East African embassy bombings. The Jordanians managed to uncover the operation's code name, The Big Wedding. A Taliban official even provided warnings to US officials, so afraid was he of possible American retaliation against an al-Qaeda attack planned on Afghan soil. By the summer of 2001, more alarm bells were going off in local FBI bureaus where agents were growing concerned over the possibility of jihadi terrorists trying to get flight training. Later, the head of the CIA, George Tenet, admitted to the federal commission that examined the intelligence failures that "the system was blinking red" with warnings. Such warnings were also making their way into President George W. Bush's daily briefings. One he received a little more than a month before the attack was headlined "Bin Ladin Determined To Strike in US" (quoted in *9/11 Commission*, 259, 261).

But the CIA and NSA refused to share most of their best information with the FBI, a continuation of a syndrome that plagued American intelligence agencies in the 1990s. Even when organizations shared intelligence, the absence of established links, clear chains of command, and sufficient numbers of analysts meant that critical information often languished until it was too late to be useful. Another problem was that terrorism ranked rather low on the list of priorities drawn up by the new administration of President Bush. In fact, his National Security Advisor, Condoleezza Rice, downgraded the standing of Richard Clarke, the leading interagency figure involved in counter-terrorism, so that he no longer had access to department heads.

September 11, 2001

On the morning of September 11, nineteen al-Qaeda agents operating in four teams hijacked commercial jetliners, using only box cutters to carry out their task. They seem to have met little resistance, since passengers probably assumed that the planes would be diverted to a different airport where the hijackers would make demands – this was the pattern, after all, that hijackings had followed for decades. Instead, the terrorists crashed the planes into each of the main towers of the World Trade Center, as well as the Pentagon. Less than two hours after the first flight slammed into the North Tower, both towers collapsed. The fourth plane was hijacked slightly later, giving passengers the chance to learn through airphone and cell phone calls the fate that was likely in store for them. Passengers decided to try to storm the cockpit. One man's final words, heard over a phone, were "Let's roll!" The passengers of the fourth flight failed to get through the cockpit door, but the hijackers sensed they were about to be overwhelmed and intentionally crashed the plane into a field in Pennsylvania. The plane's likely target was the US Capitol or the White House. American officials responded as if the United States were under attack. In fact, for the first time in its history, NATO invoked Article Five of its charter stating that an attack on one member is considered an attack on all, and Europeans flew over three hundred sorties in radar-laden surveillance planes in American airspace from October 2001 to May 2002. Suspicion immediately turned to al-Qaeda.

Casualties from the 9/11 attacks were enormous: 2,998 killed or missing (not including the nineteen hijackers). The economic cost of the attacks was also catastrophic. Lower Manhattan lost nearly 30 percent

Figure 16.1: United Airlines flight 175 veers toward the south tower of New York's World Trade Center. Smoke pours from the north tower, which had been hit seventeen minutes earlier
(© AFP/Getty Images)

of its office space. The value of physical assets lost and the cost of rescue and cleanup totaled over $27 billion. Wall Street shut down trading for the rest of the week, but when it reopened it promptly lost nearly 15 percent of its value, or $1.2 trillion. The International Monetary Fund estimated that the attacks cost the US economy $75 billion in gross domestic product by the end of 2001. Several economic sectors, including airlines, tourism, insurance, and shipping, were greatly hurt in both the short and medium-term. By comparison, the entire operation cost al-Qaeda between $400,000 and $500,000 (*9/11 Commission*, 169).

The Anthrax Attacks

In the weeks following 9/11, five American news outlets and the offices of two US senators received letters containing anthrax spores – only the second time that biological weapons have ever been used in a terrorist attack. The attack led to the temporary closure of the US Senate, House, and Supreme Court, as well as several postal facilities. At least twenty-two people were infected, including several at mail handling facilities where the letters were processed. Five people eventually died from inhalation anthrax. In August 2008, FBI officials announced that a scientist employed in a US government biodefense lab, Bruce Ivins, was the sole suspect in the case. When informed a week earlier of his pending arrest, Ivins committed suicide. The US government now considers the case closed, but questions remain, including Ivins' possible motive. One FBI report estimates that the cost of the attacks, including clean up, topped $1 billion (*The Washington Post*, September 16, 2005).

It appears that the anthrax attacks were unrelated to the 9/11 attacks, but the timing of the events magnified the sense that America was under siege. The United States had long known terrorism on its own soil – from Klan violence during Reconstruction to the Oklahoma City bombing in 1995 – but Americans generally considered terrorism to be a problem "over there," associated with areas with long histories of violence, such as Northern Ireland, Latin America, and the Middle East. Despite previous attacks and a "declaration of war" from al-Qaeda, the 9/11 attacks came as a paradigm-shifting surprise to Americans, entering the pantheon of era-defining moments such as the Japanese attack on Pearl Harbor and the assassination of John F. Kennedy. The immediate response across the country was an outpouring of patriotism, emotional expressions of grief and unity, and not a few revenge attacks on Arab-American citizens. "Let's Roll" became a ubiquitous rallying cry. There were also jokes, reflecting the deep-seated but incorrect sense that al-Qaeda's fundamental goal was the disruption of the American routine: "If I don't get my coffee [meal, raise, vacation, etc.] now, then the terrorists have already won!"

The War on Terror

In the immediate aftermath of 9/11, Americans rallied around President Bush, the percentage of citizens who approved of his job performance temporarily spiking above ninety. Nine days after the tragedy, Bush announced to the nation in a speech before a joint session of Congress, "On September the 11th, enemies of freedom committed an act of war against our country. . . . " He went on to introduce the umbrella phrase and lofty purpose that would define America's response to the attacks: "Our war on terror begins with al Qaeda, but it does not end there. It will not end until every terrorist group of global reach has been found, stopped and defeated" (Whitehouse.gov, 9/20/01). Several weeks later, Bush further clarified his intentions: "You're either with us or against us in the fight against terror" (CNN.com, 11/6/01).

While the phrase "war on terror" has struck a chord with the public and been embraced by the media, it presents a number of problems. As many critics have noted, the word "war" is highly inappropriate to the current struggle. Wars, after all, are traditionally fought between states, using uniformed, organized armies, on clearly defined territory. None of those criteria apply in the case of Bush's War on Terror (the term is routinely capitalized, signifying its acceptance as standard nomenclature). How, many have asked, will victory be defined? Occupation of some undetermined piece of land? Indeed, is al-Qaeda the sort of "army" that will surrender when it is defeated? The problems extend well beyond the semantic or philosophic. The use of the word "war" elevates the terrorists to the level of legitimate combatants – after all, one does not fight a "war" against pirates or criminals. A "war" also demands that the US, as a signatory to the Geneva Conventions, must provide captured enemy combatants the status of "prisoner of war," which is to say, humane treatment and the promise of repatriation at the conclusion of the conflict. But if these enemies are not soldiers, but rather criminals, as our rhetoric typically describes them, then there is a prescribed method for dealing with them as well: the criminal courts. The Bush administration steadfastly refused to use the civilian judicial system to prosecute terror suspects, in part, because the accused would be entitled to legal rights and protections. In the meantime, members of al-Qaeda captured by US forces have fallen into the rabbit hole of Guantanamo Bay, a special facility whose prisoners qualify neither as POWs nor criminal suspects. This is simply one of the great dilemmas encountered by a liberal democracy struggling against terrorism. Bush's rhetorical declaration of war, presumably, was not meant to answer any of these questions but rather to rouse Americans to a great "crusade" – a word that Bush used not long after 9/11. Not surprisingly, Islamists pounced on the gaffe. To sidestep the problems posed by the use of the phrase War on Terror, some in the President's administration at one time sought to replace it with the more accurate and more concrete, but less euphonious rubric, the Global Struggle Against Islamic Extremism. The phrase has not found an audience. For good or ill, the phrase War on Terror has stuck.

The first action in the War on Terror was an ultimatum to the Taliban to hand over al-Qaeda's leaders, including bin Laden, who were sheltering in Afghanistan. When Mullah Omar refused, the US and Britain introduced special forces, commenced aerial bombardment, and closely worked with the anti-Taliban Northern Alliance. Via a recording – the first of many – bin Laden spoke to the Muslim world, calling for a new jihad that would defeat the United States as the mujahideen had defeated the Soviets two decades earlier. No such jihad materialized – or even had time to. Kabul fell to the Northern Alliance within a month and a half,

but bin Laden and other key al-Qaeda leaders escaped. Despite the introduction of American, British, and eventually NATO troops in 2002, bin
Laden has still never been captured. He is presumed to still be hiding in
the nearly impenetrable mountains along the Afghan–Pakistan border.

September 11 gave the US tremendous moral capital throughout
the world. For instance, the most influential French newspaper, *Le
Monde*, published a front-page editorial immediately after the attacks
that declared, "We Are All Americans." The US and British invasion
of Afghanistan enjoyed wide support around the world, as well. The
US also reached out to other countries around the globe to forge the
links necessary to fight al-Qaeda and other terrorist organizations. This
unprecedented level of cooperation led to new agreements for basing US
troops abroad, sharing critical intelligence, and cutting off sources of
financing for jihadists. Unglamorous work, yes, but the sort that reflected
a fundamentally sound understanding of terrorist tactics.

Driven into hiding, bin Laden and 9/11's principal architect, Khalid
Sheikh Muhammad, continued to plot against the United States and its
allies. American agents supposedly foiled an al-Qaeda plot to hijack
planes and crash them into West Coast targets in the US in 2002. In
2003, Muhammad was captured in what seems to have been a combined
US-Pakistani operation. By that time, perhaps two-thirds of al-Qaeda's
upper-level leadership at the time of 9/11 had been captured.

The Iraq War

At this critical juncture the Bush Administration shifted its attention and
its resources to Saddam Hussein and Iraq. Many critics have claimed
that the President and a core of his closest advisors were devoted to the
idea of removing the dictator from the moment the President took office
and quickly seized upon 9/11 as an opportunity to do so. According
to Richard Clarke, America's counter-terrorism czar in the National
Security Council, Bush asked him on September 12 to "see if Saddam
did this." Clarke's report indicated that no evidence for such a link
existed, and Bush decided not to invade Iraq immediately (quoted in *9/11
Commission Report*, 334). But in October 2002, the President categori-
cally stated in a major speech that Iraq had "given shelter and support
to terrorism" and that "Iraq and al-Qaeda have had high-level contacts
that go back a decade. . . . Alliance with terrorists could allow the Iraqi
regime to attack America without leaving any fingerprints" (Whitehouse.
gov, October 7, 2002). As it turns out, no credible evidence has ever been
produced linking al-Qaeda and Saddam Hussein. Nonetheless, the US

Congress shortly thereafter authorized the use of force to compel Hussein to relinquish his possession of so-called weapons of mass destruction. Despite mounting international opposition, the United States and several allies invaded Iraq in March 2003. The invasion quickly toppled Hussein, who was captured in December and executed three years later.

The end of conventional fighting in May 2003, however, was just the beginning of the violence. Emboldened and empowered by the US government's inept post-invasion plans, an insurgency coalesced during the summer. At this stage, most of the combatants were elite troops or former members of Hussein's Baath Party, and they used classic guerrilla tactics against American and allied troops. In 2004, the nature of the insurgency began to change, as Baathist cells were replaced as the primary combatants by sectarian groups. Some Sunnis took up arms in hopes of regaining what had been their favored status under Hussein, while Shiites, particularly the so-called Mahdi Army, fought for the creation of an Islamist state. Both increasingly targeted the newly created Iraqi Security Forces, US-armed and -trained police and army units meant to eventually replace US forces.

That fall, another new group appeared: al-Qaeda in Iraq, which has primarily been composed of foreigners nominally loyal to bin Laden. Although its announced aims are the eviction of US forces and the creation of an Islamic state, the group has principally targeted Shiite civilians, security forces, and infrastructure using a range of terrorist tactics. In May 2005 alone, over seven hundred civilians, mostly Shiites, died in wave after wave of suicide bombings. In February 2006, agents, presumably from al-Qaeda in Iraq, blew up the al-Askari Mosque in Samarra, one of the holiest of Shiite shrines. The goal was to enflame sectarian passions between Shiites and Sunnis, which is exactly what happened. In the aftermath of the bombing, the average daily murder rate in Baghdad tripled from eleven to thirty-three. Many observers, including the UN, claimed that Iraq had slipped into a full-blown civil war. But this was a civil war marked mostly by suicide bombings, assassinations, kidnappings, and murders, with the United States and a dwindling number of allied troops caught in the middle.

The insurgency was fueled by a number of factors, including the chaos itself, which provided a clear field for terrorists who generally thrive in the absence of strong, popular central governments. An additional critical factor was the behavior of American forces, who were poorly prepared to fight a counterinsurgency operation. Heavy-handed US tactics, including the use of overwhelming firepower, massive round-ups of suspects, and allegations of prisoner abuse (all errors committed by the French in Algeria), contributed immensely to the impression many Iraqis held of Americans as illegitimate occupiers. In a National Intelligence Estimate prepared in April 2006, the US intelligence community admitted that "the Iraq jihad is shaping a new generation of terrorist leaders and . . . the Iraq conflict has become the 'cause celebre' for jihadists" ("Trends in Global Terrorism: Implications for the United States").

This dawning awareness of the US role in enabling the nearly unprecedented campaign of terrorism in Iraq prompted American military leaders to revisit their basic approach to the struggle. A team of soldiers and academics led by General David Petraeus produced a nuanced field manual on counterinsurgency, well informed by the history of such conflicts in Malaya, Algeria, and Vietnam. Officers in the US military were quickly introduced to the ideas contained in the new manual, and Petraeus was tapped to command all US forces in Iraq in early 2007. Shortly thereafter, more troops – the so-called surge – were committed to Iraq, where they began to implement the "Petraeus Plan" based on key elements of the new manual. Even more importantly, Sunni tribesmen, fed up with al-Qaeda in Iraq's brutal terrorism against civilians, largely abandoned the insurgency and sought cooperation with the United States, which began to fund the tribesmen's security operations. These developments have collectively led to a decrease in violence, but flare-ups and questions about the Iraqi government's political will leave the situation in Iraq still in doubt.

Jihad Spreads

The Iraq War certainly added new grist to the mill in the jihadist campaign against Western power and influence. But there have been changes in the way that jihadist terrorism has been organized and carried out. Although al-Qaeda certainly continues to develop plots against the West, most jihadist terrorism around the globe in the last five years has been carried out by homegrown groups inspired, but not directly organized or even funded by bin Laden. Some commentators have referred to this as the "franchising" of terrorism. There is much debate about the degree to which these local groups are branches of al-Qaeda or international jihadist examples of leaderless resistance. In fact, there are cases of both.

The clearest examples of al-Qaeda's efforts to use terrorism to foment unrest in the Muslim world since 9/11 can be found in Saudi Arabia and Southeast Asia. Fifteen of the nineteen hijackers were Saudi citizens, causing, once again, the country's Wahhabist establishment and its teachings to come under scrutiny. There were no official American attempts to punish the Saudi government for allegedly nurturing Islamism, but US authorities increased pressure on the Saudis to step up their level of cooperation in terms of intelligence gathering and analysis. Initially, Wahhabist clerics and other conservative elements in the country pointed to this pressure as proof of a larger pattern of American arrogance and intimidation – a position that bore startling similarities to other forms of Islamist criticism of the West.

In 2003, groups with probable links to al-Qaeda stepped up their recent efforts, unleashing a campaign of terrorism in Saudi Arabia. They particularly targeted foreigners and the country's economic interests through kidnapping, assassination, and suicide bombing. Over the next two years, there were more than two dozen attacks that produced nearly one hundred fatalities. This wave of sustained violence directed against the economic well-being of the state fully awakened the Saudi government to the extent of the jihadist threat it faced. What followed was a string of fatwas from the state's Wahhabist clerics condemning jihadism and approving closer cooperation with American intelligence. Since 2005, the Saudis, with help from the United States, have largely clamped down on al-Qaeda violence in the Kingdom, aided in no small part by the fact that the country remains authoritarian, with few civil liberties and broadly empowered security organs.

In Southeast Asia, the most significant and dangerous jihadist group is the Islamic Group (not to be confused with Omar Rahman's similarly named group), a radical militant organization with roots dating back to the 1970s. It has been based principally in Malaysia and Indonesia, and its goal is the creation of a new caliphate stretching across Southeast Asia. Some of its members took part in the mujahideen's struggle against the Soviets in the 1980s, and the organization provided some support to Ramzi Yousef and Khalid Sheikh Muhammad in the Philippines in 1993 and 1994. The Islamic Group began cooperating with al-Qaeda in the mid-1990s, a partnership that grew closer after 9/11. In October 2002, on the second anniversary of the bombing of the USS *Cole*, the Islamic Group set off two bombs on the Indonesian resort island of Bali, killing over two hundred people, including almost ninety Australian tourists. In the past few years, the Islamic Group and al-Qaeda have almost completely merged.

Elsewhere, bin Laden and al-Qaeda are merely the godfathers of terror, inspiring it from afar. The clearest examples of this have been in Europe, where hate-spewing radical clerics have gathered small but devoted followings among disaffected members in large Muslim communities. As has been the pattern for over two decades, those militant Islamists attracted to terrorism typically come from relatively affluent and educated backgrounds. In March 2004, a series of coordinated explosions on commuter trains in Madrid killed 191 and wounded over seventeen hundred people. The blasts came late in a general election campaign in which polls indicated the incumbent ruling party, the Populist Party, held a slight lead over its Socialist rivals. Despite evidence to the contrary, Populist leaders announced that they suspected Basque separatists in ETA were behind the blast – evidently to curry sympathy with the electorate. A group linked to al-Qaeda eventually claimed responsibility, stating that the blasts were meant to punish Spain for participating in the Iraq War. Spanish voters blamed the Populists both for the deception and the attack; the Socialists eked out a narrow victory and promptly withdrew Spanish troops from Iraq. The subsequent investigation suggested that the bombings were carried out by a recent offshoot of an established Moroccan jihadist group working in concert with local Spanish jihadists with no direct links to al-Qaeda. In July 2005, one Jamaican-born and three British-born jihadists carried out suicide bombings in a bus and three subway cars in London, killing 52 people. The investigation that followed revealed that these were home-grown terrorists who were inspired by, but unaffiliated with bin Laden.

Counter-Terrorism in the US

In the United States, one of the government's first official reactions to 9/11 was the creation of new agencies to counter or combat terrorism. In a bid to better secure air travel, the US government created the Transportation Security Administration, which effectively nationalized all airport security – at an annual cost of $4.7 billion for the most recent fiscal year. Airline security procedures have become more standardized and more stringent but often as a reaction, not a precaution. In the wake of an attempt by Richard Reid, a British jihadist and possible al-Qaeda member, to set off explosives hidden in his shoe, passengers traveling in the US are now required to pass through security without footwear. After American authorities got wind of al-Qaeda efforts to bring aboard fluid explosives, they severely restricted the quantities of liquids that passengers are allowed to bring on planes. Several studies have suggested that as restrictions on passengers grow, their sense of security actually decreases. Meanwhile, little has been done to secure other possible terrorist targets or means of entry to the country. One frequently cited example is that of American ports, through which seven million shipping containers pass each year. The dramatically uneven amount of resources devoted to airline travel and port security is alarming to many experts, who note that terrorists specialize in finding weaknesses – if one target is too heavily guarded, terrorists tend to move on to other, less secure targets.

In 2003, the US Congress created a new cabinet-level Department of Homeland Security – the third largest department in the federal government – devoted to the prevention of and responses to terrorism. Dozens of offices and bureaus were amalgamated into Homeland Security, including bodies in charge of border control and immigration. The FBI and CIA remained outside the new department. The degree to which Homeland Security was scrambling to provide some level of comfort to a rattled nation was exemplified – and greatly mocked – by recommendations issued in February 2003 that duct tape and plastic sheeting were viable short-term defenses against nuclear, radiological, biological, or chemical (NRBC) attacks. The announcement set off waves of panic shopping that emptied stores of those items (CNN.com, February 11, 2003). Homeland Security has also administered a multibillion dollar grant program that hands out funds to local and state government "to prevent, prepare for, respond to, and recover from terrorist attacks, major disasters, and other emergencies." Many critics have complained that such a use of public funds is simply pork-barrel spending that has had little to do with the pursuit of a rational plan to counter terrorism.

Another much maligned creation of the Office of Homeland Security has been the Homeland Security Advisory System. Better known as the "terror alert level," the system makes use of a color-coded chart to communicate to federal, state, and local officials and organizations the degree of danger posed by terrorists at any given moment. The system is meant to be used to trigger specific security responses and precautions from various agencies but has been mocked by critics and comedians as a kind of weather forecasting system for terrorism. It might also be decidedly counterproductive, for a recent study suggests that the act of raising the terror threat level triggers an increase in public fear – exactly the sort of reaction sought by terrorists.

Bibliography

The best study of the history of al-Qaeda is Lawrence Wright, *The Looming Tower: Al-Qaeda and the Road to 9/11* (Knopf, 2006). The events of 9/11 themselves are chronicled and analyzed in detail in the US government's official investigation, National Commission on Terrorist Attacks upon the United States, *The 9/11 Commission Report* (Norton, 2004). A valuable study of the hijackers is Terry McDermott, *Perfect Soldiers: The 9/11 Hijackers* (Harper, 2005). A helpful study of the economic impact of 9/11 is Robert Looney, "Economic Costs to the United

States Stemming From the 9/11 Attacks," Center for Contemporary Conflict, *Strategic Insights*, Volume I, Issue 6 (August 2002).

The War on Terror is the study of an enormous number of books. The most insightful are Ian S. Lustick, *Trapped in the War on Terror* (University of Pennsylvania Press, 2006); Louise Richardson, *What Terrorists Want* (Random House, 2006); John Robb, *Brave New War: The Next Stage of Terrorism and the End of Globalization* (Introduction by James Fallows, John Wiley & Sons, 2007); Michael Scheuer, *Imperial Hubris: Why the West IS Losing the War on Terror* (Brassey's, 2004); and Ron Suskind, *The One Percent Doctrine: Deep Inside America's Pursuit of Its Enemies Since 9/11* (Simon & Schuster, 2006).

On the Iraq War and its connection to the War on Terror, see Mark Danner, *Torture and Truth: America, Abu Ghraib, and the War on Terror* (New York Review Books, 2004); Thomas Ricks, *Fiasco: The American Military Adventure in Iraq* (Penguin, 2006); and Bob Woodward's three volumes on the subject, *Bush at War* (Simon & Schuster, 2002); *Plan of Attack* (Simon & Schuster, 2004); and *State of Denial: Bush at War, Part III* (Simon & Schuster, 2006). The new US counterinsurgency doctrine has been made widely available: *The U.S. Army/Marine Corps Counterinsurgency Field Manual* (University of Chicago Press, 2007).

The future of terrorism is the subject of Marc Sageman, *Leaderless Jihad: Terror Networks in the Twenty-First Century* (University of Pennsylvania Press, 2008).

Index

Page numbers in italics refer to illustrations.

Abane, Ramdane, 202–3, 210
Abbasids, 40–1, 44
Abbey, Edward, 327
Abdullah (King of Saudi Arabia),
    330–1
abortion, 322–3
Abu Nidal, 226–7, 230–1, 300
Abu Sayyaf Group, 303, 321
Achille Lauro, 230
Action Directe, 266
action-repression-action spiral theory,
    249–50
Adams, Gerry, 239, 240, 242–4
*A Defense of Liberty against
    Tyrants* by de Mornay,
    51–2
Afghanistan, 295–9, 304–6, 330–1,
    335–6
agents provocateur, 69, 94, 101–2,
    109–10
air travel, 278
    see also hijacking
Alabama, 128, 131, 138–9
al-Amir (Fatimid Caliph) *see* Amir, al-
    (Fatimid Caliph)
Alamut, 40–1, 43–4
al-Aqsa Martyr Brigades *see* Aqsa
    Martyr Brigades, al-

al-Askari Mosque *see* Askari Mosque,
    al-
al-Assad, Hafiz *see* Assad, Hafiz al-
al-Banna, Hasan *see* Banna, Hasan al-
al-Banna, Sabri Khalil *see* Abu Nidal
Alec Station, 307
Alexander I (Yugoslavia), 156
Alexander II (Russia), 75, 82–4, 100
Alexander III (Russia), 84, 161
Alexander the Great, 12–13, 33
Alexandria, Egypt, 29
Alfred P. Murrah Federal Building,
    321
al-Gaddafi, Muammar *see* Gaddafi,
    Muammar al-
al-Gamaa al-Islamiyya *see* Islamic
    Group (Egypt)
Algeria, 179, 200–14, 313–14
Algerian Civil War, 313–14
Algerian War for Independence, 180,
    200–12
Algiers, 201–7, 211–12
Ali (Caliph), 38–9
Alipore Bomb Conspiracy, 150
al-Jihad *see* Jihad, al-
al-Khattab, Amir *see* Khattab, Amir
    al-
Alleg, Henri, 208

al-Ma'mun *see* Ma'mun, al-
al-Qaeda *see* Qaeda, al-
al-Qaeda in Iraq *see* Qaeda in Iraq, al-
al-Qassam Brigades *see* Qassam
    Brigades, al-
al-Turabi, Hasan *see* Turabi, Hasan
    al-
al-Utaybi, Juhayman *see* Utaybi,
    Juhayman al-
al-Zawahiri, Ayman *see* Zawahiri,
    Ayman al-
Amir, al- (Fatimid Caliph), 42
ammonium nitrate and fuel oil bomb,
    237, 302, 321
Anabaptists, 57–8
anarchism, 77–8, 85–6, 107–8,
    111–12, 123, 144
  in Europe,98–112
  in Russia, 77, 90–92, 160
  in United States, 116–24
Anarchist Fighters, 122–4
anarcho-terrorism *see* anarchism
Andrianov, S., 93
Ángel Blanco, Miguel, 251
Anglican Church, 58, 196
Anglo-Irish Agreement, 241
Anglo-Israelism, 318
Angry Brigade, 266
Animal Liberation Front, 327–8
Antenor, 18
anthrax, 325–6, 333–4
anti-Semitism, 137, 167–8, 174–5,
    181, 187, 318
  see also pogroms
Anti-terrorist Liberation Groups,
    251
Antony, Mark, 24–6
Apis *see* Dragutin Dimitrijevich
Aqsa Martyr Brigades, al-, 309
Aquinas, Thomas, 36
Arab Afghans, 297–9, 303, 308, 311,
    313
Arab–Israeli War (1948), 188, 217
Arafat, Yasser, 218–221, 223,
    225–33, 291, 309–10
Argentina, 259–60, 294–5

Argentine Anticommunist Alliance,
    259
Aristotle, 18–19, 35
Arkansas, 127, 130
Armed Forces of National Liberation
    (Venezuela), 255
Armed Islamic Group (Algeria),
    313–14
Armed Revolutionary Nuclei, 273
Army of God, 322–3
Arnett, Peter, 305
Arthashastra by Kautilya, 13–14
Aryan Nations, 318–20
Asahara, Shoko, 325–6
Askari Mosque, al-, 337
Assad, Hafiz al-, 291
assassin, origin of term, 43
assassination, 52, 55
  attitudes toward, 13, 20, 40
  state-sponsored, 48–9, 52, 55, 153
  vs. murder, 32–3
  see also attentat; tyrannicide; and
    individual victims
Assassins, 39–45, 324, *43*
Assurnasirpal II, 12
Assyrians, 11–12, 15
asymmetric warfare, 54
Athens, 13, 18
Atlantic Charter, 180
Atta, Muhammad, 331
attentat, 99
Augustine of Hippo, 33
Augustus (Emperor), 24, 26
Aum Shinrikyo, 325–7
Aussaresses, Paul, 205–6
Austria, 156
Austro-Hungarian Empire, 151–5
Ayers, Bill, 265
Azev, Evno, 94
Azzam, Abdullah, 297–9, 301, 309

Baader, Andreas, 267–9
Baader-Meinhof Gang *see* Red Army
    Faction
Baath Party, 285, 337
Babeuf, François-Noel, 67

Badreddin, Mustafa, 292, 294
Bakunin, Mikhail, 77–8, 90, 116
Balfour Declaration, 181
Balkans, 151–8
Baltic Exchange bombing, 243
Banna, Hasan al-, 283
Banna, Sabri Khalil al- *see* Abu Nidal
Barcelona, 106–7
Bartholdy, Jakob, 68
Barthou, Louis, 156
Basayev, Shamil, 311–12
Basque Nation and Liberty *see* ETA
Basques, 179, 249–51
Battle of Algiers, 201–7, *204*
Battle of Algiers by Pontecorvo, 202, 206
Beam, Louis, 316–17, 319
Becket, Thomas, 34
Begin, Menachem, 183–5, 229
Beirut, 228, 292–4
Belfast, 234, 237
Bely, Andrei, 93
Bengal, 149–50
Beres, Louis René, 275–6
Berg, Alan, 319
Berkman, Alexander, 120–1, 123
Beslan school crisis, 312
Bible, and descriptions of tyrannicide, 15–16
Bible, used as justification for violence, 34–5, 323
bin Laden, Osama, 297–301, 304–8, 313, 330–2, 335–40, *305*
and Afghan-Soviet War, 297–9
forms al-Qaeda, 298
grievances against West and Arab states, 299–300, 305–6
patron and inspiration to other jihadists, 337–40
and September 11 attacks, 331–2
use of terrorism to unite Islamists, 300–1, 330–1
bioterrorism, 324–7
Birds of Freedom, 248
Birmingham, Alabama, 139
Birmingham (UK) Six, 239

Birth of a Nation by Griffith, 137, *136*
Bishopsgate bombing, 243
Bismarck, Otto von, 102, 105
Black and Tans, 146–7
Black and Tan War *see* Ireland, Irish War of Independence
Black Banner, 90
Black Codes, 127
Black Hand (Serbia), 152–3
Black Hand (Spain), 102
Black Hundreds, 93
Black Reichswehr, 168
Black September, 223–5, *224*
Blackshirts, 169–70
Black Skin and White Mask by Fanon, 213
Black Sunday, 274
Black Tigers, 248
Blair, Tony, 244
Bloody Friday, 237
Bloody Sunday (1905), 88
Bloody Sunday (1920), 146
Bloody Sunday (1972), 237
Böll, Heinrich, 269
Bollardière, Jacques de, 208
Bologna, 273
Bolsheviks, 76–7, 91–2, 160–2
see also Communist Party of the Soviet Union
Bonnot Auto gang, 111
Bordaberry, Juan María, 259
Borgia, Cesare, 48, 50
Boscoli, Pietro Paolo, 48
Bosnia and Herzegovina, 152–3, 311
Boupacha, Djamila, 209
Bradshaw, John, 59
Branch Davidians, 320, 323
Bray, Michael, 322–3
Briggs, Henry, 191
Briggs Plan, 191–3
Britain *see* United Kingdom
Brownshirts, 170–2, 174–6
Brown v. the Board of Education, 138
Brunhilda of Austrasia, 37
Brüning, Heinrich, 172

Brutus (pseudonym) *see* de Mornay, Philippe
Brutus, Lucius Junius, 19
Brutus, Marcus Junius, 24
    invoked, 25, 48–9, 51, 61, 71, 128
Brzezinksi, Zbigniew, 295, 298
B-Specials, 234–5
Buda, Mario, 124
Buenos Aires, 294–5
Bulgaria, 154–7
Buonarroti, Filippo, 67
Bureau of Alcohol, Tobacco, and Firearms, 320–1
Burke, Edmund, 65
Burke, Thomas, 143
Bush, George W., 331–2, 334–6

Caesar, Julius, 23–5, 55
Café Libman, 91
Cahill, Joe, 243
Cairo, 42, 183, 284, 290
caliphate, 38, 282
caliphs, 38–9, 281–2
Callistratus, 18
Callwell, Charles, 147–8
Calvin, John, 50
Canada, 266
Cánovas del Castillo, Antonio, 107
Caravaggio, *Judith Beheading Holofernes*, 16
Carbonari, 67–8
Carlos the Jackal, 227, 300
Carnot, Sadi, 105
carpetbaggers, 127
Carrero Blanco, Luis, 250
Carter, Jimmy, 289, 295
Casbah (Algiers), 202, 204–6
Caserio, Santo-Geronimo, 105
Casey, William, 276
Cassius Longinus, 20, 24, 49
Catechism of the Revolutionist by Nechaev, 78–9
Catholic Church, 33–4, 37, 50, 59–60
    see also Christianity
Catholics (Northern Ireland), 234–9, 241–4

Catiline, 21–2
Catullus of Cyrene, 29
Cave of the Patriarchs Mosque massacre, 310
CBS, 210
Central Intelligence Agency, 306–7, 331–2, 341
    covert operations, 288, 306–7
    interpretation of international terrorism, 274, 276–7
    and jihadism, 298, 306–7, 331–2
Challe Plan, 207–8
Chamber of Deputies (France), 104, 106
Chandragupta, 13–14
Charles I (England), 54, 59
Charles VI (France), 36
Chechnya, 306, 311–13
Cheka, 95, 161–4
Chernyshevsky, Nikolai, 76, 155
Chesterton, G. K., 109–10
Chicago, 117–19, 263–4
China, and Cold War, 188–9
Chin Peng, 190–2
Christian Democratic Party (Italy), 271
Christian Identity, 318–21, 323
Christian Patriotism, 320, 322–3
Christianity, 33, 50–1
    see also Bible; Catholic Church; Reformation; tyrannicide in early modern Europe; and tyrannicide in medieval Europe
Christ the Savior on the Spilled Blood, Church of, 84, *84*
Churchill, Winston, 186
Cicero, Marcus Tullius, 21–3, 25–6, 29, 33, 36
Cinna, 21
City of God by Augustine, 33
Civil Rights Movement (Northern Ireland), 234
Civil Rights Movement (United States), 138–9
Civil War (United States), 126, 132
Clarke, Richard, 307, 332, 336

Clinton, Bill, 243, 300, 306–7
Clodius Pulcher, 23
COINTELPRO, 264–6
Cold War, 188–9, 200, 254–5, 275–6, 295–6, 298
    aftermath of, 5, 307
    end of, 320
    and ethno-nationalist terrorism, 188–9
    and international terrorism, 275–6
    and revolutionary terrorism, 254–5
Collins, Michael, 145–6, 148, 182, 241
Colombia, 260
colons (Algeria), 200, 202, 205–8, 211
Combat Organization (of PSR), 87–9, 94, 160
communism, 164, 189, 193, 200, 250, 256, 261, 295–6
    fear of, 122–3, 137, 167–75, 259, 264, 272, 320
    international terrorism as communist conspiracy, 275–7
    see also individual communist parties and movements
Communist Party of Germany, 168, 170–2, 174
Communist Party of Italy, 270–1, 273
Communist Party of the Soviet Union, 162–6
Communist Terrorists see Malayan Communist Party
concentration camps, 148, 174–6, 196, 208
Confederates (United States), 127–9, 131–2
Congress Party see Indian National Congress
Connolly, James, 144–5
Conrad, Joseph, 105, 109–10
conservatism, 65
Conspiracy of Equals by Buonarroti, 67
Constitutional Democrats (Russia), 92

Continuity Irish Republican Army, 244
Convention (France), 60–4
Convention on the Prevention and Punishment of Terrorism, 156
Corday, Charlotte, 60–2
Council of Constance, 37
Council of Ten (Venice), 48–9
counter gangs, 196
counter-insurgency, 189, 199–200, 203, 207–9, 337–8
    see also counter-terrorism
counter-terrorism, 7, 147, 199-200, 278
    dual meaning, 7
    in Argentina, 259–60
    in France, 106
    in Imperial Russia, 93–5
    in Northern Ireland, 238
    in Peru, 261–2
    in Spain, 107, 251
    in United States, 340–1
    in Uruguay, 258–9
    vs. Assassins, 42
    see also counter-insurgency
criminology, 108
Croatia, 156
    see also Yugoslavia
Cromwell, Oliver, 54
Cronaca Sovversiva (The Subversive Chronicle), 120–1
cross burnings, 137
Crusades, 35, 43–4
Cuba, 227
cults, 324–7
Cyprus, 197–9
Cyrene, Libya, 29
Czolgosz, Leon, 120

Dante, 49
David, Jacques-Louis, The Death of Marat, 61
Dayan, Moshe, 188
Days of Rage, 263–4
Dees, Morris, 319
DeFreeze, Donald, 265

de Gaulle, Charles, 210–11
de la Hodde, Lucien, 69
Delchev, Goce, 154
Demaris, Ovid, 275
democracy, 18, 212
  and modernity, 110, 112
  and revolutionary terrorism, 67–8,
    71
  and state terror, 63, 65
  terrorism in democracies, 184, 262,
    266, 273, 335
  see also nationalism; popular
    sovereignty
Democratic Party (United States), 132,
  263
De Officiis by Cicero see On Duties
Department of Homeland Security
  (United States), 341
de Valera, Eamon, 145, 148
Devils by Dostoevsky, 79, 109
Dimitrijevich, Dragutin, 152–3
dirty war (Ireland), 238
dirty war (Latin America), 277
dirty war (Spain), 251
Divine Comedy by Dante, 49
Dixon, Thomas, 137
Docklands bombing, 244
Donatello, 48
Dorhn, Bernardine, 265
Dostoevsky, Fyodor, 79–80, 109
Dozier, James, 272–3
Dublin, 143–4, 146
Dubrovka Theatre, 312
dynamite see explosives
Dzerzhinsky, Felix, 161

Earth First!, 327
Earth Liberation Front, 327–8
Easter Uprising see Ireland, Easter
  Uprising
Eban, Abba, 232
Eglon, 15, 35
Egypt
  and Israel, 188, 218–19, 286
  and Islamism, 283–90, 296–8,
    300–4, 306, 331

  and Palestinians, 217–19
  and United Kingdom, 283–4
Ehud, 15, 35
El Al airline, 221, 230
Eleazar ben Yair, 29
Elizabeth I (England), 52–3
Enabling Act, 174
England
  and Ireland, 142
  in early modern era, 51–5
  medieval, 34–5, 37–8
  see also United Kingdom
English Civil War, 54–5
Enlightenment, 57, 59–60, 66, 110
Ensslin, Gudrun, 267–9
EOKA, 198–9, 240
EOKA B, 199
Erzberger, Matthias, 168
ETA, 240, 249–51, 266, 340
Eugénie (Empress of France), 71–2
Evian Accords, 212
explosives, 71, 83–4, 106, 121, 303
expropriations, 89, 91–2, 111, 161
External Macedonian Revolutionary
  Organization, 155
Extremists (India), 149–51

Fadlallah, Muhammad Hussein,
  291–2
Fanon, Frantz, 213–14, 240
Farouk (King of Egypt), 284
fascism, 168–70
  see also Nazi Party
Fatah, 218–21, 223, 225–8, 230,
  232–3, 309–10
Fatahland, 220, 222–3
Fatah Revolutionary Council, 226
Fatimids, 40, 42
fatwas, 285, 287, 300, 302, 306,
  339
Fawkes, Guy, 53
fedayeen
  defined, 42,
  modern, 218–20
  see also Assassins; Palestine
    Liberation Organization

Federal Bureau of Investigation
(United States), 341
COINTELPRO, 264–5
and Islamism, 302, 307, 331–2
Palmer Raids, 123
and recent domestic terrorism,
320–1, 327–8, 334
Fenian Brotherhood, 143
Fenians see republicans (Ireland)
feudalism, 32–3, 35, 59
Fighting Leagues (Germany), 168
FLN see National Liberation Front
(Algeria)
Ford, Franklin, 51
Forrest, Nathan Bedford, 128–9,
132
Fourteen Points, 180
Fourteenth Amendment to US
Constitution, 127
France, 154, 180, 283
and Algeria, 179, 200–13
anarcho-terrorism, 103–6, 111
and Basques, 250
and counter-terrorism in Algeria,
203–10
early modern, 59
French Indochina, 180, 201, 203
French Revolution, 59–67, 161
and Islamic Jihad/Hezbollah, 292–3
medieval, 36–7
Resistance, 175, 203
revolutionary terrorism, 266
secret societies in, 68–9
Wars of Religion, 51–2
Franco, Francisco, 249–50
Franklin, Benjamin, 59
Franz Ferdinand, 152–4, 157
Freedmen's Bureau, 127
Freedom see Die Freiheit
Freedom Riders, 139
Freemasons, 66
Free Officers, 284
Freiheit, Die (Freedom), 100–2, 116
Freikorps, 167–8, 170
French Revolution, 59–67, 161
Frick, Henry Clay, 120

Fronterlebnis, 167, 170–1
Fürstenfeldbruck, 224–5

Gaddafi, Muammar al-, 230–1,
277
GAL see Anti-terrorist Liberation
Groups
Galleani, Luigi, 120–3
Galleanists, 121, 123–4
Galula, David, 207–8
Gamaa al-Islamiyya, al- see Islamic
Group (Egypt)
Gandhi, Mahatma, 150–1
Gandhi, Rajiv, 247
Gaza Strip, 217, 219, 231, 233, 310
Geneva Conventions, 335
Georgia (country), 311
Georgia (US state), 137
Gérard, Balthasar, 52
German Autumn, 268–9
Germany, 66, 153–4, 162
Imperial era, 99–102
Nazi era, 172–6
Weimar, 167–72
see also West Germany
Germany in Autumn, 269
Gerson, Jean, 37
Gestapo, 174
Gilded Youth, 64
Golan Heights, 219
Goldman, Emma, 108, 120, 123
Goldstein, Baruch, 310
Gompers, Samuel, 119
Good Friday Accords, 244
Gorbachev, Mikhail, 298
Göring, Hermann, 174
Gowen, Franklin B., 115
Gracchus, Tiberius and Gaius, 14,
20, 22
Grand Hotel (UK) bombing, 239
Grand Mosque (Mecca), 291
Great Depression, 170, 179
Great Fear (France), 60
Great Reforms (Russia), 75
Great Terror (Soviet Union), 165–6,
179

Greece
  ancient, 12–13, 17–19
  modern, 68, 154–5, 199
Greek Cypriots, 197–9
Green Book, 239
Greenwich Observatory, 109
Gregory VIII (Pope), 34
Griffith, D. W., 137
Grivas, George, 197–9
GSG 9, 268
Guantanamo Bay, 335
Guatemala, 255
guerrilla war, 147, 189
  and terrorism, 179, 190, 237, 239, 266
  see also urban guerrilla
Guerrilla Warfare by Guevara, 255
Guevara, Che, 189, 255
Guilford Four, 239
Gulag, 166
Gulf War, 232, 299
gun control, 317, 320
Gunpowder Plot, 53–4, *53*
Gúzman, Abimael, 261–2

Haase, Hugo, 168
Habash, George, 220–1, 223
hadith, 38–9, 281–2
Haganah, 181, 183
Haig, Alexander, 276
Hamas, 231–3, 300, 308–10
Hardman, Jacob, 179
Harmodius and Aristogeiton, 18
hashishiyyin, 43
  see also Assassins
Hasmoneans, 27
Hassan-i Sabbah, 40–1, 43–4, *43*
Hayes, Rutherford B., 134
Haymarket Riot, 106, 117–20, *118*
Hearst, Patty, 265
"hearts and minds," phrase coined, 191
Hebrews, 15–17, 35, 55
Heinzen, Karl, 70–1
Henry, Emile, 103–6
Henry I (England), 37

Henry II (England), 34
Herodotus, 18
Hezbollah, 229, 232–3, 247, 292–5, 300
hijacking, 221, 225, 268, 278, 294, 307, 332
Hill, Paul, 323
Hindenburg, Paul von, 172
Hinduism, 324
Hindu nationalism, 149, 151, 247
Hindustan Socialist Republican Association, 150–1
Hipparchus, 18
History of Secret Societies in France by de la Hodde, 69
Hitler, Adolf, 168–70, 172, 174–6
Holocaust, 175, 179, 182, 224
Holofernes, 15, 35, 48, *16*
Homeland Security Advisory System, 341
Homer, 12
Hoover, J. Edgar, 123
Hotman, François, 51
Huguenots, 51–2
Hume, John, 243
Hungary, 156
Hussein (King of Jordan), 218, 222–3
Hussein, Saddam, 232, 298, 336–7

ibn 'Abd al-Wahhab, Muhammad, 282
ibn Taymiyya, Ahmad, 282–3, 287, 300
illegalism, 111
Illuminati, 66
Immigration Act of 1917, 122–3
Immigration Act of 1924, 124
India
  ancient, 13–14
  modern, 149–51, 156, 247, 324
  and Tamil Tigers, 246
Indiana, 137
Indian National Congress, 149–51
individual exaction, 103–8, 111–12
individualism, 32, 47, 76, 95–6, 110, 112

Indonesia, 339
industrialization, 69–70, 98, 114
Internal Macedonian Revolutionary
    Organization, 154–7
International Association of Bridge
    and Structural Iron Workers,
    121
International Workers of the World,
    122–3
International Workingmen's
    Association, 99, 102, 105, 116
internet, 317–18, 323
Interservices Intelligence, 296, 298
Intifada, First, 231–2, 301, 308
Intifada, Second, 233, 309
Invisible Empire see Ku Klux Klan
Iran, 285, 288–9, 292–4
Iran-Contra Affair, 294
Iranian Revolution, 288–9
Iranian Revolutionary Guard, 292
Iran-Iraq War, 294
Iraq, 188, 232, 309, 336–8
    backs Middle East terrorist factions,
        226–7, 230
    breeding ground for new terrorists,
        337–8
    opposed by Islamists, 285, 299
Iraq War (2003-), 337–8, 340
Ireland, 58, 114–15, 142–8, 157–8
    Easter Uprising, 144–5, 157–8
    Irish War of Independence, 146–8,
        157
    Republic of, 236–7, 241–4
    see also Northern Ireland
Irgun Zvai Le'umi, 181–8, 229
Irish National Invincibles, 143
Irish Northern Aid Committee, 240
Irish Republican Army, 145–8, 233–5
    see also Irish Republican
        Brotherhood; Provisional Irish
        Republican Army; Official Irish
        Republican Army
Irish Republican Brotherhood, 143–5
Islam
    and Europe, 35, 43–4, 282–3
    and Islamism, 281–7

Ismaili, 40, 44
    medieval, 38–45
    Nizari, 40–1
    Shia, 39, 282, 289, 291–2, 337
    Sunni, 39, 42, 282
    Sunni-Shiite rivalry, 39, 44, 285,
        300, 337
    Twelver Shia, 42
Islamic Group (Egypt), 287, 290, 300,
    303–4
Islamic Group (Malaysia and
    Indonesia), 339
Islamic Jihad (Lebanon), 229, 292–4
Islamic Resistance Movement see
    Hamas
Islamic Salvation Front (Algeria),
    313
Islamic Society (Palestine) see Hamas
Islamism, 281–7
    in Algeria, 313–14
    in Bosnia, 311
    in Chechnya, 306, 311–13
    in Egypt, 283–90, 303–4
    and ethno-nationalism, 294, 309,
        311–12
    in Europe, 331, 339–40
    in Indonesia, 339
    in Iraq, 337
    in Kashmir, 306
    in Lebanon, 229, 291–3
    in Palestine, 231, 308–10
    in Philippines, 302–3
    in Saudi Arabia, 286–7, 290–1,
        338–9
    in Syria, 291
    in United States, 301–2
Ismaili see Islam, Ismaili
Israel
    ancient, 16
        see also Hebrews
    Arab-Israeli wars and relations,
        188, 218–19, 228–9, 286, 289,
        291–2, 294–5
    counter-terrorism, 220, 225, 229,
        231, 310
    creation of Israel, 187–8, 199

Israel (*cont.*)
  Israel Defense Forces, 188, 220,
    225
  modern state's double standard
    regarding terrorism, 30, 229
  and Palestinians and PLO, 179,
    188, 217–21, 223–33, 291–2,
    301, 308–10
Italian Combat League, 169–70
Italy
  anarcho-terrorism, 85, 99, 102,
    105, 111, 119–20
  fascist, 155–6, 168–70,
  nineteenth-century nationalists, 66,
    68, 71
  Red Brigades and neo-fascist
    terrorism, 266–7, 270–3
  Renaissance, 47–50
Ivins, Bruce, 334

Jabotinsky, Ze'ev, 181
Jacobinism, 67, 70
Jacobins, 60–4, 161
Jael, 35
jahiliyyah, 283, 285, 288
Jallianwala Bagh Masacre, 150
Jamaat al-Jihad *see* Jihad, al-
James, Henry, 109
James I (England, James VI of
    Scotland), 53
Japan, 180, 190, 325–7
Japanese Red Army, 268
Jean the Fearless, 36–7
Jefferson, Thomas, 59
Jehu, 16
Jerez, 106
Jerusalem, 27–8, 44, 185–6, 219
Jesus Christ, 33
Jewish Agency (Palestine), 183, 185
Jewish War, 27–30
Jewish War by Josephus, 27–30
Jews, 169
  of ancient Judea, 26–30
  in Palestine, 180–8
  see also Hebrews; Israel; Judah;
    Judea; pogroms; anti-Semitism

Jezebel, 16
jihad, 282, 285, 288, 300
  greater, 282
  lesser, 282
  transnational, 288, 296–308,
    311–13, 330–40
Jihad, al-, 288–90, 300, 303–4, 306,
    309
Jihad Group *see* Jihad, al-
jihadism, 45, 282, 287–8, 291
  see also Islamism
Jim Crow, 134–5, 137–8
John (King of England), 37–8
John Chrysostom, 33
John of Salisbury, 15, 34–6
Joint Terrorism Task Force, 302
Jonathan of Cyrene, 29
Jonathan the high priest, 27
Jordan, 179, 188, 218–20, 222–3,
    228, 230
Josephus, 27–30
Judah, 16
  see also Hebrews
Judah the Maccabee, 26–7
Judea, 26–30
Judeo-Bolshevism, 169
Judith, 15, 35, 48, 16
Jugantar (*The New Age*), 149–50
just war, 22
Juvayni, 44

Kaczynski, Theodore, 328
Kadets *see* Constitutional Democrats
Kaliaev, Ivan, 87
Kanafani, Ghassan, 219
Karakazov, Dmitrii, 78
Karameh, 220
Kashmir, 306
Kautilya, 13–14
Kenya, 193–7, 307–8
Kenya African Union, 193–4
Kenya Police Reserve, 194, 196
Kenyatta, Jomo, 193–4, 197
Khaled, Leila, 221, 222
Kharijites, 39, 313
Khattab, Amir al-, 311–12

Khobar Towers bombing, 295
Khomeini, Ayatollah Ruhollah, 288–9
Khrushchev, Nikita, 166, 189, 254
Kikuyu, 193–7
Kikuyu Home Guard, 194, 196
"Killing No Murder" by Saxby, 54–5
Kimathi, Dedan, 195–6
King David Hotel, 185–6, *186*
Kirkpatrick, Jeane, 277
Kirov, Sergei, 165
Klan *see* Ku Klux Klan
Klinghoffer, Leon, 230
Knights of Labor (United States), 116, 119
Knox, John, 51–2
Koppel, Ted, 5
Kravchinsky, Sergei, 81–2, 155
Kristallnacht, 175
Kropotkin, Peter, 85–6, 90, 100, 108, 111–12, 214
Ku Klux Klan
    during Reconstruction, 126, 128–33, 135–7
    in 1910s-1940s, 137–8
    during post-war era, 138–9, 318–19
Ku Klux Klan Act of 1871, 133
Kuwait, 232, 294, 299

labor, laborers, and labor organizations, 69–70, 99, 111, 115–22, 137–8
Land and Liberty (Russia), 80–82, 86
Latin America, 255–62
latro, 22, 29, 33
Law on Suspects, 62
leaderless resistance, 316–17, 327, 338
League of Nations, 156, 184, 283
Lebanese Civil War, 228–9
Lebanon, 188, 217, 223, 225, 228–9, 285, 291–4
Left Socialists-Revolutionaries, 162–4
Legislative Assembly (India), 151
LEHI, 182–8, 229, 284
Lenin, Vladimir, 76–7, 91, 161–4
liberalism, 55, 68, 75, 98

liberal paternalism, 99, 102, 110–11
Liberation Tigers of Tamil Eelam *see* Tamil Tigers
Libya, 226–7, 230–1, 277
Livy, 19, 22
Lloyd George, David, 148
Locke, John, 55, 58–9
Lockerbie, Scotland, 231
Lod airport, 223
lois scélérates, les ("the villainous laws"), 106
Lombroso, Cesare, 108
London, 143, 243–4, 340
Long War (Ireland), 238–9
Los Angeles Times, 121
Lost Honor of Katharina Blum by Böll, 269
Louis, Duke of Orleans, 36
Louisiana, 129–30, 134
Louis XVI (France), 59–60
Lubbe, Marinus van der, 172–3
Luddites, 69–70
Luther, Martin, 50
Luxor temple massacre, 304
lynching, 135–8

Maccabee revolt, 27
MacDonald, Andrew *see* William Pierce
Macedonia, 154–5
Machiavelli, Niccolò, 49–50
MacMillan, Harold, 196–7
Madrid, 339–40
Maelius, 20
Magna Carta, 35, 38
Mahdi Army, 337
mail bombs, 101, 122, 328
Major, John, 244
Makarios III, 198
Malaya, 148, 189–93
Malayan Communist Party, 190–93
Malayan National Liberation Army, 190
Malvern Street Murders, 234
Ma'mun, al-, 42
Manchester Guardian, 187

Manlius, 20
Man Who Was Thursday by
    Chesterton, 110
Mao Zedong, 189–90, 254
Marat, Jean-Paul, 60–2, *61*
March on Rome, 169–70
Marighella, Carlos, 249, 256–9, 264
Marius, 21
Marx and Marxism, 77, 98, 116, 162,
    188–9, 254–5, 274–5
    see also Mao Zedong; Russia,
    Marxism in; individual
    communist parties and
    movements
Mary I (England) ("Bloody" Mary),
    51–2
Masada, 27–30, 229
Massu, Jacques, 203–6
Mattathias, 26–7
Mau Mau, 194–7
Maze, 241
McCormick Harvesting Machine
    plant, 117
McGuinness, Martin, 242, 244
McKay, Jim, 223
McKinley, William, 120
McParlan, James, 115
McVeigh, Timothy, 321
Mecca, 286, 291
media
    growth of in 19th century, 72
    in Imperial Russia, 75, 92
    see also terrorism, and media
Medici family, 48
Meinhof, Ulrike, 267–8, *269*
Meir, Golda, 220
*Memoirs of the Secret Societies of the
    South of Italy* by Bartholdy, 68
Menachem, 28
Mencken, H. L., 123
Merrill, Lewis, 133
Meunier, 103, *103*
Mezentsev, Nikolai, 82
Middle Ages, 32–45, 49
Milan, 271
Milestones by Qutb, 284–5

Militia-at-Large for the Republic of
    Georgia, 321–2
militias (United States), 317–18,
    320–2
Mini-Manual of the Urban Guerrilla
    by Marighella, 256–7, 259
Mirbach, Count, 162
Mississippi, 128–9, 134, 139
Mississippi Plan, 134
Mitchell, George, 244
Mitrione, Dan, 258
Molly Maguires, 58, 114–15
monarchomachs, 50
Monde, Le, 336
Mongols, 44
Monkey Wrench Gang by Abbey, 327
monkeywrenching *see* terrorism, eco-
    terrorism
Montesquieu, 59
Montevideo, 256
Montjuich, 107
More, Thomas, 49
Mornay, Philippe de, 51–2
Moro, Aldo, *271*, 272
Morozov, Nikolai, 80, 82–3
Moscow, 312
Mossadegh, Muhammad, 288
Most, Johann, 100–2, 108, 116–17
motiveless terror, 90
Mountbatten, Louis, 239
Moyne, Lord, 284
Mubarak, Hosni, 289, 302, 330–1
Mughniyeh, Imad, 292–5, 300
Muhammad, 38–9, 41, 281
Muhammad, Khalid Sheikh, 331, 336,
    339
Muhammad Reza Pahlavi *see* Shah
    of Iran
mujahideen, 295–7
Münster, 57–8
"Murder" by Heinzen, 70–1
Muslim Brotherhood, 283–5, 287,
    289, 291, 295, 308
Muslims *see* Islam
Mussolini, Benito, 156, 168–70
Muzzafarpur, India, 150

Nakba, 188, 219
Napoleon Bonaparte, 64–5, 68
Napoleon III, 71–2
Narodnaia Volia *see* People's Will
Nasser, Gamal Abdul, 218, 284–6
National Assembly (France), 59–60
National Intelligence Estimate (United
    States), 337–8
nationalism, 64–5, 69, 98, 110–11,
    181
    see also democracy; popular
    sovereignty
National Labor Union (United States),
    116
National Liberation Army (Algeria),
    201
National Liberation Front (Algeria),
    201–3, 205–12, 257, 313
National Liberation Movement
    (Uruguay) *see* Tupamaros
National Organization of Cypriot
    Fighters *see* EOKA
National Rifle Association, 320
National Security Agency (United
    States), 331–2
National Socialist Worker's Party *see*
    Nazi Party
Nazi Party, 167–72, 174–6, 182
Nechaev, Sergei, 90
Nechaev Affair, 77–81
neo-fascism, 270–1, 273
New Left (United States), 262–3, 265
New Prison, 143
New York City, 123–4, 143, 264,
    301–2, 332–333, *333*
New York Times, 238
Nicholas I (Pope), 33
Nichols, Terry, 321
Night of the Long Knives, 174
nihilism *see* Russia, nihilism in
Nikolaev, Leonid, 165
9/11 *see* September 11, 2001
Nixon, Richard, 265–6, 307
Nizam al-Mulk, 40
Nizar, 40
Nizaris *see* Assassins

Nobel, Alfred, 83
Non-Cooperation Movement (India),
    150
North Atlantic Treaty Organization,
    272, 332, 336
Northern Ireland, 142–3, 148
    Irish-Americans and Anglo-Irish
    conflict, 143, 240–1
    The Troubles, 179, 233–45
Northern Ireland Assembly, 244
North Ossetia, 312
NRBC, 324–7, 341
nuclear weapons, 326
Nuremberg Files (website), 323
Nuremberg Trials, 176

Occupied Territories *see* Gaza Strip;
    West Bank
Octavian *see* Augustus, Emperor
October Manifesto, 88–9
Odessa, 91
Odyssey by Homer, 12
Official Irish Republican Army, 236
*Of the Right that Princes Have to
    Compass the Lives of Their
    Enemies' Allies*, 49
oil, 286–8, 300
Oklahoma City bombing, 320–1
Old Man of the Mountain *see*
    Hassan-i Sabbah
Olympics
    Atlanta (1996), 322–3
    Munich (1972), 223–5, 268, *224*
Omagh, 244
Omar, Muhammad, 304
Omar, Mullah (Afganistan), 335
On Duties by Cicero, 25
O'Neil, John, 307
Operation Rescue, 322–3
Operation Spring of Youth, 225
Operation Wrath of God, 225
Orange Order, 58, 143
Order, The (fictional), 319
Order, The (organization), 319
Organization of the Armed Arab
    Struggle,

Organization of the Petroleum
    Exporting Countries, 227
Orsini, Felice, 71–2
Oslo Peace Accords, 233, 310
Ottoman Turkish Empire, 152–5,
    181, 282

Paisley, Ian, 244
Pakistan, 295–8
Palestine, 180–8, 308–10
Palestine Liberation Organization,
    183, 218, 220–33
  and Arab states, 218–20, 228, 230
  and the IRA, 240–1
  in Jordan, 220–3
  in Lebanon, 223, 225, 228–9,
    291–2
  popularity of, 219–20
  and the RAF, 267–8
Palestinian Authority, 233, 310
Palestinian Islamic Jihad, 309
Palestinians, 213, 217–19, 223,
    225–6, 228–9, 231–2
  and Arab states, 217–9, 226, 230
  in Jordan, 188
  nationalism, 217, 219
  in Palestine, 179–82, 185, 187–8
  pre-PLO terrorism, 218
Pallás, Paulino, 106–7
Palmer, A. Mitchell, 123
Palmer Raids, 123
Pan Am Flight 103, 231
pan-Arab nationalism, 218, 230, 232,
    284, 286
Papen, Fritz von, 172
Paris, 101, 103–5
paternalistic reform see liberal
    paternalism
Paul, Apostle, 33
Pavelić, Ante, 156
Pelloutier, Fernand, 111
Pennsylvania, 114–15
Pentagon (United States), 264, 332
People's Vengeance, 79
People's Will, 80, 82–4, 86
Perceval, Spencer, 70

Persia, medieval, 40–2
  see also Iran
Peru, 260–2
Peruvian Communist Party, 261
Petersburg by Bely, 93
Petit, Jean, 36–7
Petraeus, David, 338
Philippines, 302–3, 339
Philip II (Spain), 52
Phoenix Park, 143–4
Piazza Fontana bombing, 270–1
pieds noirs (Algeria), 200, 203, 211
Pierce, William, 319
Pinkertons, 115
piracy, 245
Pisacane, Carlo, 85
Plato, 18–19
Plehve, Vyacheslav von, 87
Plessy v. Ferguson, 135
Plutarch, 19, 24–5
pogroms, 85, 93, 175, 181
Point, Ali la, 203, 206
Policraticus by John of Salisbury,
    34–6
Politics by Aristotle, 18–19
Polo, Marco, 43
Pompey Magnus, 23–4
Pontecorvo, Gillo, 202, 206
populares, 20–1, 24
Popular Front for the Liberation of
    Palestine, 220–3, 226–7, 275
popular sovereignty, 51, 54–5, 57, 60,
    65–6
  see also democracy; nationalism
populism see Russia, populism in
Populist Party (Spain), 340
Posse Comitatus, 317
Possessed see Devils
Prabhakaran, Velupillai, 245, 247–8
Prince by Machiavelli, 50
Princess Casamassima by James, 109
Princip, Gavrilo, 153
propaganda of the deed, 85–6,
    99–107, 110–12, 116, 119,
    143–4, 164, 172, 214
proscription, 21

Protestantism *see* Reformation
Protestants (Northern Ireland), 234–5,
    236–7, 242–4
Provisional Irish Republican Army,
    236–244, 266, 275
Putin, Vladimir, 312

Qaeda, al-, 183, 298–9, 304–8, 311,
    330–6, 338, 340
Qaeda in Iraq, al-, 337–8
Qassam Brigades, al-, 309–10
Québec Liberation Front, 266
Quran, 38–9, 281–2
Qutb, Muhammad, 297
Qutb, Sayyid, 284–5, 300
    influence of, 285–7

Radio Athens, 198
Rahman, Omar Ahmad Abdel, 287,
    289, 301–3
Rajneesh, Bhagwan Shree, 324
RAND Corporation, 274
Raspe, Jan-Carl, 268–9
Rath, Ernst vom, 175
Rathenau, Walther, 168
Ravachol, François-Claudins, 103–6,
    111
ravacholiser, 103
Reagan, Ronald, 230, 276–7, 289,
    293–4
Real Irish Republican Army, 244
Rebel Armed Forces (Guatemala), 255
Reconstruction (United States),
    126–37
Reconstruction Acts, 127–8
Red Army Faction, 240–1, 266–70,
    276
Red Brigades, 240, 266–7, 271–3
Red Front Fighter's League, 168,
    170–1
Red Scare (1880s), 117–19
Red Scare (1910s and '20s), 179
Red Scare (1910s-20s), 122–4
Red Terror (Soviet Union), 162–4,
    163
Reformation, 50–5, 58

Reichsbanner Black-Red-Gold, 168,
    170
Reichstag Fire, 172–4, *173*
Reid, Richard, 340
Reign of Terror (France), 62–4
reigns of terror, 21, 57–8
Reinsdorf, August, 101
Rejectionist Front, 226–7, 230
Remembrance Day bombing, 242
Remirro de Orco, 50
Renaissance, 47–50
reprise individuelle see individual
    exaction
republicans
    Ireland, 58, 143–8, 213
    Northern Ireland, 233–245
Restoration (1815), 65, 68
"Returning to Haifa" by Kanafani,
    219
Revolutionary Armed Forces of
    Colombia, 260
Revolutionary Armies (France), 62
Revolutions of 1848-9, 69–70, 98,
    116
Reynolds, Albert, 243
Ribbonmen, 143
Rice, Condoleezza, 332
Rida, Rashid, 283, 285
Robespierre, Maximilien, 62–4, 70,
    214
Rockefeller, John D., Jr., 121
Romanticism, 110
Rome Conference, 105
Rome
    ancient, 14, 19–26, 32
    and Jewish War, 27–30
Roosevelt, Franklin Delano, 180
Ropshin, V. *see* Savinkov
Rousseau, Jean-Jacques, 60
Royal Irish Constabulary, 145–7
Royal Ulster Constabulary, 233–5,
    237, 244–5
Ruby Ridge, Idaho, 320
Rucks, Michael, 195
Rudolph, Eric, 323–4
Rukn al-Din, 44

Russia
    anarchism in, 77, 90–2, 160
    civil war, 161–4
    counter-terrorism in, 312
    Empire, 74–96, 152, 154–5
    liberalism in, 92
    Marxism in, 76–7, 85, 90–1, 161
    nihilism in, 76, 78–9
    populism in, 75–6, 80–2
    post-Soviet era, 311–13
    Revolution of 1905, 88–96
    Russian Revolution (1917), 122,
        160–1
    see also Russian Method; Soviet
        Union
Russian Method, 148–51, 155, 183

Sabra and Shatila camps, 228–9
Sacco, Nicola, and Bartolomeo
    Vanzetti, 124
Sadat, Anwar, 284, 286–7, 289–90
Sadducees, 27–8
Saladin, 44
Salafi, 282
salafism, 282
Salafist Group for Preaching and
    Combat, 314
Salameh, Ali Hassan, 225
Sallust, 22
Salvador French, Santiago, 107
San Francisco, 121
Sánchez, Ilich Ramírez see Carlos the
    Jackal
Sands, Bobby, 241
sans-culottes, 60–2
Sarajevo, 152–3
sarin nerve gas, 325–6
Sartre, Jean-Paul, 208, 214
Saudi Arabia, 232, 286–7, 290–1,
    295–6, 299, 338–9
SAVAK, 288
Savinkov, Boris, 87–8, 93
Saxby, Edward, 54–5
scalawags, 127, 134
Scheuer, Michael, 307
Schleyer, Hanns-Martin, 268–70

scholasticism, 34–5
School of the Americas, 277
Science of Revolutionary Warfare by
    Most, 101, 117
Science of Wealth see Arthashastra by
    Kautilya
seajacking, 230
Secret Agent by Conrad, 105, 109–10
Secret Army Organization (Algeria),
    211–12
secret societies, 58, 66–9
Security Service (Nazi Germany),
    174–5
Sedition Act of 1918, 122
Seljuk Turks, 40–1
Senate (Rome), 19–26
Sendero Luminoso see Shining Path
Sendic, Raúl, 256–9
September 11, 2001, 5, 330–4, 336,
    333
Serbia, 151–4, 157
    see also Yugoslavia
Sergei Aleksandrovich (Grand Duke),
    87
Services Bureau, 297
Servius Tullius, 19
Shah of Iran, 288
Shamir, Yitzhak, 182, 185–6, 229,
    232
sharia, 38–9, 45, 281–2, 285–6, 288
Sharon, Ariel, 228–9
Sheikh Omar see Rahman, Omar
    Ahmad Abdel
Shia see Islam, Shia
Shining Path, 260–2
Sicarii, 27–30, 182, 229
sicarius (assassin), 29
Silent Brotherhood see The Order
    (organization)
Simmons, William, 137
Sinai Peninsula, 218–19
Sinhalese, 245–6
Sinn Féin, 145, 239, 242–4
Sisera, 35
Six Day War, 219
Sixteenth Street Baptist Church, 139

Sixtus V (Pope), 52–3
Slepian, Barnett, 323
*Small Wars – Their Principles and
    Practice* by Callwell, 147
Social Brigade (Spain), 107
Social Democratic and Labour
    Party (Northern Ireland),
    243–4
Social Democratic Party of Germany,
    99–100, 167–8, 170, 172
socialism, 98–100, 102, 106, 111,
    116, 167, 169
Socialist Law (Germany), 100–1
Socialist Party (Italy), 270
Socialist Party (Spain), 340
Socialists-Revolutionaries, Party of,
    85–90, 92, 94, 162
    see also Combat Organization
Somalia, 299–300
Sophie (Empress of Austria-Hungary),
    152–3
South Africa, 213
South Carolina, 133–4
Southern Poverty Law Center, 319
Soviet Union, 169, 175–6
    and Afghanistan, 295–8, 301
    and Cold War, 188–9
    collapse of, 301, 311
    and international terrorism, 155,
        276
    state terror in, 160–6
    see also Russia
Spain
    anarchism in, 102, 106–7, 111
    and Basques/ETA, 179, 249–51
    Carbonari in, 68
    Islamism in, 339–40
Special Air Service, 238
Special Irish Branch, 144
Spence, Gusty, 237
Spies, August, 117, 119
Squad (IRA), 146
squadristi see Blackshirts
Sri Lanka, 245–9
Stalin, Joseph, 92, 164–6
Stammheim prison, 268–9

Statesman's Book see Policraticus
state-sponsored assassination *see*
    assassination, state-sponsored
state-sponsored terrorism *see*
    terrorism, state-sponsored
state terror, 7, 179
    in ancient world, 11–12, 21
    in French Reign of Terror, 62–4
    in medieval Europe, 37–8
    in Nazi Germany, 172–6
    in Renaissance Europe, 50
    in Russia/Soviet Union, 91,
        160–6
    in United States, 135–6
    vs. terrorism, 7
stay-behind force, 175–6
St. Bartholomew's Day Massacre,
    51–2
Steinberg, Isaac, 164
Stephen (King of England), 37
Stepniak *see* Kravchinsky
Sterling, Claire, 276
Stern, Avraham, 182
Stern Gang *see* LEHI
Stinger missiles, 296, 311
Storm Division *see* Brownshirts
St. Petersburg, 88, 93
St. Petersburg Protocol, 105
strategy of tension, 270–1, 273
Struve, Peter, 89–90
Students for a Democratic Society,
    263, 266
submachine gun, 184
Sudan, 299, 304, 308
Suez Crisis, 218
suicide terrorism
    in Egypt, 303,
    Hezbollah/Islamic Jihad, 292–4
    in Iraq, 337
    in Israel and Palestine, 309–10
    in Russia and Chechnya, 312
    and September 11, 2001, 278,
        331–3
    in Sri Lanka, 245, 247–8,
Sulla, 21, 29
Sunni *see* Islam, Sunni

Switzerland, 105
Symbionese Liberation Army, 265–6
syndicalism, 111–12
Syria
    and Arab-Israeli wars, 188, 219
    ancient, 26–7
    Islamism in, 285, 291–2
    and Lebanon, 228, 292–3
    and Palestinians, 217, 219
    and PLO factions, 226–8

Taber, Robert, 240–1
takfir, 39, 282, 298, 313
takfirism, 282
Taliban, 304, 331, 335
Tallien, Jean Lambert, 64
Tamil Tigers, 213, 245–9
Tankosich, Vojin, 153
Tanzania, 307–8
tawhid, 38, 45, 281, 285
Tehran hostage crisis, 289
Teitgen, Paul, 206
Templer, Gerald, 191
Tenet, George, 331
Tennessee, 128–30
Tenth Parachute Division (France),
    203–8, 211, *204*
terror, as weapon of war, 11–12
Terror, The *see* Reign of Terror
    (France)
terrorism
    animal rights, 327–8
    and Cold War, 188–9
    as communicative act, 3
        see also propaganda of the deed;
        terrorism, as a symbolic act
    and criminal behavior, 22, 29,
        70–1, 77, 90–1, 94, 103, 111,
        132, 147, 155, 256, 260, 265,
        267–8, 324, 335
        see also expropriations
    as cultural, linguistic, or social
        construct, 3, 176, 327
    definitions of, 2–7
    eco-terrorism, 327–8
    as ideology, 95

depicted in literature and film, 53,
    79, 87–8, 93, 105, 109–10,
    137, 195, 202, 206, 269, 274,
    319
effect on terrorist, 88, 93, 157, 212
ethno-nationalist, 142–58 passim,
    178–251 passim
    and religious and ideological
        terrorism, 178
    and revolutionary terrorism,
        148–9, 157–8, 178–80
    varieties of, 178–9,
    see also individual movements
        and locations
explanation of, 69, 79–80, 108–10,
    150
funding of, 240, 260–1
    see also state-sponsored
        assassination; state-sponsored
        terrorism
and guerrilla war, 179, 190, 237,
    239, 245–7, 266
and historians, 5–6
and humor, 82, 92–3, 268, 334
international, 221, 274, 277–8
    and revolutionary terrorism,
        274–6
international efforts against, 105,
    156
and media, 5, 72, 75, 103–5, 109,
    115, 119, 131, 134, 138–9,
    158, 184, 195, 210, 223, 227,
    266, 305, 322, 328, 335–6
and mercenary violence, 156–7,
    226–7
and modernity, 95–6, 98, 108–10,
    112
and morality, 2, 70–1, 78, 89–90,
    93, 210
narco-terrorism, 260–1
and personal motives, 81, 103, 105,
    107–8, 237
as provocation, 94, 108, 146–7,
    155, 157, 170, 178, 198, 200,
    209, 212–13, 239, 249, 301,
    304, 337

purpose of, 82–3, 129, 132, 146,
149–50, 183, 202, 234, 243,
249, 278, 301, 323
as rational act, 3–4
religious *see* individual religions;
terrorism, as sacramental act
revolutionary, 27, 57, 74–96
passim, 179, 254–73
and ethno-nationalist terrorism,
148–9
and international terrorism,
274–6
see also Russian Method;
individual movements and
locations
as sacramental act, 4, 45, 324
and social science, 5–6
solipsistic, 214
state-sponsored, 156–7, 230,
276–7, 294
success of, 28, 45, 95, 112, 126,
135, 192–3, 197, 199, 259,
273
support for, 81, 147, 199, 246–7,
303–4, 309, 312, 316, 322
as symbolic act, 4, 45, 64, 70, 83,
86, 100–1, 106, 108, 111, 124,
129, 131, 135, 157–8, 170,
178, 190, 200, 289, 301
see also propaganda of the deed
as tactic, 2–3, 275
as violence against civilians, 2
vs. state terror, 176
vs. tyrannicide, 14–15, 55–7, 59,
61–2, 71, 80
and warfare, 13, 22, 146, 203,
245–7, 335
terrorist, first use of word, 63, 65
Terror Network by Sterling, 276
Terry, Randall, 322
Texas, 132, 136–7
Thatcher, Margaret, 239, 241
Thebes, 13
Theodosius I, 33
Thirteenth Amendment to US
Constitution, 127

"Threshold" by Turgenev, 81
Thucydides, 18
Thuggees, 324
Tikhomirov, Lev, 81, 83
Tilak, Bal Gangadhar, 149–50
Tokyo subway attack, 325–6, *325*
Tolstoy, Leo, 94
torture, 175, 204–6, 208–9, 238
Transportation Security
Administration, 340
Treaty of Versailles, 167–9
Trepov, Teodor, 81
Trinquier, Roger, 203–5
Trotsky, Lev, 91, 162, 164–6, *163*
Troubles *see* Northern Ireland
truck bomb, first, 186
Tunisia, 228, 230
Tupamaros, 256–9, 264, 266
Turabi, Hasan al-, 299, 304
Turgenev, Ivan, 81, 92
Turkey, 199
Turkish Cypriots, 197, 199
Turner Diaries by Pierce, 319, 321
Twelver Shiites *see* Islam, Twelver
Shia
tyrannicide, 14–15, 153
in ancient Greece, 17–19
in ancient Rome, 19–21, 23–6
defined, 14
in early modern Europe, 47–56
and Hebrews, 15–17
in medieval Europe, 32–7
in medieval Islam, 38–9
vs. terrorism, 14–15, 55–7, 59,
61–2, 71, 80
see also assassination; individual
assassins and victims
tyranny, 34–6, 93
in ancient Greece, 17–19
in ancient Rome, 19, 25
in early modern Europe, 48
as a system, 58–9
see also tyrannicide

ulema, 286
Ulster *see* Northern Ireland

Ulster Freedom Fighters, 242
Ulster Unionist Party, 243–4
Ulster Volunteer Force, 234–5, 237
ultras (Algeria), 202, 205, 211
Umberto I, 120
Unabomber, 328
Union or Death *see* Black Hand
unionists (Ireland), 142–6
unionists (Northern Ireland), 234–8, 241–5
unions *see* labor and labor organizations
United Kingdom, 105, 154, 266, 335–6, 340
  and Cold War, 200
  and colonies, 180, 283
  and counter-insurgency, 147
  and counter-terrorism, 199-200, 238
  and Cyprus, 197–200
    and Egypt, 180, 283–4
  and India, 149–51
  and Ireland, 142–8
  and Kenya, 193–7, 199–200
  Luddites, 69–70
  and Malaya, 148, 189–93, 199–200
  and Northern Ireland, 233–45
  and Palestine, 181–8, 284
  see also England
United Nations, 180, 184–5, 187, 199, 207, 210, 220, 226, 299, 320–1
United States
  and Afghan resistance, 295–6, 298
  anarchism in, 116–24
  anti-immigrant attitudes, 117, 119–20, 122–4, 137
  Capitol, 264, 332–3
  and Cold War, 188–9, 254, 275–6, 295–6, 307
  condemns colonialism, 180, 184
  Constitution, 59
  embassies in East Africa attacked, 307–8, 330
  and international terrorism, 274–7, 307

  interests targeted in Europe, 268, 270, 272–3
  and Iran, 288–9, 294
  and Iraq, 232, 299, 336–8
  and Ireland, 243–4
  and Lebanon, 228–9, 277, 292–4, *293*
  leftist terrorism and violence, 1880s-1920s, 114–24
  leftist terrorism and violence, 1960s-70s, 262–6
  and Libya, 230–1
  and al-Qaeda, 299–301, 306,
  recent domestic terrorism, 317–24, 327–8, 333–4
  and Saudi Arabia, 295
  September 11, 2001, 330–3
  visited by Sayyid Qutb, 284–5
  white supremacist terrorism, 126–39, 318–19
  War on Terror, 334–9, 340–1
  World Trade Center attack (first), 301–3
urban guerrilla, 256–9, 263–73
Uritsky, Moisei, 162
Uruguay, 255–9, 266
USS Cole, 308
USSR *see* Soviet Union
Ustaša, 156–7
Utaybi, Juhayman al-, 291
Uthman (Caliph), 38

Vaillant, Auguste, 104–6
Vail Ski Resort, 327
Valdinoci, Carlo, 123–4
Valerius Publicola, 19
Venezuela, 255
Venice, 48–9
V for Vendetta, 53–4
Victor Emmanuel III (Italy), 170
Videla, Jorge, 259–60
Vietnam War, 263–4
vigilantism, 20, 130

Waco, Texas, 320
Wahhabism, 282, 286–7, 290, 306

Wall Street, 123–4, 333
War of the Flea by Taber, 240–1
War on Terror, 334–5
Washington Post, 238
waterboarding, 205
Watergate, 307
Weathermen, 263–4
    see also Weather Underground
Weather Underground, 264–6
    see also Weathermen
Weaver, Randy 320
Weishaupt, Adam, 66
Werewolf, Operation, 175–6
West Bank, 217–19, 230–1, 233, 310
West Germany, 223–5, 266–70
What Is to Be Done? by
    Chernyshevsky, 76
*What Never Happened: A Novel of
    the Revolution* by Savinkov, 88
White Aryan Resistance, 318–19
Whiteboys, 58, 70, 115, 143
Whites (Soviet Union), 161–4
white supremacy, 126–39
white terror, 64
Wilhelm I (Germany), 99–100
William of Orange, 52
William the Conqueror, 37
Wilson, Charlie, 296
Wilson, Woodrow, 180

Wobblies *see* International Workers of
    the World
Wolves of Islam, 311
World Trade Center attack (1993),
    301–3
World Trade Center attack (2001),
    332–3, *333*
World War I, 95, 111, 122, 144, 150,
    154–5, 167, 169, 180
World War II, 156, 167, 175–6, 179,
    180, 182
Wretched of the Earth by Fanon,
    213–14
Wright, Richard, 135

Yacef, Saadi, 202–3, 206
Yassin, Ahmad, 308–10
Yemen, 299
Young Bosnia, 152–3
Yousef, Ramzi, 301–3, 321, 331, 339
Yugoslavia, 155–6, 311

Zabrezhnev, Vladimir, 112
Zasulich, Vera, 81, 88
Zawahiri, Ayman al-, 287–9, 297–9,
    303–4, 306, *303*
Zealots, 28
Zia-al-Haq, Muhammad, 295
Zionism, 180–1, 183